1999

Marketing Ethics: An International Perspective

agement,

I⟨T⟩P An International Thomson Publishing Company

London • Bonn • Boston • Johannesburg • Madrid • Melbourne • Mexico City • New York • Paris
Singapore • Tokyo • Toronto • Albany, NY • Belmont, CA • Cincinnati, OH • Detroit, MI

Marketing Ethics: An International Perspective

First published by International Thomson Business Press

I(T)P® A division of International Thomson Publishing Inc.
The ITP logo is a trademark under licence

British Library Cataloguing-in-Publication Data
A catalogue record for this book is available from the British Library

First edition 1998

Typeset by J&L Composition Ltd, Filey, North Yorkshire
Printed in the UK by TJ International, Cornwall

ISBN 1–86152–191–X

International Thomson Business Press
Berkshire House
168–173 High Holborn
London WC1V 7AA
UK

International Thomson Business Press
20 Park Plaza
13th Floor
Boston MA 02116
USA

http://www.itbp.com

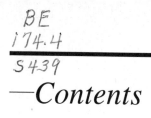

—*Contents*

—List of figures

—List of tables

—List of exhibits

—About the author

Bodo B. Schlegelmilch (Dipl. Betriebswirt, MSc, PhD, FCIM, MMRS) is Chair of International Marketing and Management at the Vienna University of Economics and Business Administration (Wirtschaftsuniversität Wien). He was previously Professor of Marketing at Thunderbird, The American Graduate School of International Management in Arizona, where he headed the marketing group and founded the US Government-supported Institute of International Business Ethics. He also held academic posts as the British Rail Chair of Marketing at the University of Wales, Swansea, as lecturer of Marketing and International Business at the University of Edinburgh in Scotland and visiting positions at the University of California at Berkeley and the University of Miami in Florida. At the beginning of his career, he also worked for Deutsche Bank and Procter & Gamble.

Professor Schlegelmilch is president of Canyon Consulting Inc. and has conducted executive education work in strategic marketing for major multinationals, including Allied Signals, Anheuser Busch, AT&T, BellSouth, Black & Decker, Cable & Wireless, Citibank, Dow Chemical, Eastman Kodak, EDS, Estée Lauder, Goldman Sachs, Goodyear, MCI, Merck Sharp & Dohme, KPMG, Phillip Morris, Pharmacia & Upjohn, Samsung, Schlumberger, Sunkyong and Universal Flavors. He has taught in international marketing programmes in Austria, Britain, Egypt, France, Germany, New Zealand, the United States and Russia.

The research of Professor Schlegelmilch has been published in over 100 academic papers, including the *Journal of International Business Studies, Journal of Business Ethics, Business Ethics: A European Review, Journal of International Marketing, Management International Review, International Marketing Review, Managerial and Decision Economics, European Journal of Marketing, Journal of Marketing Management and Industrial Marketing Management*. He is on the editorial board of nine leading academic journals, including the *International Journal of Research in Marketing*, the *Journal of International Business Studies*, the *Journal of World Business*, the *Journal of International Marketing*, the *Journal of Business Research and Marketing – Zeitschrift für Forschung und Praxis*.

—Acknowledgements

I would like to thank all who have contributed to the development of this text. I am particularly indebted to my students at Thunderbird, The American Graduate School of International Management, who provided many helpful comments and insights and made me appreciate the importance of cultural differences in the discussion of business ethics. I am also grateful to Professor Dale Littler at the Manchester School of Management, UMIST, the editor of the *Advanced Series in Marketing*, and Julian Thomas, the commissioning editor at International Thomson Publishing, for their support and encouragement during the project. Most importantly, however, I would like to thank my wife, Irene for spending long hours in reviewing the draft and keeping good humoured during the inevitable periods of frustration.

To Irene and Roger

—PART I
Fundamentals of marketing ethics

1 *Introduction*

1.1 WHAT IS INTERNATIONAL MARKETING ETHICS?

The last decade has witnessed a remarkable increase in ethical concern. In the UK, leading business schools (including London Business School and Manchester Business School) have introduced courses in business ethics and appointed professors to teach and research in the field. In the US, business benefactors have endowed more than 25 chairs in ethics (*US News and World Report* 1995) and ninety per cent of business schools now have ethics courses in their programmes (Schlegelmilch and Robertson 1995). More than 150 research centres and organizations now exist in the US alone. Long-established business periodicals regularly devote lead articles to the subject of business ethics and hardly a day goes by without television and radio unearthing ethically questionable business practices. Books, articles and new journals exclusively devoted to business ethics (e.g. *Business Ethics*) are covering subjects ranging from unethical marketing practices to harassment in the workplace. In 1997, two of the main academic publications, the *Journal of Business Ethics* and *Business Ethics Quarterly* are in their 16th and 7th year of publication, respectively.

Consumers' concern about unethical business practices is reflected in a number of surveys. In the US, a Business Week/Harris poll indicated that 49 per cent view white-collar crime as very common (Robin and Reidenbach, 1989). In a more recent Gallup Poll, only the US government scored lower marks than corporations in terms of trustworthiness (*US News and World Report* 1995). In the UK, Schlegelmilch (1994) reports that only 17 per cent of the public rates the honesty of top business people as 'high'. Inevitably, this concern has influenced shopping practices. Two-thirds of consumers now claim that their purchasing habits are influenced by ethical considerations (BARB/Mintel 1991). Neil Garnet, director of corporate communications at Grand Metropolitan, states: 'There is no doubt that consumers are tending to reject some products on ethical grounds' and Jack Mahoney, Professor of Business Ethics at London Business

School, generalizes: 'Every purchase is an economic vote' (*The Sunday Times* 1994: 10).

Private and institutional investors are also increasingly scrutinizing the ethics of the companies they invest in (Schlegelmilch 1997). Indeed, *The Sunday Times* (1993) reported that ethical investment funds represent one of the fastest growing components of the financial sector. In the US, it has been reported that 182 major investment institutions – including pension funds, foundations and community development funds – manage socially responsible investments totaling $639 billion (Ericson 1995).

In the light of growing ethical concern, corporations have also been taking steps to incorporate ethics into their organizations (Robertson and Schlegelmilch 1993). Nearly all Fortune 1000 companies have now formulated corporate codes of ethics (Weaver 1993; Center for Business Ethics 1992) and more than half of the largest corporations teach ethics to their employees (*US News and World Report* 1995). Many companies have set up reporting channels to ensure that their policies are adhered to (Schlegelmilch and Robertson 1995). In addition, companies have also recognized the marketing potential of exemplary ethical behaviour, either in the form of cause-related marketing campaigns (Varadarajan and Menon 1988) or in terms of corporate ethical positioning (Trommsdorff and Schlegelmilch 1996).

But although business ethics appears to have made significant inroads into teaching and research at universities, although consumers and investors appear to shy away from companies with questionable business practices, and although companies appear to have institutionalized business ethics in the form of codes of ethics, policies, procedures and training, there still appears to be a widespread ignorance of and scepticism about business ethics. Not surprisingly, marketing ethics, a subset of business ethics, is viewed very much in the same light.

1.1.1 The public perception

Mentioning that one is writing a book on marketing ethics typically provokes three kinds of reactions. The first reflects the perception that it is not a 'proper' subject, since marketing managers do not have any ethics in the first place! This view tends to be packaged in remarks like 'This won't take you long, there is no ethics in marketing in the first place' or, 'Marketing ethics is even more of an oxymoron than marketing academics.' The second type of reaction, more positive but equally wrong, is to place you firmly in the corner of those who are about to enter priesthood or have decided to embark on some sort of alternative lifestyle. People reacting in this way usually comment that 'Business and ethics do not mix', and that 'Business is mostly immoral or, at best, amoral.' Last, there are those who recognize the importance of ethical decision making, but question the attempt to discuss business ethics in a book. They view ethics as an individual, private affair. Typical comments are: 'Ethics is something one learns at childhood; an adult either is ethical or is not,' or 'Ethical decisions are based on everyone's own conscience and are not a matter for public debate.'

None of these views is correct. Managerial decision making very often calls for ethical judgements, in particular in marketing. Indeed, because marketing represents the interface between a company and its customers, ethical misconduct in marketing is particularly visible and, consequently, particularly dangerous for the reputation of the firm. Moreover, one does not have to leave business and enter priesthood to be concerned with ethics. Ethics and business are inextricably mixed together. Management decision making regularly involves tradeoffs between economic and social performance. The manager who decides to recall a potentially dangerous product might, at least in the short term, compromise profits for the sake of consumer protection. In contrast, the manager who decides to delay the installation of pollution control equipment will, at least in the short term, increase shareholder value. Thus, business decisions almost always involve value judgements. Depicting business as something which merely follows scientific decision making rules ignores the fact that business is a human activity and, as such, has a moral perspective. Finally, there are those who view ethics *exclusively* as a private issue. Although private ethics is undoubtedly important, this view neglects the influence of corporate cultures and the influence of society at large on decision making. Surveys have shown that managers frequently feel pressured to sacrifice their personal values for corporate goals (Posner and Schmidt 1984) and that industry and country affiliations shape their attitudes towards ethics (Schlegelmilch and Robertson 1995). Thus, business decision making does not only rest on personal ethics, but is also impacted by organizational and societal pressures. The latter, of course, becomes more complex when managerial decision making affects more than one country or culture.

The previous paragraph hinted at a distinction between a short- and a long-term impact of decision making. This distinction is important as some ethicists and practising managers believe that good business ethics is, in the long run, synonymous with good business. Typical is the view expressed by Laczniak and Murphy (1993: ix) who state that 'While being ethical sometimes reduces short-term profits, it should enhance long-range shareholder value.' James Burke, who decided during the Tylenol crisis (see Exhibit 1.1) to remove every bottle of this headache medicine from the shelves, expresses a similar view when asked what discourages him about the state of American business ethics: 'Getting caught in these conflicting forces that all business leadership is brought up in has, in too many instances, caused people to think short rather that long term; and that's the key to all of this' (Burke 1996: 14). Contrary to such views, Hoffman and Moore (1990: 13) argue that: 'The ethical thing to do may not always be in the best interests of the firm . . . We should promote business ethics, not because good ethics is good business, but because we are morally required to adopt the moral point of view in all our dealings with other people – and business is no exception.'

EXHIBIT 1.1

The Tylenol crisis

In 1982, seven people died after taking Tylenol Extra-Strength capsules, marketed by Johnson & Johnson. The medicine was poisoned with cyanide. During this crisis, James Burke was chairman and CEO of Johnson & Johnson. He decided that this crisis demanded absolute honesty with the media and set up an executive team which was devoted full time to handling the crisis. Subsequently, he took the unprecedented step and ordered that every single bottle of Tylenol should be removed from the shelves. The crisis was resolved – although the culprit was never caught. James Burke, one of the most respected senior executives in America, retired from Johnson & Johnson in 1989 and became chairman of the Partnership for a Drug-free America and The Business Enterprise Trust.

Source: Adapted from Burke, J. (1996) The Fine Art of Leadership, Interview in *Management Review*. October, pp. 13–16.

1.1.2 A working definition

While the previous section discussed some commonly-held misperceptions of business ethics, it carefully avoided defining what business ethics, let alone marketing ethics, actually is. This is because an attempt to define ethics is notoriously difficult, a bit like nailing jelly on a wall. Using statistical terminology, ethics would be characterized as a latent construct, i.e. something which is not directly measurable but can be represented or measured through other variables. Thus, by observing a person's conduct, for example whether he or she is lying, stealing, harming others, etc. we can attempt to capture whether a person is ethical, namely whether he or she has a conception of right and wrong. However, the fact that we cannot measure ethics directly is only the start of the problem. Defining ethics as a concept of right and wrong raises the question from where such concepts originate. The answer to this can be found in the upbringing of a person, the influences of family, school, religion, friends, role-models, the media to name but a few. Thus, ethics is something which is learned, a belief system which guides moral judgements and actions.

However, arguing along these lines inevitably leads to the observation that the upbringing and learning experiences of individuals may vary widely. Consequently, it is not surprising that ethics, the concept of what is right or wrong, may vary greatly from one person to the other. Indeed, perceptions of right and wrong may vary in particular when people have been brought up in different religious or cultural environments. What might be perceived as ethical in one country or culture might be viewed as unethical in another. Even studies of value systems in different European countries, which are relatively homogeneous, revealed major differences in tolerances on issues like euthanasia (highest tolerance in Denmark, lowest in Ireland), under-age sex (highest tolerance in Holland, lowest in Ireland), accepting a bribe (highest tolerance Belgium, lowest Denmark) or lying in your own interest (highest tolerance Holland, lowest Italy).

The existence of differences in the perception of right or wrong raises a further question, namely that of ethical relativism. In essence, this controversial issue, which will be discussed in more depth in Chapter 2, focuses on whether there are universal ethical standards or whether ethical principles should be defined by various societal traditions, circumstances of the moment or opinions of decision makers. For multinational companies with business activities in numerous countries, the issue of ethical relativism assumes great importance. The answer will determine whether the company will act according to the same ethical principles world-wide, or will follow the motto: 'When in Rome, do as the Romans do.'

So far we have talked about ethics in general. Focusing on business ethics in particular, the first thing to note is that business ethics does not represent a separate set of ethical norms, only applicable to business situations. If an action is considered unethical outside a business context, it should be considered equally unethical within business. Indeed, business ethics is merely the application of general ethical ideas to business situations. For example, business ethics would ask how ethical principles can be used to deal with the following questions:

- Which minimum working standards and environmental standards should be adhered to in global manufacturing operations?
- How should multinational companies deal with corrupt political regimes? When should a company decide to withdraw from a country?
- What should international managers do when different cultural attitudes clash, for example, with regard to diversity issues?

Marketing ethics, finally, deals with ethical dilemmas pertaining to the marketing function. Laczniak and Murphy (1993: x) define marketing ethics as 'the systematic study of how moral standards are applied to marketing decisions, behaviors and institutions.' Among the ethical issues frequently arising in marketing situations are the ethics of gift-giving to customers, deceptive advertising, misleading pricing, unsafe products, anti-competitive distribution agreements (e.g. slotting allowances), high pressure sales tactics, misrepresentation of services, privacy in marketing research, etc.

1.1.3 Ethics and the law

Although ethics and law are related, they are not the same. The law tries to codify what a society defines as right and wrong, but can rarely do this comprehensively. To this end, ethics often deals with responsibilities which go beyond the law, i.e. situations, which are legal but nevertheless unethical. Two situations will illustrate this point. First, consider a chemical company that voluntarily installs a system which will cut the pollution from its manufacturing operation far more than would be required by law. Now compare this with a company that just meets the minimum pollution standards defined by the law and is unwilling to invest into more sophisticated equipment, which would cut emission of pollutants further. Both companies are operating within the law, but the first one is arguably more ethical. Second, it may be perfectly legal to lay off an employee just before he or she will become entitled to costly retirement benefits, but many observers would regard such action as unethical. Thus, the equation 'if it is legal it is ethical' does not always hold. A course of action may be legal, but not necessarily ethical.

But what about the reverse situation? Are all illegal actions also unethical? Although, in the large majority of situations one would hope that this would be the case, in some instances, it may not be. At one stage, for example, trade laws permitted manufacturers to determine the retail price of their products. Retailers who undercut these prices were violating the law. However, some people saw such illegal price cutting as ethical, although it broke the law (Hartley 1993). In some countries, for example in Germany, accountants are not allowed to advertise. However, it is debatable whether an accountant who advertises in such a situation should be regarded as unethical.

Thus, there is no one-to-one match between ethics and law. The law is not infallible, and, conversely, staying within the legal requirements is sometimes not enough for businesses to be regarded as ethical.

1.1.4 Ethics and culture

The subtitle of this book is: 'An International Perspective'. This is important, since it is the international side of business ethics that causes some of the most difficult dilemmas. Many companies operate in a wide variety of cultural environments which differ in their understanding of right and wrong. Such differences may be as fundamental as agreeing on what constitutes human rights (see, for example, the ongoing debate between the US and China), and whether and how far women, or different racial and ethnic groups are to be treated equally. In such situations, executives of multinational companies are frequently faced with difficult ethical dilemmas, since they have to decide whether they want to confirm to the standards of their host country, to insist on their own perception of right or wrong, or find some middle ground. Areas where cultural differences often cause ethical dilemmas particularly often include employment practices, such as equal opportunity issues and non-discriminatory treatment of workers, pollution standards and bribery. For example, in some cultures, the differences between genders is regarded as so fundamental that equality in employment is completely out of the question. For example, in Saudi Arabia the role of women in society would prevent a company from including females in a sales force that visits customers.

In debating ethical differences between cultures, a link is frequently made between ethics and level of economic development (Donaldson 1989). Essentially, it is argued that actions, which would be regarded as morally unacceptable in economically well-off, wealthy societies, might be permissible – *under certain circumstances* – in economically underdeveloped societies (this argument will be scrutinized in more depth in Chapter 2). However, linking the morals of other societies to their lack of economic development implies that the values in highly developed countries, although not absolute, are at least exemplary in the sense of being the best so far developed. Sorell and Hendry (1994: 213) view this line of argument as dangerous: '. . . for who is to say which of the world's cultures is the "most" developed? Only in economic terms can any kind of objective answer be given, and it is far from obvious why economic development should provide a touchstone for morality: "rich" is not necessarily right.' Moreover, there are plenty of ethical differences which are completely unrelated to economic development but, instead, are primarily related to religion. Consider, for example, the differences in values between Islamic, Buddhist, Christian and Hindu societies. Who could prove that one religion and value system is better than the other?

But do the above arguments inevitably lead to the acceptance of ethical relativism? Not necessarily – ethical relativism can be refuted by carrying it to its extreme. If one would view ethics as completely relative, one would also have to accept the 'ethics' of a culture where cannibalism is viewed as morally permissible, where murder and torture are acceptable and where stealing is admissible. Few would accept such a position. However, stating that there are limits to what is ethically acceptable and, at the same time, acknowledging different ethical standards between cultures inevitably leads to the question of the extent of moral common ground. DeGeorge (1993: 10) argues 'all countries hold that it is wrong for one person to kill another arbitrarily . . . nor is lying and stealing acceptable in any country.' Thus, at best, supporters of ethical relativism can claim that not all ethical rules are universally accepted.

Taken collectively, it appears that neither the extremes of relativism, nor the ethnocentric belief that our ethics represents the only reasonable approach provide suitable guidance to managers grappling with cross-cultural business dilemmas. Instead, what is called for is careful managerial judgement of the impact a decision will have on all affected parties. In short, there is a strong link between ethical decision making and leadership, an issue which will now be explored further.

1.2 ETHICAL DECISION MAKING AND LEADERSHIP

1.2.1 Characteristics of a good leader

Attempts to identify the characteristics of a good leader are as old as the need for leadership itself (Bass 1990; Wilner 1984; Nadler and Tushman 1990). In management, a range of characteristics have been identified as beneficial for leadership. Business schools and universities that teach management concentrate on techniques, implying that a sound knowledge of the latest management techniques is necessary for future business leaders. Other observers view leadership in management primarily as a question of charisma, the elusive special charm and personal qualities which enable a person to win and keep the interest and love of ordinary people. A third view concentrates on style, arguing that the 'correct' approach to leading always depends on the idiosyncrasies of a given situation and, consequently, a manager's 'style' should vary from situation to situation.

All three arguments, although not completely wrong, have their deficiencies. The latest management techniques tend to be disseminated so quickly through conference papers, journal articles, consultants, books, etc. that a knowledge of such techniques can merely provide a short-term advantage. Therefore, knowledge of management techniques can, at best, only be viewed as a necessary but not a sufficient characteristic of leadership ability. Reducing leadership to charisma ignores the fact that 'The vast majority of business leaders have succeeded, not through charisma, but through experience, judgment, boldness, tenacity, and hard work' (Badaracco and Ellsworth 1989: 4). Relying on style, finally, also has its share of problems. Apart from the fact that most people cannot, or do not want to change their style like a chameleon each time they face a different situation, simply stating that managers should adapt their style to the circumstances does not provide any guidance on how to gain leadership qualities.

But what characterizes a good business leader? And where is the link to business ethics? In interviews with chief executives, Badaracco and Ellsworth (1989: 100) found that 'strong personal ethics' emerged as a dominating trait of good leadership: 'Again and again, executives told us that these characteristics [honesty and fairness] are the fundamental source of loyalty and trust in an organization.' A link between ethics and leadership has also been made by the management guru Peter Drucker (1968: 461), who stated that 'It [management] has to consider whether the action [it takes] is likely to promote the public good, to advance the basic beliefs of our society, to contribute to its stability, strength and harmony.' Even more clearly is the connection established by Kanungo and Mendonca (1996: 33), who observed that 'Effective organizational leaders need ethics as fish need water and human beings need air.'

Thus, integrity in the sense of seeing the whole picture, as well as in the sense of attempting to achieve a congruence between personal beliefs, management decision making and organizational aims is a core leadership characteristic. Managerial integrity, of course, also means doing 'the right thing.' This is where ethical judgement inextricably links with leadership qualities.

1.2.2 Ethics and trust

An insightful perspective into the nature of business ethics can also been gained by exploring the link between ethics and trust. Laczniak and Murphy (1993: xi) state that 'some of the elusiveness about what constitutes an ethical person could be overcome if people substituted the word trust for ethics; that is, ethical marketing managers are trustworthy in that they can always be counted on to try to do the right thing.' Thinking along these lines also clarifies the need for ethics in a company. For example, consider the typical budget debate. During the debate, trust in the decision makers will facilitate open information exchange. In the aftermath of the debate, in which some managers lost and others gained, trust and respect in the people who made the decision will make it more likely that the affected managers will work together in implementing the decision. Trust is also required when managers bestow authority on other people and expect them to make various decisions independently. Finally, trust and fairness are necessary in any evaluation process which attempts to capture the performance of individual managers at the end of a budget cycle. Thus, within a company, trust, and therefore ethics, is like a lubricant which facilitates transactions between the people working in that company.

Trust not only facilitates interaction within the company, but also the interaction between a company and external constituencies, such as suppliers, customers and the communities in which it operates. In this context, Hartley (1993: 2) points out that managers need to be ethical and trustworthy out of enlightened self-interest since 'a firm that violates the public trust today stands to be surpassed by competitors more eager to please customers and develop a trusting relationship with its various publics.' For marketing managers, it is of fundamental importance to develop ethical and trusting relationships with customers. Looking at the prerequisites of exchange relationships, Chapter 2 will pursue this issue in more depth.

1.3 OBJECTIVES AND STRUCTURE OF THE BOOK

So far, we looked at some frequently held (mis)perceptions of business ethics, offered a working definition of the subject, clarified the relationship between ethics and law and pointed out some of the complexities arising when ethical issues transcend cultural boundaries. Moreover, we have argued that ethics is a core leadership characteristic and have shown that ethics, in particular when interpreted as trust, facilitates smooth internal and external company relationships. This discussion made clear that business ethics touches on virtually all aspects of business. However, this book concentrates on a sub-set of possible ethical issues, namely those connected to international marketing management. What follows are some recommendations on who should read the book and an outline of the main components of the text.

1.3.1 Who should read the book

The target audience of this book is business students and practising managers.

Business students, both at graduate and advanced undergraduate level, can use this book as a main text for a business ethics course or self study of the subject. Alternatively, the book can be used as a supplementary source for courses in marketing management or international marketing. In both applications, the text will offer three main benefits: first, the conceptual framework in Part I will introduce the key concepts of business ethics. Second, the cases in Part II will serve as a platform for discussing these concepts in an applied context. Third, the readings in Part III will deepen the understanding of selected topics and, in some instances, might even entice readers to engage in their own research on business ethics.

Practising business managers, who are challenged to make ethical decisions and aim to derive a better understanding of principles that can guide their decision making, can use the book in a different way. They should also begin with Part I to familiarize themselves with the key issues in business ethics. Next, they should work through some selected cases in Part II to facilitate the knowledge transfer into practical settings. But instead of the readings in Part III, mangers will gain most from the Business Ethics Resource Guide at the end of the text. Here, they will find useful addresses, web-sites, examples of codes-of-ethics, etc.

1.3.2 Part I: key concepts

Chapter 2 reviews the role of business ethics in corporate decision making. It introduces the fundamentals of a stakeholder approach to business ethics, broaches the main stream theories and discusses different approaches to analysing business ethics across country borders.

Chapter 3 highlights some of the idiosyncrasies in the practice of business ethics and focuses on the factors impacting on the development of business ethics in the triad, i.e. the United States, Europe and Japan. Specifically, it demonstrates how history and geography have shaped business ethics in these three regions, analyses the impact of religious and philosophical traditions on the perception of ethical issues in business, and compares the nature of public discussion across the triad countries.

Chapter 4 focuses on ethical issues connected to the analysis of international marketing opportunities. Both marketing research in general and competitive intelligence gathering in particular can help international marketing managers to understand their environment, customers and competitors. As such, these activities provide very valuable information that can be the basis for the development of a competitive advantage. Consequently, there are ample temptations to engage in questionable marketing research and competitor intelligence-gathering methods. This chapter identifies some important ethical principles in this arena.

Chapter 5 discusses various ethical aspects in the management of international product-and-price. This includes, among others, unethical product labelling, product packaging and product recall issues. In terms of pricing, the chapter discusses misleading pricing, anti-competitive pricing, price fixing, discriminatory pricing and predatory pricing.

Chapter 6 continues the discussion of ethics in the context of marketing mix instruments by focusing on distribution and promotion policies. Among the topics discussed are the use of unauthorized distribution channels and truth in advertising. Where appropriate, these issues are considered in an international context.

Chapter 7 investigates the means for implementing ethics in corporate decision making. Among the issues raised are the use of training initiatives, the role of corporate codes of ethics and credos, and the function of ethics ombudsmen, offices and committees. In addition, the nature of 'whistle blowing', whereby an employee or manager reports wrong doing to authorities, the purpose of ethics hotlines, and the scope of ethics audits are also explored.

Chapter 8 draws together some of the learnings of the previous chapters and looks at some of the future challenges in business ethics. Three areas are emphasized: ethics and cross-cultural diversity, ethics and multinationals and ethical issues beyond the corporate scope. This first area is mainly concerned with dilemmas arising from clashes between corporate ethics and national culture. The second area explores ethical leadership expectations one might have of multi-nationals. Finally, the limitations of corporate ethics initiatives are highlighted by looking at the need for industry wide and international initiatives.

1.3.3 Part II: cases

The cases in Part Two of the book place some of the key concepts developed earlier into a practical context. The first case **RU 486**, describes the controversy surrounding the so called 'abortion drug'. Based on the French drug developed to abort foetuses at an early stage, this case can be used to illustrate different ethical norms, such as cultural relativism, universalism and utilitarianism. The next case, **The Starnes-Brenner Machine Tool Company – To Bribe or Not to Bribe**, illustrates that bribery does not only involve direct payments to senior decision makers. The case can be used as a platform to discuss the differences between bribery and facilitating payments. Case 3, **Levi Strauss & Co: Global Sourcing**, looks at the span of corporate responsibilities. Among the pertinent case issues are the degree to which manufacturers are to be held responsible for unethical actions of suppliers and how companies should deal with unethical host countries. Case 4, **Audi of America**, deals with the ethics and legality of Audi's rebate and promotion programme. It is questioned whether the policies pursued by Audi represent a bait-and-switch approach.

1.3.4 Part III: readings

The readings presented in this part of the book focus on different international business ethics topics. They all attempt to provide in-depth insights into these particular issues. However, in doing so, the authors utilize rather different methodologies. **Ernest Grundling**, *Ethics and Working with the Japanese: The Entrepreneur and the 'Elite Course'*, uses a number of mini-cases to depict differences in Japanese and American business ethics and to present possible explanations. **Lynn Sharp Paine**: *Corporate Policy and the Ethics of Competitor Intelligence Gathering*, focuses on methods of acquiring competitor information and uses powerful examples to separate legitimate from illegitimate approaches. The paper also suggests steps managers can take to provide ethical leadership in the area of competitor intelligence gathering. **Jack Mahoney**, *Ethical Attitudes to Bribery and Extortion*, represents a conceptual paper. Nearly every international manager will sooner or later come in contact with the issues raised. Having a clear understanding of the differences between bribery, in various shapes and forms, and extortion is required when ethical leadership is called for. The article by **Bodo B. Schlegelmilch and Diana Robertson**, *The Influence of Country and Industry on Ethical Perceptions of Senior Executives in the US and Europe*, uses statistical tests to analyse ethical perceptions of senior executives. The findings suggest that country and industry affiliation have significant effects on the identification of ethical problems and the comprehensiveness of ethics policies and training. **Robert S. Tancer**, *International Marketing of Organs for Transplantation*, tackles a contentious and emotionally charged topic when reviewing various national approaches to the increasing commercialization of organ transplants. Paying for organs and equitable access to the supply of available organs are among the issues discussed in this paper. Staying with health related issues, **Richard Spinello**, *Ethics, Pricing and the Pharmaceutical Industry*, explores the ethical obligations of pharmaceutical companies to charge a fair price for essential medicines. He argues that Rawl's notion of distributive justice is both compelling and practically feasible in industries which are supplying essential commodities. **Catherine Langlois and Bodo B. Schlegelmilch**, *Do Corporate Codes of Ethics Reflect National Character? Evidence from Europe and the United States*, analyse the results of a large survey to explore the usage and contents of corporate codes of ethics in the United States and Europe. The findings indicate that codes of ethics made their way into Europe via subsidiaries of US firms. However, notwithstanding this American influence, a distinctly European approach to codifying ethics has emerged. The final article by **Lyn S. Amine**, *The Need for Moral Champions in Global Marketing*, emphasizes the ethical responsibilities of western managers for the well-being of consumers in the developing world. Particular focus is placed on the 'opportunity' for managers to become involved in dubious ethical decisions and practices when marketing potentially harmful products to consumers in LDCs.

1.3.5 Part IV: resources guide

The final part of the book offers a number of different resources which are useful for practising managers as well as research students. Appendix A contains a list of addresses of **Centres and Institutes of Business Ethics**. These centres are either focusing on particular industries, are engaged in academic research on business ethics or provide advice to companies on a variety of ethical issues (see also Appendix E: Consulting Companies). Appendix B, **Business Ethics Related Sites on the World Wide Web**, addresses the internet users among the readers. It contains the addresses of institutes that have established web-sites, some web-pages of companies that are related to business ethics (e.g. British Petroleum's 'What we care about.') and on-line journals that can be accessed through the internet. Appendix C provides **Examples of Credos and Corporate Codes of Ethics**. Practising managers may want to use these to benchmark their own attempts to formulate or revise similar documents for their companies. Appendix D, **Example of an Ethics Audit Report: The Body Shop**, includes the full Body Shop audit report as distributed by the company to their customers. It provides insights into the topics an ethics audit could address and shows how the findings of such an audit might be distributed. Appendix E, finally, provides a list of companies that offer **Consulting Services in Business Ethics**. There is some overlap between these companies and the addresses given in Appendix A, since some of the centres and institutes also offer services to companies.

1.4 REFERENCES

Badaracco, J. and Ellsworth, R. (1989) *Leadership and the Quest for Integrity*, Boston, MA: Harvard Business School Press.

BARB/Mintel (1991) *The Green and Ethical Shopper*, London: BARB/Mintel.

Bass, B.M. (1990) *Bass and Stogdill's Handbook of Leadership* (3rd edn), New York: Free Press.

Burke, J. (1996) The fine art of leadership. Interview in *Management Review*. October, pp. 13–16.

Center for Business Ethics (1992) Installing ethical values in large corporations. *Journal of Business Ethics*, 11, pp. 863–67.

De George, R.T. (1993) *Competing with Integrity in International Business*, New York: Oxford University Press.

Donaldson, T. (1989) *The Ethics of International Business*, Oxford: Oxford University Press.

Drucker, Peter F. (1968) *The Practice of Management*, London: Pan Books.

Ericson, R. (1995) Socially responsible investing is turning mainstream. *Business Ethics*, Vol. 9, No. 6. p. 43.

Hartley, R.F. (1993) *Business Ethics: Violations of the Public Trust*, New York: John Wiley & Sons, Inc.

Hoffman, M.W. and Moore, J.M. (1990) *Business Ethics* (2nd edn), New York: McGraw-Hill.

Kanungo, R.N. and Mendonca, M. (1996) *Ethical Dimensions of Leadership*, Thousand Oaks: Sage Publications.

Laczniak, G.R. and Murphy, P.E. (1993) *Ethical Marketing Decisions: The Higher Road*, Boston, MA: Allyn and Bacon.

Nadler, D.A. and Tushman, M.L. (1990) Beyond the charismatic leader: leadership and organizational change. *California Management Review*, Winter. pp. 77–97.

Posner, B. and Schmidt, W. (1984) Values and the American manager: an update. *California Management Review*. Spring, pp. 202–16.

Robertson, D.C. and Schlegelmilch, B.B. (1993) Corporate institutionalization of ethics in the United States and Great Britain. *Journal of Business Ethics*. Vol. 12, No. 4, April, pp. 301–12.

Robin, D.P. and Reidenbach, R.E. (1989) *Business Ethics: Where Profits Meet Value Systems*, Englewood Cliffs, NJ: Prentice-Hall.

Schlegelmilch, B.B. (1994) Green, ethical and charitable: another marketing ploy or a new marketing era, in M.J. Baker (ed.) *Perspectives on Marketing Management*, Vol. 4, Chichester: John Wiley & Sons, pp. 55–71.

Schlegelmilch, B.B. (1997) The relative importance of ethical and environmental screening: implications for the marketing of ethical investment funds. *International Journal of Bank Marketing*. Vol. 15, No. 2, pp. 48–53.

Schlegelmilch, B.B. and Robertson, D.C. (1995) The influence of country and industry on ethical perceptions of senior executives in the US and Europe. *Journal of International Business Studies*. Vol. 26, No. 4, pp. 852–81.

Sorell, T. and Hendry, J. (1994) *Business Ethics*, Oxford: Butterworth-Heinemann.

The Sunday Times (1993) Investors see red over green funds. 18 April, Section 4, p. 1. Green Co-op Invested in Animal Testing Laboratories. 4 November p. 1.

The Sunday Times (1994) The growing business of ethics. 8 May, p. 10.

Trommsdorff, V. and Schlegelmilch, B.B. (1996) Ethische Unternehmens-positionierung. Working Paper, Technische Universität Berlin.

US News and World Report (1995) The bottom line on ethics. 20 March, pp. 61–6.

Varadarajan, P.R. and Menon, A. (1988) Cause-related marketing: a coalignment of marketing strategy and corporate philanthropy. *Journal of Marketing*, 52, pp. 58–74.

Weaver, G.R. (1993) Corporate codes of ethics: purpose, process, and content issues. *Business & Society*, 32, pp. 1, 44–58.

Wilner, A.R. (1984) *The Spellbinders: Charismatic Political Leadership*, New Haven, CT: Yale University Press.

2 *Key concepts and approaches*

2.1 THE ROLE OF ETHICS IN CORPORATE DECISION MAKING

Should we expect a company to 'do good' by contributing money to charity? Should a drug company willingly limit its profits in the Third Word? Should a paper manufacturer voluntarily exceed pollution standards set by a host government? In short, how far should a company's social responsibility stretch? The famous Chicago economist and Nobel Laureate Milton Friedman (1962: 33) perceives little scope for corporate social responsibility: 'There is one and only one social responsibility of business – to use its resources and engage in activities designed to increase its profits as long as it stays within the rules of the game, which is to say, engages in open and free competition, without deception or fraud.' This classic statement, widely misunderstood and frequently used by ethicists as an example of unadulterated capitalism, raises some important issues. First, there is the notion of the costs of corporate social responsibility. Are the costs of 'doing something good' not born by the shareholders in the form of lower dividends, by the customers through higher prices, and by the workers via lower wages? Managers deciding to support 'worthy causes' spend someone else's money! Second, there is the notion of competitive disadvantage. If only one company voluntarily sacrifices profits, how will this affect its stock market value? Do managers not put the company into a situation where it places itself at a disadvantage? Finally, there is the notion of managerial competency and legitimacy. Do managers have the right skills to decide which social causes to support and which to ignore? Moreover, managers are not democratically elected. Do they have the legitimacy to deal with social issues?

Despite the weight of the above concerns, most scholars and managers now reject Friedman's argument. They point out that Friedman's neoclassical model of capitalism is inaccurate; companies are not operating in conditions of perfect competition, managers do exercise discretion, even individual companies are powerful and managers often see a positive relationship between 'enlightened self-interest' and long-term profitability (Smith and Quelch 1993).

De George (1993) refers to Friedman's sentiment as the 'Myth of Amoral Business.' This myth, which dominates the thinking of many people on the national and international level, assumes that companies conduct their business transactions with no, or little, regard for personal or professional ethics. The myth's basic flaw is its assumption that companies are operating in a realm unaffected by moral considerations. In reality, every time managers make decisions, they are influenced by a variety of internal and external moral pressures.

Carroll (1978) categorizes these internal and external moral pressures into five different levels:

1   individual;
2   organizational;
3   associational;
4   societal;
5   international.

The individual level is concerned with personal ethical codes. The organizational level maps out the corporate procedures, policies and codes of ethics. The associational level refers to professional guidelines and codes of conduct. The societal level is concerned with the laws, cultures, and traditions which determine the acceptability of actions. The international level focuses on the laws, customs and norms of foreign countries. An example of how various levels can affect a manager's actions may be shown through a company's decision to conduct business in China (refer to the Levi Strauss case in Part Two of this text). Some consumers may boycott products from China because they are offended by China's human rights record on an individual level. On an organizational level, these companies may decide that it is lucrative to continue conducting business in China. Some of these companies may find themselves under pressure from the societal and international levels, when claiming that human rights violations are a matter of domestic Chinese politics and unrelated to their businesses. By ignoring the different moral pressures, companies may jeopardize their reputation and profits.

De George (1993: 5) argues that, 'business, like most other social activities, presupposes a background of morality, and would be impossible without it.' If customers did not trust a particular company, they might not buy its products, fearing that product claims would be untrue. The marketplace is built on trust between the company and the consumer. Any breakdown in this trust will have a detrimental effect on the company's sales. This argument can be linked to marketing theory, which suggests that a business transaction between a buyer and a seller requires the participation of at least two parties, and that each of these parties has something which the other party desires. However, as illustrated in Figure 2.1, every decision is also subject to organizational, personal, and macro-ethical considerations. The ethical compatibility between the two parties is a central factor which affects the trust between the buyer and the seller. Thus, ethical considerations are likely to determine whether each party deems it appropriate to conduct a business transaction with the other party and, therefore, some ethicists will argue that ethics has a direct and positive impact on profit.

However, many times acting 'ethically,' especially in the short run, may hurt the company's profit. Consider a company which discovers that one of its products could endanger the lives of its customers. If it decides to recall the product, it faces indirect and direct costs. The company must not only recall the product from its distributors, but it also needs to inform its customers of the product's potential dangers. Moreover, the company must consider the impact of a recall on its reputation. Publicly admitting that it had developed and gone to market with an unsafe product could cause society to question the company's responsibility. On the one hand, Johnson & Johnson recalled all Tylenol products (a non-prescription pain killer) when there was suspicion that some bottles had been laced with cyanide (see Chapter 1: Exhibit 1.1). The company suffered an approximate $100 million loss in recalling Tylenol from all shelves. But once the product had been completely recalled, society's faith in Tylenol was restored, and it regained its market share almost immediately (De George 1993). On the other hand, Ford Motor Company did not recall its passenger car, the Pinto, even though the company realized it had a defect which could cause the gas tank to explode. The company knew that it would be less expensive to settle law suits

Figure 2.1 Ethical dimensions of the exchange relationship between buyer and seller

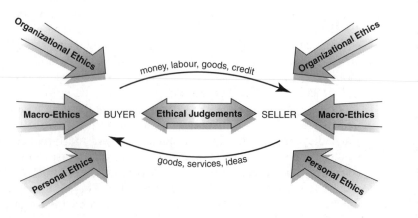

with the families of those killed or injured by the defect than recalling all of the cars. However, when the media discovered this, it led to a serious crisis for Ford Motor Company, which was called upon to justify its inhumane decision.

These cases illustrate that companies are not acting in a vacuum. As such, society will condemn or reward companies on the basis of their moral decisions. As Donaldson (1982:106) puts it: 'defending unadulterated profit maximization tends to generate a vicious circle. If corporations neglect moral issues, society will look outside the corporation for remedies.' Whether companies act philanthropically or merely in 'enlightened self-interest,' it is essential for them to weigh the consequences of their actions.

As multinational corporations become larger and span more countries, the problems facing the corporations become more complex. What is considered 'appropriate' in one country, will not necessarily apply in others. Sometimes corruption will be far greater in a host country than it is in the home country. Sometimes a corporation will find that it wields considerable economic power in smaller, less developed countries (De George 1993).

Marketing managers, in particular, will often come up against some difficult ethical issues. This is due largely to the fact that their business function involves dealing with many different groups of people who have many, and sometimes conflicting, agendas. External forces with which the marketing managers come into contact can include: the media, customers, suppliers, unions, governments, professional investors, special interest groups, and the legal community. In addition to the various pressures marketing managers face from these groups, they must also try to satisfy the needs of internal forces in their organization, such as the board of directors, fellow managers, and employees. Many times the interests of the various forces can come into conflict with each other. For example, a company might want to move its plant to a country where the cost of labour is lower. This decision would save on production costs and increase profits and, thus, be in the best interest of its shareholders. However, a relocation to another country might create negative publicity because it will lead to unemployment for many of its domestic workers. Finally, if the company is moving into a country with an unsavoury human rights record, a special interest group could decide to use it as an example of an 'unethical' company, which could further damage the company's reputation. Trying to balance the needs of the different stakeholders is never easy; there would be no ethical dilemma if it was obvious that one course of action was in all the stakeholders' best interests. However, a company sometimes encounters 'grey areas' where different forces are pulling it in different directions. Consequently, marketing managers need to balance the responsibilities of their companies to each of their different stakeholders and decide how much importance should be given to one stakeholder's interest in relation to another.

Laczniak and Murphy (1993) classify stakeholders into two categories: namely, primary and secondary stakeholders. Primary stakeholders include all 'those who have a formal, official, or contractual relationship with the firm' (p.14). Secondary stakeholders include the external forces which are interested in the company's achievements and actions, but do not have specific ties to the company. They then argue that a company subscribing to the stakeholder concept should see that its primary stakeholders attain their objectives, while at the same time keeping the other stakeholders satisfied. An important but often ignored question, in this context, is the ranking of primary stakeholders (see Chapter 8, Section 8.4.2). Should there be one group of stakeholders, such as the shareholders or customers, whose interests and wishes are paramount and ought to determine company policy and actions? Does it make sense to argue that the interests of some stakeholders always outweigh the interests of others? The following pages provide a closer look at the main groups of stakeholders and illustrate how they influence the decisions made by marketing managers.

2.2   PRIMARY STAKEHOLDERS

2.2.1   Customers

Marketing managers usually argue that customers are the most important stakeholder group for a company, because they are the ones who buy its products or services, thereby keeping the company in business. Since it is the marketing manager who must manage a company's relationship with its customers, it is also mostly the marketing manager who needs to justify the company's actions to the customers. In order to keep customers buying its products or services, a company must obtain and maintain its customers' trust. To do this, a company must be perceived as responsible, receptive to customers' needs, and honest. To build and maintain customer loyalty, marketing managers often act as 'customer-advocates' (Smith and Quelch 1993) by articulating the customers' concerns and needs to their companies. Consequently, marketing managers are often caught in the middle, trying to fulfil their customers' needs as well as meeting their performance targets.

2.2.2   Employees

The ethical environment in a company can influence the attitude and performance of its current employees, as well as the calibre of future employees which the company can entice to work for them. On the one hand, if a company promotes a cut-throat environment, the employees will be less likely to have any loyalty towards fellow employees or to the company as a whole. On the other hand, an environment in which employees are encouraged to act ethically will inspire a cooperative atmosphere which will create motivated and loyal employees. Consider, in this context, the experience of GE Plastics and Borg-Warner Chemicals described in Exhibit 2.1.

EXHIBIT 2.1

GE Plastics and Borg-Warner Chemicals

The need for team building among employees took on a new meaning when, in 1988, GE Plastics purchased Borg-Warner Chemicals. The two companies had been competitors for years. Furthermore, both had two very different corporate cultures. As a result, morale took a dive after the purchase. GE Plastics managers knew that they were faced with the major challenge of integrating the two discordant work cultures and making the two workforces become a single team. Therefore, the managers created a team-building experience called 'Share to Gain' that would make a lasting impression on the participants. The idea was that the employees would work together to renovate dilapidated facilities that were open to and served the entire local community. The feelings of camaraderie and accomplishment experienced by the employees were more than the planners could have hoped for. These projects were the turning point in the integration of GE Plastics and Borg-Warner Chemicals. Source: Adapted from Bollier, D. (1996) Building Corporate Loyalty while Rebuilding the Community. *Management Review*, October, pp. 17–22.

Society expects companies to take a certain degree of responsibility for their employees. If a company fails to look out for the welfare of its employees, its ethical stance may be called into question. Sometimes a company's treatment of its employees is viewed as an indication of how the company treats people in general.

2.2.3 Suppliers

Companies must also consider the suppliers with whom they choose to associate. Being linked to a supplier who violates human rights can be very damaging to a company's image. As Veverka (1993: 3) puts it, 'No executive wants to wake up to a headline screaming that his or her company sells products made by Chinese prisoners or Bangladeshi children.' Companies can no longer plead ignorance. They are expected to be informed, thus not unwittingly perpetuating human rights violations. To this end, companies are establishing policies regarding their suppliers. For example, in 1992, Sears, Roebuck and Co. signed an agreement with the American Clothing and Textile Workers Union, promising to reject Chinese goods made with forced or child labour. Salton-Maxim, which imports about 60 per cent of its inventory from Hong Kong, personally inspects its suppliers' factories to make sure that there are no human rights violations occurring.

Unfortunately, even establishing such policies does not necessarily ensure that human rights violations will not occur. However, it does show that social responsibility now stretches beyond the confines of both corporate and country lines. Companies can no longer justify their position by pleading ignorance or excuse their actions by cultural relativism (see Section 2.4.1).

2.2.4 Shareholders

Most people would argue that a company's ultimate responsibility is to the people who own the company, *i.e.* the shareholders. Since it is the shareholders' capital which allows the company to stay in business, the company will strive to do what is in the shareholders' best interests.

To illustrate the power one individual shareholder can have, consider the example of a Procter & Gamble shareholder who submitted a resolution in 1990 to boycott coffee from El Salvador. Initially, Procter & Gamble did not respond to the shareholder's resolution, who, in the meantime, gathered support from other shareholders around the country. Procter & Gamble's lack of responsiveness eventually led to media coverage of the problems in El Salvador, which in turn forced the company to reconsider its business dealings in El Salvador. The shareholder's concern has led Procter & Gamble to become more careful in its dealings with El Salvador and to adopt a policy where it deals with small coffee growers and is more sensitive to the political situation of the country (Henry 1993).

2.2.5 Institutional investors and ethical investment funds

Closely related to the shareholders are the institutional and professional investors themselves, who are becoming increasingly concerned with the ethical practices of the companies in which they are investing. Institutional and professional investors can have a major impact on companies because they screen and help direct the portfolio choices of their clients. A company known as the Informed Investors Group, based in Seattle, Washington, can serve as an example. The managers counsel clients on investment decisions and help them to create customized portfolios in accordance with their social beliefs. Their commitment to ethical investment extends beyond their immediate pool of clients. The managers of the group also appear on

Table 2.1 Investment criteria of the Friends Provident Stewardship Unit Trust

Positive	Negative
Conservation/anti-pollution	Armaments
Community responsibility	Gambling
Socially useful products	Tobacco
Quality and safety	Alcohol
Progressive employment practices	Oppressive regimes
Equal opportunities	Exploitation of animals
Training	Environmental damage
Standards for overseas conduct	
Advertising standards	
Customer relations	
Openness	

television, produce newsletters, and provide handouts concerning the ethical stances and infractions of companies.

The demand for ethical investment funds, an attempt to combine profit-making with an ethical orientation, has been growing quickly in recent years (Cooper and Schlegelmilch 1993). Although the primary goal of these funds is to make a profit, the investors choose the companies in which they want to invest on the basis of their ethical beliefs. For example, an investor may choose not to invest in companies which test their products on animals or which conduct business in countries controlled by oppressive regimes. Investors may also use positive choice criteria such as investment in companies which produce or sell basic necessities or which contribute to charities and their communities. The criteria used by the Friends Provident Stewardship Unit Trust, one of the oldest ethical investment funds in the United Kingdom, are shown in Table 2.1.

2.3 SECONDARY STAKEHOLDERS

2.3.1 The media

As the rapid advancement of information and communication systems is bringing the world closer together, society is becoming more aware of the actions of companies. An event which occurs in one country can become common knowledge world-wide virtually instantaneously. The power of the media to sway public opinion can greatly impact the sales and the reputation of a company. Management must consider how any decisions may be conveyed in the media and how it will affect the public's perception. The media increasingly acts as a 'watchdog,' sniffing out and revealing underhanded business decisions. However, media power can also have some undesirable consequences. Audi, for example, received negative publicity in the

1980s for a supposed acceleration problem. Television and papers reported the dangers of the car, and Audi's sales and reputation suffered. Eventually, the US federal government released a study which concluded there was no acceleration problem. However, the damage had already been done and the media's retraction of its accusations did little to compensate for the company's tarnished reputation (Jennings 1995).

2.3.2 Special-interest groups

Special-interest groups work closely with the media. These groups seek to inform the public about specific issues, such as environmental protection, arms control, and human rights violations. Through economic and political leverage, these groups can wield considerable power over companies' business practices. An example of the success of a special-interest group is demonstrated by the aforementioned American Clothing and Textile Workers Union, which persuaded Sears to sign an agreement not to buy any products made by prison or child labour. But even charities can exert pressure. Following widespread media coverage detailing the squalid living conditions of Third World agricultural workers, Christian Aid, a British charity, recently launched a campaign to persuade British consumers to put pressure on supermarkets not to source from suppliers that do not conform to certain minimum standards (*The Economist* 1996).

2.3.3 Government/legal environment

There are also a number of governmental and legal considerations which continue to shape the institutionalization of corporate codes of ethics. Among the most important are:

- the US Federal Sentencing Guidelines, which encourage companies to create codes of ethics and to provide ethics training for their employees;
- Foreign Corrupt Practices Act, which sets out guidelines concerning the difference between a 'grease payment' and a bribe;
- US state laws, which are legally deciding matters previously considered ethical issues;
- the US Commerce Department's voluntary business ethics code, which provides guidelines for US companies' business dealings with foreign countries.

(a) US Federal Sentencing Guidelines

The Federal Sentencing Guidelines took effect on November 1 1991. They provide far-reaching guidelines which serve as directives for federal judges to follow in white-collar crime sentencing. Among others, they mandate strict punishments including financial settlements which may exceed $500 million (Ettorre 1994).

The sentencing guidelines establish a procedure to follow in order to minimize managers' and companies' liability if ethical infractions do occur. Specifically, the guidelines provide that a key mitigating factor for judges handing out sentences is the prior existence of a formal ethics effort (Henricks 1995). This provision was designed to encourage organizations to maintain internal mechanisms for preventing, detecting, and reporting criminal conduct and to provide incentives for organizations to hire ethics officers to develop policies and training programmes (Austin 1994). Moreover, top management should be responsible for assuring that the codes of conduct are complied with and behaviour within the organization is monitored. Thus, the impact of the Federal Sentencing Guidelines is threefold. First, companies are encouraged to implement codes of conduct and ethical training. Second, when companies have implemented the guidelines, financial penalties are likely to be lower if an unethical and illegal act is committed by an individual employee. Finally, the guidelines also give the government and the legal profession a basis for determining if a company has done everything within its power to assure that legal infractions will not occur (Paine 1994).

Will the guidelines help further corporate social responsibility and ethical conduct in the workplace? Once again opinion is divided. Some are highly doubtful while others, like W. Michael Hoffman, Director of the Center for Business Ethics at Bentley College, believe that the new regulations will have a watchdog effect on businesses (Austin 1994). There is compelling evidence to support this latter view. According to a Conference Board Study, most large companies had ethical codes of conduct by the early 1980s, but it was not until the Federal Sentencing Guidelines that companies developed an ethics officer position. A 1995 study by the Center for Business Ethics showed that 70 per cent of companies with an ethics officer position had developed it in the past 6 years (Henricks 1995).

(b) Foreign Corrupt Practices Act

Another important consideration, especially in the international arena, is the payment of bribes. In some countries, the payment of bribes is still a widespread practice, which is used to influence officials to exercise their duties improperly. Refusal to make a payment to officials can often leave a manager at an impasse, unable to obtain the necessary paperwork or forms to conduct business in the country. However, bribery is by no means confined to Third World countries. Recent business history contains abundant examples of bribery and corruption in virtually all of the highly developed industrialized nations, including the US, Britain, Germany, and Japan (see

Jack Mahoney's paper on 'Ethical Attitudes to Bribery and Extortion' in Part Three of this text).

After a series of bribes of high-placed foreign officials had been revealed, the Foreign Corrupt Practices Act (FCPA) was passed by the United States in 1977. It was enacted to help define ethical and legal behaviour and to limit the payments of fees, gifts, or bribes (Pitman *et al.*, 1994). The FCPA has three main provisions:

1   an antibribery section;
2   an accounting/record keeping section;
3   a penalty section.

Recognizing that bribes are a common practice in a number of countries, the antibribery section limits the payments of fees, gifts, or bribes to low ranking government officials. The accounting section mandates the financial reporting of such 'grease' expenditures. Finally, the penalty section stipulates the consequences for US companies who fail to comply (Pitman *et al.* 1994).

The FCPA helps to establish the difference between a bribe and a 'facilitating payment.' To this end, the original act specified the individuals to whom it was acceptable to give a 'facilitating payment.' These individuals include low-level officials, who have little power to influence a company's business transactions. In 1988, the act was further refined and now permits payments for routine governmental action, such as processing papers, stamping visas, and scheduling inspections without subjecting the exporter to the worry of whether this type of payment may lead to criminal liability. In contrast, a bribe is defined as a payment which allows a company to receive preferential treatment over competitors, and is strictly prohibited. Indeed, the penalties for paying a bribe are severe: a company can be fined up to $1 million and the manager responsible can be fined $10,000 and/or given 5 years' imprisonment.

The FCPA has been very controversial since its inception. Introduced as an amendment to the Securities Exchange Act, it represented the most significant intrusion of government into corporate affairs since the original enactment of the Securities Exchange Act in 1934 (Pitman *et al.* 1994). Many believe that this unilateral effort by the United States Government to impose international ethical business standards has hurt US exports by giving foreign firms, who are not obliged to follow the FCPA, an unfair competitive advantage over their US counterparts. This was the conclusion reached by a study by Harvard University economist James R. Hines Jr. (Koretz 1996). Others, like Kate Gillespie, are unconvinced. Her 1987 study concluded that the FCPA's potential to hurt US exports remained unproved (Cascini *et al.* 1992).

(c) US state laws regarding ethical issues

US States are increasingly entering the realm of ethical issues and attempting to determine these matters legally. For example, under a new law signed by Governor Wilson in 1996, it is now illegal for the State of California to purchase any items made by foreign slave labour. It is the first State law in the United States to deal with this issue. The state purchasing power covered by the bill is estimated to be between $2 and $4 billion (*Business Ethics* 1996). Similar bills are being introduced in other States. In the state of Massachusetts, companies with six or more employees must comply with a new State law that requires employers to have specific written sexual harassment policies. This new law requires employers to distribute to all employees a written policy statement prohibiting sexual harassment in the workplace (*Investor's Business Daily* 1996).

(d) The US Commerce Department's voluntary business ethics code

The US Commerce Department offers annual awards to US companies judged to be complying the best with its voluntary code of ethical practices in business dealings with foreign countries. The Model Business Principles urge employers to provide a safe and healthy workplace, avoid discrimination on race, religion or sex, avoid the use of child labour or forced labour and promote free expression. The US government plans to encourage foreign governments to draw up similar guidelines for their own companies and will seek international support for its code in such bodies as the Paris-based Organization for Economic Cooperation and Development (see Chapter 8: Section 8.3.2) and the International Labor Organization in Geneva (Lewis 1995).

2.4 THEORIES

After identifying the key stakeholders and defining the interests of each group, a manager must then decide on the best course of action. Ethicists and philosophers have developed theories to explain various ways in which people approach ethical decision making. These theories address age-old questions such as: Is it ever justified to take an action that would sacrifice the well-being of one person if this action would, in turn, benefit many others? Are morals relative or are there certain moral norms which extend beyond all geographic and cultural boundaries? What rights do people possess which should never be violated? Although a manager may not adhere exclusively to one theory or school of thought when faced with a difficult moral decision, a basic knowledge of the different ethical theories will be helpful as a framework in the systematic analysis of ethical issues.

2.4.1 Relativism

Relativism states that there are no universal standards which can be used to judge the morality of a person's actions. Differing views on morality should all be considered equally valid, and everyone should be judged on the basis of their own moral codes. For this reason, all actions must be taken on a case-by-case basis because what is considered 'wrong' in one situation may be considered 'right' in another. When transacting business in the international arena, a relativist's advice might be: 'When in Rome, do as the Romans do.' A foreign national should respect and follow a host country's laws and moral codes even if they are different from his or her own.

The strength of this theory is its respect for the values and practices in different countries. Different religious and cultural ideologies create various moral filters for judging morality. For example, it may not be appropriate to advertise women's clothing in the same way in Europe as in Saudi Arabia, where it is forbidden to show a scarcely-dressed woman on the television. Unfortunately, the relativist theory is often used as a justification for immoral behaviour. The justification is 'everybody else is doing it.' A manager representing a multinational company must realize that an action taken in one country will not always be judged exclusively by local standards. Instead, interested stakeholders from the manager's home country and third nations will also be judging his or her decision. Thus, 'when in Rome, do as the Romans do' does not provide a multinational with an easy fix for ethical dilemmas.

2.4.2 Utilitarianism

Utilitarianism judges the ethical quality of a decision by its consequences. An action is morally right if it produces the greatest good for the greatest number of people affected by the action.

Utilitarians believe that people should follow the course of action which does the most to further the common good. This theory is also referred to as a *consequentialist theory*, because it emphasizes that actions should be judged by their end results and not by the means used to achieve them. When making a decision, a Utilitarian first identifies all the stakeholders and then estimates the costs and benefits for the affected groups. The manager should decide on the course of action which will result in the most good for the largest number of the stakeholders.

The strength of the Utilitarian school of thought lies in its broad picture approach and its emphasis on doing what is best for the collective good. The theory is often used by business managers because it seems to make inherent sense and is compatible with traditional business thinking in terms of costs and benefits. As Lacz-niak and Murphy (1993) argue, this theory emphasizes maximizing happiness or goodness, just as a business manager seeks to maximize profits or return on investment.

The strength of this theory may also provide cause for criticism. Sometimes an action taken for the collective good comes at an unreasonable expense to an individual; aggregate good can some-times causes undue individual suffering. Take for example, a phar-maceutical company selling a drug which will cure 75 per cent of patients suffering from a disease but causes side-effects which will result in the death of the other 25 per cent. Simply speaking, a Utilitarian might argue that the drug should be sold because it would be beneficial to the majority of users as well as the company itself, which would profit from selling the drug.

2.4.3 Universalism

Universalism, or duty-based theory, determines moral authority by the extent to which the intention of a decision is to treat all persons with respect and requires that everyone should act in such as way that the act could be taken as a universal rule of behaviour. The Prussian philosopher, Immanuel Kant, developed two guiding principles in *Kant's Categorical Imperative*, which sum up the essence of univers-alism, namely:

1   act only according to the maxim by which you, at the same time, will that it should become a universal law;
2   act so as to never treat a human being merely as a means to an end.

Universalists, also referred to as deontologists (based on the Greek work *deon*, meaning duty), believe that an individual's well-being is the most important component of any decision. Therefore, the *golden rule*, 'do unto others as you would have them do unto you,' should be applied to all decision making. Universalism is also considered a non-consequentialist theory, signifying that all means to achieve an end are considered in judging an action. No matter how much 'good' results as a consequence of an action, it never justifies using unethical means to achieve it.

The strength of this theory is its emphasis on a decision maker's responsibility to examine the inherent wrongness or rightness of an action and its impact on all affected individuals. Universalism con-siders individual human welfare as the primary stake in any decision (Weiss 1994). In the above example regarding selling the new, but potentially dangerous drug, the Universalist would believe the new drug should not be sold because of the potential danger it could cause some of the users. Unfortunately, the Universalist maxim is often difficult to apply. When a manager is weighing the interests of different stakeholders, situations arise which cannot produce a 'win-win' situation and might be required to sacrifice the interests of one individual for the good of another. Consider the classic dilemma which philosophers use to illustrate the point (see Exhibit 2.2.).

EXHIBIT 2.2

A classic dilemma

You are traveling alone in a remote corner of the world when you stumble upon a primitive tribe. You are in luck. The chief of the tribe likes you and you are fortunate to have arrived in time to partake in a tribal custom, which takes place every full moon. As demanded by the gods, there is a sacrifice of ten members of the tribe. The chief gives you the honour of killing one member of the tribe. Suspecting you may not be skilled with the sacrificial knife, he has suggested that there should be only one victim on this occasion. However, if you refuse the honour, he would conduct the ceremony with the full sacrifice. Your choice is to kill one person and save nine, or not to kill and see ten die. You would be reluctant to offend your host by exploring other options.

What would the Universalist's and the Utilitarian's response be?

Source: Adapted from Smith, C.N. and Quelch, J.A. (1993) *Ethics in Marketing*, Boston, MA: Richard D. Irwin, Inc., p. 16.

2.4.4 The theory of justice

John Rawls' (1971) *A Theory of Justice* is considered an important contemporary approach to moral philosophy. Rawls criticizes the Anglo–Saxon tradition of utilitarianism as introduced by John Stuart Mill (1806–1873) and Jeremy Bentham (1748–1832) for its teleological conception of justice. Rawls points out that defining justice as the greatest good for the greatest number of people denies any categorical rights and duties. For example, according to the utilitarian calculus that treats potential victims of such an apportionment as means and not as ends, slavery would be permissible as long as it generates the greatest happiness for the greatest number. Consequently, Rawls argues that a trade off relationship between basic rights of individuals and the hedonic goals of a society as it is suggested by the principle of utility does not lead to justice.

Rawls suggests a contractarian approach to moral justice, which applies primarily to the relations between institutions (Ricoeur 1990).

Justice as fairness in a social contract implies that an agreement is fair if the circumstances of the choice are fair. This fairness is based on the idea of the original position which hypothetically assumes that no one knows his position in society, not even his place in the distribution of natural talents and abilities. In Rawls' famous allegory of the veil of ignorance, the principles of justice are chosen in the absence of any specific information. A veil of ignorance prevents anyone from being advantaged or disadvantaged by the contingencies of social class and fortune. Hence this hypothetical equality of individuals precludes the bargaining problems which arise in real life. Therefore, the traditional foundational approach to moral justice is replaced by a procedural approach. Based on the imagination of the original position, Rawls formulates two principles of justice (Rawls 1971: 302):

> *First Principle*: Each person is to have an equal right to the most extensive total system of equal basic liberties compatible with a similar system of liberty for all.
> *Second Principle*: Social and economic inequalities are to be arranged so that they are both: (a) to the greatest benefit of the least advantaged, and (b) attached to offices and positions open to all under conditions of fair equality of opportunity.

These principles are to be ranked in a serial or lexical order. A lexical order implies that a loss of liberty cannot be compensated by an increase in economic efficiency. Well being cannot be traded in at the expense of liberty. The lexical order applies also to the two parts of the second principle. Justice is achieved when 'the advantages of the more fortunate promote the well being of the least fortunate, that is, when a decrease in their advantages would make the least fortunate even worse off than they are' (Rawls 1979: 227).

The two principles reflect the maximin solution of rational decision makers as it is suggested by game theory for situations characterized by uncertainty. 'The two principles are those a person would choose for the design of a society in which his enemy is to assign him his place' (Rawls 1971: 153).

The practical application of Rawls' theory cannot avoid measurement problems because elusive expressions such as liberty or benefit would have to be defined and gauged (Rusche 1992). Therefore, it does not seem to be trivial to derive concrete recommendations from Rawls' abstract contractarian approach to moral justice.

2.4.5 The virtue theory

Virtue theory, which has existed for a long time, has enjoyed renewed interest since the mid 1980s. The cornerstone of virtue ethics is 'seeking to live a virtuous life' (Laczniak and Murphy 1993). This means acting beyond duty and beyond self interest in the true spirit of goodness and virtuousness.

Virtue theory finds its roots in the teachings of Aristotle. Three concepts lay the foundations for virtue theory (Laczniak and Murphy 1993). First, virtues are 'good habits' which must be learned, practised and nurtured. Second, virtuous people should be seen as role models to emulate and learn from. Third, a healthy balance of desirable, virtuous qualities should be sought.

In an organization, virtue ethics could be fostered through the inclusion of its desirable and virtuous qualities in its code of ethics. The ensuing corporate culture is then the living result, whereby managers and employees learn from and strive to emulate their virtuous leaders.

2.5 FRAMEWORKS FOR ANALYSING BUSINESS ETHICS ACROSS COUNTRIES

Developing frameworks for a meaningful study and comparison of international ethical standards and practices in business is almost as challenging as the actual analysis itself. Scholars and theorists have struggled over finding the most suitable approach and have proposed different analytical models. Before the next chapter turns to the analysis of various environmental components affecting the character and development of business ethics in different countries and regions, it is useful to consider some frameworks that have been suggested by various scholars as a means for analysing ethical issues across countries. Among the frameworks which have been proposed are:

- A three-pronged approach evaluating business ethics at the individual, organizational, and system-wide levels (Enderle 1995).
- A systematic treatment utilizing general principles in order to reduce the volume and variety of values, whether the values are of an ethical nature or not. In other words, reduce the importance of the number of different values (Donaldson 1992, 1996).
- A micro-ethical framework assessing value systems of individual firms, as opposed to institutionalized values internationally co-ordinated (Schokkaert 1992).
- An approach which analyses ethics problems by categorizing ethical dilemmas into two types: Acute Dilemmas and cases of Acute Denial (Nash 1992).
- Dialogic idealism, which posits that through communication it is possible to find mutually acceptable norms (Nill 1995).
- A suggestion to focus on broad-based issues, and the corresponding input and influences of the many stakeholders in addressing these issues (van Luijk 1992).
- The suggestion to develop true international practices/forms of doing

business so as to minimize nationalistic differences which are presumed to complicate the analysis of international business ethics (Bowie 1993).

Each of these proposed frameworks provides insight into the challenges of studying international business ethics. A closer look at these ideas reveals some of these challenges and indicates how scholars have proposed addressing them.

2.5.1 Enderle's three-pronged approach

Enderle has developed a grid comparing different approaches to business ethics (specifically between Europe and the US, but presumably the framework would work for comparisons between other regions and countries as well). One dimension of comparison is the level of analysis: individual/micro-level; organizational/meso-level; and system-wide/macro-level. The second dimension of comparison represents three qualitatively different levels of acting: speaking about business ethics/semantics; acting ethically/practice; and thinking about business ethics/theory. This approach is summarized in the following matrix (Enderle 1995).

	Semantics (speaking about business ethics)	*Practice (acting ethically in business ethics)*	*Theory (thinking about business ethics)*
Micro-level (persons)			
Meso-level (organizations)			
Macro-level (systems)			

This approach neither distinguishes specific issues of ethical dilemmas, nor does it focus on environmental differences of different countries. Instead, by its very nature it assumes that actors at all three levels (individual, organization and systemic) are exposed and forced to make decisions and take actions which necessarily involve ethical dimensions, but not a particular set of values, specific rationality, or world view. Instead, this method of comparisons focuses primarily on 'human action, the independent variable of all morality' (Enderle 1995).

2.5.2 Donaldson's simplified approach: general principles

Donaldson posits that 'The key issues of business ethics have more to do with how rules are made, than with what rules are made' (Donaldson

1992: ix). His proposal is to develop a systematic treatment of business ethics by developing a set of general principles which can be applied in order to evaluate all situations. For example, he suggests to assign any given situation to one of two categories detailed below. Such categorization, in turn, would help to analyse systematically whether a given course of action is ethical or not. This would reduce the volume and variety of individual values, whether ethical or not, to a set of general principles. The outcome of the approach would avoid arbitrary treatment by individuals. Donaldson indicates that the subjective element in judgements about values is not the most serious problem for anyone attempting the systematic handling of values, but that the 'more formidable' problem is the sheer number and variety of values that enter into business and what people say and do within and about it.

In developing general principles, he suggests that similar cases should be treated alike and assigned to various principles. Specifically, in case of a given ethical difference between two societies, Donaldson suggests to analyse this difference by assigning it to one of two categories:

- Category 1: The reason underlying the host country's view that the practice is permissible lies in the country's *relative level of economic development.*
- Category 2: The reason underlying the host country's view that a given practice is permissible is *independent of* the country's *relative level of economic development.*

When faced with a category 1 situation, Donaldson argues that the different standards should be accepted if the members of the home country, under conditions of economic development relatively similar to the host country, would regard the practice as permissible. Thus, he suggests to make allowances for local conditions when dealing with a developing country and judging issues like environmental standards, work-safety conditions, etc.

In a category 2 situation, Donaldson calls for a second level of analysis in order to decide whether a different ethical standard should be condoned. He argues that a practice should be viewed as permissible if it is *impossible to conduct business successfully* in the host country without engaging in the practice, and if the practice *does not violate 'fundamental international rights'.* These rights are: freedom of physical movement, ownership of property, freedom from torture, a fair trial, non-discriminatory treatment on the basis of such characteristics as race or sex, physical security, freedom of speech and association, minimal education, political participation and subsistence.

Sorell and Hendry (1994) criticize Donaldson's algorithm on a number of accounts. Among others, they argue that in Donaldson's category 2 situation, the use of the word 'successful' leaves too much room for interpretation. This is illustrated by the following example. If it is necessary to make a large cash payment to a senior government official to conduct any type of business in a country, such conduct would appear to be permissible on Donaldson's criteria, as it does not breach any international right and it is clearly necessary for any (successful) business. Consequently, they conclude that '. . . there are unlikely to be any simple rules or algorithms that can determine what is ethically acceptable practice across cultures' (Sorell and Hendry 1994: 221).

2.5.3 Schokkaert's approach: global issues

Schokkaert (1992) makes a case that some environmental issues are so large and technically complex that they can only be reasonably addressed from a global perspective. An example provided is the greenhouse effect. The value systems of individual firms (and even less so of individuals, by extension of this approach), even if in total support of policies that would provide for reduction of pollution, are by themselves insufficient to produce necessary changes. The need for an international political debate is paramount, and is the only reasonable approach for addressing such global, complex types of issues.

Schokkaert acknowledges conflicting forces between market desires and the role and responsibilities of government in addressing such global and political problems. Addressing these immense problems must be undertaken with an understanding that there will always be a trade off between different objectives, which all cannot be obtained to the same degree. Thus, ethical questions must be weighted in effect. Considering the question of global pollution, the question of the first order is what weight should be given to the material welfare of present and future generations?

Furthermore, the well being of millions of poor people in the less developed countries remains a dominant challenge to the economic system. With the conflict already acknowledged between market and government forces, how economic systems deal with the extremely poor economic status of many Third World countries is another global question that cannot be addressed by evaluating and studying ethical values of smaller components of business systems (firms and individuals). Environmental degradation and pollution cannot be fully addressed without taking these other global problems into consideration at the same time.

Obviously, these issues and how to approach them are huge and volatile questions. Getting local and national governments to address these questions in a meaningful and productive way happens rarely enough. Global efforts are even more complicated. There are a myriad forces and demands, which are often in conflict with one another and need to be addressed. Yet dialogue does occur on a global basis to address pollution, decimation of natural resources, etc.

To state that international debate is required in order to address global problems can hardly be criticized. Mobilizing governments and convincing groups with different motivations and goals to give up some of their demands is without doubt a situation requiring international focus and effort. It seems self-evident that some of the largest problems facing our global society can only be solved, or even adequately addressed, from an international political perspective.

Yet using this framework as a means for studying international business ethics may in fact be a situation of putting the cart before the horse. Shared values leading to shared perceptions as to the existence and need for the resolution of issues needs to precede any efforts to resolve these issues.

2.5.4 Nash: two types of ethical problems

Almost refreshing in its approach, after considering the truly weighty problems of the world Schokkaert wrestles with above, is Nash's (1992) suggestion for evaluating ethical problems by type. Nash proposes dividing ethical problems into one of two types. Type A problems are 'acute' dilemmas, which are characterized as 'situations of moral uncertainty, where we don't automatically know right from wrong, where two or more ethical values are in conflict' (Nash 1992: 172). In such situations, faced most often by senior management, Nash believes, it is the *process* for resolving such dilemmas that may provide the appropriate focus for analysis. In these situations, the outcome will probably always appear flawed to some extent (a result of two ethical values being in conflict), so the process provides the moral test. The honesty of the deliberation process and assurance of representation of affected parties' points of view become the primary elements of consideration of the ethical values in use.

Type B problems are those categorized as 'cases of acute denial'. These problems arise when the right action is objectively known, but is not followed. These are often moral and ethical issues of compliance and implementation, often encountered by line managers. Nash proposes ways businesses can address both types of problems, utilizing different strategic approaches, including training and dissemination of corporate standards to workers.

The benefit of this approach is its simplicity. The question as it applies to international business ethics is: does it provide a sufficiently flexible and comprehensive model for comparative analysis of issues arising in different cultures, business and legal environments, business practices, etc.?

2.5.5 Nill: dialogic idealism

Dialogic idealism is a contemporary approach to business ethics in the Kantian tradition (Nill 1995). Dialogic idealism abandons any attempts in searching for universal ethical principles that are both valid and practical at the same time. Instead, communication is viewed as a way to find mutually acceptable norms. These norms, which are generated in an open dialogue, may not be universally valid but they are acceptable to the specific participants of a given dialogue. As participants naturally have conflicting interests, they may not be able and willing to come to a communicative agreement. Therefore, the dialogic idealist theory suggests two levels: level one, which represents the concept of the ideal dialogue, and level two, which represents the actual dialogue.

2.5.6 Van Luijk: a broader discussion

In keeping with Schokkaert's position that a broad, large-scale approach is required to adequately address large-scale issues, van Luijk (1992) maintains that analysing business ethics from the level of the corporation is an 'uninteresting frame for debate'. There is a need to escape the prior restrictive and opposing views that the proper, ethical role of corporations is to either increase profits, or alternatively, to contribute to the common good regardless of the impact on the corporation's profitability. Neither of these views has proved adequate as an analytical framework.

Van Luijk suggests changing the framework by rethinking basic concepts such as collective responsibility, mixed motives, and shifting social coalitions. He, like Schokkaert (1992), believes that the future will require coalitions of stakeholders perhaps never brought together before, for example, government agencies, interest groups, and the media.

2.5.7 Bowie: a true international society

Bowie (1993) suggests that the proper approach to ethical analysis is to develop international forums and collaborations. His suggestion is to internationalize *keiretsu* (Japanese business) practices and to develop joint venture *keiretsu* organizations. Bowie sees this as a natural development of companies as they expand their international customer base. They should develop international *keiretsu* partnerships which serve as international supplier bases. This in turn will lead to the internationalization of financial markets, leading to global mutual funds.

What Bowie suggests is occurring already to some degree. How the development of international trade and financial markets naturally leads to a consensus of international agreement as to necessary ethical practices or even ethical debate has yet to be seen. It is not certain at this point whether one trend automatically will lead to the other.

Indeed, at present, ethical differences between countries still appear to be rather pronounced. Consider the results of a recent survey on corruption summarized in Exhibit 2.3.

EXHIBIT 2.3

Survey determines the 10 most corrupt countries
Merchant International Group, a London-based corporate research firm, recently compiled a list of the world's most corrupt countries. The list is primarily based on a survey of 2,500 foreign corporations operating in the countries. The results are calculated according to the number of incidents of corruption each corporation claimed to have experienced. This firm's research highlights 'grey-area dynamics' in different countries and aims to give investors an idea of the level of institutional corruption and other types of fraud (such as counterfeiting) that exists. Heading the list is Russia, followed by Venezuela, Mexico, Pakistan, Brazil, China, Indonesia, the Philippines, Turkey, and India.
Source: Adapted from Larner, D. (1996) A Top-10 List that Nations would Love not to Make: U.K. Survey Ranks Countries by Corruption. *The International Herald Tribune*, October 26, p. 21.

2.6 SUMMARY

This chapter introduced some key concepts and approaches to analysing business ethics. It opened by exploring Friedman's views on the role of ethics in corporate decision making and by highlighting the need for ethics to facilitate business exchanges.

Subsequently, stakeholder analysis has been presented as a useful means of approaching ethical issues. Corporations and the marketing functions, in particular, are constantly being pushed back and forth, jostled between interests in and responsibilities toward various stakeholders. These stakeholders' different moral beliefs and interests influence managers' decisions by pressuring managers into certain solutions in response to social commitment and concern for the company's reputation.

Next, the discussion focused on some important ethical theories. While the treatment of these theories had to be brief, even a rudimentary knowledge of alternative approaches should improve a manager's ethical reasoning skills. The fact that different theories often lead to different conclusions should not be taken as evidence to dismiss business ethics as a futile exercise, but viewed as an opportunity to improve one's understanding of ethical dilemmas and decision making.

As businesses cross borders and internationalize, ethical dilemmas and issues become more complex. Therefore, much thought has been given to the overall question of how to engage in meaningful discussion concerning international business ethics. The chapter closed with a look at some frameworks which suggest how to best address this subject. As increasing internationalization of finance and trade occurs, ethical issues across borders will become more acute and widespread. New ideas will undoubtedly be proposed and current proposals refined.

2.7 REFERENCES

Austin, N. (1994) The new corporate watchdogs. *Working Woman*, 19(1), pp. 19–20.

Bollier, D. (1996) Building corporate loyalty, while rebuilding the community. *Management Review*, October, pp. 17–22.

Bowie, N.E. (1993) *International business, a universal morality and the challenge of nationalism*, in Thomas W. Dunfee and Yukimasa Nagayasu (eds), *Business Ethics: Japan and the Global Economy*, Norwell, MA: Kluwer Academic Publishers.

Business Ethics (1996) Progress on sweatshops, November/December, p. 12.

Carroll, A.B. (1978) Linking business ethics to behavior in organizations. *Advanced Management Journal*, Vol. 7, Summer 1978, pp. 110–112.

Cascini, K. and Vanasco, R.R. (1992) FCPA: the American antibribery legislation. *Managerial Auditing Journal*, 7(2), pp. 24–9.

Cooper, M. and Schlegelmilch, B.B. (1993) Ethical investment: a review of key issues and a call for future research. *Business Ethics: A European Review*, Vol. 2, No. 4, pp. 213–27.

De George, R.T. (1993) *Competing with Integrity in International Business*, Oxford: Oxford University Press.

Donaldson, J. (1992) *Business Ethics: A European Casebook*, London: Academic Press, Inc.: Harcourt Brace Jovanovich, Publishers.

Donaldson, T. (1996) Values in tension: ethics away from home. *Harvard Business Review*, Vol. 74, No. 5, September/October, pp. 48–59.

Donaldson, T. (1982) *Corporations and Morality*, Englewood Cliffs, NJ: Prentice Hall.

The Economist (1996) Ethical shopping: bananas, November 2, p. 59.

Enderle, G. (1995) A comparison of business ethics in North America and Europe. *Working Paper*, University of Notre Dame, College of Business Administration, Notre Dame, Indiana.

Ettorre, B. (1994) Crime and punishment: a hard look at white-collar crime. *Management Review*, 83(5), pp. 10–16.

Friedman, M. (1962) *Capitalism and Freedom*, Chicago: University of Chicago Press.

Henricks, M. (1995) Ethics in action. *Management Review*, 84(1), pp. 53–5.

Henry, K. (1993) Investment firm capitalizes on social responsibility. *Puget Sound Business Journal*, Vol. 13, February 26, 1993, p. 1.

Investor's Business Daily (1996) Law requires companies to deal with sexual harassment, September 24, A4.

Jennings, M. (1995) Confessions of a business ethicist. *The Wall Street Journal*, September 25, 1995, p. A-14.

Koretz, G. (1996) Bribes can cost the US an edge. *Business Week*, 3471, p. 30.

Laczniak, G.R. and Murphy, P.E. (1993) *Ethical Marketing Decisions – The Higher Road*, Boston, MA: Allyn & Bacon.

Larner, D. (1996) A top-10 list that nations would love not to make. *The International Herald Tribune*. October, 26, 1996, p. 21.

Lewis, P. (1995) U.S. provides first details of its business ethics code. *The New York Times*. May 27.

Nash, L.L. (1992). *American and European Corporate Ethics Practices: A 1991 Survey*, in Jack Mahoney and Elizabeth Vallance (eds), *Business Ethics in A New Europe*, Norwell, MA: Kluwer Academic Publishers.

Nill, A. (1995) *Strategische Unternehmensführung aus ethischer Perspektive*, Münster: LIT Verlag.

Paine, L.S. (1994) Managing for organizational integrity. *Harvard Business Review*. March-April, 1994, pp. 106–17.

Pitman, G.A. and Sanford, J.P. (1994) The foreign corrupt practices act revisited: attempting to regulate 'ethical bribes' in global business. *International Journal of Purchasing and Materials Management*, Vol. 30, Issue 3, Summer, pp. 15–24.

Rawls, J. (1971) *A Theory of Justice*, Cambridge, MA: Harvard University Press.

Rawls, J. (1979) *Distributive Justice*, in Thomas Donaldson and Patricia Werhane (eds), *Ethical Issues in Business*, Englewood Cliffs, NJ: Prentice Hall.

Ricoeur, P. (1990) On John Rawls' *A Theory of Justice*: is a pure procedural theory of justice possible? *International Social Science Journal*, November 1, 42, (4) pp. 553–64.

Rusche, T. (1992) *Philosophische versus ökonomische Imperative einer Unternehmensethik*, Münster: LIT Verlag.

Schokkaert, E. (1992) *Business ethics and the greenhouse problem, the world environment: a critical challenge to Europe*, in Jack Mahoney and Elizabeth Vallance (eds), *Business Ethics in A New Europe*, Norwell, MA: Kluwer Academic Publishers.

Smith, C.N. and Quelch, J.A. (1993) *Ethics in Marketing*, Boston, MA: Richard D. Irwin, Inc.

Sorell, T. and Hendry, J. (1994) *Business Ethics*, Oxford: Butterworth-Heinemann.

van Luijk, H.J.L. (1992) *A Vision of Business in Europe*, in Jack Mahoney and Elizabeth Vallance (eds), *Business Ethics in A New Europe*, Norwell, MA: Kluwer Academic Publishers.

Veverka, M. (1993) China syndrome: firms struggle on rights issue. *Crains Chicago Business*. July 5, p. 3.

Weiss, J.W. (1994) *Business Ethics: A Managerial, Stakeholder Approach*, Belmont, CA: Wadsworth Publishing Company.

3 *Environmental influences on business ethics in the triad*

3.1 FACTORS IMPACTING THE DEVELOPMENT OF BUSINESS ETHICS

The development of business ethics in different countries or regions is heavily influenced by the environmental conditions in which businesses operate. For example, some issues regulated by law in one country may be left to the discretion of individual businesses in another country. Laws have, in addition to a possibly moral imperative, the requirement of compliance, a threat of penalties and fines. Some may claim that laws are nothing more than a matter of compliance: 'that it is not the purpose of laws to make people ethical in their behaviour. Their purpose is less ambitious – to compel people to behave or not to behave in certain ways which are designated from time to time either as legally mandatory or as crimes, *i.e.*, as actions which are legally forbidden and punishable' (Harvey 1994: 33). There is no guarantee, though, that actions judged to be illegal are necessarily ethically wrong, or that all immoral or unethical acts are illegal (see Chapter 1, Section 1.1.3). However, in the study of comparative international business ethics, it is important to recognize that laws established by governments may obviate the need for businesses to devise their own ethical standards in certain areas. One such example is the US Foreign Corrupt Practices Act (FCPA) discussed in the previous chapter. The point here is that with the FCPA providing a firm with legal guidelines which may or may not correspond with a company's ethical guidelines, the law supersedes a firm's need to establish a separate policy in the matter of bribery. The same holds true for operations in other areas and countries as, for instance, in terms of hiring and firing, environmental protection, and so forth.

There are not only differences in laws in the different countries of Europe, in Japan and in the United States, but also differences in other environmental factors such as the economic systems, the extent of nationalism, the history and geography of the countries, and the religious and philosophical traditions. Indeed, there is a vast body of literature addressing each of these factors within the United States, Japan and Europe, and a comprehensive discussion of all of these factors would be clearly beyond the scope of this book. However, this chapter attempts to provide at least a brief outline of some of these important issues. This will help to set the stage for a subsequent comparison of ethics initiatives in the triad.

3.2 HISTORY AND GEOGRAPHY

3.2.1 The United States

'Advanced' society in the United States is relatively young, especially when compared to Japan and Europe. Physically, the country is a huge land. Individual states are larger than some European countries. During its settlement by Europeans (and others), natural resources were abundant. The wide oceans on the borders have provided natural defences, which have allowed focus on individual needs without fear of foreign intrusion. Self-sufficiency was therefore possible and prized as a value of the individualistic society that was built. This self-sufficiency and the related bootstrap mentality of the 'American dream' were quick to become societal norms. The Protestant ethic (discussed in more detail below) exerted a strong influence on the development of the nation's self-identity and personality.

This strong independence, individualism and self-sufficiency resulted in less involvement with other countries, and less influence and definition imposed by outsiders. Americans are noted for their tendency 'to say what they mean and mean what they say,' even when engaging in business negotiations.

Another distinctive element of America's historical development as noted by Vogel (1993: 31), is

'the considerable emphasis that historically has been placed on the social obligations of business. Because corporations played a critical role in the development of cities and the shaping of communities in the United States, they long have been perceived as social institutions with substantial responsibility for the moral and physical character of the communities in which they have invested.'

Related practices of corporate philanthropy and this history of social responsibility have existed for more than a century.

3.2.2 Europe

Europe, on the other hand, has traditionally had more international relations. The creation of the Single European Market and the European Union are the most recent and clearest manifestations of this fact. Even countries not included in these pacts think and adapt to concerns broader than merely national issues. Small countries, for example Belgium, the Netherlands, and Switzerland, have always been forced to have an international outlook. The larger countries that have been colonial powers, such as France, the United Kingdom, Spain, and Portugal are still linked with their former colonies in numerous ways. This international experience and outlook has resulted in more exposure and more familiarity with international ethical challenges.

However, even with the experience and geographical proximity of foreign countries to one another in Europe, there is no certainty or guarantee of agreement as to ethical standards or practices. Jackson (1992), has examined the issue of trust in a pluralist culture. Her analysis begins from the premise that trust is the underpinning of all moral virtues. She identifies three obstacles to trust in modern Europe, which assist in the understanding of the impact of history and geography on the development of European and international business ethics. These three obstacles are pluralism, liberalism, and mobility.

Pluralism, the coexistence of numerous and diverse nationalities within Europe, naturally results in a community that is most definitely not homogenous. The result of cultural and national diversity is that shared understanding cannot be assumed: 'The same code might turn out to lend itself to startlingly different interpretations in different corners of the community' (Jackson 1992: 36).

Liberalism is identified as a shared commitment to tolerance of personal freedoms and lack of stereotyping. Jackson argues that in efforts to avoid stereotyping, real cultural and traditional differences may be brushed aside as irrelevant, when acknowledgement of these differences might lead to better understanding between people.

Mobility as the third obstacle might better be defined as 'technological distancing' from one another. Modern communications devices increasingly replace face-to-face contact. Lack of regular physical contact with business associates reduces opportunities and, indeed, the necessity for establishing trust and co-operation.

Jackson's discussion helps in understanding that although Europe's history, geography and experience have fostered international dealings with its own neighbours, this does not necessarily ensure a smooth route to consensus toward international ethical analysis.

3.2.3 Japan

Japan is far enough from the Asian continent to have escaped involvement in continental upheavals, but close enough to have benefited from its culture. Japan's history is vastly different from both Europe and the United States. Its prior feudal society, coupled with its geographic and self-imposed isolationism in its early history, established exceedingly different historical traditions and outlooks toward the conduct of business inside and outside its borders. Under centralized governments which regulated their lives in detail, the Japanese culture is perceived to be homogeneous; primary importance has always been placed on the group rather than the individual, accounting for the uniformity of Japanese culture.

Tsunehiko Yui (1993) examines Japanese history in three phases. The first, the Tokugawa feudal society (1600–1867), was a formal and stylized feudal society, with strong hierarchical authority permeating all classes and relationships of work and society. Work was closely bound to Confucian beliefs and loyalties. While the Tokugawa was a period of economic activity and domestic commerce, merchants were closely bound to guilds which fostered group responsibility and ethical norms. The rigid roles and duties defined by the Tokugawa society discouraged the rise of individual capitalism in spite of the growing wealth of the merchant class.

The second phase of Japanese history Yui discusses is the Meiji Restoration (1868–1912), which abolished the feudal system without abolishing the horizontally structured, group-oriented societal structure. The Meiji Restoration was a period of slow change and did not result in a revolutionary rejection of traditional, social values. Western technology was desired, while the materialism of the West was rejected. Harmony and loyalty continued to be emphasized as important social values. Continuing subservience of individual rights to the welfare of the group led to the beginning of Japanese management models of lifetime employment and seniority systems.

It was not until the end of World War II that Japan entered the third phase Yui analyses, 1945–1980. Post-war Japan was a period of extreme and numerous, sometimes conflicting, changes and motivations. The country was eager to adopt changes, with the United States serving as a model. Economic growth, growth of individual freedoms and rights, and social mobility occurred after the war. During this time, there was also an almost nationalistic drive to produce wealth for the country. Emphasis on maximizing GNP motivated economic activity and individual work efforts for a number of years. The concepts of loyalty and duty to one's company, which began during the Meiji Restoration, continued during this period and provided workers with a sense of purpose.

Changes are still taking place in Japan's modernization, with the GNP maximization being questioned, amid the rise of individual rights and individual mobility. In summarizing the changes Japan has experienced in its post-war era, Yui states the dilemma well: 'Western commentators have often underestimated the extent to which Japanese society has changed' (Yui 1993: 272). And on the following page, 'It is impossible to overemphasize the impact of changing values and ethical norms.'

3.3 RELIGIOUS AND PHILOSOPHICAL TRADITIONS

3.3.1 The United States

The United States is as known for its emphasis on independence and individual freedoms as Japan is known for its emphasis on group loyalties. The reward for individual initiative, the 'boot-strap' mentality, is inculcated throughout society. This began with the Puritan ethic, which provided a moral justification, if not imperative, for pursuing wealth. Hard work in the name of God was to be rewarded on earth, as well as in heaven. 'Profit was praised as a moral and spiritual achievement; the road to riches coincided with the road to virtue' (Chang 1993). Individuals were rewarded individually for their efforts. The Protestant Ethic viewed work as a worldly sign of salvation rather than a means for attaining salvation. Indeed, the Puritans likely had the most profound influence on early American ideology and values, since they came to the United States very early.

Since Puritans were not to be consumed by their own successes or failures, self-discipline was important (Cavanagh 1990). Puritans fully integrated business with worship. God was often mentioned in invoices, thanking Him for profit or accepting losses for His glory. Work was done individually, and salvation was achieved individually as well. This mutual understanding and support between religion and business became a hallmark of early American society.

Alexis de Tocqueville, a French observer of early American life, saw Americans as hardworking and individualistic; the only rationale Americans might have had for their actions and attitudes, according to Tocqueville, was enlightened self-interest (Cavanagh 1990). He felt Americans were disinclined to reverence tradition, reflect, or philosophize. Self-interest could not, however, make people good and virtuous on its own, and thus could not effectively serve as a cornerstone for morality.

Freedom is another important American value, and the one that is most discussed. It is the cornerstone of the *laissez-faire*, free-enterprise economic system and the rest of American life (Cavanagh 1990). Freedom permeates business ideology. Other values include equality, patriotism, material comfort, external conformity, rationality and measurement, optimism and the inevitability of progress. These values make up the ideology which is so important for business; without an ideology, a mission statement and co-operation, decisions, and implementation of business initiatives is difficult.

Capitalism provided the economic framework for these values and views, with its concepts and goal of a free market and the promotion of individual wealth. Yet it should be understood also that the Protestant heritage has greatly contributed to the defining of American values and that the United States still remains a highly moralistic society. 'Americans are more likely to believe that business and

Table 3.1 Change of values which underlie the American business system

Protestant Ethic	Pluralism and Self-fulfilment
1 Hard work	1 Salary and status
2 Self-control and sobriety	2 Self-fulfilment
3 Self-reliance	3 Entitlement
4 Perseverance	4 Short-term perspective (if not successful here, move on)
5 Saving and planning ahead	5 Immediate satisfaction (buy on time, little savings)
6 Honesty and observing the 'rules of the game'	6 Obey the law (in any case, don't get caught)

Source: Cavanagh 1990: 216. Reprinted by permission of Prentice-Hall, Inc., Upper Saddle River, NJ.

morality are, and should be, related to each, that good ethics is good business, and that business activity both can and should be consistent with high personal moral values' (Vogel 1993: 32). It should not be forgotten though, that the purpose of business in America is to make a profit. Vallance (1992) points to the importance of defining the place of ethics in business properly. She argues that within Capitalism, the aim of business is not itself a moral aim; it is a commercial one and that commercial organizations would be wrong to believe themselves to be in business to dispense social justice and create human fulfilment. However, 'this does not mean that business has, should have, or can afford to have, no morality' (ibid.: 45). The Protestant ethic has shifted to pluralism and self-fulfilment, as demonstrated in Table 3.1.

Despite the legalistic separation of the Church from the government and business that is a part of the American Constitution, religious organizations have persisted in ethical and moral issues that have pervaded American business practices. Exhibit 3.1 illustrates one example of this.

EXHIBIT 3.1

Social investors triumph with 3M tobacco ban

The nation's third-largest billboard company, St. Paul, Minnesota-based 3M Media, a subsidiary of 3M, announced in mid-May that effective December 31 1998, it will withdraw from billboard advertising of tobacco products and promotions, including tobacco-sponsored events.

The announcement came in response to efforts by the Interfaith Center on Corporate Responsibility (ICCR), the New York-based coalition of 275 Protestant, Catholic, and Jewish institutional investors who raise social issues with corporations. In the past eight months, four members submitted four different shareholder resolutions. In addition, health care systems belonging to ICCR threatened to stop buying various 3M health products.

The gradual withdrawal was necessary from 3M Media's point of view to avoid significant adverse impact on its business.

'The three most highly advertised cigarettes, Marlboro, Camel, and Newport, are the three most used by teenagers,' says Reverend Michael Crosby, ICCR's tobacco programme coordinator. 'And being a responsible company, their involvement in cigarette advertising was, to us, a huge contradiction,' he says. 3M products include the litmus stethoscope, nitrogen patches, and various other hospital products.

Crosby says ICCR has also approached Gannett, the country's leading billboard advertiser, but says the company refuses to discuss the issue. 'They've been hiding behind the First Amendment,' says Crosby.

Source: Adapted from Scott, M. (1996) Social Investors Triumph with 3M Tobacco Ban. *Business Ethics*. Volume 10, Number 4. July/August, p. 13.

The profit motive leads to distinctly different attitudes of the purpose and goal of corporations in Japanese and American societies. In Japan, because of the group normative environment discussed above, 'the corporation is thought to exist for its employees rather than for its shareholders' (Taka 1993: 45). In the United States it is commonly accepted, and in fact the law, that the corporation which is owned by the shareholders, has as its highest duty to increase the wealth of those shareholders, even if this requires the disappearance of the corporation through merger or acquisition (compare to the discussion of stakeholders in Chapter 2).

Corporate downsizing, mergers and acquisitions, and divestitures are commonplace experiences these days, with little concern given to the situations of the affected workers, all in the pursuit of maximizing shareholder wealth. At the same time, individual workers experience great freedom in seeking their own wealth without being duty-bound to their corporation. While American workers are not devoid of a sense of corporate loyalty, it is not uncommon for workers and executives to change jobs and companies in search of better work and compensation possibilities. Chasing the literal pot of gold during the Gold Rush, or crossing over the Oregon Trail to seek fortune on the Pacific coast, or merely moving from depressed areas to boomtowns, is all part of the American culture. There is not a limitation on individual movement as can be found in the Japanese system due to the sense of group loyalty.

3.3.2 Europe

The Founding Fathers of the United States were influenced by European thinkers like John Locke, Jean-Jacques Rousseau, and Adam Smith, so Western European traditions are not totally unlike those of the United States. Ancient Greeks thought of work and business as demeaning (Cavanagh 1990). Work was seen as a necessary evil, a burden required to survive. Plato viewed work as something to avoid because it hinders the ability to live and to contemplate. Aristotle found crafts, trade, and business detrimental to one's health and character. He considered work the deprivation of the leisure necessary to contemplate the good, the true, and the beautiful; it hinders the proper physical, intellectual, and moral development. In addition, it is 'illiberal' because it is performed for pay and is less perfect because its end is outside itself.

The Christian tradition has also contributed to the European attitude toward work. Christianity holds that work is necessary to earn a living, but also out of love and concern for one's fellow human beings. Many scholars hold Christianity as an important step forward in the foundation for work and business values, especially in its emphasis on love of neighbour (Cavanagh 1990). By 1700, Christianity had aided in the development of business and commerce. Work was considered as something valuable for the first time because it provided self-discipline and an integrating force in a person's life. Even better, work often enabled one to help family and neighbours; the Catholic Church made efforts to foster community and co-operation among all people, rich or poor. However, because of its 'otherworldly theology,' the Catholic Church thwarted the onslaught of capitalism. The modern European perspective on work and family is illustrated in the commentary by Patricia Hedberg (see Exhibit 3.2).

EXHIBIT 3.2

The European perspective on work and family

Four-week summer vacations. Two-hour lunch breaks. Thirty-hour work weeks. Compensated child care. When it comes to balance, it seems our European counterparts are doing it right.

In ranking the number and importance of work-family initiatives, the United States lags far behind its Western industrial counterparts.

This low performance may result from the way we provide family support. In Europe political units provide government-supported child care, regardless of income. While 21 per cent of

U.S. children live under the poverty line, 2.5 to 12 per cent do in Western European countries.

In the United States, programmes such as Head Start, food stamps, and Medicaid help poor families only.

Many Western European countries, however, provide generous parental work leave, subsidies for children's food and clothing, government-run child care programmes, and national health insurance for all family members. And its cost is borne by everyone. Europeans pay more taxes than Americans. But, to them, it's not a question of money but of values. And how Europeans spend their tax dollars demonstrates how important family life is to them. They believe that the larger society is responsible for healthy families, and consequently, they distribute resources through national programmes. In the United States, however, corporations now provide the leadership in delivering work-family programmes.

Though Europeans and Americans may disagree about how to legislate family initiatives, both share a common problem. Regardless of whether family support comes from the government or the corporation, workers struggle, though less than their American counterparts, with balancing work and family. That struggle is rooted in a shared belief about the importance of work.

Most Europeans view work as a social privilege, a basic human right. Work provides social status, giving people a sense of identity and meaning as both an individual and a member of society. 'It is deeply embedded in the social market economy of Germany, and is the foundation of the Scandinavian welfare state system,' says Heide von Weltzien Hoivik, who runs the Center for Ethics and Leadership, Norwegian School of Management.

Source: Adapted from Hedberg, P. (1996) Work and Family: A European Perspective. *Business Ethics*, 10(5). September/October, p. 30.

After the Reformation, the Protestant Ethic became a dominant philosophy in Europe. Adam Smith, a political economist and moral philosopher, also contributed a great deal to what was to become the European tradition. His theories of exchange and the division of labour, the free market, competition, and profit maximization laid the foundation for business and social policy. Along with the Industrial Revolution, Adam Smith shifted people's view of society so that it was conceived as a machine rather than an organization, as had formerly been the case.

With the fall of the Iron Curtain, European diversity has come to the forefront, affecting ethical initiatives. As Jackson (1992) pointed out, the cultural diversity of the European community is a real factor which can impede the establishment or development of trust. Donaldson (1992) also raises the issue of a lack of common ground in theoretical approaches and terminology of European business ethics, citing different philosophical traditions found in Europe as contributing factors to this diversity.

Donaldson compares the different and strong philosophical traditions of northern and southern Europe. Southern Europe has a strong Aristotelian tradition, arising in part from differing religious histories. The Anglo-Saxon tradition is one of 'analytical philosophy', which is not widely accepted by southern Europeans. Likewise, the positivism viewpoint that values and beliefs (and thus ethics and business ethics) cannot be discussed on theoretical grounds has strongly influenced northern Europe. This particular positivism approach has produced a strong tradition of scepticism, which influences business and economic policy. The modern European attitude is that work is an exchange of labour for money and that neither the work nor the act of working has any inherent value.

The difficulty of attempting to gain an overall understanding of the religious and philosophical traditions of Europe is succinctly summarized in the following statement: 'Europe is a politically diverse continent with conservative Irish Catholics to the north, conservative Spanish Catholic socialists to the west, Italian Catholic communists to the south and Protestant Social Democratic Germans and Danes to the east' (Devinney and Hightower 1991: 193).

3.3.3 Japan

While not adhering to any single religion, the Japanese have a reverence for all things which stems from their affinity with nature and search for rewards in this life. Japan's business environment is influenced by both religious and social norms. Taka (1993) notes that Confucianism, Buddhism, and other traditional Japanese religions combine to emphasize that each individual has a soul or spirit (*numen*) which is connected to the ultimate reality, or unique *numen* of the universe. Work provides one means for individuals to connect to this ultimate reality, to reach beyond the secular, tangible world. This transcendental belief instils a work ethic in the Japanese worker, encouraging continuous improvements in products, work methods and decision-making processes. The act of working is accepted as a spiritual discipline in which enlightenment (in the spiritual sense) is the prize to be gained through devotion to work; this orientation lives on in Japanese companies. Work is not only a means to an end, but rather it is seen as fulfilling to the Japanese.

There are several reasons for the Japanese 'custom' of hard work. First, Japanese society was traditionally agrarian; farmers had no choice but to work hard. Second, the Meiji Restoration eliminated the old social order and paved the way for social mobility through individual efforts; consequently, everyone began to work hard to attain higher positions. Third, post-war inflation made people work harder just to survive the hardship following World War II. Finally, Japanese businesses tend to take good care of their employees, inducing loyalty and hard work for the success of the business. All of these traditions and historical consequences have contributed to the Japanese work ethic as it is known today.

Japanese society contrasts sharply with American and European societies in that Japanese society is characterized by its predominant group orientation, whereas American and European societies are largely individualistic. The Japanese pressure to conform is demonstrated by a Japanese proverb: 'The nail that sticks out is pounded down.' In general, the group has defined the individual in Japanese society, and the individual is significant in so far as he or she represents the group. This group orientation has historical, philosophical, and logistical bases.

Groups are also believed to possess their own *numen*, which may be superior to those of the individual members. Activities of the group provide another means for individuals to connect to the ultimate reality. Thus, groups help their members fulfil their potentials, while at the same time individuals attempt to maintain harmonious relations with other group members to contribute to the continuing existence of the group.

Underlying the perceived efficiency of Japanese business are the concepts of *giri* (duty) and on (indebtedness); these are the deep-rooted concepts of Japanese ethics. *Giri* is a concept which drives the Japanese to fulfil their life duties as Japanese. They feel morally obligated to return the favour of someone who has helped them in some way. Conversely, *on* refers to the social and psychological indebtedness incurred when a favour from someone in a superior position is received. Japanese society is still largely vertically structured, and those in higher positions are expected to bestow paternal-like favours on their subordinates both publicly and privately. Those receiving the favours, then, are expected to demonstrate respect and loyalty and feel *on*.

Japanese businesses are often described as family-like; management plays the role of parent, and the employees play the role of children. Management provides employees with tangible and intangible benefits much as a parent cares for his children. In return for these benefits, the employees feel loyal to the company, have a strong sense of belonging, and work hard for it. Feelings of obligation also extend between companies, emphasizing long-term relationships.

These individual and group norms apply to businesses, through the practice of *keiretsu*, *i.e.*, closely connected firms that work cooperatively toward common goals. *Keiretsu* follow the framework of the social normative environment, which may be viewed as four concentric circles similar to a water ring. These circles represent family, fellows or close associates, the nation of Japan, and the world. It is important to recognize that different ethical rules govern in the respective circles: filial piety, long-term give-and-take relations, a combination of competition and long-term give-and-take, and open competition (Taka 1993).

Vertical *keiretsu* are combinations of 'suppliers . . ., manufacturers and distributors; whereas, firms associated with a horizontal *keiretsu* operate at the same level of the marketing structure' (Dunfee and Nagayasu 1993: 9).

These vertical or horizontal corporate relationships can be considered to fall within certain circles, with social status and responsibilities toward other members defined by religious and societal norms, expectations, and obligations. Business modes of operation and business ethics are strongly influenced by these values and practices. '*Keiretsu* enables Japanese firms to take a longer view, to spend more on research and development, to improve product quality and to provide more employee job security' (Bowie 1993: 110).

These belief structures and sociological traditions impact individuals in ways that affect business ethics. There is a strong tendency for the subordination of individual rights to duties and loyalty owed to the 'group', whether that be family, company, or merchant guild. Individuals become dependent on their work group, which may lead to overwork. An extreme example of this is *karoshi*, death caused by overwork. This represents the ultimate abandonment of individual rights for the sake of the group. Even without going to this extreme, the devotion of individuals to their business groups results in a general unwillingness of individuals to express their opinions. This can lead to an unwillingness to speak out concerning ethics, and a tendency to obey organization orders, even if they are not agreed with (Taka 1993).

Today, the Japanese tradition of corporations providing a sense of identity and belonging to their workers is undergoing transformation, as market and competitive forces lead to changes within the employment practices. However, the cultural values and social structure of Japan have played an instrumental role in its economic development. What has emerged is a uniquely Japanese form of capitalism which embodies the essence of its culture (Yui 1993).

3.4 PUBLIC DISCUSSION OF BUSINESS ETHICS

In the first part of this chapter, some of the environmental factors which impact the development of ethical initiatives and frameworks in the triad were introduced. Based on these observations, it is not surprising that the nature of public discussion of business ethics differs substantially across countries. As Enderle (1995: 2–3) puts it,

> 'The attitudes toward speaking about ethics, and the terms used and not used, in one cultural setting may significantly differ from those in another cultural setting. Moreover, talking about business ethics is usually not identical with ethical conduct: one can do the former without doing the latter, resulting in a lack of credibility and moral authority.'

Subsequently, some of the idiosyncrasies in the public debate of business ethics are outlined.

3.4.1 The United States

The United States, with its history of individualism and freedom of speech, is a relatively outspoken society. The country has a long tradition of talking about ethical issues in business (Donaldson 1992), yet, the discussion may be more outspoken in expressing ethical concerns in ethical terms without addressing the real ethical concerns (Enderle 1995). In other words, the expression of concern may be louder than the actual concern. Vogel (1993) seconds this understanding and adds that some of these concerns about business ethics amount to little more than public relations. But not all public expressions are of such a nature. Vogel goes on to say that '. . . it is impossible to read through the various reports on business ethics in the United States without being struck by the sincerity of the concerns of the executives whose view they report' (ibid.: 32).

Managers understand that without ethics, the only restraints are legal. Government regulation may be perceived as unnecessary and constraining, but less regulation requires more managerial ethical skills in decision making. According to Cavanagh (1990), business managers act ethically under these conditions:

- when they believe that a moral principle has bearing on a situation;
- when they perceive themselves as powerful enough to affect a situation.

Enderle (1995) notes that the discussions that do occur are predominantly concerned with 'micro-issues', those concerned with persons. He also observes an increase in discussion of meso-level ethics, those concerned with organizations; but still rarely are there discussions of ethics at the macro-level, those concerned with overall systems. These discussions are practical in nature, reflecting a tradition of pragmatism. The role of corporate law and the litigant nature of society contributes to the openness of discussion of ethical, right and wrong, and responsibility issues. The existence of strong consumer organizations in a very large and relatively uniform market-place also contributes to the openness of discussion.

Much of the public discussion of ethics in the corporate environment has been the result of exposure and conviction of unethical and illegal activities by several prominent American companies. Thus, the media plays a key role in the publicizing of ethical issues, and will likely continue to do so.

The commentary in Exhibit 3.3 illustrates many American attitudes toward business ethics, and demonstrates how religious and spiritual issues often overlap with business, as mentioned previously.

EXHIBIT 3.3

Ethics in a plain manila envelope

At my company we adhere to a simple creed that sees no division between ethics in business and ethics in life. In other words, we hold that it is impossible to be ethical in business and unethical in everything else we do, and vice versa. Simply said, ethics is a matter that is inseparable from the whole person; it cannot be changed for different occasions.

On the practical level, it boils down to three basic premises. First, for a person to be ethical, he or she must respect other people. Respect encompasses many things: respect for their personal rights, respect for their property, and respect for their opinions and judgments.

The lack of respect becomes evident in the absence of warmth and the person's tendency to do whatever may be expedient at a given time. It indicates a total selfishness and an inward-directed preoccupation. In other words, a characteristic lack of respect for others ultimately means that the individual is setting himself or herself apart from and above fellow human beings.

The second premise is that ethics is learned, not an innate sense. Selfishness, unfortunately, is linked to the survival instinct. Left to our own devices, we tend to become completely selfish and self-centered, ignoring or becoming insensitive to the rights and feelings of others. The character revelations in Lord of the Flies is a classic portrayal of selfishness in a survival setting.

Experience tells us that respect for others is something we must be taught from infancy and childhood. We simply do not grow up with the Ten Commandments programmed in our internal memories, ready for an on-screen application. We have to see and imitate ethical conduct to be able to comprehend the basic laws of human relations.

> The third, and perhaps most important, premise is that the root of all truly ethical conduct is a genuine spiritual life. This applies whether those roots are Christian, Jewish, Muslim, Buddhist, agnostic, or atheistic.
>
> A spiritual life implies a transformation from basic selfishness and self-centeredness to a concern for others. Society recognizes a life of commitment and concern for others. With a genuine transformation, ethical decisions derive not only from intellectual judgments of what is right or wrong; they literally flow from a depth of character.
>
> Source: Holland, W. (1996) Ethics in a Plain Manila Envelope. Simple Guidelines for Doing Business Honestly. Reprinted with permission from *Industry Week*, March 18, p. 20. Copyright Penton Publishing, Inc., Cleveland, Ohio.

3.4.2 Europe

In Europe, a rather different attitude prevails; there is a reticence in discussing ethical issues publicly. In fact, there appears to be even a tendency of understating the importance of ethics. Possibly, this can be explained by a greater implicit agreement about ethical issues within *individual* European countries or by a perception that too much talk about business ethics may draw public criticism if something goes wrong.

One factor contributing to the lack of public discussion of business ethics issues across European countries is the existence of numerous languages, which makes it inevitably more difficult for consumer groups and other organizations to monitor business conduct. There is evidence that there is none the less some commonality of identification of issues and principles, through the existence of the European Business Ethics Network. Members are found in most countries within Europe. Annual conferences that are well-attended indicate an interest in international ethics and some recognition of commonality of issues and values (Donaldson 1992).

European discussions of business ethics issues are connected to social sciences and have a weak practice focus (Enderle 1995). The focus is mostly on macro-issues, although there are some discussions of micro-issues, especially as related to psychology. Due to its cultural diversity and the proximity of nations, European discussions of business ethics are much more international than those of the United States and Japan.

3.4.3 Japan

In Japan, too, there is increasing activity in the area of business ethics. International conferences on international business ethics were held in 1989, 1991 and 1995, co-sponsored by the Institute of

Moralogy in collaboration with universities and governmental ministries. Discussions in Japan tend to focus on meso-level issues, reflecting the importance of groups and group thinking (Enderle 1995). As one Japanese saying goes, 'One step by 100 persons goes further than 100 steps by one person' (Reinemund 1991). There are also some macro-level discussions, but micro-issues, dealing with the roles and responsibilities of individuals, are almost entirely absent from public debate.

Exhibit 3.4 illustrates the extent to which the public, and changing technology has dictated a change in ethics policies in Japanese business.

EXHIBIT 3.4

Sega to remove sex and violence from video games

Sega Enterprises, the leading Japanese games maker, announced plans to remove all sex and violence from its computer games.

The new rules stipulate that photographs and animated images of naked women will not appear in any games. Women in swimsuits or underwear will be permitted, but only in games labelled for those over 18 years of age.

The change has been brought on, not by pressure or complaints, but by technology. With the new generation of 32-bit and 64-bit games machines, stunningly realistic animation is possible making the images on the screen all the more realistic. This, coupled with the much wider customer base that the better systems are attracting, has led to the change in rules.

The change has not been restricted to Sega either. Sony Corporation's Sony Computer Entertainment and Nintendo Co. have already banned naked women from games for their new systems. Some games also carry warning labels advising of graphically violent scenes.

The Computer Entertainment Software Association, an industry association, recently polled its members and has decided to draw up a code of ethics regarding sexually explicit and violent content in video games. Such a code would have to be followed by members of the association. These include leading software producers such as Namco, Konami and Square.

Estimates put the number of software developers that make solely adult games at around 200 in Japan.

Source: Adapted from Williams, M. (1996) Sega to Remove Sex and Violence from Video Games. *Newsbytes*, August 23, 1996.

3.5 SUMMARY

While a discussion of environmental factors, including the history of several centuries ago in Japan, may initially seem far removed from a comparison of business ethics in different countries, such background is crucial in gaining an understanding of the handling of contemporary business ethics issues. The first part of this chapter has therefore attempted to give a basic overview of some key environmental influences in the US, Europe, and Japan. Any one of these areas is worthy and pithy enough for full-scale study; the goal here has been to provide an overview and perhaps whet the appetite for additional individual study.

The chapter also tried to convey an awareness of the differences in the public debate of business ethics in the triad. Interest, and correspondingly, public discussion of ethics in general and international business ethics in particular seems to be undoubtedly on the rise everywhere. However, the nature and focus of the debate differs widely, both in terms of the willingness to discuss ethical issues in business as well as in terms of the level at which issues are debated.

3.6 REFERENCES

Bowie, N. (1993) International business, a universal morality and the challenge of nationalism, in Thomas W. Dunfee and Yukimasa Nagayasu (eds), *Business Ethics: Japan and the Global Economy*, Norwell, MA: Kluwer Academic Publishers.

Cavanagh, G.F. (1990) *American Business Values* (3rd edn), Englewood Cliffs, NJ: Prentice Hall.

Chang, Han-Yu (1993) The Japanese view of business and work, in Thomas W. Dunfee and Yukimasa Nagayasu (eds), *Business Ethics: Japan and the Global Economy*, Norwell, MA: Kluwer Academic Publishers.

Devinney, T. and Hightower, W. (1991) *European Markets After 1992*, Lexington MA: Lexington Books.

Donaldson, J. (1992) *Business Ethics: A European Casebook*, London: Academic Press, Inc.: Harcourt Brace Jovanovich.

Dunfee, T.W. and Nagayasu, Y. (1993) Global business ethics and Japanese economic morality: an introduction and overview, in Thomas W. Dunfee and Yukimasa Nagayasu (eds), *Business Ethics: Japan and the Global Economy*, Norwell, MA: Kluwer Academic Publishers.

Enderle, G. (1995) *A Comparison of Business Ethics in North America and Europe*, Notre Dame, IN: University of Notre Dame.

Harvey, B. (ed) (1994) *Business Ethics: A European Approach*, Hertfordshire, UK: Prentice Hall International (UK) Ltd.

Hedberg, P. (1996) Work and family: a European perspective. *Business Ethics*. 10(5) September/October, p. 30.

Holland, W. (1996) Ethics in a plain manila envelope: simple guidelines for doing business honestly. *Industry Week*, March 18, p. 20.

Jackson, J. (1992) Preserving trust in a pluralist culture, in Jack Mahoney and Elizabeth Vallance (eds), *Business Ethics in a New Europe*, Norwell, MA: Kluwer Academic Publishers.

Reinemund, S.S. (1991) Defining the ethical challenge – a view from above, in Theresa Brothers (ed.), *Corporate Ethics: Developing New Standards of Accountability*, New York, NY: The Conference Board, Inc.

Scott, M. (1996) Social investors triumph with 3M tobacco ban. *Business Ethics*. 10(4), July/August, p. 13.

Taka, I. (1993) Business ethics: a Japanese view, in Thomas W. Dunfee and Yukimasa Nagayasu (eds), *Business Ethics: Japan and the Global Economy*, Norwell, MA: Kluwer Academic Publishers.

Vallance, E. (1992) Never the twain? Ethics and economics in Eastern and Western Europe, in Jack Mahoney and Elizabeth Vallance (eds), *Business Ethics in A New Europe*, Norwell, MA: Kluwer Academic Publishers.

Vogel, D. (1993) Is U.S. business obsessed with ethics? *Across the Board*, November/December, pp. 31–2.

Williams, M. (1996) Sega to remove sex and violence from video games. *Newsbytes*. August 23, p. 6.

Yui, T. (1993) Economic development and ethics in Japan – a historical perspective, in Thomas W. Dunfee and Yukimasa Nagayasu (eds), *Business Ethics: Japan and the Global Economy*, Norwell, MA: Kluwer Academic Publishers.

4 *Ethical dimensions in the analysis of international market opportunities*

4.1 ETHICAL ISSUES ARISING FROM SPECIFIC MARKETING TASKS

So far, we have introduced some key concepts and approaches to business ethics and discussed the impact of certain environmental factors on the development and debate of the subject in different countries. Having covered this groundwork, the following three chapters will turn to ethical issues inherent in specific marketing tasks. Following a standard sequence of opportunity analysis and policy setting, this chapter focuses initially on ethical issues in marketing research and competitive intelligence. The following two chapters will then look at issues involved in managing the marketing mix elements in an international setting.

4.2 MARKETING RESEARCH

When discussing the implications of ethics in marketing research, the old adage, 'figures lie and liars figure' comes to mind. This is not to say that marketing researchers are all liars or that all data is misleading, but there is a kind of mystique surrounding marketing research. Almost as if by magic, consumers' preferences and thoughts are quantified and transformed into a series of numbers, statistical terms, and pie charts. Unfortunately, most marketing researchers are also familiar with presentation techniques which make even weak numbers look good (Ramsey and Kaufman 1982). But why would there be an inducement to make weak numbers look good? For a start, most marketing research is conducted by commercial research companies where the profit motive may 'cause researchers, their managers, or clients to occasionally compromise the objectivity or precision of the project' (Laczniak and Murphy 1993: 55). Suppose a large British company is interested in discovering how well their product would perform in Chile and hires a Chilean research firm to conduct a study. If the British company decides to enter the market, the company could become a lucrative client who might continue to use the services of the market research firm. For this reason, it is in the best interest of the researchers to present the data in a positive way in order to encourage the British firm to enter the Chilean market.

Conversely, perhaps the marketing manager in the British firm has already decided that Chile would be a lucrative market for his company's products. However, he does not have any hard data to back up his 'hunch'. When he decides to contact a marketing research firm, he already has a set agenda as to the data which he would like to see in the study. This, in turn, may place the research firm in an awkward position because it already knows what information the client prefers to receive. Although professional ethics dictates that the research firm conduct an objective study, it also knows that being the bearer of bad news might adversely affect the relationship with the client.

In the non-commercial sphere, there is also a temptation to 'tweak' the data in order to make the results of a marketing research study more interesting, more impressive and thus more publishable. Indeed, the scope for falsifying data to be able to finish a Ph.D. earlier or to publish something in an academic journal has led some advisers, journal editors and reviewers now routinely to demand the original data sets on which results are based.

Another major issue associated with marketing research involves the trust relationship between marketing researchers and the general public as provider of research information. When the public experiences more and more telephone sales or fundraising approaches disguised through bogus telephone 'surveys', genuine marketing research efforts suffer; people will become increasingly reluctant to co-operate in surveys (Brannigan 1987) Moreover, marketing researchers routinely gather sensitive information from the general public which is subject to potential misuse. The public needs to be able to trust assurances of anonymity and, for example, needs to be able to rely on promises that individual responses will not be passed on to direct sales organizations. If this trust is undermined, marketing researchers will be unable to enjoy the continued support of the public.

When marketing researchers are working in the international arena, the room for bias increases (Douglas and Craig 1983). Mentalities and culture are more diverse and can interfere in every step of the research process. For example, when conducting marketing research studies in a foreign country, a marketing researcher might notice a tendency to provide more favourable information than domestic respondents. Subsequently, the researcher may decide to use mathematical formulae to 'adjust' the data to make it more suitable for cross-national comparison. But if the data are adjusted, how objective does the study remain and how much of it is subject to the whim of the researcher? In a complex, cross-cultural study, marketing managers often have to depend on the expertise of the researchers to provide reliable, valid and useful data. Such reliance on the researchers' expertise provides the researchers with the power to influence the outcome of the study and perhaps the outcome of important marketing decisions. Exhibits 4.1 and 4.2 illustrate how marketing researchers can impact even such important figures as the consumer price index (CPI) or, perhaps inadvertently, bias personal interviews.

EXHIBIT 4.1

A matter of formula bias

The Finance Committee's Advisory Commission to 'Study the CPI' uncovered a problem of formula bias. They found that the weight given to replacement items, which were to enter the CPI calculation, was being tied to its expected price change. Researchers concluded that this method could lead to an over-statement of inflation whenever new items were introduced into the CPI sample. Changes to correct this bias were being made effective with the CPI calculation for July 1996.

Source: Adapted from Parker, R.P. and Grove, C.B. (1996) 'The Statistics Producers' Corner. *Business Economics*, 31(3), pp. 59–60.

EXHIBIT 4.2

A matter of culture and gender bias

A study to analyse the effects on response quality by respondents when their interviewer possessed different culture and/or gender characteristics from their own had interesting results. Using Hispanic and Anglo interviewers and Hispanic and Anglo respondents of both sexes, the study concluded that response quality was affected significantly by the interaction effects of the different interviewer/respondent combinations. For the most part, the highest response quality was generated by having an interviewer of the same culture, but the opposite gender, of the respondent.

Source: Adapted from Webster, C. (1996) Hispanic and Anglo Interviewer and Respondent Ethnicity and Gender: The Impact on Survey Response Quality. *Journal of Marketing Research*, 33(1), pp. 62–72.

The ethical dilemmas and temptations in market research to give in to unprofessional behaviour are well recognized. As one marketing researcher put it: 'Much marketing research is only an "eye wash" . . . to convince that the product is indeed needed and will sell in volume – almost a "fraudulent" situation' (Hunt *et al.* 1984: 313). Although most reputable market research firms want to steer clear of 'fraudulent' situations, one of the most often cited ethical dilemmas for both marketing research firms and in-house research departments involves balancing their duties and responsibilities towards managers, companies, self, society, competitors and respondents.

4.2.1 Stakeholders in marketing research

The most important stakeholders involved in the marketing research process are the general public, the respondents of a specific study, the client, and the researcher. All four groups have their own concerns and agendas, but must work together in order to successfully bring a research study to fruition. Below, each group is examined in more detail.

(a) The general public

In many ways, the public reaps the benefits of marketing research studies. Gathering marketing research information allows companies to find better ways to serve customers. Disclosing the results of studies, in turn, permits the public to make better purchasing decisions. In return for the benefits to the consumer, the general public provides researchers and clients with a pool of respondents which give companies the information necessary to continue making improvements. To maintain the goodwill of the public and ensure future support of marketing research efforts, it is important that the marketing research profession understands the implications of ethical misconduct, including the potential misuse of their findings.

Frequently, the general public only becomes familiar with the results of a marketing research study through advertising. How many times, for example, has a TV ad proclaimed that 'four out of five doctors surveyed recommend product X' to cure any possible ailment? But, how valid are these surveys? How was the study conducted and were the respondents representative of the population as a whole? What were the methods employed to reach these conclusions? The general public is often bombarded with impressive sounding statistics which resulted from a marketing research survey. What responsibilities do companies and researchers have to the general public?

The general public has the right to expect integrity in the practice and reporting of research. To deny the public this right is equivalent to lying and not providing them with the information to make informed decisions. In fact, many surveys conducted by companies are conducted in order to provide information for competitive marketing. In the US, for example, the Federal Trade Commission (FTC), who helps to regulate the claims made in advertising, requires companies to substantiate such claims through, among others, producing appropriate marketing research results. However, even though these FTC requirements exist, there are always means by which results can be skewed. For a research executive, it is important to remember the ramifications of manipulated results, not only because they misguide consumers and undermine the public's willingness to participate in market research studies, but also because they pose a potential legal risk to the company (Neuborne 1987).

(b) The respondents

When participating in a study, respondents should expect that certain rights are respected by researchers. These include the *rights to privacy, to anonymity, to safety, to be informed, to free-choice, to be heard, and to redress* (Churchill 1991). The respondents in most cases have the upper-hand on the bargaining table because they are donating their time and opinions for little, if any, material gain. It is therefore in the best interest of the researcher and the client to respect the needs of the respondent.

Many research associations address the rights of individuals to *privacy* in their guidelines. For example, Article 2 of the Code of the International Chamber of Commerce and the European Society for Opinion and Marketing Research (ICC/ESOMAR) states that: 'No information which could be used to identify informants, either directly or indirectly, shall be revealed other than to research personnel within the researchers' own organization who require this knowledge for the administration and checking of interviews, data processing, etc' (Worcester and Downham 1986).

In an age in which many people have access to a caller identification feature on their telephone, it is always possible for the researcher to be privy to more personal information than the respondent realizes. Combining information from a survey with an address and phone number on the caller identification feature could provide valuable information to a sales force. However, this action would be considered an infringement of the individual's right to *privacy* and *anonymity* (Smith and Quelch 1993). By not respecting the customer's anonymity, the researcher may also affect subject responses.

Another issue which potentially impinges a whole host of respondent's rights, such as the rights to *privacy, anonymity, free-choice*, as well as on the right to be *heard* and the right to *redress*, involves the use of 'hidden cameras' in conducting behavioural research. Is it ethical to film unsuspecting consumers? Advertising agency J. Walter Thompson has launched a new consumer research technique called InSitu, which involves filming unsuspecting shoppers in stores and then questioning them about their shopping decisions (Snowdon 1995). This raises the question of whether consumers/respondents should be asked for their consent prior to being filmed, even if this could result in biased responses. The Professional Marketing Association of Canada (PMRS), the ICC/ESOMAR, and the Council of American Survey Research Organization (CASRO) all agree that participants should have *advance* knowledge of observation and recording techniques. However, the ICC/ESOMAR code allows an exception to this rule if a respondent is in a public place and the following conditions are observed (Smith and Quelch 1993):

1   all reasonable precautions are taken in order to preserve the respondent's anonymity;
2   the respondent is told immediately after the event that his/her actions have been filmed or recorded;
3   the respondent is given the opportunity to see or hear the relevant section and, if he/she wishes, have this record destroyed, i.e. has the right to redress.

The *safety* right, finally, is primarily interpreted in terms of providing safe physical conditions for the respondent. This can be an issue where the measurement of physiological reactions involves the use of machines, such as in measuring the response to advertising (Churchill 1991). However, one can also expand the interpretation of the safety right to preventing undue mental stress in research participants. Such stress can often be dispelled through an adequate debriefing process during which the researcher gives the respondent the opportunity to voice concern.

While the protection of the respondent's rights sounds fine at face value, there is also a downside, as illustrated in Exhibit 4.3.

EXHIBIT 4.3

Testing without consent?

An important aspect of public health surveillance in Australia and New Zealand involves the testing of patients for human immunodeficiency virus (HIV) on an anonymous, unlinked basis. However, this testing, without the specific knowledge and consent of the patients, raises ethical and legal issues. An interesting debate has emerged with one view arguing that the research is in the interest of the public good and should be allowed. On the other hand, as another view argues, specific consent by patients should be enforced in view of privacy concerns, the importance of patient autonomy, and the potential for conflict of interest.

Source: Adapted from Magnusson, R.S. (1996) Testing For HIV Without Specific Consent: A Short Review. *Australian & New Zealand Journal of Public Health*, 20(1), pp. 57–60.

(c) The client

The relationship between the client and the researcher can often be conflictual because of the clash of the objectives of these two groups. Sometimes, companies come to a researcher desiring to obtain specific results. In such cases, the client is not interested in obtaining objective results, but in proving a pre-formulated point. Although it is easy to say that a researcher should remain objective, it can become a difficult decision to make if the researcher knows that failure to provide the anticipated data could result in the loss of a customer. Or, in the case of an in-house marketing research department, the failure to produce particular results could damage either the career opportunities of certain researchers or cause complications in office politics. In order to maintain the integrity and confidence in marketing research, it is important that researchers maintain objectivity, and that clients do not ask them to sacrifice this objectivity for corporate goals. Therefore, it is the responsibility of the client not to encourage the researchers to conduct studies which produce leading results and the right of the researcher not to misrepresent the findings of the research. Exhibit 4.4 illustrates this point.

EXHIBIT 4.4

Providing what the client wants
Often the client will commission a research study because (1) they want to prove something that they 'think' or (2) they want to prove something that they 'know'. In either case, the researcher is pressured to provide the desired results. Rather than educate the client about the realities and limitations of survey research, an act that would be likely to reduce future market demand for their services, the researchers generally tell the client what he/she wants to hear. Researchers routinely engage in puffery that hides the limitations of survey research behind a screen of high-quality, high-tech language designed to paint a glowing picture of quasi-scientific competence and sterling reliability and sets up unrealistic expectations for research results. These unrealistic research expectations fuel the demand for further research.
Source: Adapted from Semon, T.T. (1996) Can We Afford To Be Honest? *Marketing News*, 30(12), p. 5

Of course, the client has not only responsibilities but also rights. Specifically, the client has the right to accurate, understandable presentation of data, which the company can utilize. *Accuracy* of the information has become an important issue, especially in the field of advertising. Because competitors and, sometimes, governments monitor the claims used in advertising, in order to avoid litigation, it is important that the data are gathered in a scientific manner (see Section 4.2.1(a)). For this reason, it is in the best interest of both the company and the researcher to provide and publish data which is as unbiased as possible.

Another right which the researcher should afford the client, is the right to *anonymity*. There are some instances in which a company may not want its name mentioned in connection with a survey, for fear that the research it is doing might give information about future strategies to its competitors or that using the company's name might bias the results.

Finally, researchers should respect the confidentiality of research results in their client relationships. In particular, they should be careful not to pass on information from one company to another. In practice, this is sometimes a tall order. When designing a study for a new client, it literally requires the researcher to ignore information which has already been collected for clients in the same industry and might be useful in the design of the new study.

(d) Researchers

In the last few decades, the marketing research profession has boomed. There are now more marketing research firms than ever before. The increase in competition and the advancements in technologies have added more pressures on the research profession (Akaah 1990). The deadlines for collecting and analysing data have grown shorter. One American marketing researcher, Ruth Nelson (1990: 27), expressed concern that demands for speed and low costs were negatively affecting the quality of the collected data (compare Exhibit 4.5). She claims that 'the term "quick and dirty" is a permanent part of [the modern marketing researchers'] vocabulary'. Conducting 'quick and dirty' research does not present an ethical problem as long as both the client and the researcher are aware of the quality of the research provided. Ethics only becomes an issue when the researcher conducts a study but does not fully reveal the accuracy and reliability of the data. Nelson blames the lack of quality control and uninformed managers, who are not knowledgeable enough about the marketing research process to interpret the data. However, the responsibility for shoddy data cannot be blamed solely on uninformed managers. The reason why companies consult marketing research firms is because they lack the time or expertise to conduct the studies on their own. Since the marketing researchers possess such 'exper-tise,' it is their responsibility not to take advantage of their knowledge to the disadvantage of their clients. This includes persuading the client to commission unnecessary research in order to pad the researchers' fee.

EXHIBIT 4.5

Do interviewers follow telephone survey instructions?
Telephone surveys are currently the most popular mode of data collection in marketing research in the US. However, studies show that 'misbehaviour' by telephone interviewers is ordinary and normal. 'Misbehaviour' can include: interviewers reword-ing questions, interviewers answering questions when intervie-wees refuse to respond, or interviewers fabricating answers to entire questionnaires.
Source: Adapted from Kiecker, P. and Nelson, J.E. (1996) Do Interviewers Follow Telephone Survey Instructions? *Journal of the Market Research Society*, 38(2), pp. 161–76.

4.2.2 Privacy

The importance of privacy has already been stressed in the context of the rights of respondents. However, the privacy issue should also be seen in the wider context of marketing research as a whole. Indeed, it is in the very nature of marketing research to invade individual privacy and the ethical issue at the core of the debate is whether the need to know outweighs the right to individual privacy? As technology continues to improve, the voices questioning the amount of information researchers are allowed to gather become louder. People are beginning to feel that their privacy is being threatened by an information-hungry world (Bowers 1994).

In the United States, at this point in time, it only takes a name and a phone number to enable a researcher to discover a person's credit history, demographic information, mortgage figures, and police records (Smith and Quelch 1993). The fact that technology has made this information so easily accessible is causing widespread concern (Blackmer 1994). It has been reported that in the United States alone, about 500 bills concerning consumer privacy abuses and protection issues have been introduced (Norwood 1994). Hong Kong has also recently introduced some new regulations concerning privacy (*Business Asia* 1994), and the European Union has just issued a privacy directive which must be implemented by the EU member countries within the next three years (Platten 1995). The European Union's new directive specifies that data concerning ethnicity, race, political and religious beliefs, health, and sexual interest may only be gathered with explicit consent of the person concerned.

Outside Western Europe and the United States, nations' policies range from little or no formal privacy measures to intensive regulation and self-regulation in particular sectors. When doing business in a foreign country, it is important to be aware of the laws in that country, as well as the cultural sentiments of what constitutes an invasion of privacy. In many Latin American countries, for example, telephones are viewed as a vehicle for communication with close friends and family members; consumers therefore might not respond favourably to a cold call from a marketing researcher (Hernandez and Kaufman 1990). What is considered an invasion of privacy in one country may not be considered as such in another. But even within a country it is often strongly debated which information should and should not be private – Exhibit 4.6 illustrates this point.

EXHIBIT 4.6

Who should have access to your medical record?

The US congress introduced a bill in October, 1995, called the 'Medical Records Confidentiality Act' which has since been the subject of heated debate. While the bill provides for the right to confidentiality of medical records, there are notable exceptions granted to: public health, law enforcement, and medical research. Proponents argue that 'to foreclose the ability to offer the benefits of research to the entire community because some individuals wish to exempt their data from scientific analysis would hold the entire society hostage.' Those opposed to these exceptions argue that they effectively provide a major loophole which allows for 'millions of persons to access your medical records without your consent and without any notice.'

Source: Adapted from Detmer, D.E. and Love, J. (1996) Who Should Have Access to Your Medical Record. *Business & Health*, February 1996, pp. 59–60.

4.2.3 Self-regulation

Due to the fact that marketing research is so dependent on the co-operation of the general public as a pool from which researchers draw their respondents, it has been in the interest of the marketing research profession to be proactive, and to provide guidelines which aim to maintain the trust between the researchers and the general public. As one marketing research professional put it: 'Let's face it, we are able to collect our research data only because the general public continues to be willing to submit to our interviews. This acceptance of us by the public is the basic natural resource on which our industry is built. Without it, we would be out of business tomorrow' (Carlson 1967: 5).

In order to protect the rights of this 'natural resource', many marketing research associations world-wide have adopted guidelines for conducting research in which they attempt to define what is considered ethical and what is not. The list of associations which have written such guidelines includes the International Chamber of Commerce in conjunction with the European Society for Opinion and Marketing Research (ICC/ESOMAR), the Professional Marketing Research Society (PMRS) in Canada, the American Marketing Research Society (AMR) and the Market Research Society (MRS) in Britain.

4.3 COMPETITIVE INTELLIGENCE

Ethical issues do not only arise in conjunction with classical marketing research methods which involve surveys and statistical analyses. Other practices, focusing on the collection of trade secrets, pose even more serious ethical challenges. Commonly referred to as competitive intelligence, this field has gained increasing importance in recent years. Many companies have either developed internal competitive intelligence units (CIUs) or hired outside consulting firms to perform analyses of the competition.

The words 'ethics' and 'grey areas' appear many times in the literature on competitive intelligence. In this field more than in many others, the line is blurred between what is legal and what is ethical. In the United States, many companies still hesitate to adopt competitive intelligence units, because they consider it 'distasteful', or think that intelligence gathering suggests spying or 'illegal skullduggery' (Ettore 1995). However, much of the information which is gathered is both legal and necessary for a company to survive in today's competitive environment. Gary Costly, former president of Kellogg Co. North America, even contends that managers who do not do competitive intelligence are incompetent and irresponsible for not understanding their competitors (Ettore 1995).

Professionals employ many different techniques to acquire information on competitors' products, pricing strategies, operational details or advertising campaigns. Information can be gained by means as innocent as reading trade journals, analysing databases and public financial statements, or could be gathered by more surreptitious means (see Exhibit 4.7). Questionable practices include posing as a potential customer at a trade fair, rummaging through a competitor's trash can, masquerading as a graduate student in order to gather pricing and promotion information, or taking a camera on a tour of competitors' facilities to gather information about production processes. While collection of information in the public domain is considered ethical and theft of information would be regarded as illegal across most cultures, there are many other practices which are not illegal but can be considered unethical. The question is where one draws the line between competitive intelligence and corporate espionage. The definitions differ from country to country. If only to protect its own trade secrets, an enterprise doing business in another country must be aware of what is considered unethical and what is regarded as 'fair game'.

EXHIBIT 4.7

Straight out of a spy novel

With the explosion of electronic information tools and resources into the marketplace, corporate facilities may be increasingly exposed to security threats that would have once seemed straight out of Cold War spy novels. Unless companies take measures to encrypt, encode, or otherwise protect their information assets, no form of communication is entirely secure. That is, in this age of 'wireless communication', concrete barriers and computer system fire walls only protect against certain forms of larceny, terrorism, and espionage. New high-tech threats to corporate security now include electronic eavesdropping – gleaning corporate secrets from the very airwaves. Thus, devices to protect phones, faxes, modems, and other data devices are increasingly important.

Source: Adapted from Brown, R. (1996) Not Enough Secrets. *Buildings*, 90(3), pp. 36–8.

4.3.1 Common ethical problems

Because the competitive intelligence field involves collecting trade secrets, the very premise of the profession involves discovering something which one company does not want another to know. The line between legal and illegal does not always help define what is ethical. Paine (1991) sees three common ethical problems which can arise in the information gathering process:

- misrepresentation;
- inducements to influence those who have trade secrets;
- covert surveillance.

Misrepresentation is widespread throughout the competitive intelligence profession. Common practices include anything from posing as a prospective company employee, client, or student in order to gain access to information which would not be available to the general public. One US competitive intelligence professional describes that he and his colleagues approach employees, friends and families of companies disguised as fellow clerks, engineers, or managers. He says, 'we don't break laws ever. We just tell little fibs'. Is telling these 'little fibs' unethical or is it just part of the game that must be played in order to maintain a competitive advantage in today's society?

Techniques in the second category, inducements to influence those with trade secrets, could be as blatant and simple as giving a disgruntled employee a bribe. However, companies also use more sophisticated tactics such as offering positions to an executive of a competitor who could give them valuable trade secrets. The ethical misconduct in this category is mutual, because the practices involve both parties agreeing to the terms and inducements offered by the company attempting to collect information.

Covert surveillance could include bugging telephones or installing hidden cameras, but it is not always that glamorous. In a survey of British executives, only a very small percentage admitted that they would be willing to bug another's conversation. However, the vast majority conceded that they would position themselves at a gathering so they could eavesdrop on their competitors (*Management Today* 1995).

The three problem areas described above must be faced by the competitive intelligence professional every day. Because circumstances and situations vary, self-regulatory codes are difficult to formulate and even more difficult to enforce. When conducting competitive intelligence in an international environment, Jones (1991) recommends that professionals must also consider the '*moral intensity*' of the government, people, and company they are representing. 'Moral intensity' describes the emphasis and acceptability of questionable research techniques which can depend upon the situation and characteristics surrounding a particular circumstance. Perhaps, if a country was facing continuous political turmoil and civil war, such as is the case in Northern Ireland, questionable research would be viewed differently than it would in a more stable situation. One research study supported a hypothesis which showed that Northern Irish consumers, due to the tenuousness of life in its culture, led citizens to be less concerned with the ethical nature of their problems for the simple reason that they had little time to consider these problems (Rawwas *et al.* 1995). However, this line of argument implicitly supports ethical relativism. It is questionable if the so called 'moral intensity' should become the sole measurement by which one should judge whether actions are ethical. Ethics in decision making is influenced by different factors such as personal beliefs, the government/legal environment, the social environment, and the corporate environment. History, culture, and religion also shape different beliefs regarding the appropriateness of intelligence gathering techniques which fall into the 'grey area.'

4.3.2 Governments as stakeholders

In the world of competitive intelligence, the stakeholders include companies, competitive intelligence consulting firms and, perhaps most importantly, governments. In many countries, governments play an active role in the collection and dissemination of information about foreign companies to domestic companies (Herring 1992). Immediately following World War II, for example, Japan realized that it needed to modernize its industrial base. Since 1957, the government has established a variety of agencies to collect and distribute foreign business information to Japanese firms. Often, countries with a large number of state-owned companies are more likely to take an active role in protecting and assisting these companies. Even in countries which have begun to privatize their state assets, the history of government involvement can lead to a different attitude towards government involvement (Prescott and Gibbons 1993).

Governments' approaches to competitive intelligence gathering also have a considerable influence in shaping their citizens' vision of what is ethical. In a country where information gathering is condoned and practised openly by the government, people are more likely to accept the practice and to engage in intelligence gathering. In both France and Japan, competitive intelligence is considered an important element in making business decisions and is sponsored and encouraged by the government. In Japan, almost every company has a competitive intelligence unit, and intelligence gathering is considered an essential and acceptable part of doing business (Herring 1992).

One of the most infamous scandals of corporate espionage in recent history took place in 1993. French agents admitted to bugging the seats of two American executives in order to gain access to corporate secrets (Day 1995). It is not surprising that French attitudes towards the role of government agencies in competitive intelligence gathering and the line between competitive intelligence and corporate espionage are frequently criticized. Jean Bonthous (1993: 14) stated: 'The French business intelligence system faces few pressures from lawmakers or from constituents. There is a wide popular consensus that in matters of intelligence, morals and ethics do not apply. French do not maintain codes of ethics, which they perceive as an irrelevant Anglo-Saxon concept.' This is not to say that French agencies are routinely operating amorally regarding intelligence gathering, or that the French public believes that the above-mentioned agents were acting with integrity. Still, there might be a rather different mindset as to what intelligence and ethics mean to the French as opposed to what they mean to an Anglo-Saxon.

Many Americans, in particular, are still fairly squeamish when it comes to competitive intelligence and tend to view gathering information about competitors as a game of cloak and dagger. This is compounded by the fact that companies, in general, harbour a deep-seeded suspicion of government motives (Brod 1995). An illustration of this is the recent debate on whether to let the CIA get more involved in competitive intelligence. Suggestions along these lines met resistance, both from the government and private industry; many CIA agents viewed corporate intelligence as trivial, while companies did not like the idea of having a government agent in the boardroom (Brod 1995). The American ideology, which distrusts government intervention and equates competitive intelligence with 'spying', emanates throughout American corporate culture today which, in turn, influences how Americans view the ethicality of competitive intelligence. However, US attitudes are also changing. Even though American executives still view competitive intelligence with some reservations, the competitive intelligence industry is now booming. As American companies scramble to gather strategic information about their competition, values appear to be compromised.

4.3.3 Society of Competitive Intelligence Professionals

The Society of Competitive Intelligence Professionals (SCIP) is a nonprofit organization devoted to furthering the art and science of competitive intelligence. The society was founded in the United States in the mid-1980s and now has an associated European affiliate. As of spring 1996, SCIP has chapters in 35 different countries and is actively attempting to continue global expansion. Even the Japanese, who are considered the leaders in business intelligence, are reaching out to the SCIP for new ideas. Alan Eastwood, a member of the SCIP, describes some of the intelligence gathering techniques published in the society's magazine as a 'little out of bounds', even though they are, strictly speaking, legal (*Management Today* 1995). However, the society, which acts as a forum for discussing competitive intelligence issues, has actually assembled an ethics committee to address the problems and dilemmas related to this profession. But although the ethics committee represents a move in the right direction, it does not have any power to enforce its code, and there remains a lack of consensus on what is an ethical practice. The code (see Exhibit 4.8) is also rather general and, consequently, open to very different interpretations.

EXHIBIT 4.8

Society for Competitive Intelligence Professionals: code of ethics

- To continually strive to increase respect and recognition for the profession on local, state, and national levels.
- To pursue his or her duties with zeal and diligence while maintaining the highest degree of professionalism and avoiding all unethical practices.
- To faithfully adhere to and abide by his or her company's policies, objectives and guidelines.
- To comply with all applicable laws.
- To accurately disclose all relevant information, including the identity of the professional and his or her organization, prior to all interviews.
- To fully respect all requests for confidentiality of information.
- To promote and encourage full compliance with these ethical standards within his or her company, with third party contractors and within the entire profession.

Cohen *et al.* (1992) suggest that an international code of conduct for the competitive intelligence profession needs to meet two criteria: first, the code needs to be consistent with the consensus of professionals world-wide and, second, it needs to be relevant to professional practice in the companies in which it is adopted. Although this is a lofty goal, reaching consensus with competitive intelligence professionals world-wide is easier said than done. For this reason, Prescott and Gibbons (1993) suggest a 'geocentric view' of competitive intelligence practices and recommend that organizations adapt their practices to different national environments while continuing to maintain world-wide integrity in their identity and policies.

4.4 SUMMARY

The ethical problems in marketing research and competitive intelligence will continue to become more complex as technology advances and business continues to expand across national borders. In the future we can expect to witness attempts toward a global harmonization of codes of conduct and legislation. But even if a standardization of these measures can be achieved, differences in culture will continue to influence the observation and interpretation of these codes. It is therefore necessary for a marketing manager to be aware not only of the legislation but also of the country-specific attitudes towards the collection of information.

4.5 REFERENCES

Akaah, I. (1990) Attitudes of marketing professionals toward ethics in marketing research: a cross-national comparison. *Journal of Business Ethics*, Vol. 9, p. 52.

Blackmer, S. (1994) Privacy in cyberspace. *International Corporate Law*, October, pp. 19–23.

Bonthous, J. (1993) Understanding intelligence across cultures. *Competitive Intelligence Review*, Summer/Fall, p. 14.

Bowers, D.K. (1994) Privacy concerns and the research industry. *Marketing Research: A Magazine of Management and Applications*, 6(2), Spring, p. 48.

Brannigan, M. (1987) Pseudo polls: more surveys draw criticism for motives and methods. *The Wall Street Journal*, January 27, p. 27.

Brod, E. (1995) This is the CEO – get me the CIA. *Wall Street Journal*, November 14, p. A15.

Brown, R. (1996) Not Enough Secrets. *Buildings*, 90(3), pp. 36–8.

Business Asia (1994) Coming up . . . Vol. 26, Issue. 26, December 19, p. 9.

Carlson, R.O. (1967) The issue of privacy in public opinion research. *Public Opinion Quarterly*, Spring, p. 5.

Churchill, G.A. (1991) *Marketing Research Methodological Foundations*, Hinsdale, IL: Dryden Press, p. 54.

Cohen, J.R., Pant, L.W. and Sharp, D.J. (1992) Cultural and economic constraints on international codes of ethics: lessons from accounting. *Journal of Business Ethics*, Vol. 11, pp. 687–700.

Day, Bill (1995) The Spying Game: Staying competitive takes more than tracking competitors' products and prices. *Business Record – Des Moines*. 91(29) July 17, p. 10.

Detmer, D.E. and Love, J. (1996) Who should have access to your medical record. *Business & Health*, February, pp. 59–60.

Douglas, S.P. and Craig, S.C. (1983) *International Marketing Research*, Englewood Cliffs, NJ: Prentice Hall.

Ettore, B. (1995) Managing competitive intelligence. *Management Review*, October, p. 16.

Hernandez, S.A. and Kaufman, C.J. (1990) Marketing research in hispanic barrios: a guide to survey research. *Marketing Research*, March, p. 78.

Herring, J. (1992) Business intelligence in Japan and Sweden: lessons for the U.S. *Journal of Business Strategy*, March/April, pp. 44–9.

Hunt, S.D., Chonko, L.B. and Wilcox, J.B. (1984) Ethical problems of marketing researchers. *Journal of Marketing Research*, Vol. XXI, August, p. 313.

Jones, T.M. (1991) Ethical decision making by individuals in organizations: an issue-contingent model. *Academy of Management Review*, April, 16(2), pp. 366–95.

Kiecker, P. and Nelson, J.E. (1996) Do interviewers follow telephone survey instructions? *Journal of the Market Research Society*, 38(2) pp. 161–76.

Laczniak, G.R. and Murphy, P.E. (1993) *Ethical Marketing Decisions: The Higher Road*, Boston, MA: Allyn and Bacon.

Magnusson, R.S. (1996) Testing for HIV without specific consent: a short review. *Australian & New Zealand Journal of Public Health*, 20(1), pp. 57–60.

Management Today (1995) The listening society, September, p. 17.

Nelson, R. (1990) Ethics, quality control and data collection. *Applied Marketing Research*, Vol. 30, First Quarter, p. 27.

Neuborne, E. (1987) Researchers see chill from suit. *Advertising Age*, 58 (July 20), pp. 3 and 50.

Norwood, G. (1994) Trend 3: hostility is growing. *Managers Magazine*, Vol. 69, January, p. 32.

Paine, L.S. (1991) Corporate policy and the ethics of competitive intelligence gathering. *Journal of Business Ethics*, Vol. 10, pp. 423–36.

Parker, R.P. and Grove, C.B. (1996) The statistics producers' corner. *Business Economics*, 31(3), pp. 59–60.

Platten, N. (1995) The impact of new EU rules on data protection. *Marketing and Research Today*, 23(3), August, pp. 147–52.

Prescott, J. and Gibbons, P. (1993) *Global Perspectives on Competitive Intelligence*, Society of Competitive Intelligence Professionals, USA.

Ramsey, P. and Kaufman, L. (1982) Presenting research data: how to make weak numbers look good. *Industrial Marketing*, 67, March, pp. 66, 68, 70, 74.

Rawwas, M., Patzer, G., and Klassen, M. (1995) Consumer ethics in cross-cultural settings: entrepreneurial implications. *European Journal of Marketing*, 29(7), pp. 62–78.

Semon, T.T. (1996) Can we afford to be honest? *Marketing News*, 30(12), p. 5.

Smith, N.C. and Quelch, J.A. (1993) *Ethics in Marketing*, Homewood, IL, and Boston, MA: Richard D. Irwin, Inc., pp. 145–95.

Snowdon, R. (1995) Why JWT is now asking the obvious. *Marketing*, September 19, p. 16.

Webster, C. (1996) Hispanic and Anglo interviewer and respondent ethnicity and gender: the impact on survey response quality. *Journal of Marketing Research*, 33(1), pp. 62–72.

Worcester, R.M. and Downham, J. (eds) (1986) *Consumer Market Research Handbook*, Amsterdam: North-Holland.

5 Ethical dimensions in international marketing management: product and pricing policies

5.1 THE ROLE OF ETHICS IN MARKETING MIX DECISIONS

Marketing managers face a barrage of ethical issues which concern all aspects of the job on a daily basis. In the international arena, differing regulations and cultures further add to the complexity of ethical dilemmas. Having explored some ethical issues involved in the analysis of international business opportunities in the previous chapter, we shall now discuss some ethical questions concerning the main elements of the marketing mix, *i.e.*, the product, price, distribution, and promotion policies.

5.2 ETHICAL ISSUES IN PRODUCT POLICY DECISIONS

The choices a firm makes regarding its product design clearly affect all other aspects of the marketing mix. As an increasing number of firms are starting to focus on expanding their sales in overseas markets, the variety of ethical standards further compounds the difficulty of the decisions that have to be made. What one country considers as 'ethical' may not be viewed as such in another country. Due to these differences, most firms use the least common denominator approach – making product decisions based on the strictest requirements in the countries in which they operate. However, it is sometimes argued that this is not enough and that marketing managers should deal with ethical issues on a basis of virtue ethics (see Chapter 2, Section 2.4.5). In this context, following the principles of virtue ethics means doing what is 'right', rather than just what is required by law.

There are a number of different views on the responsibility multinational companies have for their customers. Smith and Quelch (1993) present an 'ethics continuum' and suggest that product decisions can be based on different values. *Caveat emptor*, on one end of the spectrum, maintains a 'buyer beware' philosophy in which consumers have knowledge about the product, and the company's policy is based on observing legal restrictions. On the opposite end, *Caveat venditor* maintains that the manufacturer should be responsible for informing the consumer of all aspects of the product or service, even if this goes beyond the legal requirements. Proponents of this position argue that consumers, especially those in less developed countries (LDCs), often lack the basic skills and knowledge that typify customers in Western markets, and/or are unable to express, claim, or defend their rights as consumers (Compare Part Three, Chapter 22). According to this position, a corporation has a moral duty to take whatever steps necessary to ensure the product is as safe as possible. Another option is to take a middle ground, because 'consumers purchasing many different kinds of commodities cannot be as knowledgeable as a manufacturer specializing in particular products' (Smith and Quelch 1993: 27). The pros and cons of these different positions will become more apparent below, where we examine six elements of product policy that raise significant ethical issues for the international marketing manager: product safety, product positioning, product packaging and labelling, product recall policy, and counterfeiting.

5.2.1 Product safety and design

Companies should clearly be responsible for the safety of their products, a view which is increasngly shared in countries all around the world. An OECD study conducted in 1995 found 'the general trend (in member countries) has been to make it progressively easier for consumers to bring product liability lawsuits' (OECD 1995: 7). This is important, because consumers want and expect safe products although they seldom actively seek safety. Instead, they tend to make their choices for other reasons (Smith and Quelch 1993). Consequently, consumers depend on governments to guarantee that manufacturers and retailers will not sell unsafe products.

Due to the current legal environment and the volatility of a company's reputation, decisions about product safety should be easy to make. However, firms sometimes face an interesting challenge: safer products cost more but consumers are not willing to pay for the increased cost. Even worse, in some countries, highlighting safety features could cause some consumers to question what they previously had assumed was a safe product. For example, Regina Corporation, a small appliance manufacturer in the United States, devised an immersion detection circuit interrupter for its home spa products. This device interrupts the circuits should someone accidentally drop an appliance in the water. Regina Corporation did not advertise the benefits of this new device because they believed it would frighten potential buyers (Nelson-Horchler 1988).

Another issue marketing managers face is that of differences in safety legislation across governments. Consider, for example, the chemical chlembuterol, which is an anabolic steroid that increases the appetite and sleeplessness of cattle. Chlembuterol is given to cattle to speed development, to increase the percentage of flesh and to decrease the fat, giving the meat a better appearance. Usage of this chemical is illegal in the United States. After 200 people were poisoned by consuming cow's liver treated with the substance in several parts of Spain, the country also outlawed its use (Harvey 1994). Although the rest of the European Community soon joined Spain in banning the substance, a spot done on the popular American news television show *Prime Time Live* found that many European breeders are still using chlembuterol in cattle feed (*Prime Time Live* 1996). *Prime Time* found that the ban on the chemical was revoked pending investigation of the incident in Spain, and that most of the imports from Europe of beef and beef products contain chlembuterol. Should the European beef manufacturers change their standards to that of the United States? Do the benefits of this chemical outweigh the risks? Although chlembuterol is effective in speeding growth in cows, there are safer options to do this on the European market, but they cost more. Is the producer or the purchaser of this chemical responsible for any side effects it might cause?

Laczniak and Murphy (1985) use the chemical insecticide DDT as another example to demonstrate the impact of different product safety standards across countries. Although DDT was banned in the US in 1972, it is still being sold to Third World countries to control malaria. DDT is effective in stopping the spread of malaria; however, there are safer but more expensive chemicals available. Should the producer of DDT take it off the market, even when Third World countries cannot afford to pay a higher price for safer options? Should the producer absorb the difference in price to supply a safer product?

Furthermore, does a manufacturer have the responsibility to do what is good for customers, even if customers do not want it? Consider seat belts, which are standard safety equipment in automobiles. A large number of motorists in the United States refuse to wear safety belts. Furthermore, what if customers demand features which the company perceives to be bad for the consumer (like too much sugar in children's cereal)?

5.2.2 Product positioning

Positioning a product correctly is critical in reaching the intended target market and in gaining a competitive edge. This is especially important in the international arena, where competition is intense and positioning may differ by country.

However, product positioning and target marketing can be unethical, even if the product itself is perfectly ethical. This could be the case where the target market is unable to think rationally through the information and will therefore make uninformed or poor choices. Smith and Quelch (1993) cite a well-known case concerning the positioning strategy of the Suzuki Motor Company, Ltd. for its Suzuki Samurai four-wheel drive vehicle in the United States. The car was positioned as 'a unique, exciting, fun vehicle (alternative to small-car boredom) that stands in a class by itself'. Although disclaimers and warnings regarding seat belt usage were provided by Suzuki, roll-over incidents were so high that the Consumers Union in the US brought complaints to the Federal Trade Commission (FTC), stating that because the car was positioned as a sport utility car, consumers – many of whom were young, first time buyers – tended to drive it more recklessly and have more accidents.

5.2.3 Labelling and packaging

Firms that sell their products in international markets are challenged to achieve, as much as possible, economies of scale to save costs. Companies, therefore, not only strive for the standardization of product and promotion, but also attempt to achieve standardization of packaging and labelling. Labels are important to a product's success, because they capture attention and communicate details about the product and its usage to the consumer. If markets are similar, economies of scale are easily attained. English has traditionally been thought of as the 'international' language for commerce, and hence many European and American manufacturers have used English labels on products shipped for sale in the Far East. Many goods produced in Europe (such as Procter and Gamble's Head & Shoulders), make use of a 'Eurobottle' label in eight languages to reach the consumer. But what about customers in nearby Eastern Europe who purchase the product, who may not be able to read one of the languages and misuse the product (Jeannet and Hennessy 1995)? The mobility of people in today's world further increases the dilemma. Is Procter and Gamble responsible?

Labels can also communicate quality. This also applies to country-of-origin labels. By identifying the product's origin, the marketer is hoping to invoke certain quality perceptions that will help to sell the product in the world market (Samli 1992). In some cases, the country-of-origin label can be deceiving. Consider the manufacturer who produces in (for example) Russia, and then ships the product to Germany to be packed for export to Japan with the 'Made in Germany' label. Is the manufacturer taking advantage of the perceptions consumers have of quality products coming from Germany? In this case, it would be safe to say 'yes'. But what about a situation when the finishing touches are done in Germany? In that case, would the country of origin label also be deceiving to consumers?

Warning labels are also an issue (see Exhibit 5.1). Warning labels are being increasingly used by firms to reduce their exposure to product liability suits. However, warning labels are sometimes overused. A study done by Schwartz and Driver (1983: 60) found that 'as the number of warnings increases, consumers may not take the time or be able to differentiate the relative magnitude of risks between products, and consequently they will ignore the risk'. The ethical concern firms face is how to effectively communicate warnings to consumers in each country. Can the firm fulfil its responsibility by placing a warning obscurely on the label? On the other hand, would distinct placement of a warning on a label be the responsible action to take, yet scare away the customer?

Yet another aspect of labelling, which has become increasingly important in recent years, is the abuse of labels stressing health or ecological product attributes (Schlegelmilch 1994). For example, one might question the motivation and ethics of stressing that a washing powder is phosphate free while it still contains other environmentally harmful substances. Similarly, there are food products which stress the absence of monosodium glutamate (MSG) although they contain other artificial additives. It is also questionable whether the emphasis on waste redution through the use of refill packages or concentrates in products like fabric softeners, which many people regard as both useless and environmentally harmful in the first place, does not mislead consumers into thinking that the product, overall, is ecologically sound.

EXHIBIT 5.1

All part of the product

Product labels and packaging are part of the product. As such, manufacturers must consider the following key packaging concerns:

1 Labels must be accurate, brief, and easy to understand.
2 Warnings must be conspicuous and designate the degree of hazard.
3 Warnings and instructions should be repeated in the various languages of primary users.
4 Warnings should convey consequences of failure to heed (i.e. causes burns).
   Labels should describe proper disposal of a container if its contents are toxic, corrosive, caustic, or flammable.
5 Labels must be firmly attached so they remain in place and are legible for the product's life.
6 Packaging should minimize harm to contents and handlers.

Source: Adapted from Ryan, K. (1996) Product Liability: An Overview of Critical Loss Control Factors. *American Society of Safety Engineers*, April, pp. 33–4.

Packaging makes up on average 40 per cent of the world's solid waste (Alexander 1993). As consumers and governments become more concerned about the effects of solid waste on the environment, they are expecting companies to develop packaging that is environmentally friendly. The issue of 'slack fill' (packages being only partially full with the product) is becoming even more important with respect to the growing interest in environmental issues. Is slack fill used to protect the product or to make the product look bigger than that of the competition? Obviously the answer to this depends upon the product. Slack fill is needed to protect potato chips; however is it necessary in the case of perfumes or computer CD-ROM games? Is slack fill perhaps used to gain shelf space? Furthermore, what about the waste generated by slack fill? When dealing with slack fill, the marketing manager not only needs to consider the ethical implications of the excessive environmental waste, but also the possible charge of misguiding consumers.

5.2.4 Product recalls

Although companies strive to produce reliable and safe products, defective items may still reach the market. Products may be flawed due to intrinsic problems, external ones caused by users, or problems caused by people who tamper with products. In any event, defective products are dangerous not only to the consumer but also to the firm itself in terms of reputation and sales. Because companies must react swiftly to the problem of defective products on the market, decisions on whether to inform consumers, modify the product, or recall it can raise ethical issues. The pressure to market new products quickly and sometimes without adequate testing will ensure that this problem will stay with us for some time to come (see Exhibit 5.2).

EXHIBIT 5.2

Switching the switches

Switching kingpin 3Com Corp. is quietly replacing thousands of its LANplex 2500 data center switches because of a flaw in a 25-cent component that has paralyzed some networks. 3Com blamed the problem on 'a connector manufacturer that did not meet their published specifications' for the 25-cent part. Consumers should be aware that there will likely be more problems, in general, in software and hardware as vendors truncate product testing cycles and reduce costs to keep pace with plummeting product prices. Consumers should wait for six to nine months before buying new products. Otherwise, users will

> become part of the vendors' testing processes whether they like it or not.
> Source: Adapted from Wallace, B. (1996) 3Com Pulls Switches. *Computerworld*. May 27, p. 15.

Recalling a product is a costly operation, especially if a firm has to recall products world-wide. However, when considering a recall, a company not only needs to consider the costs in terms of lost earnings or company reputation, but also the implications of potential non-action. Furthermore, how consumers perceive the negative news about a product and evaluate the risk is important; consumer perceptions held in one country can soon spread to others. For example, in 1990 the French manufacturer of Perrier bottled water had to remove its product from US retail stores after the product was found to contain benzene above the legal limit. Other countries were influenced by the publicity and conducted tests of their own. 'Soon Perrier had to withdraw its products in other countries eventually resulting in a world-wide brand recall' (Jeannett and Hennessy 1995: 355).

5.2.5 Product counterfeiting

The special properties and traits of a product provide the firm with competitive advantages and product differentiation, and firms protect these traits with patents. With increasing global competition, companies place a greater importance on the protection of patents for their products. Even so, differences in intellectual property rights legislation among countries make this a daunting task. For example, in India process patents (not *product* patents) are granted, thereby facilitating the copying of products. Firms spend a great amount of money on developing new products through innovation and research. The world-wide pharmaceutical industry, in particular, spends billions on research and development of new products. Pharmaceutical companies 'do not often compete on the basis of price differentials to sell their drugs, leaving two possibilities for competition: original research which produces significant improvements over existing therapies and product differentiation based on marketing skills' (Chetley 1990: 36). Firms that infringe on patents justify their position on a humanitarian level – being able to provide necessary goods to the market at a price the market can afford as opposed to the 'market price'. Pharmaceutical firms justify the high prices of their products with the need to finance research and development of better, more effective drugs to benefit humanity. Which side is the truly humanitarian is often debated.

It is not just the pharmaceutical industry that is placing importance on the issue of intellectual property rights. In 1994, US companies are said to have lost $1.3 billion in pirated copyrighted works to Japan, and $1.2 billion to Germany (Lii 1996). Furthermore, in 1995, 220 million cassette tapes and 45 million CDs (worth a total of $250 million) were copied illegally in China (Faison 1996). Indeed, the International Anti-Counterfeiting Coalition estimates that some 5 to 8 per cent of all products and services world-wide are counterfeit (Nill and Shultz 1996)

Pirates look at themselves as providing a social service – products at a price the market can afford. Are these pirates thieves of someone else's hard work or do they, indeed, provide a 'social service'? In a roundabout way, illegal copies can sometimes increase brand awareness, a fact which will not usually console the holder of the copyright. A related issue is where to draw the line in terms of copying. For example, consider a household in France with two computers. Does purchasing one software programme used on both computers infringe on copyright laws? If so, should the copyright police be able to enter a home to enforce copyright law? Exhibit 5.3 illustrates the severity of the problem:

EXHIBIT 5.3

The crime of the 21st century . . .

Product forgeries are affecting everything from Windows 95 to Similac baby formula to ACDelco auto parts. In fact, according to federal and industry surveys, America's annual losses from the problem have quadrupled over the past decade to a staggering $200 billion. An estimated 5 per cent of products sold world-wide are phony. Indeed, the money US companies have saved by moving manufacturing operations to developing nations has been offset by a huge hidden cost: 'knockoffs' of their products. The problem is extremely serious for high-margin products such as software and pharmaceuticals. Says Microsoft attorney Anne Murphy: 'We refer to some countries in Asia as one-disk markets. More than 99 per cent of the software is illegitimate copies'.

Source: Adapted from Stipp, D. (1996) Farewell, My Logo. *Fortune*, 133(10), pp. 128–38.

5.3 ETHICAL ISSUES IN PRICING POLICY DECISIONS

Ms Kiyono Seto received her yearly bonus from the company and promptly went shopping in Tokyo's fashionable Ginza district for a new business suit. At one of the designer stores, Kiyono was quite attracted to the fine fabric and cutting of a suit, but the price was a concern. However the clerk assisting her assured her that it was unlikely the suit would become a sale item, so Kiyono spent close to JPY100,000 (about US$1,000) on the suit. Two weeks later, she found the boutique had a sale and had reduced the price of the suit to JPY45,000. Six months following, the price had been reduced even further to JPY25,000. Why was the price so high in the first place? Is the store making any money at JPY25,000? 'I should have waited two weeks,' she said. Although cultures and tastes are quite diverse across the globe, experiences like Kiyono's are growing, especially in the triad. Is such a pricing system fair to the consumer?

This is only one of a variety of ethical pricing issues, and the issues tend to become more complex when pricing decisions in more than one country are involved. Smith and Quelch (1993) divide ethical pricing issues into two broad categories – fairness in consumer pricing and anti-competitive pricing. Fairness in consumer pricing looks at how the consumers are affected by pricing decisions; for example, can pricing mislead the consumer? Anti-competitive pricing deals with the antitrust laws in the United States and similar regulations in other countries, which are designed to protect small businesses and to maintain free competition.

5.3.1 Misleading pricing

Sale pricing, the use of price comparisons, and the provision of manufacturer's suggested retail prices have been the target of complaints from consumers all over the world. Recently in the United States, a court ruled against May D & F (a division of May Department Stores), finding the prices in the housewares department to be deceiving. Customers criticized the company for setting the initial price of goods at a high level for a brief period of time (in some cases only 10 days) in order to advertise a sale and draw customers. The accusations of price deception are not limited to the United States. With the introduction of seasonal sales in Japan, consumers have complained that the regular prices are exorbitant. Although no regulation has been passed in Japan as of yet, it is highly likely that such legislation will appear as competition becomes more fierce.

But are consumers influenced by reference pricing? Research has shown that although consumers are sceptical of reference pricing, they are 'nonetheless influenced by them in assessing the value of a sale offering' (Smith and Quelch 1993: 399). However, retailers that have these pricing policies argue that consumers are sceptical and are conditioned to thinking rationally because they have been exposed to this environment for a long time. Although this argument may hold true for the United States, the conditioning of consumers varies by country. Moreover, while most governments do not provide guidelines on how long merchandise must be quoted at the regular price before it can go on sale or when sales periods are to be scheduled, some countries, notably Germany, provide some very specific regulations on such issues.

5.3.2 Anti-competitive pricing

When looking at ethical issues in pricing a product internationally, one can find a diverse landscape of antitrust laws in each country in which multinational corporations compete. The basic antitrust law in the United States, the Sherman Act, was enacted under the power of Congress to regulate commerce with foreign nations and among the States.

The European Union has developed antitrust laws that cover business practices in the EU. The EU's competition policy is designed to prevent artificial distortion of the market and to stimulate the free enterprise system. Enforcement of the policy is the responsibility of the executive branch of the European Committee, called the Commission. Article 85 prohibits the following pricing practices: 'price-fixing agreements, uniform pricing, and price discrimination arising from concerted practices' (Van Bael and Bellis 1987: 231). However, Article 85 is not applicable when (a) one party has no commercial autonomy *vis-à-vis* another and is treated as part of the same economic grouping, and/or (b) there is no effect on interstate trade.' (S.J. Berwin & Co, 1992: 65). In the case of (b), the matter is handled at the national level.

Japanese antitrust laws are similar to the Sherman Act of the United States. This is due to the US Occupation after World War II. The 'Act Concerning Prohibition of Private Monopoly and Maintenance of Fair Trade' (sometimes called ACT), was a result of US demands on the Japanese government which would 'eliminate and prevent private monopoly and restrict trade'. The ACT is enforced by the Fair Trade Commission (FTC) in Japan, which is modelled after the FTC in the United States. The law prohibits cartel arrangements, unfair business practices (including price discrimination, dumping, using economic advantage to coerce customers or competitors), private monopolization, and unreasonable restraint of trade (Kintner and Joelson 1974). The ACT was amended in 1991 to strengthen deterrence by drastically increasing surcharges to be imposed on firms engaging in cartels. Exhibit 5.4 gives an example of the work conducted by the Japanese Fair Trade Commission.

EXHIBIT 5.4

Cartels and collusion

According to Masanari Iketani, president of Tokyo Steel, Nippon Steel regularly acts behind the scenes to control who the major Japanese trading companies (Marubeni, Mitsubishi, and

Mitsui) do business with. That is, every time that Tokyo Steel introduces a new product, such as H-beams and hot-rolled coil, Nippon pressures the big trading companies not to broker the products. According to the Wall Street Journal, these kind of cartels and collusion cost Japanese consumers up to $140 billion a year. Now, however, the Fair Trade Commission is stepping up its investigations of illegal price fixing.

Source: Adapted from Anonymous-1 (1996) Breaking the Oligopoly: Tokyo Steel vs. Nippon Steel. *Iron Age New Steel.* 12(1), pp. 66–7.

5.3.3 Price fixing

In the United States, a 'suggested retail price' is not considered a form of price fixing. In Japan the price of a product is set by a *'gentlemen's agreement'*; however, should a retailer violate the 'agreed-upon' retail price, traditionally the manufacturer or wholesaler could stop sales to the retailer. Shisedo, a major cosmetics manufacturer in Japan, attempted to do this in 1995, when a retailer for Shisedo sold Shisedo products below the suggested market prices. The issue went to court and the court ruled in favour of the retailer, citing Shisedo's practices as a violation of Japanese anti-monopoly law (Fukunaga and Chinone 1994). Shisedo would have never discovered the violation of this 'gentlemen's agreement' (now illegal), had it not been for complaints from stores nearby. Consumers argue that manufacturers' suggested retail pricing strategies are unfair and do not reflect free market forces.

In all triad countries, the *explicit* agreement to fix prices is illegal. An oligopolistic market provides the atmosphere in which it is most attractive and easy to establish a price fixing agreement with competition. So why are companies attracted to do so? Proponents of price setting agreements argue that the purpose is 'to get a fair market value and produce a fair profit for the industry to keep it healthy' (Velasquez 1988: 211). They further justify price-fixing arrangements by arguing that without such an agreement, a price war will erupt, eventually causing bankruptcies and loss of employment. However, opponents argue that in a society that values justice, freedom, and social utility, price fixing is unethical because it restrains the consumer's freedom of choice and interferes with each firm's interest in offering the consumer products of the highest-quality and reliability at the best price. Price-fixing becomes more of an issue for multinational corporations when operating in countries in which anti price-fixing laws do not exist. Here, it is easy for the corporation to use the excuse that everyone is doing it, so why should the company not participate, too? Consider Exhibit 5.5 for an example of a report on alleged price fixing in the explosives industry.

EXHIBIT 5.5

Explosive price fixing

The six largest explosive makers in the US face a new antitrust lawsuit, this time brought by several explosives users who allege that producers conspired to fix prices. The suit against ICI Explosives USA, Dyno Nobel, Mining Equipment and Mill Supply, Austin Powder, ETI Explosives Technologies International, and El Dorado Chemical, is being pursued by 70 different mining and electric power companies. They allege that these six producers violated the Sherman Antitrust Act by artificially raising and fixing prices, allocating customers, and rigging commercial bids for explosives between 1988 and 1992.

Source: Adapted from Fattah, H. (1996) Explosives Producers Face Lawsuits. *Chemical Week*, June 26, p. 18.

5.3.4 Price discrimination

Price discrimination occurs usually in business-to-business transactions, for example, suppliers to retailers. A seller may offer a better price to a favoured buyer, thereby giving an unfair competitive advantage. Price discrimination can also affect competition at the seller and consumer level. Many firms justify price difference with differences in the cost of production, delivery and selling, or that they must adjust prices to stay competitive in a market where competition is high and consequently does not have to adjust as much in markets where direct competition is not as big a threat.

The United States has a rather controversial law called the Robinson–Patman Act, which makes price discrimination illegal. The act, adopted in 1936, was designed to protect small companies from being put at a disadvantage by suppliers who gave discounts to big companies. Critics of the legislation argue that it protects competitors rather than competition and hence the FTC does not currently enforce it. Similarly, Article 85 of the Competition Law of the European Economic Community 'prohibits agreements between undertakings or concerted practices which apply dissimilar conditions to equivalent transactions with other trading parties, thereby placing them at a competitive disadvantage' (Van Bael and Bellis 1987: 232). However, multinational corporations argue they must price their products differently according to the economic situation and competition in each country, and justify their prices with differences in distribution. Is price discrimination unethical by giving an unfair advantage to distributors and retailers who purchase large quantities? Or do those large quantities justify a significant cut in price? Exhibit 5.6 provides two recent legal perspectives.

EXHIBIT 5.6

Recent judgements

A) California recently enacted the Gender Tax Repeal Act of 1995 which prohibits businesses from discriminating on the basis of gender with respect to the price charged for services of similar or like kind (Anonymous-2 1996).

B) A federal judge, Judge Charles P. Kocoras, has approved a $351 million settlement that forces pharmaceutical manufacturers to offer the same discounts to independent pharmacists as they extend to managed care organizations. This signals the end of two-tier pricing based on retail status. In practice, this means that discounts enjoyed by managed care can no longer be refused to buying groups who are able to demonstrate a similar ability to affect market share (Conlan 1996).

Source (A): Adapted from Anonymous-2 (1996) Civil Rights – Gender Discrimination. *Harvard Law Review*, 109(7) pp. 1839–44.
Source (B): Adapted from Conlan, M.F. (1996) Finally Settled. *Drug Topics*, 140(13), pp. 22.

5.3.5 Predatory pricing (dumping)

Predatory pricing refers to a situation in which a company cuts its prices to unreasonable low or unprofitable levels in order to drive the competition out of the market. The firm incurs losses with the intent that profits will be gained once the competition is eliminated. The reason why a company would be tempted to do this appears obvious – to obtain a monopoly position in the market. However, as a side note, there are some economists who argue that predatory pricing is *not* a suitable tool for gaining monopoly power (Yamey 1972).

A specific form of predatory pricing exists in the form of dumping, i.e. 'selling goods overseas for less than in the exporter's home market or at a price below the cost of production, or both' (Czinkota and Ronkainen 1996: 519). The issue of dumping is certainly not a new one. Even before World War II, cases of dumping were levied against the Japanese, the most famous one being 'Alaska's Salmon War' (1937), in which Japanese caught salmon outside the 300 mile coastal area of Alaska, canned it, and exported it to the United States to sell at prices way below market value (NHK Television: Special Documentary, March 1996). Finally, with the General Agreement on Tariffs and Trade (GATT), antidumping regulations were permitted by Article VI. This Article defines dumping and establishes several basic conditions in which action against dumping is permissible.

According to Article VI, dumping must cause material injury (however, stabilization programmes for primary commodities do not cause material injury) and cannot occur solely because internal consumption taxes are not levied on exports (Hawk 1983).

The controversy surrounding dumping laws focuses primarily on what proves *intent* and what constitutes *unreasonably low* or *unprofitable* prices (see Exhibit 5.7). The standards to determine *unreasonably low cost* differ around the globe almost as much as cultures do. In the United States, prices set below the average variable or marginal cost (whichever is lower) are considered unreasonably low, whereas the EU defines 'unreasonably low' when the export price to the Community is 'less than the comparable price actually paid in the course of trade for the like product intended for consumption in the exporting country or country-of-origin' (Hawk 1983: 43).

EXHIBIT 5.7

Predatory pricing or not?

Trade relations between the US and Japan were dealt a blow recently as the sole US producer of sodium azide levied dumping charges against three competitors in Japan. In a petition filed with the International Trade Commission in January, 1996, American Azide Corp., a subsidiary of American Pacific Corp., stated its sodium azide business was in imminent peril because of predatory pricing by Japanese producers. Other, non-Japanese competitors of American Azide agree. ICI Canada indicated it would file a so-called third country antidumping petition and India's Amindo Chemical said it would submit a letter in support of American Azide's position. A spokesman for Mitsui & Co., one of two importers in the US, denies that the Japanese producers – Masuda Chemical Corp., Toyo Kasei Kogyo Ltd., and Nippon Carbide Co. Ltd. – are dumping and claims that American Azide's costs are too high.

Source: Adapted from Chapman, P. (1996) Sodium Azide Woes Seen in Japanese Dumping Suit. *Chemical Marketing Reporter*, 249(7), pp. 3, 18.

In the United States, if a product is found unsafe by the Consumer Product Safety Commission it can no longer be sold in the country. This stipulation often provides a different motivation for US companies to dump the product in other countries. For example, in 1988, the Commission outlawed three-wheel cycles, citing they were dangerous to the consumer. Many companies recalled their products and dealt with the large inventories by dumping them at low prices in other countries. 'Often the firms are faced with the decision of "dumping" the product in other countries or taking a large write-off that negatively affects earnings, stock price, and employment stability' (Jennings 1993: 124).

5.4 SUMMARY

This chapter provided an overview of some of the ethical issues marketing managers face when making marketing mix decisions. Although it was not possible to pursue individual topics in depth, it has become evident that numerous ethical issues surround each marketing mix element. Ethical choices are called for in all aspects of product policy decisions, starting at the design stage with safety questions and ending at the final stage of a product's life with recycling issues. Pricing decisions also provide ample opportunity to demonstrate ethical leadership. The temptations and scope for misleading pricing, discriminatory pricing, price conspiracies, etc. appears to be relatively large, and enforcement agencies and consumer interest groups have been set up world-wide to protect fair competition and to prevent unfairness in consumer pricing.

5.5 REFERENCES

Alexander, J.H. (1993) *In Defense of Garbage*, Praeger Publishers Inc., US, p. 63.

Anonymous-1 (1996) Breaking the oligopoly: Tokyo Steel vs. Nippon Steel. *Iron Age New Steel*, 12(1), pp. 66–7.

Anonymous-2 (1996) Civil rights – gender discrimination. *Harvard Law Review*, 109(7), pp. 1839–44.

Chapman, P. (1996) Sodium oxide woes seen in Japanese dumping suit. *Chemical Marketing Reporter*, 249(7), pp. 3, 18.

Chetley, A. (1990) *A Healthy Business? The Global Pharmaceutical Industry*, London: Zed Books Ltd, pp. 36, 40.

Conlan, M.F. (1996) Finally settled. *Drug Topics*, 140(13), p. 22.

Czinkota, M.R. and Ronkainen, I.A. (1996) *Global Marketing*, Fort Worth, Philadelphia: The Dryden Press.

Faison, S. (1995) Copyright pirates prosper in China despite promises. *The New York Times*, February 20, front page.

Fattah, H. (1996) Explosives producers face lawsuits. *Chemical Week*, June 26, p. 18.

Fukunaga, H. and Chinone, K. (1994) Taking on the system. *Tokyo Business Today*, Vol. 62, Issue 5. May 1994, pp. 4–13.

Harvey, B. (1994) *Business Ethics: A European Approach*, Hemel Hempstead: Prentice Hall International.

Hawk, B.E. (1983) *Antitrust and Trade Policies of European Eco-*

nomic Community, New York: Fordham Corporate Law Institute, pp. 41–3.

Jeannet, J.-P. and Hennessey, D. (1995) *Global Marketing Strategies* (3rd edn), UK: Houghton Mifflin Company.

Jennings, M.M. (1993) *Case Studies in Business Ethics*, St Paul, MN: West Publishing Company.

Kintner, E.W. and Joelson, M.R. (1974) *An International Antitrust Primer*, New York: Macmillan, p. 253.

Laczniak, G. and Murphy, P.E. (1985) *Marketing Ethics: Guidelines for Managers*, Boston, MA: Lexington Books, pp. 29, 77, 85.

Lii, J.H. (1996) Boom-at-a-Glance. *The New York Times Magazine*, February 18, Section 6, p. 27.

Nelson-Horchler, J. (1988) Safety: a tough sell. *Industry Week*, 236(3), February 1, pp. 49–50.

NHK Special Documentary (1996) *Eizo no 20 Seki*: The world that viewed the Meiji, Taisho and Showa eras of Japan. Television show.

Nill, A. and Shultz, C.J. (1996) The scourge of global counterfeiting. *Business Horizon*, November–December, pp. 37–42.

Organization for Economic Cooperation and Development (1995) *Product Liability Rules in OECD Countries*, Paris, France: OECD, p. 7.

Prime Time Live, aired on ABC (The American Broadcast Company) on February 7, 1996.

Ryan, K. (1996) Product liability: an overview of critical loss control factors. *American Society of Safety Engineers*, April, pp. 33–4.

Samli, A.C. (1992) *Social Responsibility in Marketing: A Proactive & Profitable Marketing Management Strategy*, Quorum Books, US, pp. 122–3.

Schlegelmilch, B.B. (1994) Green ethical and charitable: another marketing ploy or a new marketing era, in M.J. Baker (ed) *Perspectives on Marketing Management*, Vol. 4, London: Wiley, pp. 55–71.

Schwartz, V. and Driver, R.W. (1983) Warnings in the workplace; the need for a synthesis of law and communication theory. *University of Connecticut Law Review*, 52(1), p. 60.

S.J. Berwin & Company (1992) *Competitions & Business Regulation in the Single Market*, Confederation of British Industry, p. 65.

Smith, N.C. and Quelch, J.A. (1993) *Ethics in Marketing*, Times Mirror International Publishers Ltd.

Stipp, D. (1996) Farewell, my logo. *Fortune*, 133(10), pp. 128–38.

Van Bael, I. and Bellis, J.-F. (1987) *Competition Law of the EEC*, Bicester, UK: CCH Editions Ltd, pp. 231–2.

Velasquez, M. (1988) *Business Ethics Concepts and Cases*, Hemel Hempstead: Prentice Hall, p. 211.

Wallace, B. (1996) 3Com pulls switches. *Computerworld*, May 27, p. 15.

Yamey, B.S. (1972) Predatory pricing: notes and comments. *Journal of Law and Economics*, Vol. 15, pp. 129–47.

6 *Ethical dimensions in international marketing management: distribution and promotion policies*

6.1 ETHICS IN DISTRIBUTION AND PROMOTION POLICY DECISIONS

The previous chapter illustrated the complexity of ethical issues in product policy and pricing decisions. This chapter continues the focus on marketing mix decisions by looking at ethical questions arising in the context of distribution and promotion policy decisions. Once again, an international perspective is injected where appropriate.

6.2 ETHICAL ISSUES IN DISTRIBUTION POLICY DECISIONS

One of the key expressions in every marketing student's vocabulary is 'channel captain' or 'channel leader'. It expresses the notion that within a distribution channel consisting of, for example, a manufacturer, wholesaler and retailer, one organization holds the greatest degree of power and control. This power can sometimes be misused. Manufacturers may take advantage of small retailers or, vice versa, powerful retail chains might take advantage of manufacturers. Below, we focus on the latter and initially look at the controversial issue of slotting allowances. Next, we highlight some ethical issues surrounding direct marketing and network marketing, two distribution methods which have strongly benefited from the availability of new technologies. The section on distribution closes with a brief look at grey markets, a problem familiar to most marketers who sell branded products in multiple countries.

6.2.1 Slotting allowances

During the last twenty years, the packaged consumer goods industry has witnessed a power shift away from manufacturers in favour of retailers. Among the main contributing factors were the increasing size and, consequently, purchasing power of retailers, the introduction of scanner systems which provide the retailer with much more accurate information on the profitability of a product than ever before, and the emergence of retail brands, which attempt to replace manufacturer brand loyalty with store loyalty. Given today's bargaining power of retailers, it has become common practice for them to demand slotting allowances from manufacturers. Specifically, retailers, and sometimes also wholesalers, demand payments or 'free' goods for listing a new item and taking it into their store or warehouse. To defend this practice, which is said to have originated in Europe and entered the US via Canada, retailers often argue that their valuable shelf space is for rent, and slotting allowances represent nothing else but rent payments for shelf space. Of course, the logical extension of this thought is to charge slotting allowances not only for new products, but also to demand annual renewal fees, a practice which is becoming more wide spread (Kiley 1989). It has been estimated that some 55 per cent of promotional expenditures flow into slotting allowances (Dagnoli and Freeman 1988). However, since slotting allowances are often negotiated orally and privately (Laczniak and Murphy 1993), determining the proportion allocated to slotting allowances is likely to be a rather imprecise exercise.

From an ethical perspective, slotting allowances have been heavily criticized. Indeed, some critics have referred to them as 'ransom', 'extortion allowances' and 'institutional bribery' (Laczniak and Murphy 1993). The issues at the heart of the concern are whether such payments represent price discrimination (Freeman and Dagnoli 1988) and whether this practice stifles innovation (Therrien, 1989). As to the latter, it has been argued that smaller manufacturers, who often cannot afford to pay slotting allowances, are frequently the ones who invent new products. Whether slotting allowances are an abuse of power or a justifiable fee might be ethically debatable. Without a renewed shift in the bargaining power of channel participants, however, the slotting allowance is here to stay.

6.2.2 Direct marketing

In the triad, the use of direct marketing methods by companies has increased during the past decade (Baines 1995: 332; see also Exhibit 6.5). In Japan, there has been an increase in the usage of direct marketing *as part of* companies' sales strategies, which is due to improved delivery and payment systems, an increase in the number of working women, and computerization of mailing lists. In Western Europe, direct marketing is gaining a bigger share of companies' marketing budgets, growing at an average of 10 per cent per year (United States Postal Service 1994). In the United States, the number of direct mail shoppers rose by more than 42 per cent from 1984 to 1990 (Smith and Quelch 1993: 474).

Furthermore, the development and increase in usage of electronic media, on-line information systems, direct mail, door-to-door sales, 'micro-marketing', and telemarketing have provided for a wide range of methods which are encompassed in the term direct marketing. With companies in all countries in the triad becoming more dependent on technology to suit their communication needs, and the technological improvements that have been made as of late, the ethical issues regarding direct marketing gravitate towards questions of privacy, confidentiality, and intrusion. Compare Exhibit 6.1 for an example of the privacy debate in direct marketing.

EXHIBIT 6.1

Invasion of consumer privacy?

'Executives of Lotus Development corporation and Equifax Marketing Decision Systems canceled the release of a proposed product called "Lotus marketplace: Households" in the wake of an unprecedented storm of consumer protest regarding its alleged invasion of consumer privacy. The product would have provided operators of small businesses with information regarding American households, in compact disk (CD-ROM) form, to be used for target selection. After a number of negative news articles appeared in the press, the product began to receive legislative scrutiny, and a grass-roots protest campaign began. After over 30,000 consumers requested that they be deleted from the database, the project was canceled'.

Source: Adapted from Smith, H.J. (1994) *Managing Privacy: Information Technology and Corporate America*, Chapel Hill: The University of North Carolina Press, p. 2.

In collecting, publishing, and selling data on consumers in specific markets, does a company have the moral and legal responsibility to advise first those consumers who are included in their list? Does the collecting company have the right to publish and sell information which may or may not be considered private? Some may argue that the company is even providing an indirect service to the consumers by divulging information which would result in more satisfying product offerings being made available to them. Who actually owns the information being collected? Some of the issues are identical to those discussed in the Chapter 4 in the context of marketing research.

The above problems are exacerbated in so called 'micro-marketing' campaigns. This is a one-to-one approach, in which certain characteristics of each consumer are collected and scrutinized to develop an individualized product or service targeted directly to a small group of consumers with very specific traits. The concept itself is not the problem; rather it is the process of collecting, storing, and sharing information about individual consumers that raises ethical issues of privacy.

The differences in legislation regarding privacy rights reflect how differently each country treats this issue. In particular, 'the restrictive European position on the right to privacy contrasts with the more liberal American position, when confronted with the supply of data for direct marketing purposes' (Harvey 1994: 146). The European Commission passed a directive on data protection which not only protects consumer data within the EU but also outside the European Union. The Directive on Data Protection states that

(1) Data use is prohibited without authorization of the consumer; (2) data subjects must be personally notified to whom information has been passed and for what purpose; (3) subjects can claim compensation if the data is 'misused and causes damage'; and (4) European Community data can only be transferred out of the European Community if the receiving country can guarantee the same level of protection

(Harvey 1994: 146).

Currently consumers in all European Union countries have the legal right to have their name and data omitted from direct mailing lists; however, the number of consumers who have chosen to specify that they do not want direct mail has been relatively small. Japan, much like the United States, has relatively little regulation on the issuance and use of customer data, and direct mailing lists are increasing (United States Postal Service 1994). Exhibits 6.2, 6.3 and 6.4 provide additional insights into the privacy debate.

EXHIBIT 6.2

A critical juncture

According to a recent poll by Nielsen Media Research, 37 million people in the US and Canada – about 17% of the combined populations – have access to the Internet via home or office computers. This has led to the phenomenal growth of on-line systems, such as the World Wide Web, and has opened up a vast arena for commercial transactions. Consumers and businesses can now capture and use commercial information in ways that were unimaginable just a few years ago. Businesses, for example, have available consumer marketing information and transactional data that is much richer, more detailed, and more personalized than ever before. With this new technology come significant privacy protection obligations for all parties to on-line commercial transactions.

Source: Adapted from Varney, C.A. (1996) Privacy in the Electronic Age – Rights and Responsibilities of Business and the Consumer. *Credit World*, Jan/Feb, pp. 11–13.

EXHIBIT 6.3

Privacy issues: the US response

In June 1995 the Clinton administration's National Information Infrastructure Task Force issued an important document entitled 'Privacy and the National Information Infrastructure: Principles for Providing and Using Personal Information.' Unlike the direction taken by other countries, these principles emphasize disclosure about, rather than prohibition against, the use of personal information. Moreover, they focus on individual consumer responsibility and the sorts of empowerment (i.e. opt-out provisions and information audit provisions) needed by individuals in order to exercise such responsibility.

Source: Adapted from Varney, C.A. (1996) Privacy in the Electronic Age – Rights and Responsibilities of Business and the Consumer. *Credit World*, Jan/Feb, pp. 11–13.

EXHIBIT 6.4

Privacy issues: the global response

The New Zealand Privacy Act not only mandates that marketers ensure any information collected is relevant and essential for an organization's business purpose, but requires that personal information be collected directly from the individual. In addition, the Act mandates that reasonable steps are taken to make the individual aware that the information is being collected, why it is being collected, who is going to receive it, the name and address of any organization collecting and holding it, and the individual's right to access and correct it. Needless to say, New Zealand's direct marketing industry offered resistance to the bill since it eliminates their ability to use subscription lists. Today, Holland, Germany, and a growing list of other countries have already adopted similar types of legislation. And in July 1995, the European Parliament through its council of Europe Convention on Data Protection, adopted a directive to protect the fundamental rights

and freedoms of individuals – in particular, their right of privacy with respect to processing of personal data.
Source: Adapted from Morris-Lee, J. (1996) Privacy: It's Everyone's Business Now! *Direct Marketing*, April, pp. 40–43.

6.2.3 Network marketing

Network marketing (pyramid or multi-level marketing) has increased to the point of saturation in the United States, and companies using this marketing tool are slowly beginning to establish international networks. Amway, the oldest company to practise network marketing, has been relatively successful in Japan, and other companies such as NuSkin and Mary Kay cosmetics have been increasing their operations overseas. These companies employ thousands of part-time workers who sell door-to-door to friends and family. Most of these companies entice their employees to attract new part-time sales people by promising a percentage of the profit gained by the person recruited. Each sales person is encouraged (by promises of more money and other rewards) to develop their own network of sales people. The perception of network marketing varies greatly in different cultures. Is it acceptable to use friendships as a means to gaining sales? Should one make a profit from selling to a friend, colleague, or neighbours? By attracting part-time sales people with the promise of increasing profits and rapid promotion, is a network marketing company not promising something it can seldom deliver? Network marketing does not appear to be unethical *per se*, but even its supporters will agree that it is a marketing instrument which has often been abused through over-inflated claims and unrealistic promises. Exhibits 6.5 and 6.6 attest to the success of multi-level marketing.

EXHIBIT 6.5

Network marketing and direct selling companies rise to the top

Two network marketing and direct selling companies are now among the top five companies by sales in a *Household and Personal Products Industry* survey. Amway was fourth at $2.65 billion, and Avon fifth at $2.6 billion. They blew by many household names in the listings, including Estée Lauder and Revlon. Mary Kay placed 17th, NuSkin 19th, and Beauti-Control 49th.
Source: Adapted from Anderson, D. (1996) Accelerated Growth: Using Technology to Speed Expansion. *Success*, June, p. 17.

EXHIBIT 6.6

A new concept in multi-level marketing

In traditional network marketing companies, distributors have to buy so much a month before they can earn the top commission, and they have to maintain minimum volumes within their group. In addition, there are sign up fees, starter kit requirements, meetings, training, and retail requirements. Life Plus was started in 1992 because its founder and president, Bob Lemon, saw the need for a less complicated plan. With Life Plus, there is a simple, high-tech sign up system and all business is done over the telephone. There is no face-to-face selling and no need to ask anyone for money. Distributors simply tell others about the product and, when someone is interested in buying, tell them to call the company. When the order person asks who referred the customer, the customer provides the distributor's PIN number. The computer will keep track of referrals and lineage, paying distributors on six levels, plus an infinity bonus. Some people are being paid beyond the 150th level. Is it successful? Distributors ('members') have increased from 17,000 to more than 250,000 in the past year and wholesale sales are estimated at $60 million. Life Plus manufactures and sells products aimed at nutritional and enzyme therapy.

Source: Adapted from Anderson, D.M. (1996) Accelerated Growth: Using Technology to Speed Expansion. *Success*, June, p. 17.

6.2.4 Grey markets

When a product is sold through unauthorized distribution channels within a market, grey markets develop. In international business, parallel importing is often the word that best describes grey marketing. The products involved are not counterfeit but legitimate; it is the distribution method itself that is not legitimate. One example of this involved a high quality women's lingerie manufacturer in France. The manufacturer had developed an extensive list of exclusive importers and distributors for just about every country in the world, and international sales were a significant amount of total sales. Problems arose with their Japanese distributor after he discovered, much to his dismay, that the French products were found in a shop with which their company had no business relationship. The Japanese shop had imported the products directly from a shop in Paris, who bought the products from their domestic sales force. The French manufacturer finally had to discontinue sales with this shop in Paris, as the Japanese importer expressed concern about dilution of brand equity. Was the existence of a grey market in Japan an indication of the inefficiency of distribution on the part of the Japanese supplier? Was it unethical for the Paris shop to try to increase its sales by selling to another shop in Japan? Will not the consumer benefit from grey markets resulting in lower prices? Indeed, grey markets are not only viewed negatively. Some consumers and (unauthorized) retailers see grey markets as an opportunity to cut channel costs, increase product availability, and lower end-user prices.

However, the majority of commentators point to the negative implications of grey markets and view the practice as unethical (Duhan and Sheffet 1988). Grey markets often occur with brands which are well-recognized throughout the world, and grey marketers enjoy a free ride by marketing those products for which the manufacturer and authorized distributor provide advertising, brand demonstrations, and publicity. It is also argued that grey marketing destroys brand equity by not offering the same level of after-service that is regularly offered for a high-quality brand name product. Furthermore, consumers are not adequately protected, as grey marketers usually do not offer warranties for their products. Authorized dealers may even refuse to repair a product that has been purchased on the grey market, causing more consumer headaches. The development of a grey market decreases the amount of trust between manufacturers and their authorized distributors, and encourages other companies to practise grey marketing to remain competitive. Exhibit 6.7 illustrates the ramifications of grey markets in the context of satellite TV.

EXHIBIT 6.7

Satellite TV doesn't recognize political borders

Canada's grey market for US satellite television services continued to grow in 1995 and 1996. Entrepreneurs like Peter G. are making a nice living supplying small satellite dishes to Canadians so that they can watch banned US channels like HBO and ESPN. A 1995 venture between DirecTV, a unit of GM Hughes Electronics, and Power Corp. of Canada was to recapture satellite television viewers through a new company called Power DirecTV. However, the deal collapsed due in part to the growing grey market, estimated at more than 100,000 Canadian households, and costly regulatory requirements. With Power DirecTV out of the picture, the grey market should continue to flourish proving that satellite TV does not recognize political borders.

Source: Adapted from Johnson, S.S. (1996). Culture Cops, Part Deux. *Forbes*, March 11, p. 14.

6.3 ETHICAL ISSUES IN PROMOTION POLICY DECISIONS

Of all components of the marketing mix, advertising is, without debate, the most visible element. People of all countries and cultures are exposed to thousands of advertisements and promotions on a daily basis. However, the degree of criticism given to advertisers varies by culture (compare Exhibit 6.8).

EXHIBIT 6.8

Who trusts advertising?

When it comes to advertising, Asians are the most trusting, with Russians being the most cynical. Across the world, 72 per cent believe marketers deliberately exaggerate health benefits, 70 per cent complain that they brainwash children, while 61 per cent are adamant that they reduce the contents of packaging below that which they advertise. On the positive side, however, 60 per cent of the world's consumers find advertising entertaining, and 45 per cent believe marketers sponsor worthwhile events. But only 38 per cent say marketers provide consumers with accurate information, and a mere 30 per cent believe marketers respect consumers' intelligence.

Source: Adapted from Belgiovane, R. and Milne, J. (eds) (1996) *The Globe Report*. Sydney, Australia internet: http: //www.globe.com.au/globereport210396.html#a, March 21.

The main reason why people of all countries view advertising with such scepticism is that nearly every advertising decision has an ethical dimension. Consider, for example, the use of emotional appeals, the use of misleading or deceptive messages, the direction of advertising to child audiences or the advertising of gambling opportunities. There is also the issue of celebrity endorsements. Do these celebrities really use, let alone prefer, the washing-up liquid they are advertising? Moreover, there is a wider debate on the usefulness of advertising as such. For example, does advertising create the right values when it attempts to convince children that their happiness depends on a pair of super expensive basketball shoes? To explore some of the controversy surrounding advertising, it is required to examine both legal and ethical issues associated with promotion decisions.

6.3.1 Legal aspects

Laws can be regarded as a reflection of ethical judgements in society and, of course, it would be a much simpler environment for the international marketer if regulations were the same across the board.

However this is not the case, and country specific differences can seriously obstruct the efforts of a multinational to achieve economies of scale through the standardization of advertisements.

The United States has basic regulations on the federal and state level, outlawing false and deceptive advertising. The advertising industry also practises self-regulation through two organizations, the National Advertising Division (NAD) of the Council of Better Business Bureaus (CBBB), and the National Advertising Review Board (NARB). The objective of these two organizations is to screen for claims that are unsubstantiated, thereby promoting the highest standards of truth and accuracy in national advertising. These organizations not only 'ensure that the marketplace where advertisers compete is not corrupted by false product claims,' but also 'defend advertisers against excessive government restrictions that would severely limit their ability to function in a competitive business environment' (Boddewyn 1992: 130). The United States has a very liberal attitude toward advertising. Although strict guidelines exist for advertising to children and truth in advertising, guidelines for competitive advertising centre mainly on the issue of unsubstantiated claims.

In Japan, advertising is regulated more strictly. In addition to laws dealing with truth in advertising, the Fair Trade Commission in Japan introduced the Act Pertaining to the Prevention of Unfair Competition to eliminate false advertising and business practices that might adversely affect competitive enterprises. Accordingly, comparative advertising must meet the following criteria to be permitted in Japan (Feldman 1996):

1   the content must be proven to be true;
2   the data or facts that substantiate the advertising must be cited correctly in the advertisement;
3   the methods and manners must be 'fair'.

However, what constitutes 'fair' is not clearly defined. The advertising industry in Japan also has a centralized self-regulation organization called The Japan Advertising Review Organization (JARO), which co-ordinates the activities of a variety of specialized self-regulatory bodies.

In the European Union, there is no significant advertising legislation which encompasses all member nations. However, a European Union Green Paper on 'Commercial Communication', approved in May 1996, aims to abolish a number of restrictive practices which currently make pan-European campaigns impossible (Schröder 1996/97). Great Britain, a major proponent of advertising self-regulation (ASR), has been pushing for the standardization of advertising practices and codes throughout member states, and for a self-regulation body which will ensure free competition in Europe. However, as of today, standards are incredibly different from one member country to another. Comparative advertising, for example, is not allowed in Germany, but is allowed in France and the UK. Advertising cash discounts is limited to three per cent in Germany and there are extremely detailed regulations on trading stamps and discounts in Southern European countries. Advertisements for pregnancy testing are banned in Ireland, but not in France.

Notwithstanding the regulatory differences between the triad countries, most tend to address such issues as puffery in advertising, children's advertising, deception in demonstrations and mock-ups, bait-and-switch advertising, the use of coupons, sweepstakes and promotional games, etc. The first two issues are discussed in more detail below.

(a) Puffery

Puffery is the over-exaggeration and overstatement of claims in advertising. Sometimes these claims can be disguised as factual information, which of course then makes the advertisement deceptive in all countries. In the United States, puffery is legal providing the characteristics 'puffed' actually exist. Smith and Quelch (1993: 611) give the following examples of 'permissible puffery' in the United States: 'The legendary marquee [*sic*.] of high performance' (Alfa Romeo) and 'The lightest, most compact cellular phone on earth' (Motorola).

The United States assumes that a rational consumer will not rely solely upon such positive expressions of opinion and general statements of praise, and therefore such puffery is harmless. Furthermore, there is no objective way to determine whether such statements are false. These factors, combined with the importance Americans place on free competition in the marketplace, provide for a *caveat emptor* (or 'buyer beware') attitude towards puffery (compare Exhibit 6.9).

EXHIBIT 6.9

A close call for advertisers

In 1995 the Uniform Commercial Code was being reviewed for proposed revisions which would make companies vulnerable to lawsuits by consumers for advertising claims and promotion copy termed 'puffery'. Luckily, especially for companies with outrageous advertising, the latest revision switches the burden of proof to the consumer to prove that an advertiser's claim was meant to be taken as a promise.

Source: Adapted from Ross, C. (1996) Marketers Fend Off Shift in Rules for Ad Puffery. *Advertising Age*, 67(8), p. 41.

Like the US, most countries in the European Union also allow puffery if, and only if, it does not deceive the customer. According to a European directive on misleading advertising, the burden of proof is on the advertiser should his claims be challenged. In Japan, the Premiums and Representations Act clearly outlaws misleading representations, stating any claims made must be proven by objective means (Boddewyn 1992). For example, open ended claims such as 'My product is the best' would not only be misleading to the public, but also unfair to competitors because they cannot be proven objectively (Feldman 1996).

(b) Children's advertising

In any country, parents buy toys, clothes, and other products for their children, and give children some amount of money to make their own purchases. As the birth rate is declining throughout the triad, the amount of spending per child has risen over the past 10 years, particularly in Japan (The Japan Institute for Social and Economic Affairs 1995). Japan is one of the most lenient countries when it comes to regulation concerning advertising to children. Although some consumer groups have expressed dissatisfaction with advertising addressed to children or to which children are exposed, in general, advertising to children does not appear to be a very important issue.

This is in direct contrast to the United States. The NAD developed a special section called the Children's Advertising Review Unit (CARU) to monitor and respond to public complaints concerning advertisements to children and publish self-regulatory guidelines for children's advertising (Boddewyn 1992). Still, among consumerists in the US, there is a sense that self-regulation alone is not protecting children adequately. Rhoda H. Karpartkin, the President of the Consumers Union of the US, alludes to several ways in which marketers are unethical when targeting children:

- they mislead and manipulate kids into thinking that using the advertised product would make them more competent or better people;
- they misrepresent the size and appearance of the product;
- they omit important information from ads that would make the claims made seem implausible;
- they fail to show products being used in a normal setting;
- they make misleading claims about product performance.

The European Union, as a whole, seems to promote a sense of self-regulation when controlling advertising to children. However, there are some regulations which impact this issue. In Germany, advertising specific types of toys is banned and a law against unfair competition (UWG) gives the courts the right to handle cases of consumer complaints against advertising which is unduly appealing to children. Great Britain has laws dealing with the advertising of certain products to children, such as tobacco and alcohol, but there is no one law encompassing the subject of advertising and children (Boddewyn 1992). In France, children are not allowed to endorse products (Jeannet and Hennessey, 1995) and in Greece, TV advertising of toys is banned until 10 o'clock in the evening (Schröder 1996/97).

How different views on advertising to children can impact the content of a TV commercial can be illustrated through a General Mills example. When marketing its Action Man soldiers in Germany, the company was forced to make a very different television commercial by reducing the tone of the speaker's voice and the violence. Although the original commercial, made for view in the US and other countries, had toy soldiers holding machine guns and driving tanks, in Germany the toy soldiers were shown unarmed and driving a jeep (Jeannet and Hennessey 1995).

There are great differences in opinion across the globe on what is harmful to society. However, there is agreement that children are especially vulnerable, as they are less able to make rational decisions and are influenced more by advertising. To act in a socially responsible manner, the international marketer should make an effort to explain the product honestly and not exploit the vulnerability of children.

6.3.2 Ethical evaluation

Is advertising itself manipulative? Does the way the claims are made put 'wrong ideas' in the mind of consumers? Apart from the legal discourse, some philosophers and ethicists argue that even if advertising is legally not deceptive to the consumer, it may not necessarily be the right thing to do.

Throughout the triad, there are a diverse set of groups within each country who argue about the 'right thing to do.' For example, one set, the so-called 'Moral Majority' maintains that advertising leads to the moral breakdown of society; on the opposite side of the continuum, left-wing Marxist philosophers argue that the potentially revolutionary class is controlled by the false promises of advertising (Smith and Quelch 1993). Others, including the eminent economist John Kenneth Galbraith (1958; 1967) argue that advertising creates false needs among consumers with the inherent use of a pull strategy, promoting an unhealthy demand for something that is not necessary to society. A similar argument is made by Leiser (1979), who labels ads immoral if they promote products which are not needed or are harmful. A major question which these critics tend to ignore is: who decides what individuals really need? Do consumers 'need' an expensive Mercedes? If not, are we in fact to believe that all Mercedes ads are immoral?

Still, perceptions of what is moral and what is not clearly impact the evaluation of advertising. Consider, for example, a case from Germany: The Bahlsen Company in Hannover advertised its white chocolate by stating it is permissible to snack on sweets (*Naschen erlaubt*). Because snacking on sweets is 'allowed' (according to the advertisement), will the consumer draw the conclusion that eating Bahlsen white chocolate will have no negative effects, such as causing cavities or weight problems? Is it immoral to suggest that it is permissible to snack on sweets? Once the Berlin Consumer Protection Association forced the issue, the statement was indeed considered misleading by a Berlin Court (Harvey 1994). But is it not questionable to assume that the average consumer in Germany will be so affected by the advertisement that they will not be able to make a rational choice?

Other commonly levied criticisms of the ethics of advertising contend that advertisers are dishonest since they are only trying to make money and are not interested in communicating the truth; that persuasion of an individual violates a person's inherent rights; and can lead to human addictions and frequently degenerates into vulgarization. Moreover, advertising is often accused of creating conflict between parents and children. Atkin (1980), for example, asserts parent–child conflict is caused when parents refuse to purchase the child's request. Children also become unhappy when they are exposed to advertisements showing more affluent lifestyles than their own, and when products do not measure up to expectations created by advertising.

6.4 SUMMARY

The discussion of ethical issues associated with distribution and promotion policies illustrates the multitude and complexity of problems faced by marketing managers dealing with these two marketing mix elements. Looking at ethical issues in distribution policy decisions demonstrates once again how few issues are clear cut. Whether parallel imports, for example, are unethical, merely a result of inefficiencies in existing distribution channels, or a welcome price-break for end users will be answered differently by manufacturers, authorized dealers, unauthorized intermediaries, and different consumer groups. Advertising provides a good illustration of the connection between legislation and ethics. It is interesting to note that advertising legislation differs substantially throughout the triad, but that views on the moral aspects of advertising do not differ much from culture to culture, but rather from person to person. It can be argued though, that advertising itself is not unethical; however, the choices and actions of individual managers sometimes result in unethical advertisements.

6.5 REFERENCES

Anderson, D.M. (1996) Accelerated growth: using technology to speed expansion. *Success*, June, p. 17.

Atkin, C.K. (1980) The effects of television advertising on children, in E.L. Palmer and A. Dorr (eds) *Children and the Faces of Television*, New York: Academic Press, pp. 287–305.

Baines, A. (ed.) (1995) *The Handbook of International Direct Marketing*, London: Kogan Page Ltd, p. 332.

Belgiovane, R. and Milne, J. (eds) (1996) *The Globe Report*. Sydney, Australia internet: http://www.globe.com.au/globereport210396.ht ml#a, March 21.

Boddewyn, J.J. (1992) *Global Perspectives on Advertising Self-Regulation: Principles & Practices in Thirty-Eight Countries*, Quorum Books US, pp. 53, 56, 78, 83, 128, 130, 133, 149–50.

Dagnoli, J. and Freeman, L. (1988) Marketers seek slotting-fee truce. *Advertising Age*. February 22, p. 12

Duhan, D.F. and Sheffet, M.J. (1988) Gray markets and the legal status of parallel importation. *Journal of Marketing*, Vol. 52, July, p. 75.

Feldman, J.P. (1996) *Arent Fox Info Net*, internet: http://www.-arentfox.com/hyperout/adv/0104.html, April 17.

Freeman, L. and Dagnoli, J. (1988) FTC centers its sights on slotting allowances. *Advertising Age*, July 1, p. 35.

Galbraith, J.K. (1958) *The Affluent Society*, Boston, MA: Houghton Mifflin.

Galbraith, J.K. (1967) *The New Industrial State*, Boston, MA: Houghton Mifflin.

Harvey, B. (1994) *Business Ethics: A European Approach*, Hemel Hempstead: Prentice Hall International.

The Japan Institute for Social and Economic Affairs (1995) *Japan 1995: An International Comparison*, Tokyo: Keizai Koho Center.

Jeannet, J.-P. and Hennessey, D. (1995) *Global Marketing Strategies* (3rd edn), UK: Houghton Mifflin Company.

Johnson, S.S. (1996) Culture cops, part deux. *Forbes*, March 11, p. 14.

Kiley, D. (1989) Drug chains bleed suppliers and offer little in return. *Adweek's Marketing Week*, September 4, pp. 24–5.

Laczniak, G.R. and Murphy, P.E. (1993) *Ethical Marketing Decisions: The Higher Road*, Boston, MA: Allyn and Bacon.

Leiser, B. (1979) Beyond fraud and deception: the moral uses of advertising, in T. Donaldson, and P. Werhane (eds), *Ethical Issues in Business*, Englewood Cliffs, NJ: Prentice Hall, pp. 59–66.

Morris-Lee, J. (1996) Privacy: it's everyone's business now! *Direct Marketing*, April, pp. 40–3.

Ross, C. (1996) Marketers fend off shift in rules for ad puffery. *Advertising Age*, 67(8), p. 41.

Schröder, U. (1996/97) A harmonious eurovision. *Marketing Business*, December/January, p. 46.

Smith, H.J. (1994) *Managing Privacy: Information Technology and Corporate America*, Chapel Hill, NC: The University of North Carolina Press, p. 2.

Smith, N.C. and Quelch, J.A. (1993) *Ethics in Marketing*, Times Mirror International Publishers Ltd.

Therrien, L. (1989) Want shelf space at supermarket? Ante up. *Business Week*, August 7, pp. 60–61.

United States Postal Service (1994) *International Marketing Resource Guide*, Washington, DC: United States Postal Service, p. 36.

Varney, C.A. (1996) Privacy in the electronic age – rights and responsibilities of business and the consumer. *Credit World*, January/February, pp. 11–13.

7 Implementation of ethics into corporate decision making

7.1 CORPORATE INITIATIVES

Having illustrated the extent to which decision making in marketing is permeated by ethical issues, we will now explore how companies have reacted to growing ethical concerns and are attempting to institutionalize ethics in their organizations. To this end, we are starting at the roots of every strategic planning exercise, namely with a look at the changing nature of corporate mission statements. This is followed by a discussion of corporate codes of conducts and ethical credos. Many companies have also instituted ethics officers, established ethics hot-lines, instigated ethics training, and regularly conduct ethical audits. A review of these initiatives completes this chapter.

7.2 ETHICS AND THE CORPORATE MISSION

A mission statement aims to distinguish a business from similar ones and identifies the scope of its operations in product and market terms. The company mission embodies the business philosophy and reveals the image the company seeks to project. 'In short, the company mission describes the firm's product, market, and technology in a way that reflects the *values and priorities* of the strategic decision makers' (Graham and Havlick 1994: 4; emphasis added). Although not everyone believes in the value or necessity of mission statements, most companies find it useful to have an explicitly defined set of principles to guide their actions and embrace them enthusiastically. Mission statements are at the heart of a company's corporate philosophy (Falsey 1989) and go much deeper than mere definitions. They are documents that guide the thoughts and actions of employees; they outline goals by which a company desires to be measured, and they define priorities.

Since few things in life are static, mission statements have evolved to reflect changes in ideas, language, priorities, and goals. To be truly valuable, they must be in step with the changes taking place in the company and in the external environment – society, the political

Figure 7.1 Contents of mission statements

system, and the law. Traditionally, mission statements have focused primarily on the relationship of a corporation with its external environment. The two major issues addressed were the product-market domain and the critical factors required to be successful in an industry. More recently, companies have added an internal focus to their mission statements through addressing questions of organizational philosophy and organizational key values. Figure 7.1 illustrates the main areas covered by good mission statements.

Statements that include both a traditional external focus and a contemporary internal focus are often called 'vision statements'. Merck and Company, Inc., for example, uses the following approach to describe their values and beliefs, and to outline their purpose and vision:

Values and Beliefs

- We value above all our ability to serve the patient.
- We are committed to the highest standards of ethics and integrity.
- We are responsible to our customers, our employees, and to the society we serve.
- We expect profit, but profit from work that benefits humanity.

Purpose

- We are in the business of preserving and improving human life.
- All of our actions must be measured by our success in achieving this.

Vision

- To establish Merck as the pre-eminent drug-maker world-wide.
- We will be the first drug-maker with advanced research in every

disease category. Our research will be as good as the science done anywhere in the world. We will be at the leading edge of concern, making contributions to the problems with which society is struggling.

To maintain or build a good reputation, companies must not only state their good intentions in the form of mission or vision statements, but foremost, they need to behave in an ethical manner. This statement is reflected by the CEO of Worthington Industries, a manufacturer of metal and plastic products, who emphasized that their corporate mission is 'not something that is on the shelf; it is a way of life at Worthington. Our people understand it and have lived it' (Jones and Kahaner 1995: 253–4). The true test for a company is not in what it says, but in what it does; actions speak louder than words.

Although mission and/or vision statements sometimes provide first insights into corporate ethics, most companies issue separate documents outlining their ethics principles and policies. Such documents are called codes of ethics and corporate credos.

7.3 CODES OF ETHICS AND CORPORATE CREDOS

Most companies have introduced corporate codes of ethics, credos or both. Credos are usually brief explanations of the company's fundamental beliefs and are designed to act as guiding principles. As such, they often have an ethical component. One example is Security Pacific's credo, presented in Exhibit 7.1. Security Pacific, a Los Angeles-based national bank, identifies its major stakeholders and then describes its commitments to each of these groups.

EXHIBIT 7.1

Credo of Security Pacific Corporation

Commitment to Customer

The first commitment is to provide our customers with quality products and services which are innovative and technologically responsive to their current requirements, at appropriate prices. To perform these tasks with integrity requires that we maintain confidentiality and protect customer privacy, promote customer satisfaction, and serve customer needs. We strive to serve qualified customers and industries which are socially responsible according to broadly accepted community and company standards.

Commitment to Employee

The second commitment is to establish an environment for our employees which promotes professional growth, encourages each person to achieve his or her highest potential, and promotes individual creativity and responsibility. Security Pacific acknowledges our responsibility to employees, including providing for open and honest communication, stated expectations, fair and timely assessment of performance and equitable compensation which rewards employee contributions to company objectives within a framework of equal opportunity and affirmative action.

**Commitment of Employee
to Security Pacific**

The third commitment is that of the
employee to Security Pacific. As employees, we strive to understand and
adhere to the Corporation's policies
and objectives, act in a professional
manner, and give our best effort to
improve Security Pacific. We recognize
the trust and confidence placed in us
by our customers and community and
act with integrity and honesty in all
situations to preserve that trust and
confidence. We act responsibly to
avoid conflicts of interest and other
situations which are potentially harmful to the Corporation.

Commitment to Communities

The fifth commitment is that of Security Pacific to the communities which
we serve. We must constantly strive
to improve the quality of life through
our support of community organizations and projects, through encouraging service to the community by
employees, and by promoting participation in community services. By the
appropriate use of our resources, we
work to support or further advance
the interests of the community, particularly in times of crisis or social need.
The Corporation and its employees are
committed to complying fully with
each community's laws and regulations.

**Commitment of
Employee to Employee**

The fourth commitment is that of employees to their fellow employees. We
must be committed to promote a climate of mutual respect, integrity, and
professional relationships, characterized by open and honest communication within and across all levels of the
organization. Such a climate will promote attainment of the Corporation's
goals and objectives, while leaving
room for individual initiative within a
competitive environment.

Commitment to Stockholder

The sixth commitment of Security Pacific is to its stockholders. We will strive
to provide consistent growth
and a superior rate of return on their
investment, to maintain a position and
reputation as a leading financial institution, to protect stockholder investments, and to provide full and timely
information. Achievement of these
goals for Security Pacific is dependent
upon the successful development of
the five previous sets of relationships.

Source: Reprinted from Creating Ethical Corporate Structures, by P.E. Murphy, *Sloan
Management Review*, Winter (1989), p. 82, by permission of publisher. Copyright 1989
by Sloan Management Review Association. All rights reserved.

Another example of a corporate credo is included in Exhibit 7.2.
These 'Guiding Principles' have been published by Federal-Mogul
Corporation, a global distributor and manufacturer of a broad range of
precision automotive parts and industrial products.

EXHIBIT 7.2

The Guiding Principles of Federal-Mogul Corporation
1   Quality
Complete customer satisfaction in products and service is cru-
cial to our continued survival in a global environment.
2   Customer Response
Our customers are our reason for being. All our efforts must be

directed towards providing them with the best products and services.

3 Continuous Improvement

We must never be satisfied with our performance. We must strive to provide the very best in products, services, and value.

4 Respect for all Individuals

Employee involvement means trust and respect for each other as members of a team.

5 Ethical Conduct

Our integrity in the marketplace and with each other must never be compromised. Our conduct must be socially responsible. We are committed to equal opportunities for all individuals.

Source: Abrahams, J. (1995) *The Mission Statement Book: 301 Corporate Mission Statements from America's Top Companies*, Berkeley, CA: Ten Speed Press, pp. 245–247.

Corporate credos work most effectively in companies with cohesive cultures and free and frequent communication (Murphy 1989). In general, this is the situation at small companies. Credos are usually not detailed enough for many large multinational companies who face cross-cultural ethical issues, have recently merged, and are constantly facing ethical dilemmas.

In contrast to credos, codes of conduct are more detailed explanations of the behaviour that is expected of employees and the corporation as a whole. These codes demonstrate the importance a company attaches to certain ethical principles and behaviour and address multiple issues across a range of contexts (Weaver 1993), including conflicts of interest, gift-giving, and political contributions. Many companies require their employees to sign these codes, thus affirming that they understand and agree to follow the companies' codes.

Codes of ethics are defined as 'distinct, formal documents specifying self-consciously ethical constraints on the conduct of organizational life' (Weaver 1993: 45). A code of conduct may also be defined as: 'A statement setting down corporate principles, ethics, rules of conduct, codes of practice or company philosophy concerning responsibility to employees, shareholders, consumers, the environment or any other aspects of society external to the company' (Langlois and Schlegelmilch 1990: 522). These documents, in order to be distinguished as codes of ethics, are usually separate from the operations manual. By treating them separately from the operations manual, managers demonstrate a belief that the framing of a requirement or expectation affects the way employees respond to different situations. Moreover, the company indicates that the standards are intended for purposes other than 'routine employee guidance', such as would be found in an operations manual.

Larger firms, which generally have more public visibility, are more often subject to greater external pressure to manage (or at least appear to manage) their ethics (Weaver 1993). Since larger corporations may operate over a greater diversity of locations with greater variation of customs, they also have a stronger need to ensure a common set of behavioural assumptions on the part of their employees. Thus, larger companies are more likely to have a formal code of ethics. Of companies responding to a Fortune 1000 survey, 93 per cent stated that they had implemented codes of ethics (Center for Business Ethics 1992). However, there appear to be some differences between the United States and the other members of the triad. In one European survey, only 41 per cent of responding companies had introduced written codes, while the remainder had not yet done so (Langlois and Schlegelmilch 1990). Further analysis revealed that the proportion of companies with codes was even lower when the companies with foreign subsidiaries or parents (mostly US) were excluded from the tabulation. Among the European countries, France reported the lowest percentage of companies with codes, followed by Britain and Germany. Some 67 per cent of Japanese companies surveyed in 1991 had introduced codes of ethics (Berenbeim 1992). Although larger companies are more likely to have formalized a corporate code of ethics, the content of the codes hardly differs between companies of different sizes, except with regard to personnel issues (Robertson and Schlegelmilch 1993).

The reasons a company may advocate a code of ethics are varied (Weaver 1993). Ethical action may be seen as an end in itself, and the code may demonstrate this. Some codes attempt to respond to specific stakeholders' demands or expectations, while others may address a variety of issues in the broader business environment. Finally, codes are employed to manage or respond to internal organizational dynamics. The most likely reasons for employing a formal ethics policy as part of the overall corporate communication effort are growth and diversification of the company (Robertson and Schlegelmilch 1993). External objectives for introducing codes of ethics include efforts to generate positive public relations; firms hope to show their concern about various external relationships through the fact that they have an ethics policy. However, codes of ethics do not ensure ethical behaviour. The generality and ambiguity of the codes tends to give managers a large amount of discretion in interpreting ethical requirements.

Firms that distribute their written code to all employees, include it in socialization or training programmes for new employees, and also require current employees to read the policy are sending a powerful internal signal. Research (Robertson and Schlegelmilch 1993) has indicated that US firms are more likely than their British counterparts to distribute their ethical policies to all employees. To whom the messages are communicated sends a message about employee roles. For example, if the policy is only distributed to managers, this may be interpreted as an indication that only managers need to be concerned about ethical issues at the firm; if it is distributed only to new hires, it may be misunderstood that only they need be held accountable under this two-tiered system. Also critical to the communication effort is who does the communicating. US firms are more likely to rely on the human resources and legal departments than are firms in the UK; however, both depend on senior executives extensively.

Finally, there is a possibility that in creating an ethics code, a company creates a set of ethical problems for itself (Weaver 1993). This is because the company sets high standards for its behaviour, and a failure to measure up to some standards will be regarded as particularly bad by external observers. Thus, if a company that prides itself on observing the highest ethical standards, such as The Body Shop, is seen to engage in some ethical misconduct, the news value will be larger than in a situation in which the ethical misconduct is committed by a corporation that has not attempted to position itself as particularly ethical, like perhaps Philip Morris. Thus, to use corporate ethics as a positioning instrument is potentially dangerous. A communications programme can never be solely responsible for developing a corporate image. In addition to the written and pictorial forms of communication, corporate image is shaped by actual behaviour. Effective ethical positioning requires the firm to project a consistent pattern of ethical behaviour enhanced by co-ordinated communication efforts; this positioning is accomplished through such methods as advertising, direct philanthropy, and joint ventures with 'disadvantaged' firms. Ethics must permeate the whole firm for successful ethical corporate positioning to occur (Schlegelmilch and Trommsdorff 1996).

Focusing on the content of corporate codes of ethics, Langlois and Schlegelmilch (1990) distinguish between ethical principles that transcend culture and those which are culture-specific. The former include customer relations, shareholder interests, supplier and contractor relationships, community, environment, innovation, the use of technology, fairness, and honesty. Culturally-specific issues include political interests and employee relations. The relationship to government figures prominently in American codes; however, there is an underlying mistrust of the government evident as well. In Europe, the overall tendency is to stress employee responsiveness to company activities, while in the US it is the quality of company policy towards employees that is stressed.

Not only are there cultural variations in ethical policies, there are industry variations as well. Among the differences evidenced in a recent study are the larger concern about employee conduct in wholesaling and retailing and the greater concern about central and foreign government relations within agriculture and manufacturing (Schle-gelmilch and Robertson 1995). Moreover, there is a difference in the way these issues are addressed in firms. Manufacturing and agricultural firms address a higher proportion of ethical issues in written policies, while service firms tend to address comparatively more issues in training programmes. Whether there is convergence among codes of ethics introduced in different cultures and industries remains to be seen. But already some academics urge companies to pursue a common line (see Exhibit 7.3).

EXHIBIT 7.3

Promoting a world ethical standard

Robert W. MacGregor, president of the Minnesota Center for Corporate Responsibility, is convincing US companies to adopt a code of business conduct if they don't already have one. The guideline he is suggesting is a world standard for ethical behavior – the Caux Round Table Principles for Business. These standards were adopted in Caux, Switzerland, two years ago by business leaders from Europe, Japan, and the United States. The principles call for support of multilateral trade agreements, protection and improvement of the environment, respect for international and domestic trade rules, and avoidance of illicit operations such as bribery and money laundering. The principles also urge respecting 'the integrity of the culture of our customers' and fostering open markets for trade and investment.

Source: Adapted from Nelton, S. (1996) Promoting a World Ethical Standard. *Nation's Business*. April, p. 12.

The United States leads in the introduction of formal corporate codes of conduct. Japan follows, with European countries least likely to have written codes. The approaches to corporate codes of the ethics by each of the members of the triad are now examined in more detail.

7.3.1 The United States

The prevalence of written codes in the US can be attributed to several factors. Vogel (1993) observes that Americans tend to think in terms of rules, noting that '. . . the writing on business ethics by Americans is replete with checklists, principles, and guidelines for individual managers to follow in distinguishing right from wrong' (p. 33). Moreover, governmental influence on business practices in the US cannot be underestimated. Berenbeim (1992: 17) summarizes this situation by noting that nearly '. . . universal inclusion of the general counsel (84%) in the US ethics code deliberations' indicate that many

American companies believe their corporate codes demand the same careful attention used to draft legal documents. As a result, these statements may have implied legislative or administrative compliance purposes . . . or enforcement mechanisms. In the United States, the main purpose of a code is to 'provide guidelines for employees and management and "to communicate to all of our employees the expected behavior of each"' (Ethics Resource Center 1990). US corporate codes, because of their emphasis on rules and regulations, tend to focus on what is wrong. It is not surprising that the purpose for written codes of conduct in the US strongly influences their content as well. 'Like its Japanese counterpart, the US corporate code is, nevertheless, the voice of a culture. But it is the voice of a people who view the organization "not as a community, but as an arena in which everyone is primarily – and entirely legitimately – looking out for number one"' (Dore 1987: 239).

7.3.2 Europe

European codes are summarized as being 'social contracts between the company and its workers' (Berenbeim 1992: 17). Langlois and Schlegelmilch (1990: 531) noted that, 'French and British firms . . . tend to emphasize the importance of their employees to the organization as a whole. Rather than promoting a sense of responsibility, these firms promote a sense of *belonging*'. German codes are differentiated as focusing on the employees' and the firm's mutual responsibility and co-operation. However, attempts to standardization across different European countries do not appear to spare codes of ethics (see Exhibit 7.4).

EXHIBIT 7.4

ISO standards to include ethics?

Generally, internationally recognized standards, such as the ISO 9000 series, are now seen as a means of achieving uniformity in Europe, where, until now, a tradition of national standards has led to a degree of fragmentation. Some companies are now broadening the idea of standards to cover ethics and a company's position in the community. Benchmarking systems, such as the ISO standards, allow companies to compare themselves with others to assess their performance in specific activities.
Source: Adapted from Milmo, S. (1996) The Way To Uniformity. *Chemical Marketing Reporter*, 249 (15), pp. SR12–SR13.

Compared to the US, there is much less involvement of legal counsel in the drafting of codes of conduct in Europe (Berenbeim 1992: 17). Instead, employee representatives, human resource personnel and executives from financial, sales, and marketing departments contribute to the drafting of the ethics statements. This broad-based process further supports the perception that European codes serve as contracts between management and workers.

7.3.3 Japan

Japanese codes do differ in many respects to those in the US, highlighting aspects of the Japanese business and social culture discussed in Chapter 3. The adoption of written codes in Japan is somewhat of an 'ancient' custom, not deserving of attention as something new or unusual. In a survey conducted by The Foundation of Southwestern Graduate School of Banking, 72 per cent of the surveyed Japanese companies who dated their codes indicated that they had adopted them by 1970. This contrasts with only two per cent of US companies having such codes prior to 1970 (Schlegelmilch 1994). Key words found in Japanese codes of ethics are 'co-operation', 'prosperity', and 'happiness'. The role and responsibility of the company to transfer family values of dependency and trust to the corporation is stressed. The Japanese code of ethics is rooted in strong cultural values, and its primary role is in the effective transfer of these values from the house to the corporation. While similarities may exist between US and Japanese codes, the differences seem greater. A large number of Japanese companies emphasize their role in promoting social progress and fostering human happiness. The disarmingly simple means to achieve these goals – also spelled out in the company codes – are the encouragement of self-development, and co-operation based on trust and respect of others.

Taken collectively, ethical codes and credos of companies serve to put down in writing the company's ethical stance and inform both employees and stakeholders of the company's corporate philosophy. Both codes and credos are sometimes criticized as merely paying lip service to today's heated ethical debates, filled with lofty words, which in practice, no one heeds. Indeed, without management support, these documents are only words on a piece of paper. Many ethicists agree that ethical codes and credos are only the first steps on the road toward ethical commitment. Credos and codes form a point of departure which management can use to promote ethical behaviour and to anchor other ethics initiatives.

7.4 ETHICS TRAINING PROGRAMMES

Ethics training programmes serve to help managers and employees address, analyse, and discuss ethical problems in the workplace.

Specific professions (see Exhibit 7.5) and/or companies may consider developing ethics programmes when they have operations in need of periodic guidance. These programmes can handle international issues and peculiarities at specific locations or jobs. Programmes are particularly beneficial when similar ethical issues are encountered regularly. Ethics programmes are also useful when there are associations with outside consultants or advertising agencies whose codes and practices may be different from the company's (Murphy 1989). In these situations, training programmes can heighten the awareness and sensitivity of the outside agencies to ethical issues, as well as reinforce the ethical principles of the company.

EXHIBIT 7.5

Ethics: what do the accountants think?

Some 167 CPA's in the United States were surveyed to determine their viewpoints on the state of ethics in the accounting profession. Here are some of their responses:

- Nearly 25 per cent of the respondents had taken an ethics course in college and over a third covered ethical issues in their college accounting courses.
- 90 per cent believe that the national accounting organizations and/or state societies should offer ethics courses as part of their CPE training.
- Over half viewed ethics as critical to decision making in the profession. Only 6 per cent reported that they never had been forced to resolve an ethical dilemma in practice.
- Some 96 per cent of the CPA's considered themselves to be ethical decision-makers. However, only 62 per cent of the CPA's viewed the profession as a whole as ethical.

Source: Adapted from Eynon, G., Hill, N.T. and Stevens, K.T. (1996) Perceptions of Sole Practitioners on Ethics Training in the Profession. *National Public Accountant*, 41(4), pp. 25–7.

Martin Marietta Corporation, the US-based aerospace and defence contractor, implemented an ethics training programme in 1985. This programme included all of the Martin Marietta employees, starting with the CEO and senior executives. The training programme for managers concentrated on decision making, the challenges of balancing multiple responsibilities, and compliance with laws and regulations which are important to the company (Paine 1994).

In its ethics training, Citibank uses, among others, vignettes (like the one included in Exhibit 7.6) to discuss ethical issues with their new recruits. The aim is to heighten the awareness of these new recruits to potential ethical issues they might face. In fact, Citibank sometimes uses a selection of such vignettes already during campus visits of their recruiters to signal the importance the bank attaches to ethical behaviour to their potential future employees.

EXHIBIT 7.6

Ethics training at Citibank

Jane Coleman is a Branch Manager of a major US bank in Latin America. The bank is very interested in expanding in that country. Local law allows divulgence of information without court order. The Chief of Staff of the Minister of Finance calls and asks Jane for the exact account balance of a construction company that is a bank customer and is also doing work for the local government.
What should Jane do?

Jim Greenwell, a US Consumer Goods firm manager based in Pakistan, is dismayed when his assistant Dennis Pierre asks to be transferred back to the United States. He obliges and begins accepting applications for his assistant's position.
Jim receives numerous applications. While many of the applications are qualified, a woman named Jessica Blackstone appears to be the strongest candidate. He is hesitant to hire her, though, because the Pakistani business community does not welcome women and is often resistant to co-operating with them in transactions.
What should Jim do?

Often companies rely on the help of consultants to solve existing ethical problems, prevent them from recurring, and regain the trust of customers, employees, stockholders, and regulators. The Ethics Resource Center, an organization founded in 1922, is one of the most established organizations to provide consulting services (see Part IV, Appendix E for a list of other companies offering ethics consulting). The Ethics Resource Center aims to serve as a catalyst to improve ethical conduct in individuals and organizations and conducts workshops based on their clients' needs for practical, integrated solutions to complex and sensitive ethical issues. The Center has developed a systematic five-stage approach to designing and implementing a comprehensive ethics programme. After an overall assessment of the organizations' operating values and areas of potential risks, code development, in-house training, and re-evaluation, team members work closely with employees at all levels to ensure that their unique needs are met and that effective and lasting programmes are implemented. For those companies who already have a programme in place, the Center is available to offer its expertise in reviewing codes of conduct, surveying employees on ethical issues, assessing programme effectiveness, developing an ethics office, recommending improvements for existing ethics offices, and designing and conducting follow-up ethics awareness education.

While ethics training is now used by many large multinational companies, there are also concerns regarding the effectiveness of such measures (see also Exhibit 7.7). Landekich (1989), for example, comments on ethics training programmes as follows:

> In the course of a long training program, employees will be educated: they will get the questions and answers; discussion meetings will be held; programs will be delivered by lecturers (consultants) and/or appear on the screens; there will be tapes and guidebooks. The employees may even learn how to forget their real problems and questions, until the ethics programs are over. Yes, there is a reason for some skepticism about such quasi-rehabilitative promotion of ethical know-how.
>
> (Landekich 1989: 57).

EXHIBIT 7.7

Does ethics training work?

A recent study of collegiate business students from the US and New Zealand found that US students were less tolerant than the New Zealand students in situations involving ethical constructs of fraud, coercion, and self interest. Additionally, females are less tolerant than males in all ethical domains in both countries. However, within the group of students who reported experience in an ethics course there was no significant difference in the ethical values of the US and New Zealand students. The implication is that educational experience in an ethics course produces homogeneity and is beneficial towards obtaining cross cultural understanding and agreement in ethical values.

Source: Adapted from Okleshen, M. and Hoyt, R. (1996) A Cross Cultural Comparison of Ethical Perspectives and Decision Approaches of Business Students: United States of America versus New Zealand. *Journal of Business Ethics*, 15(5), pp. 537–49.

Nash (1992) reports that in 1986, 44 per cent of US companies with corporate codes had some type of training or discussion programme concerning corporate ethics, compared to 19 per cent of companies without written codes. These responses compared to 15 per cent of European companies having 'some type of ethics program' (1992: 164). Berenbeim (1992) also points out that new ethics programmes are less common in Europe and Canada: 'one-fourth of the US code companies and one-fifth of the European code organizations started new ethics training courses for middle managers during the past three years' (1992: 19). Top managers and entry-level employees were also reported to have received ethics instructions. A popular means for conveying ethics information was videos. More recently, Schlegelmilch and Robertson (1995) found that 33 per cent of their sample of large US and European (UK, Germany, Austria) companies did conduct some type of ethics training.

7.5 ETHICS OFFICES AND COMMITTEES

In many larger companies, ethics offices, committees, hot-lines, compliance review boards, and ombudsmen have been established to identify potential ethical problems as well as track the number and types of cases and complaints brought against companies. These offices serve as an early warning system for problems such as poor management, quality and safety defects, racial and gender discrimination, environmental concerns, inaccurate and false records, and personal grievances regarding salaries, promotions, and layoffs (Paine 1994). The anonymity of the hot-lines allows people to be more candid about their ethical concerns while the offices and committees create a solid foundation for the implementation of ethical policy within the company.

In recent years, ethics officers in particular have become more significant players (see Exhibit 7.8). In the past, the ethics officers would fall under the human resources function and did not have enough power to influence the decisions of high-level executives. Recently, many companies have taken this position out of the human resources department to make it a more influential, higher level position. This allows the officer to have a greater impact on decision making across the corporation (Henricks 1995).

EXHIBIT 7.8

The number of ethics officers continues to grow
At least one third of all Fortune 1000 companies now have ethics officers, officials who serve as corporate moral touchstones. And, the number of ethics officers continues to grow.

This is impressive considering that five years ago ethics officers were virtually nonexistent. Large numbers of companies only began hiring ethics officers in earnest in the early 1990s after strict mandatory federal-sentencing guidelines for organizations were passed. By creating an effective ethics program, a company can reduce any fines under the new laws by up to 60 per cent.

By writing codes of ethics, running ethics-training programs, overseeing internal investigations, and sitting on committees, the ethics officer is becoming a confidant to top executives. As such, they are now playing a role in even the highest level decisions.

Source: Adapted from Freeman, L.L. (1996) The Latest in Executive Counselors: 'EOs'. *Investor's Business Daily*, June 10, p. A1.

Nash (1992) found that ethics committees are still relatively uncommon. Only about 10 per cent of US companies reported having ethics committees consisting of members of boards of directors, with only two companies in Europe reporting such committees. These committees were composed entirely of corporate insiders. The make-up of the committees in the US was very different, with all headed by an outside director and none made up entirely of corporate insiders. The purpose of these US committees seems similar to audit committees, namely '. . . to provide independent oversight of reporting and compliance procedures' (p. 165).

7.6 WHISTLE-BLOWING/HOT-LINES

Sometimes the avenues provided by guidelines and written codes are not sufficient for reporting ethical violations, or for questioning certain activities. Hot-lines provide means for employees and other interested parties to report suspected wrong-doing, or to explore the appropriateness of certain activities. Whistle-blowing is a parallel activity, whereby employees report wrong-doing to authorities.

These mechanisms are sometimes established in light of the ineffectiveness of regulatory guidelines. Whistle-blowing has been described as a limited course of action, bringing often 'huge personal risks to the individual' in a 'hit-and-miss method' of investigating and researching wrong-doing (Vinten 1992: 117–18). Ethics hot-lines, where employees can anonymously report infractions or unethical business behaviour (act as a 'whistle-blower'), or call to discuss questions of an ethical nature, seem to be decidedly American practices. Pickard (1995) reports that 'only two British companies are known to have confidential hot-lines for employees to report concerns,' and comments that hot-lines are perceived as an American invention.

These differences in perception may be explained by the strong historical US tradition of individualism discussed in Chapter 3. One result of this individualistic view is that ethical dilemmas are often perceived to require an individual to make a choice based on his or her own set of moral values and judgements. The company's goals and objectives may or may not be in conflict with the individual's values. This tension created in the decision maker can lead to whistle-blowing. Legal actions have been taken to a certain degree in the US to protect whistle-blowers. And in some cases, failure to report wrong-doing can lead to penalties (Vogel 1993).

However, protection for whistle-blowers is very limited in countries other than the US. In Japan, it is likely that whistle-blowers would be considered traitors against the group. The tension described above is 'thoroughly alien' to Japanese business culture. And in capitalist nations other than the US, loyalty to the company and respect for authority would probably prevent the whistle-blowing from occurring in the first place.

Chemical Bank developed a hot-line for a purpose other than anonymously reporting ethical infractions: its goal was to provide financial counselling to employees facing or suffering significant financial difficulties. In such instances, emergency loans could be given to head off the potential of stealing from the bank. Thus, Chemical Bank's hot-line is aimed at preventing possible unethical behaviour in the future.

7.7 ETHICS AUDITS

Just as a financial audit seeks to determine the financial health of a company, an ethical audit seeks to establish the ethical well-being of a company. Firms are conducting these audits in order to trouble-shoot and determine the nature of any problems they might have. In particular, an audit will assist a corporation to determine the degree of compliance with established ethical standards, codified or not. Many audits are conducted in-house and include employee surveys and group meetings (see Exhibit 7.9). Laczniak and Murphy (1993) suggest that these audits should be conducted by an outside source, just as an accounting audit, in order to ensure impartiality.

EXHIBIT 7.9

A human rights audit?
A new type of audit could soon appear on the balance sheet: the human rights audit. This is not a new concept. Companies like

Levi Strauss and The Gap have already been monitoring the working conditions in the factories of overseas contractors for several years. Levi Strauss, for example, conducts audits with any new supplier that they are considering and also conducts audits on a regular basis with its regular suppliers. Formulating the codes of conduct on which audits are based is difficult but there usually is flexibility in the application of these codes. That is, codes usually allow for several layers of discussion and negotiation before the threat of having to terminate a relationship arises. Commercial incentives to comply can also be built into trading relationships.

Source: Adapted from Cottril, K. (1996) Another Audit in Your Future? *Journal of Business Strategy*, 17(3) May/June, p. 57.

The ethics audit conducted by The Body Shop (Values Report) is widely regarded as path-breaking and provides an example of the kind of detailed document which may result as the outcome of the examination process. The Body Shop, a large global operation with thousands of employees, published this, its first ethical audit, in January 1996 (for the full text, please see Part IV, Appendix D). The audit's purpose was to make the activities of the company and its motivations obvious to anyone. The document defines the company's future challenges and summarizes the highlights and low points of 1995 (see Appendix D). Three reasons have been given for publishing the report:

1   The Body Shop believes that business has a moral responsibility to truthfulness about itself and facing what needs to be changed.
2   The Body Shop is a high-profile advocate of social and environmental causes.
3   The Body Shop has to take its supporters and stakeholders with it, if it is to continue to mix business with politics.

The key issues that underlie this report, then, are responsibility and accountability.

The three components of the Values Report are:

1   the social audit which measures performance against policies, internal management systems, programmes and targets, shareholder expectations, and external benchmarks;
2   the environmental audit;
3   the animal protection audit.

Finally, The Body Shop's approach to ethical business operates on three levels:

- compliance, which considers the responsibilities of business not to abuse people, the environment, or animals;
- disclosure, which takes the company beyond compliance with standards and opens the record on various issues;
- campaigning, which advocates positive change in the way the business world operates, with the ultimate aim of positively impacting the world at large. These components demonstrate the dynamics of the ethical position of The Body Shop; the company's policies involve not only the employees and shareholders, but the public at large as well.

The overriding challenge of social auditing, as The Body Shop sees it, is to measure the way people think, both tangibly and intangibly. There was no international precedent in the field from which to model the audit, but the experiences of Ben and Jerry's (US), Traidcraft (UK), and Sbn (The Netherlands) were relied upon extensively. The methodology of the audit was designed by the New Economics Foundation, a UK-based 'think-tank,' and consisted of focus groups, questionnaires, one-on-one interviews, and data collection. The information was collected from staff, customers, franchisees, and suppliers; over 5,000 people were consulted. Finally, to ensure its reliability, the report and the processes that led to its compilation were subject to independent, external verification.

Although this first audit referred primarily to operations in the UK, all of The Body Shop's markets around the world are dedicated to similar core values and long-term goals. The Body Shop is committed to extending the audit process globally in the future.

The Body Shop's ethical audit, it should be remembered, is specific to The Body Shop's concerns and interests; its format is unique. This audit provides merely one example of how a company can monitor its ethical behaviour.

7.8 SUMMARY

Nash (1992) has identified three stages of corporate ethics practice which can be used to summarize the key points of this chapter: start-up, compliance, and relevancy. There can be no doubt that there is an increase in the first stage, the start-up stage, as evidenced by increases in various ethical initiatives and activities which are discussed in this chapter. The largest area of growth is the development of written corporate codes of ethics. Accompanying this is an increase in the number and breadth of individuals in companies involved in writing and disseminating these codes. A higher frequency and advanced methods of instructing employees about the corporate codes ensure that there is greater knowledge and dialogue by and among corporate employees about these codes.

The second stage of ethics practice is compliance. To be truly meaningful and effective, it is necessary that firms answer the question, 'How are we doing?' or 'Are any of the choices we've made violating the rules we have agreed to uphold?' Activities at this stage include formal discussions of the code of conduct, performance monitoring (audits and monitoring by an ethics officer or a committee, for example), communication of enforcement procedures, training, and revisions to the original document. This chapter also detailed many of these compliant practices.

The third stage of an ethics programme is relevancy. The discussion in this chapter indicated a widely spread scepticism of ethics programmes, which shows that the relevancy of the various ethics initiatives needs to be communicated in a more convincing fashion. In the relevancy stage, the ethics programme is said to move toward a proactive diffusion of ethical sensitivity; applications to business problems are explored. The relevancy stage is an outgrowth, not an abandonment, of the first two stages; it integrates their activities. The three stages are mutually reinforcing. A good corporate ethics programme will make use of and continue to modify all three stages as the firm's environment changes.

The increasing globalization of commerce and communication make it certain that international ethics initiatives will grow. As people from different cultures with different values conduct more and more business together, it will be necessary to increase the efforts to establish mutually acceptable means of conducting such business, in ways perceived as ethical by all. An example of this challenge is Eastern Europe, where the values of communism and capitalism have come to clash (Vallance 1992). Increasing the efforts and converging the perceptions of ethical behaviour will be no easy task; however, it does not mean that ethical initiatives should be abandoned or ignored.

7.9 REFERENCES

Abrahams, J. (1995) *The Mission Statement Book: 301 Corporate Mission Statements from America's Top Companies*, Berkeley, CA: Ten Speed Press.

Berenbeim, R. (1992) *Corporate Ethics Practices*, New York, NY: The Conference Board, Inc.

Center for Business Ethics (1992) Instilling ethical values in large corporations. *Journal of Business Ethics*, 11(11), pp. 863–7.

Cottril, K. (1996) Another audit in your future? *Journal of Business Strategy*, 17(3) May/June, p. 57.

Dore, R.P. (1987) *Taking Japan Seriously: A Confucian Perspective on Leading Economic Issues*, Stanford, CA: Stanford University Press.

Ethics Resource Center (1990) *Ethics Policies and Programs in American Business*, Washington DC: ERC.

Eynon, G., Hill, N.T. and Stevens, K.T. (1996) Perceptions of sole practitioners on ethics training in the profession. *National Public Accountant*, 41(4), pp. 25–7.

Falsey, T.A. (1989) *Corporate Philosophies and Mission Statements: A Survey and Guide for Corporate Communicators and Management*, New York, NY: Quorum Books.

Freeman, L.L. (1996) The latest in executive counselors: 'EOs'. *Investor's Business Daily*, June 10, p. A1.

Graham, J.W. and Havlick, W.C. (1994) *Mission Statements: A Guide to the Corporate and Nonprofit Sectors*, New York, NY: Garland Publishing, Inc.

Henricks, M. (1995) Ethics in Action. *Management Review*, 84(1), pp. 53–5.

Jones, P. and Kahaner, L. (1995) *Say It and Live It: The 50 Corporate Mission Statements that Hit the Mark*, New York: Doubleday Publishing.

Laczniak, G. and Murphy, P.E. (1993) Marketing ethics: onward toward greater expectations. *Journal of Public Policy and Marketing*, 12(1), p. 91.

Landekich, S. (1989) *Corporate Codes of Conduct*, Montvale, NJ: National Association of Accountants.

Langlois, C. and Schlegelmilch, B.B. (1990) Do corporate codes of ethics reflect national character? Evidence from Europe and the United States. *Journal of International Business Studies*, 21(4), pp. 519–39.

Milmo, S. (1996) The way to uniformity. *Chemical Marketing Reporter*, 249(15), pp. SR12–SR13.

Murphy, P.E. (1989) Creating ethical corporate structures. *Sloan Management Review*, Winter, pp. 81–9.

Nash, L. (1992) American and European corporate ethics practices: A 1991 Survey, in J. Mahoney and E. Vallance (eds) *Business Ethics in a New Europe*. Norwell, MA: Kluwer Academic Publishing.

Nelton, S. (1996) Promoting a world ethical standard. *Nation's Business*, April, p. 12.

Okleshen, M. and Hoyt, R. (1996) A cross cultural comparison of ethical perspectives and decision approaches of business students: United States of America versus New Zealand. *Journal of Business Ethics*, 15(5), pp. 537–49.

Paine, L.S. (1994) Managing for organizational integrity. *Harvard Business Review*, March–April, pp. 106–17.

Pickard, J. (1995) Prepare to make a moral judgment. *People Management*, 1(9) May 4, pp. 22–5.

Robertson, D. and Schlegelmilch, B.B. (1993) Corporate institutionalization of ethics in the United States and Great Britain. *Journal of Business Ethics*, 12(4), pp. 301–12.

Schlegelmilch, B.B. (1994) International business ethics and the corporate mission, in F. Hoy and C. Ghiselli, *Challenging Assumptions*: Proceedings of the 1994 Family Firm Institute Conference, Scottsdale, Arizona, October 5–7, 1994.

Schlegelmilch, B.B. and Robertson, D. (1995) The influence of country and industry on ethical perceptions of senior executives in the US and Europe. *Journal of International Business Studies*, 26(4), pp. 859–81.

Schlegelmilch, B.B. and Trommsdorff, V. (1996) Ethische Unternehmens-positionierung. *Jahrestagung der Kommission Marketing im Verband der Hochschullehrer für Betriebswirtschaft*. Fürth, Germany. January 25–27.

Vallance, E. (1992) Never the twain? Ethics and economics in Eastern and Western Europe, in J. Mahoney and E. Valance (eds), *Business Ethics in a New Europe*, Norwell, MA: Kluwer Academic Publishers.

Vinten, G. (1992) Ethical aspects of mergers and acquisitions in Europe, in J. Mahoney and E. Vallance (eds), *Business Ethics in a New Europe*, Norwell, MA: Kluwer Academic Publishers.

Vogel, D. (1993) Is US business obsessed with ethics? *Across the Board*, 30(9), November/December, pp. 30–3.

Weaver, G.R. (1993) Corporate codes of ethics: purpose, process and content issues. *Business and Society*, Spring, pp. 44–58.

8 *Future ethical challenges*

8.1 THE STATUS QUO

Previous chapters have provided an overview of some key issues in marketing ethics and, where possible, placed ethical questions into an international context. The picture that emerged points to increased ethical concerns from corporations, consumers, as well as governments and multinational bodies. However, we appear to be far from having solved all ethical dilemmas in business – a state which is most likely unattainable in the first place – and countless ethical challenges remain in virtually every single topic discussed so far.

Indeed, it is not difficult to single out a topic, such as Ethics Audits, and come up with a list of unresolved issues that need to be addressed in future. In this final chapter, a different approach is taken. Instead of focusing on a host of unresolved micro-issues, three major groups of challenges to the advance of business ethics are highlighted.

The first relates to the problems companies face when dealing with cultural diversity. It can be foreseen that increased globalization of corporate activities will result in more and more companies having to deal with such challenges. The second group of challenges to be discussed arise from diverse economic conditions of countries. Here we attempt to identify the ethical implications of conducting business in nations with different levels of economic development and introduce some guidelines for conducting ethical business in LDCs. The third group of challenges, finally, deals with the expectations different stakeholders have of corporations. In this context, we discuss potential limits to ethical leadership and look at the appropriateness of stakeholder theory as a guide for corporate behaviour.

The chapter ends with a look at ethical initiatives that transcend the scope of single corporations. This rests on the belief that some ethical problems can only be solved successfully if governments and international organizations set appropriate signals.

8.2 CHALLENGE ONE: CULTURAL DIVERSITY

8.2.1 Corporate ethics versus national culture

Perhaps as a backlash to the uniformity of technology driven cultural convergence, the last decade has witnessed an increased recognition of the value of cultural diversity. But while most of us enjoy cultural diversity at the workplace, an over-emphasis of cultural differences can have downsides. The former Yugoslavia has disintegrated largely along ethnic and religious boundaries. In Spain, the Basques and the Catalans are concerned with preserving their cultures, and in the UK, the Scots and the Welsh are striving for more independence. Given such trends, the world has be careful not to regress into small principalities that are unable to see beyond their immediate boundaries.

For multinationals, cultural diversity can also cause major headaches. Consider the dilemma of a US multinational company that is formulating its hiring practices for its new operations in Japan and Saudi Arabia. It quickly learns that the local culture in both of these countries discourages gender equality in the workplace. The multinational has, thus far, been very conscious of not wanting to offend the values of the host country. However, to adopt the local attitudes towards gender equality is to violate the US policies of Title VII of the Civil Rights Act of 1964 (Mayer and Cava 1993). What should the company do?

Consider now an equally perplexing dilemma encountered by Walt Disney Co. In 1992 Walt Disney Co. was renowned around the world for providing wholesome, clean, family entertainment within the magical setting of its theme parks in Florida, California, and Japan. Disney achieved this through insisting upon a strong set of corporate values which dictated not only how employees should behave but also what customers should expect. One such value was exemplified in its strictly enforced alcohol ban in all of its parks.

When Disney proceeded with the opening of Euro Disneyland near Paris in April 1992, it assumed that the same successful principles would automatically work in France. However, after several years of poor results, Disney was forced to admit that, unlike the Japanese, the European market was not as willing to embrace 'American values'. The standards it had been determined to impose for 'clean, family fun' were simply not shared by the European market. Disney was faced with the decision of whether or not to yield on, among other things, its policy of 'no alcohol' within the parks. Should it adapt to local values or stay true to its corporate ethics?

8.2.2 Finding the balance

The two dilemmas described above demonstrate how corporate ethics can clash with a national culture. But how should organizations resolve situations in which practices which work in the home country do not work in a foreign country due to its different standards of ethical conduct? The discussion in Chapter 2 has already shown that neither cultural relativism ('when in Rome, do as the Romans do') nor utilitarianism ('the greatest good for the greatest number of people') always lead to satisfactory solutions. But how does universalism fare? Could one argue that a multinational desiring to develop global ethical standards should start by identifying those values and beliefs which are shared by cultures all over the world? One such attempt was made by Rushworth Kidder, of the Institute of Global Ethics, who conducted a global values survey and discovered these common values: love, truth, freedom, fairness, community, tolerance, responsibility, and reverence for life (Richter and Barnum 1994). However, the problem arises in reaching a global consensus as to the exact interpretation of each of these values in a given situation. To illustrate, with respect to hiring of men and women, 'fairness' in the Europe and the United States leads to 'equal opportunity' measures. Conversely, an Islamic society would be led to discriminate against women to ensure that men, the traditional heads of households, are not deprived of jobs (Sorell and Hendry 1994). Such differences in 'interpretation' of values are a direct result of fundamental cultural differences.

But how, then, can the ethical dilemmas introduced at the beginning of this section be resolved? In 1994, Disney decided to lift its alcohol ban at Euro Disneyland. This appears to have been the right decision as the issue of offering alcohol in Europe represents more of a cultural idiosyncrasy than a fundamental ethical clash. However, the first dilemma is more complex. Cultural relativism is not a panacea because it is morally blind. Equally, ethical imperialism appears unacceptable because it would ignore fundamental cultural differences. The answer seems to lie somewhere in between these two extremes. Thus, it appears impossible to provide a definite answer; corporations will have to resolve such ethical dilemmas on a case by case basis, very carefully balancing the interests of all stakeholders, both those in the host and those in the home countries.

8.3 CHALLENGE TWO: DIFFERENT ECONOMIC CONDITIONS

8.3.1 Ethics and economic development

Multinationals frequently face ethical dilemmas when dealing with LDCs. Recently, for example, the National Labor Committee reported that 'Haitian workers making Disney licensed products earn 28 cents an hour' whereas Disney's CEO Michael Eisner's 1995 compensation of $15 million works out to $7,100 an hour (*Business Ethics* 1996: 28). While, at face value, this appears to slap any concept of social justice in the face, it is questionable whether the above should be considered unethical. What are the options of a multinational that pays lower wages in developing countries? If one demands that the wages to be paid by the multinational should be on a par with North American, European or Japanese standards, there may not be sufficient incentives for multinationals to invest in LDCs in the first place. But even if the multinational decides to pays significantly above the LDC's wage average, local firms will charge that the multinational distorts the local labour market. This might even drive local firms out of business since they are unable to pay higher wages. Regardless of the wage level, other critics will argue that the American or European multinational destroys American or European jobs and, thus, weakens the appropriate home economies. In summary, it appears that multinationals are frequently in a no win situation when dealing with LDCs. Regardless of what they do, someone will criticize the multinational.

While some criticisms will be justified, others will not. In the future, managers need to be increasingly able to sort through a large number of – partly conflicting – challenges and be prepared to justify the way their companies act in LDCs. But what type of behaviour is ethically justified and what is not? Because rules and regulations differ around the world, and the implementation and enforcement of these rules and regulations differ even more, some companies might simply be tempted to locate in counties with lax labour regulations or low environmental concern. In contrast, it is now widely argued that multinational companies have an obligation to meet minimum moral standards, regardless of where they operate. But what can reasonably be expected from multinationals?

8.3.2 Guidelines for conducting ethical business in LDCs

A number of institutions, including the OECD (1984) and the UN Commission on Transnational Corporations (1990) have developed guidelines (see also section 8.5.2). Moreover, US companies can look to the Statement of Business Principles to provide guidelines for operating abroad (see Exhibit 8.1). These principles, set forth by the Clinton administration, are explicitly voluntary and recommend the following:

EXHIBIT 8.1

Statement of business principles

1 Provide a safe and healthy workplace
2 Avoid the use of child and forced labour
3 Respect the right of association and the right to organize and bargain collectively

4 Uphold responsible environmental practices
5 Comply with US and local laws promoting good business practices
6 Maintain a corporate culture that respects freedom of expression

Source: Adapted from Kapp, R.A. (1995) Does Business Need a Code of Ethics. *China Business Review*, 22(3), pp. 6–7.

Another set of guidelines, developed by De George (1993: 45) also has considerable practical appeal and is intended to 'provide the basis for evaluating and responding to the charges of unethical behavior'. Exhibit 8.2 includes these recommendations. Perhaps the most interesting of De George's guidelines is the last, calling for the development of background institutions. Such institutions, he argues, should guarantee fair competition, the protection of human rights and the conservation of the country's resources. Essentially, this demand acknowledges that not all multinationals can be relied upon to act ethically, but that adequate watchdogs are needed to ensure that everyone plays by the rules (see also section 8.5). The challenge for multinationals, in this context, is to decide when 'co-operation with local government' turns into interference in internal affairs. Moreover, it raises the question of how far companies can be expected to work for the development of institutions that will ultimately interfere and control their activities.

EXHIBIT 8.2

De George's guidelines for dealing with less developed countries

1 Multinationals should do no intentional harm.
2 Multinationals should produce more good than harm for the host country.
3 Multinationals should contribute by their activity to the host country's development.
4 Multinationals should respect the human rights of their employees.
5 To the extent that local culture does not violate ethical norms, multinationals should respect the local culture and work with and not against it.
6 Multinationals should pay their fair share of taxes.
7 Multinationals should cooperate with the local government in developing background institutions.

8.4 CHALLENGE THREE: DEALING WITH EXPECTATIONS

8.4.1 Limits to ethical leadership

There are suggestions that companies should not only be held accountable for their own actions but also for the behaviour of their suppliers. Indeed, some well-meaning companies have learned the hard way that the public also holds them responsible for the actions of their business partners. Consider, in this context, the Levi Strauss case in Part II, Chapter 11 and the experience of the Starbucks Coffee Company described in Exhibit 8.3.

EXHIBIT 8.3

Starbucks: the ethics of sourcing coffee beans

In 1994 the Seattle-based Starbucks Coffee Company was the fastest-growing specialty company in the US, with more than five-hundred company-owned stores throughout the country. The company prided itself on being progressive as evidenced by especially generous employee remuneration packages which aimed to put the 'employee first' as opposed to the old edict that the 'customer always comes first'. Also, Starbucks annually gave six-figure donations to nonprofit organizations.

Then, one day, the company found itself at the centre of criticism and controversy. A Chicago-based US/Guatemala Labor Education project was citing Starbucks for unethical conduct in the sourcing of its coffee beans. Starbucks, it claimed, was selling coffee beans at $8 per pound while labourers in Guatemala were picking beans, and toiling in inhumane conditions, to earn two cents per pound.

Starbucks was pressured to adopt a 'code of conduct' which would encourage Third World employers to ban child labour and to provide workers with increased wages, improved working conditions, and minimal health care. It released this code of conduct in late 1995 and thereby joined other companies, such as Levi Strauss & Co. and Reebok International Ltd., in establishing guidelines not only for itself but also for its suppliers.
Source: Adapted from Scott, M. (1995a) An Interview with Howard Schultz, CEO of Starbucks Coffee Co. *Business Ethics Magazine*, Nov/Dec issue, pp. 26–9.

The previous example illustrates one of the future challenges companies will have to deal with, namely assuming responsibility not only for their own actions, but also for the actions of their suppliers. Arguments that companies should go beyond minimum standards of behaviour and should act as moral champions (see Part III, Chapter 20 The Need for Moral Champions in Global Marketing) present additional challenges. But what can reasonably be expected of multinationals? Consider a profitable multinational company operating in a developing country. Suppose the company learns of local inhabitants suffering terribly? Does it have an obligation to render aid to help alleviate the problem? Does the obligation change if the company is only marginally profitable? How about if the company is unprofitable? These questions provide a glimpse of the complexities involved in trying to assess where ethical leadership should begin and where it should end.

Most observers would agree that multinationals should observe a moral minimum which is anchored in the concept of basic human rights as its starting point. The trickier part is in determining what further obligation, in excess of basic human rights, the company has. This may involve acting in ways which may be termed 'ideal' and which clearly go beyond the expectations of any stakeholder. These sorts of actions are ones in which the company would not garner criticism, from any of the stakeholders, for failure to meet these 'ideal' standards. A company which chooses to pursue this is doing so, not out of obligation, but because it aims to achieve its goal of integrity (De George 1993). A vivid example of an 'ideal' ethical standard being achieved is provided in Exhibit 8.4. It illustrates how Merck was clearly acting well beyond any expectations and was, therefore, exemplifying an 'ideal' standard of ethical leadership.

EXHIBIT 8.4

Merck is fighting river blindness

When the pharmaceutical firm Merck & Company developed a drug to prevent river blindness, a disease afflicting millions of people in Africa, it found that the people who needed the drug could not afford it. Merck also found that governments and international groups were not willing to buy the drug. Merck finally decided to distribute the drug free of charge and to incur the necessary expenditures to develop the needed distribution systems to ensure the drug reached those in need. Finally, Merck committed itself to continue distributing the drug free of charge indefinitely.
Source: From *Competing with Integrity in International Business* by Richard T. De George, p. 184. Copyright © 1993 by Richard T. De George. Used by permission of Oxford University Press, Inc.

While most companies do not strive for the 'ideal', many have already made a commitment to ethical behaviour and have taken major strides towards 'cleaning up their act'. It remains to be seen how far social responsibility will be taken as individual companies determine, for themselves, to what level of ethical leadership they will aspire. Will it be a minimum level, a more committed level, or an 'ideal' level? The final decision will undoubtedly be affected by its various internal and external stakeholders, both in the host and the home country. Unfortunately, the expectations of these various groups, as discussed previously, are often at odds with each other. This inevitably raises the question of priorities among stakeholders and, ultimately, calls into question the ability of the stakeholder theory to provide concrete managerial guidance.

8.4.2 Stakeholder theory – revisited

Jensen and Fagan (1996: 97) view it as ironical that capitalism 'will come under attack at precisely the time that it has triumphed over competing socialist and communist systems'. The means of the attack, they elaborate, will be stakeholder theory, which they regard as incompatible with capitalism. The notion that stakeholder theory represents a moral solution to deciding which interests ought to be served is regarded as wrong. Stakeholder theory, they argue, provides no guidance on the circumstances in which a particular group of stakeholders ought to have priority over another. Sir Stanley Kalms, chairman of Dixons, is equally dismissive about the stakeholder approach and describes it as 'one of the most dangerous bits of nonsense I have ever heard' (Mitchell, 1996/97: 29). His main criticism, like that of Jensen and Fagan, is that no one defines the specific rights of stakeholders.

Conversely, defenders of stakeholder theory tend to attack the unconditional priority of the shareholders among the stakeholders. Mark Goyder directs a UK research project sponsored by, among others, Blue Circle, British Gas, Cable & Wireless and Cadbury. The project, entitled 'Tomorrow's Company', published the following conclusion:

> To sustain competitive success in a global marketplace, companies need to focus less exclusively on shareholders and financial measures of success – and instead include all their stakeholder relationships and a broader range of measurements, in the way they think and talk about their purpose and performance
>
> (Mitchell 1996/97: 28).

Of course, statements like the above only provide ammunition to the sceptics. What exactly is meant by 'less exclusively'? And what should be included in 'a broader range of measurements'? But notwithstanding the critique that stakeholder theory is somewhat woolly and ill defined, its notion that profits alone cannot justify everything and that the needs of different stakeholders ought to be considered in decision making is clearly sensible. However, most of what stakeholder theory attempts to achieve is not too different from 'enlightened self-interest'. Companies that aim to maximize their profits cannot afford to ignore their stakeholders, be it in the form of customers, suppliers, or employees. The difference between enlightened self interest and a stakeholder approach lies in the clarity of the corporate objectives: following enlightened self interest, the company will be guided by value maximization; following stakeholder theory, the corporation is subject to the idiosyncrasies and biases of managerial preferences without objective means to measure managers' performance.

In practice, it is often impossible to distinguish whether companies' actions are driven by enlightened self interest or by stakeholder theory. Consider, for example, the experience of H.B. Fuller Co., an adhesives and paint maker based out of St. Paul, Minnesota. Fuller ran into trouble in 1995 when media reports claimed that thousands of Central American children were sniffing its shoe-making glue and were, in the process, permanently damaging their brains. Fuller responded to the misuse of its product by reformulating its glue, restricting its use in factories, taking the glue out of retail circulation, and giving hundreds of thousands of dollars to social programmes. Clearly Fuller has taken a stance on ethical leadership which involved balancing the expectations of its shareholders for healthy profits with the expectations of social responsibility imposed upon it by consumers at large. Chairman Anthony Andersen commented: 'If we're going to do well for our shareholders over the long term, we have to take care of our customers' (Kurschner 1996: 26). Fuller's values have paid off for shareholders. The company has reported a ten-year annual earnings growth rate of 10 per cent (Kurschner 1996).

Another company, Reebok International Ltd., has also shown that social responsibility does not need to hurt profits. It began sponsoring Amnesty International's 'Human Rights Now' World Concert Tour back in 1988 and has continued the commitment ever since. It discovered that its thoughts and actions have been reshaped by this ongoing commitment to human rights and that profits have not been hurt as a result (Duerden 1995).

The link between the two examples, then, is the realization that social responsibility need not come at the expense of the bottom line. In fact, as we discussed before, some companies argue that acting in a socially responsible manner actually enhances profits over the long run. This long term perspective is a key ingredient in fostering behaviour which surpasses the mere provision of basic human rights and actually represents a positive shift towards ethical leadership.

8.5 ETHICS BEYOND THE CORPORATE SCOPE

8.5.1 Who controls multinational corporations?

'Steal These Pants' proclaimed the headline of the *New York Post* in reference to the new campaign launched by San Francisco-based Levi Strauss & Co. In its new marketing campaign, Levi Strauss encased pairs of its $50 khakis in clear plastic and hung the displays in thirty-one San Francisco bus shelters and forty New York City shelters. On the plastic were the words 'Nice Pants.' If someone shattered the plastic and stole the khakis, an outline of the pants would remain, along with the words, 'apparently they were nice pants'.

New York City mayor Rudolph Giuliani condemned the ads, saying they were '. . . exactly the wrong message to be teaching people'. Bradford Williams, senior marketing specialist at Levi Strauss, countered, 'We were trying to be realistic that not everyone is honest. There is a difference between preparing for the worst-case scenario and encouraging the worst-case scenario.' Negative publicity finally led Levi Strauss to discontinue the ads – but not until after New York City officials banned them (Scott 1995b).

The Levi Strauss example demonstrates that companies do not always recognize when they have crossed the line between acceptable and unacceptable behaviour. Levi Strauss, a company otherwise renowned for its high ethical standards, thought it was acting within acceptable norms. However, the reaction of the media and the local government made it apparent that most people thought the ads were in bad taste. In this case, it was necessary for local officials to 'control' Levi Strauss by banning the ads.

In the above example, public opinion, the media, the New York mayor and other City officials were able to 'control' the behaviour of Levi Strauss. However, who controls multinational companies when they are overseas; especially in smaller, less developed countries? Who acts as a watchdog to ensure ethical behaviour is maintained in all facets of the companies' activities? (see Exhibit 8.5). In his article 'Ethics in the Transnational Corporation; The "Moral Buck" Stops Where?', Dobson (1992) suggests that neither management nor the typical shareholder should be expected to exercise moral judgement because they are not free agents. In other words, they have fiduciary responsibilities that must override personal moral suasion.

EXHIBIT 8.5

Report alleges that baby milk makers breach health code

A research study conducted by the Interagency Group on Breastfeeding Monitoring (IGBM), a coalition of 27 religious, health and development groups, found that many companies regularly breach domestic and international regulations on the marketing and distribution of breast milk substitutes in developing countries. Among the companies named in the report are Nestlé, long subject to an international consumer boycott because of its baby-milk marking activities, Gerber, Mead Johnson and Wyeth, and Nutricia.

The International Association of Infant Food Manufacturers rejected the study as 'biased in design and execution' stating it made 'a sham of impartiality'. Professor Andrew Tomkins of the London-based Institute for Child Health defended the study, saying it had been carried out according to the best international guidelines for medical research.

The report published by IGBM was based on interviews with pregnant women, mothers of small infants and health workers in Bangladesh, Poland, South Africa and Thailand. Commenting on the report, the bishop of Coventry stated that it 'provides compelling evidence from countries round the world that the international code is still being violated'.

Source: Adapted from Suzman, M. (1997) 'Baby Milk Companies under Fire'. *Financial Times*, January 9, pp. 1 and 12.

Mander (1992) also questions the ability of corporations to make ethical judgements. He rejects the idea that corporations can reform themselves, or that a new generation of executive managers can be re-educated. 'To ask corporate executives to behave in a morally defensible manner is absurd', says Mander. 'This is because the most basic rule of corporate operation is that it must produce income and must show a profit over time. If it is a public company, as most multinationals are, the company must expand and grow, since growth is the standard by which the stock market judges it. All other values are secondary: the welfare of the community, the happiness of workers, the health of the planet, and even the general prosperity.'

As recent evidence of his premise, Mander (1992) points to the example of the Exxon *Valdez* crash in 1989, in which oil was spilled into the sea and onto the beaches of Alaska. The corporation did respond immediately with apologies and promises to 'clean the water, clean the beaches, save the animals, pay for damages'. However, the clean up turned out to be expensive. Within six months the company ceased all of its efforts to allay the effects of the spill. In a typical corporate cost-benefit approach, it was reasoned that fighting the lawsuits and making settlements that courts might require would certainly be cheaper than cleaning the mess.

While controlling the actions of multinationals is challenging enough when traditional organizational structures are involved, it is likely to become even more challenging with the changes in the way companies will be organizing their activities. The so called 'virtual' organization of the future is predicted to consist of relatively loose alliances of individuals, coming together to achieve a specific task, and then regrouping to form a new alliance. It will typically be a 20/80 place, with only 20 per cent of the people involved being employed full-time by the organization. The others are suppliers or contractors, part-timers, or self-employed professionals. This is significant because it means that all workers will not owe all of their loyalty to one organization (Handy 1996). How such organizations can create a sense of shared values and ethics, and how such organizations can be controlled by any external bodies, will constitute one of the key challenges in business ethics in the future.

Another way to look at the control of multinationals is to focus on the internal structure of these corporations. Comparing the sales volume of multinationals with the GNP of nation states shows that many of these corporations are now larger than nation states. In fact, about half of the world's 100 largest 'economies' are now corporations. General Motors' sales revenue alone is larger than the combined GNP of Tanzania, Ethiopia, Bangladesh, Zaire, Uganda, Nigeria, Kenya and Pakistan (Handy 1996). Given the size and obvious power of these huge enterprises, it is likely that the question of who governs them will increase in importance. Internationally dispersed shareholdings, cross-holdings of shares, and shares that are held by the companies' own treasuries make it increasingly difficult to determine who actually owns the multinationals. Consequently, Handy (1996: 116) predicts that in future 'Large businesses will need to pay more heed to some form of internal democracy.' How this can be achieved in an ethical fashion without destroying many of the advantages of the current system, such as the ability to make quick decisions, will present a further challenge for the manager of the future.

8.5.2 Non-corporate initiatives: regulating and setting signals

The previous discussion has shown that individual organizations can neither solve all ethical problems on their own, nor can all organizations be trusted to behave ethically. Government involvement in guiding companies towards adopting more ethical business practices appears unavoidable. In fact, government awareness of ethical issues has been heightened in the last twenty years (see Chapter 2, Section 2.3.3). This is due to the increased liberalization of international commerce which has brought to the forefront the current lack of, and need for, international ethical standards. This recognition of the need to 'level the playing field' for all market participants also suggests the need for mechanisms to ensure compliance with and enforcement of ethical standards.

Increasingly, international organizations take it upon themselves to provide ethical guidelines and to act as ethical watchdogs. Recent examples already foreshadow what we can expect in the future. Initiatives like the 1996 resolution on bribery by the Organization for Economic Cooperation and Development (OECD), or the setting up of non-governmental bodies, such as Transparency International (TI) are likely to gain in importance as individual governments' ability to control large multinationals declines. Below, the OECD, the TI and other initiatives are looked at in more detail.

(a) OECD anti-bribery resolution

The Organization for Economic Cooperation and Development (OECD) was originally set up as the Organization for European Economic Cooperation in 1948 to co-ordinate Marshall Plan aid. This was aimed at reconstruction of post-World War II Europe. The OECD took its present form in 1961 and today has a membership of 29 countries including: Australia, Austria, Belgium, Canada, Denmark, Finland, France, Germany, Greece, Iceland, Ireland, Italy, Japan, Luxembourg, Mexico, the Netherlands, New Zealand, Norway, Portugal, South Korea, Spain, Sweden, Switzerland, Turkey, the United Kingdom, and the United States. The OECD is headquartered in Paris, France and provides a forum for the discussion of international problems (Esman *et al.* 1967).

The FCPA and the Federal Sentencing Guidelines discussed in Chapter 2 make US law the toughest in the world in forbidding its corporations from paying bribes abroad. Recognizing the potential loss to American companies of these more stringent policies, the US government launched a full-scale effort in 1994 to convince the other OECD members to adopt similar policies. They argued that for other countries to allow their businesses to bribe government officials in developing countries was to undercut the long-term goals of the industrialized nations. 'Bribes cause scarce resources to be misallocated,' says assistant secretary of state for economic and business affairs Daniel K. Tarullo, 'but more important, bribery seriously undermines the very democratic institutions which OECD seeks to promote' (Moskowitz 1994).

In April, 1996, the OECD finally passed a resolution stating that bribes made to foreign officials should no longer be tax-deductible.

This was a surprise as there had not been much consensus when the issue was first raised. The US government is hopeful that the OECD will eventually pass another resolution making bribery of a government official a criminal offence (Van Haste 1996).

(b) Transparency international

Transparency International (TI) is a non-governmental organization founded in 1993 by former World Bank director Peter Eigen to counter corruption in international business. With chapters in over 40 countries, this Berlin-based not-for-profit organization seeks world-wide legal reforms to fight governmental and corporate corruption (Kaltenhauser 1996). TI has not set out to expose particular cases of corruption, but rather to promote policy changes in the industrial north and advise leaders of developing countries who want to fight corruption (Misser 1995).

TI sees growth in international trade and communications as the cause for growth in international corruption stating that never before has there been more economic temptation and greed. Ronald Maclean-Abaroa, Latin American co-ordinator for TI, says corruption has sucked much of the economic blood out of the impoverished continent. He recommends making corruption laws and penalties more transparent, so that people know what to expect. Also, officials' discretionary powers should be reduced. Finally, the power of government monopolies must be cut back (McGugan 1995).

(c) Other initiatives

The Interfaith Center on Corporate Responsibility released a new set of principles for ethical conduct in September 1995. These principles establish clear benchmarks by which a company can appraise its performance in responsible policy and practices. Called 'Principles for Global Responsibility: Benchmarks for Measuring Business Performance', the twenty-eight page document was created by three international religious organizations representing millions of Catholics, Jews, and Protestants.

The published document includes more than a dozen sets of international principles on issues such as human rights, sustainable development, the environment, and discrimination. It also recommends standards that call for firms to provide workers everywhere with freedom of association, fair wages, a vice president with responsibilities for workplace safety, non-discrimination guidelines and, if needed, advance notification of a plant closing. Initial interest has been strong. By October 1995, AT&T, General Motors Corp., General Electric, Zenith, and others had requested a copy (Scott 1995c).

This willingness of companies to co-operate with background institutions is encouraging. It provides hope that there will also be a willingness to co-operate with Third World governments. A collaborative relationship is needed where the multinational corporations will share information based on global experiences and offer input into host governments' developmental policies, and aid their implementation. The government, in turn, will provide a reasonable regulatory environment. This calls for ongoing interactions among officials at all levels of the two institutions (Amba-Rao 1993).

Powerful pushes for ending corruption are now also coming from the Third World. At the end of 1995, 34 Latin American leaders gathered in Miami for the Summit of the Americas. Their 'No to Corruption' challenged corrupt practices in their own countries and in OECD countries for aiding and abetting the process. The Summit Agreement pledged specific actions to develop internal ethical and transparency standards to reinvent governmental regulations and process, and to strengthen inter-American banking, judicial, and extradition mechanisms. It also called on the world's governments to adopt and enforce measures against bribery in all financial or commercial transactions within the hemisphere. The Summit's anti-corruption initiative was a milestone in hemispheric coalition building (Skol 1996).

Taken collectively, it appears that two major trends can be credited with the increased focus on business ethics by governments and supranational organizations. First, market globalization and trade bloc formation have led to treaties and agreements on social responsibility. Second, pressure has been exerted on multinational corporations by consumers who increasingly shun companies' products they deem socially irresponsible (Manakkalathil and Rudolf 1995). These trends seem likely to gain momentum and further propel the world toward globalized ethical standards.

8.6 SUMMARY

This chapter examined future ethical challenges and included some current examples which enhance the understanding of the scope of these issues. At the outset, it was noted that the evidence points to a high level of ethical awareness by governments, consumers and corporations. Tangible actions aimed at creating a more ethical business environment are being taken by all three groups. However, this is by no means an easy task and there are many unresolved challenges. Some of the most complex issues arise from doing business in an international environment. To this end, three groups of challenges were singled out as particular noteworthy.

The first such challenge is that of conflicting ethical norms in different cultures. Multinationals must ensure that the ethical standards which they expound are ones which foreign customers accept, foreign employees can be motivated to uphold, and shareholders and other stakeholders can embrace. Sometimes cultural differences will necessitate having a different standard for the host country versus the home country. To judge whether different standards are ethically defensible, each case must be analysed separately as there is no single solution to all situations.

The second group of challenges arises from situations in which differences in economic conditions might cause ethical conflicts. The key challenge, in this context, is to determine the appropriate standard multinationals are required to meet. We discussed a number of guidelines and concluded that there is a movement towards a minimum standard of conduct which is based on the concept of human rights.

Having established the minimum obligations, the third group of challenges focuses on the maximum 'obligations', in other words, the limits to ethical leadership. Different groups of stakeholders are likely to define the limits to ethical leadership differently. It is one of the key challenges of senior management to reconcile such potentially conflicting demands. The discussion also revisited stakeholder theory to explore whether this approach is useful in setting priorities among demands by different stakeholders. However, it appears that the theory, although not without merits, does not provide any concrete guidance on this issue.

The final part of this chapter raised the issue of control of multinationals. The large size and power of multinationals frequently makes them the stronger partner on the bargaining table, and single nation states might find it difficult to exercise control over the behaviour of such companies. Another facet of control relates to the internal command structure of multinationals. It is expected that there will be increasing pressures towards more democratic leadership structures in future. A glance at non-corporate ethical initiatives rounded off the discussion. It is encouraging that the majority of multinationals have made positive shifts towards self regulation and appear to be willing to co-operate with social, political, and economic institutions in order to promote fair competition.

Taken collectively, the discussion illustrated that much progress has already been made in working towards ethical business practices in international marketing. At the same time, increasing globalization of industries has also led to the emergence of ethical dilemmas which are unfamiliar to many, previously domestically oriented companies. Managers are challenged to resolve increasingly complex ethical dilemmas and are charged to strike the right balance, not only between different stakeholder demands but also between cultural relativism and ethnocentricity.

8.7 REFERENCES

Amba-Rao, S.C. (1993) Multinational corporate social responsibility, ethics, interactions and Third World governments: an agenda for the 1990s. *Journal of Business Ethics*, 12(7), pp. 553–72.

Business Ethics (1996) Scandal watch: Mickey Mouse pyjamas are made in Haitian sweatshops. November/December, p. 28.

De George, R. (1993) *Competing with Integrity in International Business*, New York: Oxford University Press.

Dobson, J. (1992) Ethics in the transnational corporation; the 'moral buck' stops where? *Journal of Business Ethics*, 11(1), pp. 21–7.

Duerden, J. (1995) 'Walking the walk' on global ethics. *Directors & Boards*, 19(3), pp. 42–5.

Handy, C. (1996) *The Age of Paradox*, Boston, MA: Harvard Business School Press.

Jensen, M.C. and Fagan, P.L. (1996) Whose firm is it anyway? *The World in 1997*, London: The Economist Newspaper Ltd.

Kaltenhauser, S. (1996) When bribery is a budget item. *World Business*, 2(2), p. 11.

Kapp, R.A. (1995) Does business need a code of ethics. *China Business Review*, 22(3), pp. 6–7.

Kurschner, D. (1996) The best corporate citizens: is your company on our list of the nation's 100 most profitable, public and socially responsible companies? *Business Ethics Magazine*, May/June issue, pp. 24–35.

Manakkalathil, J. and Rudolf, E. (1995) Corporate social responsibility in a globalizing market. *SAM Advanced Management Journal*, 60(1), pp. 29–32 and Illus.

Mander, J. (1992) The myth of the corporate conscience. *Business & Society Review*, (81), pp. 56–63.

Mayer, D. and Cava, A. (1993) Ethics and the Gender Equality Dilemma for US Multinationals. *Journal of Business Ethics*, 12(9), pp. 701–8.

McGugan, I. (1995) Greed, si, but adios to bribes. *Canadian Business*, 68(2), p. 93.

Misser, F. (1995) Anti-Corruption Warriors. *African Business*, 195, pp. 27–8.

Mitchell, A. (1996/97) *Marketing Business*, December/January, pp. 28–30.

Moskowitz, D. (1994) Taking aim at bribes overseas. *International Business*, 7(2), p. 110.

OECD (1984) Guidelines for multinational enterprises. *International Investment and Multinational Enterprises* (revised edn), Paris: Organization for Economic Cooperation and Development, pp. 11–22.

Richter, A. and Barnum, C. (1994) When values clash. *HR Magazine*, 39(9), pp. 42–5.

Scott, M. (1995a) An interview with Howard Schultz, CEO of Starbucks Coffee Co. *Business Ethics Magazine*, November/December, pp. 26–9.

Scott, M. (1995b) Levis caught with pants up. *Business Ethics Magazine*, November/December, p. 15.

Scott, M. (1995c) Benchmarking your principles. *Business Ethics Magazine*, November/December, p. 17.

Skol, M. (1996) Out from under the table. *Business Mexico*, 6(2), pp. 23–5.

Sorell, T. and Hendry, J. (1994) *Business Ethics*, UK: Butterworth-Heinemann Ltd.

Suzman, M. (1997) Baby milk companies under fire. *Financial Times*, January 9, pp. 1 and 12.

UN (1990) Proposed text of draft code of conduct on transnational corporations. Economic and Social Council, E/1990/94, 12 June 1990.

Van Haste, C. (1996) Corruption, bribery, and US law: a deck stacked against US developers. *Electrical World*, 210(5), pp. 37–9.

—PART II
Ethics in international marketing practice – cases

9 *RU 486**

9.1 THE HANDLING BY ROUSSEL-UCLAF OF A DOUBLE ETHICAL DILEMMA (A)

It was Friday October 21, 1988. Catherine Euvrard, Communications Director of Roussel-Uclaf, was preparing to go to a top-level meeting called for that day regarding RU 486. Apart from herself, 19 men would be present, including members of the board and CEOs of the French pharmaceutical firm (at that time 44 per cent was owned by the French Government and 56 per cent controlled by Hoechst of West Germany).

The subject was inevitably going to provoke an unusually heated discussion. Seldom, thought Mademoiselle Euvrard, were firms faced with business decisions that generated so much passion and challenged a person's deepest convictions. The decision would be whether or not to market RU 486, an abortion inducer, also incorrectly known as the 'day-after pill'. (The temporary suspension of the sale of RU 486 was a third possibility.) Mademoiselle Euvrard summarized the information in her mind so as to anticipate the forthcoming arguments.

9.1.1 The company

The French scientist Gaston Roussel founded the pharmaceutical firm named after him at the beginning of the century. When he died in

* This case was written by Gilda Villaran, Research Associate, under the supervision of Henri-Claude de Bettignies, Professor at INSEAD. It is intended to be used as a basis for class discussion rather than to illustrate either effective or ineffective handling of an administrative situation.

Part (C) is not self explanatory – It is expected to be used after discussion of Parts (A) and (B).

The authors thank Roussel-Uclaf for its cooperation.

Reprinted with the permission of INSEAD-CEDEP.

Copyright © 1991 INSEAD-CEDEP, Fontainebleau, France. All rights reserved.

Financial support from the INSEAD Alumni Fund European Case Programme is gratefully acknowledged.

1947, he left a well-structured group to his son, Jean-Claude Roussel. Jean-Claude gave the company a more international outlook and diversified its activities to include animal health and plant care. With the backing of Hoechst of Germany, Roussel-Uclaf became a leader of the French pharmaceutical industry and developed an important presence world-wide. Today, it is a world leader in the fields of endocrinology, cardiovasculars and antibiotics. In bulk sales of cortisone, mostly to other companies, Roussel-Uclaf has 60 per cent of the present world market. Now, Roussel-Uclaf expects most of its future growth to come from health care, especially from pharmaceuticals.

Roussel-Uclaf has subsidiaries in thirty countries and partnerships in more than sixty nations. Having used its international base to overcome the limited profitability of its home market, the company seems ready to play a leading role in the global industry. Its profits have risen steadily during the past ten years as international sales grew to more than two thirds of company revenues. In 1989 Roussel-Uclaf employed 15,637 people (8,619 in France and 7,018 abroad); its annual sales amounted to FF12,369 million.

In 1990 Rhône-Poulenc acquired 36 per cent of Roussel-Uclaf's shares; Hoechst controlled 54 per cent, Elf-Erap owned 5 per cent and the public the remaining 5 per cent. According to The Pharmaceutical Executive, Rhône-Poulenc's acquisition was due to the fact that the French Government had decided that it should not have a minority participation in a company. The transfer to Rhône-Poulenc, it said, was a purely financial operation since the agreement makes absolutely no reference to the involvement of Rhône-Poulenc in the management of the Roussel-Uclaf group.

Since 1981, Roussel-Uclaf has been presided over by Doctor Edouard Sakiz. Sakiz, born in Istanbul to an Armenian family, is a medical doctor, biologist and first-rank researcher in the field of steroids.

(a) Its R&D activities

Roussel-Uclaf is proud of the importance it attaches to research and development activities. For example, in 1989 the R&D budget amounted to FF1,359 million or 11 per cent of the group's consolidated turnover. Roussel-Uclaf has entered into several co-operative agreements with French universities and research organizations, including among them Inserm (Institut National de la Santé et de la Recherche Médicale).

9.1.2 The product

(a) Its discovery

Researchers at Roussel-Uclaf had synthesized the RU 486 anti-hormone in 1980. Dr. Sakiz explained the discovery of the product to *The Pharmaceutical Executive*: 'This compound came out from research we started ten years ago into anti-hormones. There were no real anti-hormones, and what was used instead were the weak hormones. We said, it would be beautiful one day if we had a compound that gets into the receptor and has no action at all. There was no such compound available before RU 486. It was the first real anti-hormone.'

It had not been the initial intention of Roussel-Uclaf researchers to create an abortion inducer. The drug's abortion-provoking – or 'contragestive' – effects had been discovered subsequently by Professor Etienne-Emile Baulieu's team. Professor Baulieu was a researcher at Inserm and had been working in close collaboration with Roussel-Uclaf for over twenty-five years.

At that time, no top executive could have predicted the turmoil the product would cause. Doctor Sakiz later confessed: 'We never thought we would create an ethical dilemma.'

(b) How it works

The substance works by blocking the action of the hormone progesterone, which is essential to maintain a pregnancy. The administration of the product was established as follows: women in the early stages of pregnancy take a 600 mg dose of RU 486 (three pills of 200 mg each) in front of the doctor in an abortion clinic; they then go home. Two days later, the effectiveness of the product is complemented by the administration of 'prostaglandins' (which work on the muscles of the uterus, producing contractions that facilitate the expulsion of the foetus) either in the form of an injection or a vaginal pessary. Roussel-Uclaf does not produce prostaglandins, but they are available in France. The only pharmaceutical firms that produce them are Schering, and the Japanese laboratory Ono, which has licensed the product in France to Rhône-Poulenc.

RU 486 is only effective between day 35 and day 49 of the last menstrual cycle; i.e. when the pregnancy is between 21 and 35 days old. (In France, pregnancy is calculated to start on the fourteenth day of the last menstrual period.) For more details on the mode of prescription of the product, see Exhibit 9.1.

EXHIBIT 9.1

Mode of prescription of RU 486 (only in abortion clinics)

First medical visit:
The woman demands an abortion.
The diagnosis of pregnancy is confirmed and the stage of pregnancy is determined (by blood test or ultrasound).
The abortion method is chosen.
The utilization notice of RU 486 is read and the woman signs an agreement form.
An appointment is made for a psycho-social meeting and for the administration of RU 486 after a week of reflection.

Second medical visit:
The woman takes the pills in front of the doctor, who also signs the agreement form.
A blood sample is taken to determine the blood type.
An appointment is made for 36–48 hours later.

Third medical visit:
The prostaglandin is administered, either in the form of a vaginal pessary or an intra-muscular injection.
The patient is medically supervised during the next 3–4 hours.
Prevention of Rhesus immunization is done in case Rhesus is negative (gamma globulins antiD).
An appointment is made for a visit 8–15 days later.

Fourth medical visit:
The doctor verifies that bleeding has ceased.
The doctor verifies that expulsion is complete (if necessary a blood test and/or ultrasound are carried out).
The doctor prescribes a contraceptive.

(c) Its testing

Extensive clinical testing has proven the safety of the product. The drug was administered to 20,000 volunteers with a 96 per cent success rate with the supplementary administration of prostaglandins. (The success rate had been only 80 per cent in previous tests, when RU 486 alone was taken). Recent results reported by *The New England Journal of Medicine* have confirmed the 96 per cent success rate.
In none of the 4 per cent of the cases in which RU 486 failed was

there a threat to the woman's health; rather failure constituted either incomplete abortions (three per cent of the cases) or no response at all to the drug (one per cent of the cases). However, since there was no absolute certainty that the foetus had not been damaged, these women then underwent surgical abortions. During testing in England a small number of women on whom RU 486 had had no effect, although informed of the risks, decided not to undergo surgical abortion. All gave birth to healthy babies.

The World Health Organization (WHO) had had an important role in testing the substance. Following an agreement signed in 1982, WHO conducted testing and development programmes in fifteen countries, some of which were developing countries. WHO included in the agreement a clause that stipulated that, in the event of Roussel-Uclaf deciding not to continue the development of RU 486, Roussel-Uclaf should provide WHO (if it was still interested) with the product, or transfer its rights to another company that would like to continue its development. The US Population Council had also endorsed the use of RU 486, although testing in the US has been limited due to the present hostile environment.

(d) Its medical advantages

Abortion with RU 486 has some clear advantages over surgical abortion (suction): it avoids the administration of general anesthesia (surgical abortion, even under local anesthesia, is painful; therefore, in France it is mainly done under general anesthesia); it eliminates the risks of uterus perforation and laceration of the uterus neck; also, it does not require hospitalization (needed because of the administration of general anesthesia), and so its costs are lower. Studies quoted by the Population Crisis Committee (Washington, DC) have shown that most women prefer a non-surgical method of abortion because it provides greater privacy, is less invasive and avoids anesthesia.

The disadvantages of RU 486 are that it requires the patient to re-visit the doctor. In addition, the abortive pill can only be taken within a very short period of time, unlike surgical abortion.

9.1.3 The French Government's authorization

On October 9, 1987, the 'Laboratoires Roussel' (in charge of marketing the pharmaceutical products of the Roussel-Uclaf group) had applied for government authorization for the commercial use of mifepristone, which is the name of RU 486 (the commercial brand name in France is Mifegyne).

As was to be expected, Roussel's application for the commercial use of RU 486 re-kindled the whole discussion on abortion, despite the fact that the issue had been more or less dormant in France since 1975, when the Veil Law (Law of January 17, 1975, modified by Law of December 31, 1979) had legalized the 'IVG' (the voluntary interruption of pregnancy). The law allows abortion to be carried out before the end of the tenth week of pregnancy, and requires a prior discussion with a psychologist or a family counsellor and a period of reflection of one week.

The Government solicited the opinion of the French National Committee on Ethics, presided over by Professor Jean Bernard. The committee delivered its opinion on December 15 (see Exhibit 9.2, for the text). In spite of the reluctant tone of its statement, the committee approved RU 486 and recommended its use with the same legal limitations under which surgical abortions are performed. More precisely, the committee advised that the substance be administered by authorized abortion clinics only and not sold in drugstores.

EXHIBIT 9.2

Opinion of the National Consultative Committee on Ethics on the use of Mifepristone (RU 486)

The French 'Comité Consultatif National d'Ethique' was consulted for specific recommendations within the boundaries of existing law. Several committee members, whose convictions did not permit them to approve termination of a pregnancy, expressed their reservations, which were duly recorded.

The committee was asked for advice concerning the use of Mifepristone (RU 486). This compound has the property, amongst others, of preventing the progesterone hormone maintain a pregnancy. It may therefore be used as an abortive device, so that pregnancies can be terminated without surgical intervention.

With this in mind, the committee formulated on this occasion some general observations. The administering of a new product may not, whatever its intrinsic virtues, be permitted if it conflicts with existing legislation.

The relative ease of use of Mifepristone could lead potential users not to respect the measures contained in the law of 1975, modified by the law of 1979 concerning pregnancy termination. These measures correspond to general demands which the introduction of a new product cannot ignore.

Therefore, it is necessary that the use of such a product be authorized only within the framework of current laws and under medical supervision. Although the pill does not require surgery, this fact should not lead to a dramatic increase of termination cases.

> The issues thus formulated led the committee to insist imme-
> diately upon the importance of authorizing the prescription and
> use of this product only in highly specialized centres. Such
> centres already exist.'
> Source: *Le Monde*, Thursday December 17 1987, p. 14. (Trans-
> lation.)

The French press saw the committee's opinion as a warning light
to RU 486: *Le Monde* reported in big type 'Feu Orange a la Pilule
I.V.G.' and *Le Figaro* said 'Oui, mais . . . au RU 486.' However, this
was not the case for Roussel had always maintained that RU 486
should only be used under these strict conditions.

The French Government finally approved the commercial use of
RU 486. The other government which promptly authorized the drug
was the Chinese, which approved the use of RU 486 even before
France did. China runs the world's biggest abortion service; 11.5
million abortions are performed every year, legally and mostly safely.
It also conducted the largest number of clinical trials of RU 486
outside France (more than 1,600 pill-induced abortions were carried
out).

9.1.4 The debate

Mademoiselle Euvrard wondered whether the French Government's
decision would relieve the firm of its ethical responsibility. Undoubtedly, today's meeting would be one more opportunity to discuss the
fundamental values involved in the abortion issue. Someone would
probably argue that the right to life is the fundamental right of human
beings and there would be disagreement when it came to 'deciding'
whether or not a newly conceived foetus is a human being. Neither
scientists nor religious leaders have reached agreement on when
human life exactly starts. This would then perhaps lead to the issue
of weighing a woman's right to free choice against a foetus's right to
be born.

She anticipated that two conflicting views would be advanced in
today's discussion. One group would contend that while the law
might tolerate it, abortion was still morally wrong (intentional termination of a human life is intrinsically wrong) and that to facilitate
abortion was therefore condemnable. The other group would argue
that a firm had no right to place limits on the exercise of legally
enforceable rights. According to this view, personal beliefs on abortion were irrelevant; the decision to condemn or to accept abortion
only corresponded to society; and French society, through its parliament, had already decided that abortion was, if not exactly desirable,
at least tolerable and that its exercise was, with certain constraints,
legal.

Both sides were likely to invoke the firm's image as an argument for and against the marketing of RU 486. The pill's proponents would emphasize the prestige that the marketing of such an interesting and original product would give the company. RU 486 foes might counter that Roussel-Uclaf's slogan 'at the service of life' would become paradoxical if it sold a product that ended human life at its very outset. Mademoiselle Euvrard could also predict the reply that the RU 486 defenders would advance: that the product was more than merely 'interesting'; it was a life saver: WHO has estimated that out of 500,000 women per year dying from pregnancy-related complications (99 per cent of which were Third World women) 200,000 deaths were due to improperly performed abortions.

(a) Public opinion

Although public opinion was divided, those opposing RU 486 had, up to that time, expressed their views more vigorously than those in favour of it. The Catholic Church had condemned RU 486, a ruling consistent with its rejection of both contraception and any form of abortion. Archbishop Jacques Jullien, head of the Family Commission of the French Episcopate, had raised the argument of the 'banalization' of abortion. Mademoiselle Euvrard recalled Professor Baulieu's outrage when he referred to this contention, which reflected a serious misunderstanding of women. An abortion decision, he had said, can be painful; it is never banal. Baulieu had added that a pill can never eliminate a person's conscience.

The 'Laissez-les vivre' movement had used Archbishop Jullien's argument several times, contending that if abortion procedures were made too easy and commonplace, the abortion decision would be obscured. Moreover, members of the movement claimed that RU 486 favoured sexual permissiveness, which in their view was morally condemnable.

Several other French organizations, like the 'Association for Conscientious Objectors to all Participation in Abortion', and international organizations such as the 'Association of Medical Doctors for the Respect for Life', had actively campaigned against RU 486. Forming a committee called 'Save the Unborn Children', they had organized a press conference on December 7, 1987 and alerted the public to the threat posed by RU 486. The powerful International Right to Life Federation, presided over by Doctor John Willke, had initiated a crusade against the abortive pill. In June and December 1987, Doctor Willke had sent letters to the then French Prime Minister, Jacques Chirac, warning against the risks posed by RU 486, including the risk of foetus toxicity.

(b) The threat of boycott

The moral condemnation and emotive slogans (such as calling the drug the 'death pill' and 'human pesticide') contained in these and other letters had been accompanied by an important boycott threat, not only of Roussel-Uclaf products but also of the products of the parent company Hoechst. Threats made in the United States, where boycott power is strong, had already intimidated Hoechst-Roussel Product Incorporated (HRPI), the pharmaceutical division of Hoechst-Celanese (the American subsidiary of Hoechst).

As Dr Willke was prompt to remind Roussel-Uclaf, American anti-abortion groups had already defeated at least one pharmaceutical company: Upjohn had stopped research in this field in 1985 because of a hostile campaign against Prostin, a drug able to induce abortion. In fact, the large American pharmaceutical companies have long abandoned all birth-control-related research. Although right-to-lifers took the credit for this, one of the main causes of the reluctance of American firms to continue research was the relatively small size of the market. According to *The Technology Review*, the estimated US demand is 400,000 doses a year. And while estimates made by the consulting firm Intercare (of Flemington, New Jersey) determine that the world-wide market for contraceptives and abortifacient substances is worth $1 billion, the market for cardiovascular drugs in the US alone is worth $2.5 billion. Rising liability costs are a second and perhaps more important reason for the cessation of research in this field.

On the other hand, the importance of the American market for Hoechst was indisputable: a quarter of the giant's US$25 billion revenues came from the States. HRPI had a sales volume of US$485 million, which represented eight per cent of Hoechst-Celanese's sales and 11 per cent of Hoechst's total pharmaceutical sales. Hoechst-Celanese had a sales volume two-and-a-half times larger than Roussel-Uclaf's.

(c) The position of Hoechst

Hoechst was plainly against the sale of the product. Wolfgang Hilger, its President, was known to be personally opposed to abortion and had always declared: 'It is simply not company policy to sell an abortifacient.'

The position of the company's executives with respect to the marketing of an abortifacient substance reflected the fact that, in general, West Germans have more conservative views on abortion than the French. However, as Mademoiselle Euvrard understood it, religious and moral beliefs were not the most decisive reason for Hoechst's opposition. She had spoken with several of Hoechst's executives who reasoned in terms of risk. They all made the same basic point: let us put aside the moral, philosophical and religious implications of the decision and see if the international marketing of the pill makes sound business sense. What Hoechst might lose in the face of a full boycott of its products is economically much more important than the potential profits from the sale of this pill. Profits would never be considerable, given that sales of RU 486 were not expected to be very high in Western Europe, where abortion had decreased in the past few years, and that sales in developing countries, following the agreement signed with WHO, would be at cost value. Considering the credibility of the boycott threat, Hoechst's managers concluded that the product was not worth the risk. Some Roussel managers echoed this opinion.

Lastly, the possibility of conflict with the parent company Hoechst had to be evaluated. So far, differences between Hoechst and Roussel had not amounted to open controversy and both were continuing to agree on major issues. However, there remained the question of whether over-insistence on the sale of RU 486 might not lead to Roussel being excluded from future major decision making. There was a distinct possibility that Hoechst, considering the huge economic factors at stake, might decide to handle the issue itself.

(d) Potential internal problems from the sale of RU 486

Internal opposition posed a further obstacle. Shareholders' opinions were divided. On June 23, 1988, a General Assembly of shareholders had taken place. Although at that meeting no decision was taken on the future of RU 486, there was notable opposition to the very idea of selling an abortifacient. While it was true that members of the board and of the chief executive office were not bound by the opinions expressed by shareholders, it was equally true that these opinions would have some bearing on the decision to be taken today.

Mademoiselle Euvrard anticipated another source of internal opposition. Assuming that members of the board and of the chief executive's office accepted the distribution of RU 486, what if executives and employees simply refused to work on anything related to the pill because of their personal religious or moral convictions? The 'Association for Conscientious Objectors to all Participation in Abortion' had been distributing letters at Roussel-Uclaf's front door, urging employees to refuse to participate in the research and production of RU 486. (See Exhibit 9.3, a letter distributed to employees of Roussel-Uclaf at Romainville on September 9, 1988.)

EXHIBIT 9.3

Letter to the employees of Roussel-Uclaf: the truth concerning RU 486 (translation)

For several years, the Board of Roussel-Uclaf has been spreading insidiously false propaganda concerning RU 486.

It's time we re-established the truth:

Q – Is RU 486 a medicine?

A – RU 486 is mainly used (its only use up to the present time) as a POISON, acting both on the mother and the child that she is bearing, and not as a medicine or drug, which is intended to make a person well. In fact, RU 486 kills the conceived child by preventing his/her gestation – i.e. the implantation in the mother's uterus – and by causing the hormones to evacuate him/her.

Q – Is RU 486 an advance?

A – There is no law that would render acceptable the exploitation of man by man, and even more so, crime, slavery, child-labour, or forced sterilization – without mentioning the traffic of babies for organ transplants. In 1941, at the extermination camp of AUSCH-WITZ, the Nazis considered the replacement of carbon oxide by CYANIDE gas to be an advance. In the factory which produced this gas (DEGESCH in FRANKFURT), the object of the work was concealed to the workers. However, had they known (their supervisors knew), would they have felt responsible?

If RU 486 is approved, none of the weak barriers found in the French abortion law will be able to protect the unborn child.

The Chinese authorities have admitted that they compel women to have abortions strictly for political reasons, thereby denying women freedom of choice and their maternal love. We know, through reliable sources, that 95 per cent of the 10 million Chinese abortions performed per year are a result of force. Isn't this TOTALITARIAN regime ROUSSEL-UCLAF's favourite customer?

Q – Are the 'Comité d'Ethique,' the 'Population Council' and other organizations which support RU 486, legitimate scientific and humanitarian references?

A – The 'Comité d'Ethique' has some reservations concerning RU 486, and is, for the first time, divided over an issue.

The 'Population Council' is a private lobby supported by the

Rockefeller Group, whose industrial empire we know well. Their avowed objective is to reduce, by any available means, the Third World population – which is easier than helping them to develop.

The World Health Organization (its headquarters are next to the Population Council in New York) is more concerned by birth control methods than it is by actual health. In order to channel the credit it receives from the World Bank for the Third World, it demands that abortion and sterilization programmes be applied: BLACKMAIL FOR FOOD.

Q – Won't ethical, moral or religious convictions hinder research?

A – Research is not sacred. Josef Mengele, for having thought the contrary, was condemned by the Nüremberg trial, after the last World War. He and the 'accursed doctors' dedicated themselves to research of the human species (Russians, Poles, Jews, Gypsies, etc.). One of their main goals was mass sterilization . . .

Since 1982, Roussel-Uclaf has led experiments with RU 486, resulting in the elimination of thousands of children. WHAT'S THE DIFFERENCE?

Today, the conscience of employees is not always respected: they have no way of refusing to make products (of which they have not been told the truth). In a world where unemployment is always present, it's an easy task for the investigators of RU 486 to convince manufacturers to direct its production. Holding on to a job which is already threatened by upcoming restructuring, each one is tempted to collaborate. However, pursuing this RU 486 project could bring upon Roussel-Uclaf the international discrediting of all their products, which would not only be a terrible blow to the company, but to job security as well.

The directors of the board of Roussel-Uclaf would be well advised to reconsider the project of RU 486, which can only endanger the company for whom you work.

AOCPA

Association for Conscientious Objectors
to all Participation in Abortion

Whether employees would respond to this kind of invitation and whether such refusal might, at a certain point, amount to open conflict was difficult to predict. Neither did she know whether the marketing of the pill would be an issue that divided the organization's members into hostile groups. Several executives had manifested their open disagreement to the sale of an abortifacient substance and expressed their surprise at the change of attitude exhibited by Roussel-Uclaf. Only a few decades ago, the firm had the opportunity to enter the contraceptive market at an early stage; it had refused to do so because of conservative concerns, they recalled. Now, they said, the firm was in the vanguard of what it referred to as abortion methods.

Although so far the disagreements had been moderate, there was a chance that actually marketing the product would exacerbate the tone of the discussions. The issue of abortion divides countries; it could well divide organizations. The same kind of controversy could arise between Roussel and its subsidiaries; subsidiaries which were predominantly anti-RU 486 might refuse to follow instructions issued by the Paris headquarters.

Finally, Edouard Sakiz had, during the past months, been voicing his fears about the security of the company's employees. The Catholic Church had condemned the use of violence, but fanatical Catholics had recently rioted in Paris at the showing of a film perceived as disrespectful to the Catholic faith (the Saint-Michel movie theatre was set alight and several people wounded when it showed Martin Scorsese's 'The Last Temptation of Christ'). Sakiz said he did not want to jeopardize the safety of company employees by provoking the anger of such extremists. Sakiz's fears were probably exaggerated, thought Mademoiselle Euvrard, but when it comes to fanaticism, it is difficult to predict its limits.

9.1.5 World-wide distribution

In any event, an affirmative decision taken at the meeting would lead to the immediate marketing of the pill in France only. The Health Division had suggested a step-by-step strategy: having gained solid experience in France, the firm would then move to market the product in other European countries. Five conditions had been laid down that would have to be met before the pill was marketed:

- abortion must be legal;
- abortion must be accepted by political, public and medical opinion;
- synthetic prostaglandins (which Roussel-Uclaf does not produce) must be available;
- distribution circuits must be strictly controlled;
- patients must sign a consent form, agreeing to undergo surgical abortion if RU 486 failed.

After France, sales were projected to follow in England, the Scandinavian countries and Holland. Not many other countries would fulfil the conditions. Eastern European countries, which constituted an important potential market, did not meet the third and fourth requirements.

With regard to the distribution of the pill in the Third World, Roussel-Uclaf knew it had to move cautiously. Here the firm antici-pated several problems. First, it was by no means sure that the governments of many developing countries would allow use of the pill. Latin American laws, for instance, influenced by the Catholic Church, make abortion a criminal offence (for a world-wide over-view of illegal abortion, see Exhibit 9.4). As had been suggested, giving RU 486 euphemistic names such as 'menstrual inducers', while it might help relieve the conscience of Catholic women, was not likely to deceive governments. But even assuming that WHO, which would be in charge of the distribution of the product in the Third World, could break down the barriers imposed by governments, those countries would still not be in a position to fulfil the conditions required by Roussel-Uclaf. Above all, fears centred on the fact that the product can pose a risk if it is badly administered. Roussel was aware that the medical environment and the poor infrastructure of less-developed countries would not provide guarantees for the safe use of the product.

EXHIBIT 9.4

Facts on illegal abortion

FACT SHEET

For Immediate Release

- Worldwide, about 55 million unwanted pregnancies end in abortion every year. Of the total, about half are illegal abor-tions, occurring mainly in the Third World. The remaining half are legal abortions performed mainly in the developed world, China and India.
- Illegal abortion is epidemic in many parts of the developing world. In Brazil, more than three million illegal abortions take place each year – compared to 4 million live births. In Latin America as a whole, there is one illegal abortion performed for every two births. Lack of safe abortion ser-vices in India results in four to six million unregulated (performed outside licensed facilities) abortions a year, despite a 1972 law legalizing abortion.
- Illegal abortion is a leading cause of death among women of reproductive age in developing countries, killing about

100,000 women a year. In the US, a legal abortion, is 11 times safer than a tonsillectomy or childbirth. In France, an early abortion with the new RU 486 drug appears to be equally safe.

- After the 1973 legalization of abortion in the United States, abortion-related deaths dropped by more than 40 per cent. Abortion deaths in Czechoslovakia fell 56 per cent between 1958 and 1962 after liberalization. In Hungary, abortion deaths fell 38 per cent between 1958 and 1962 after liberalization. Romanian laws restricting abortion in 1966 resulted in a 700 per cent increase in abortion deaths between 1965 and 1978.

- Over the last decade 35 countries liberalized abortion laws. Canada, the Soviet Union and Spain are among those that have eased restrictions. Going against this global trend are Iran, Israel, New Zealand and the United States which have increased restrictions. Virtually all Western European countries are experiencing challenges to their Liberal abortion laws.

- A common method of illegal abortion is insertion of a sharp instrument, such as a twig, root, clothes hanger, or knitting needle, through the cervix. In Southeast Asia, Africa and the Middle East, abdominal 'massage' is common. Injection of soapy water or disinfectant into the uterus or drinking toxic herbal teas are also frequently used methods of abortion.

- These primitive, often ineffective methods of abortion frequently cause serious complications including a perforated uterus or intestine, peritonitis, shock, haemorrhage, poisoning, renal failure and infertility. Complications are often fatal.

- Treating a case of botched abortion in a Third World maternity ward can cost 12 times as much as a normal birth. As much as 50 per cent of some hospital maternity budgets are spent on treatment of abortion complications.

- According to a recent PCC review of international abortion policy data for 144 countries:
    About 1 billion people or 20 per cent of the world's population live in 49 countries where abortion is legal only to save the life of the woman, or where it is totally prohibited. Much of Muslim Asia, Latin America and Africa fall into this category. Countries include Pakistan. Venezuela, Nigeria, the Republic of Ireland and Belgium.

- About 600 million people or 11 per cent of the world's population live in 47 countries where abortion is legal on medical grounds. This includes cases of health risk to the woman and/or cases of foetal deformity. In 13 of these 47 countries, abortion is legal only in cases of risk to a woman's health, such as in Ethiopia and Costa Rica.

■ In many of the countries reviewed, where abortion is legal in cases of risk to a woman's health or life, it is also legal in cases of rape or incest.

■ Another 1.3 billion people or 95 per cent of the world's population live in 23 countries where abortion is legal on social or economic grounds. In this group of countries women can seek abortions based on familial or financial problems such as the inability to care for additional children. Examples include Japan, Poland and India.

■ About 2 billion people or 39 per cent of the world's population live in 22 countries where legal abortion is available on request usually limited to the first trimester. Examples include the United States, Tunisia, France, Greece, the Soviet Union, and the Scandinavian countries.

■ In only 3 countries – Mexico, Brazil and Ecuador – with about 5 per cent of the world's population, is abortion legal only in cases of rape or incest and to save the life of the woman.

■ Overall, 3.9 billion people, or 75 per cent of the world's population, live in countries which permit abortion on broad health or social and economic grounds.

Sources: Population Crisis Committee, International Planned Parenthood Federation, Johns Hopkins University Population Information Program, The Alan Guttmacher Institute. September 1989.

An additional fear was the possibility that a black market for the product would emerge. Traffickers could benefit from the fact that RU 486 would be sold at lower prices in the Third World and Eastern Europe. By transporting the product back to Western Europe, they could make illicit profits. More importantly, the main risk of a black market is the misuse of the pill (insufficient doses, late administration, lack of adequate medical supervision, etc.).

Thus, the day when RU 486 would be available in the Third World appeared remote, which was, in a certain way, contradictory of the aims of the product. As a colleague of Mademoiselle Euvrard graphically put it, 'RU 486 represented significant progress not as an alternative to surgical abortion, which is almost as safe although more painful and traumatizing than RU 486, but as an alternative to knitting needles.' However, it was in countries where such methods were commonplace that the product would not be available, at least not in the foreseeable future.

It was time for Mademoiselle Euvrard to leave for the meeting. She concluded that the firm was caught in a serious dilemma: whatever step it took would provoke anger from one section or another of those watching the firm's actions. She wondered how to present the arguments when her opinion was solicited, and what recommendations to make.

9.2 THE HANDLING BY ROUSSEL-UCLAF OF A DOUBLE ETHICAL DILEMMA (B)

9.2.1 The decision

Taking into account the feelings expressed by some French and foreign members of the public, together with the debate fired by the possibility of marketing the anti-hormone mifepristone (RU 486) which causes the voluntary interruption of pregnancy, the Roussel-Uclaf group has decided to suspend distribution of this product as a medical alternative to surgical abortion in France and abroad as of today. The Roussel-Uclaf group is considered to be a pioneer in endocrinology. After having developed numerous hormones (sexual steroids and corticosteroids), it has oriented its research towards the field of hormones and anti-hormones and their application. The nilutamide (anti androgen) has recently been released to the medical community as a therapy for prostate cancer. The Roussel-Uclaf group, convinced of the therapeutic effect of anti-hormones, intends to continue its research and development efforts and to maintain its world leadership in that field.

This was the communiqué by which the management of Roussel-Uclaf announced to its employees its decision to suspend distribution of its abortifacient substance RU 486. Until that time, distribution had been done free of charge and for testing purposes only. By a show of hands vote of sixteen to four, members of the executive office and the Board of directors of Roussel-Uclaf had decided, after a one-hour debate during a meeting on October 21 1988, not to market the product.

Those who voted for the suspension gave as their main reason the risk of boycott of their other products, and not only those of Roussel-Uclaf, but also those of Hoechst. 'The prospect of significant economic gains had never been a motive for developing the product; but a fear of economic losses was a reason for taking it off the market', said Madame Mouttet, Roussel-Uclaf's International Group Manager for Hormonal Products.

On the other hand, a minority had maintained that the firm should not give in to blackmail, and that the withdrawal of a first-rate medical product would deprive women of a safe and relatively painless means of ending unwanted pregnancy. Catherine Euvrard,

Communications Director and the only woman present at that meeting, had insisted on a woman's right to free choice.

Michel Delage, CEO of Roussel-France, declared to the press that 'under these circumstances, we finally decided that we did not have the right to put on one side of the scales the firm's development, and, on the other, the improvement of our group's corporate image in the medical community, which would result from the sale of such an interesting and original product'. Pierre Joly, Vice President of Roussel-Uclaf, further explained that the firm did not want to take responsibility for cases in which, due to a 'hostile religious or moral environment', women would fail to complete their treatment using the drug. To be sure, the laboratories had decided that, in addition to complying with the requirements set by French law, women considering taking RU486 should sign a consent form agreeing to undergo surgical abortion in the event of failure of the product. However, Roussel-Uclaf would not be able to enforce this agreement. Obviously, the Vice President was afraid that the firm's responsibility did not end with the signing of the consent form.

Edouard Sakiz, the group's CEO, justified the decision by saying to the press: 'Imagine your workers going back on the evening train and their children saying 'Father, is it true that you are an assassin?' He was also quoted by *The New York Times* as saying: 'We have a responsibility for managing a company; but if I were a lone scientist, I would have acted differently.' And Professor Etienne-Emile Baulieu, the 'discoverer' of RU 486, relates in his book (*Génération Pilule*, Editions Odile Jacob, Paris 1990) that, in a private meeting following the decision to suspend distribution, his good friend Doctor Sakiz had expressed the distress that this affair has exerted on him. He referred to the pressure exercised by the American subsidiary, Hoechst-Roussel Products Incorporated, and his responsibility vis-à-vis Roussel-Uclaf's personnel. However, he gave Professor Baulieu the green light to react as strongly as he wanted. 'Your position is completely different from mine; you are free to act as you see fit,' Sakiz had said.

9.2.2 Reactions

Until the decision, public pressure had come mainly from the 'pro-life' side. After the decision to withhold the product was made public, pressure from the 'pro-choice' lobby mounted. As Mademoiselle Euvrard had anticipated, the firm was caught in a unique situation; it was subject to strong pressure from opposing sides, one emphasizing the firm's moral obligation not to sell, the other emphasizing the firm's moral duty to sell the product.

The French Archbishops, in plenary session in Lourdes on October 26, were relieved by the announcement, and greeted it with long applause. Monseigneur Jacques Jullien congratulated Roussel-Uclaf for its 'courageous decision' and 'constructive attitude.'

Meanwhile, commentators in the French press debated whether the firm had the right to withdraw a pharmaceutical product whose sale had been authorized because of its usefulness, for fear of economic sanctions. Researchers at Roussel-Uclaf characterized the withdrawal of the drug as 'morally scandalous' and Professor Baulieu declared: 'The firm has given way to intolerance.'

The world's medical community protested strongly against the cessation of sales. A few days after Roussel-Uclaf decided to withdraw the abortive pill, the 1988 World Congress of Gynecology and Obstetrics was held in Rio de Janeiro, Brazil. Two thousand of its participants, mainly physicians, university professors, representatives of the World Health Organization (WHO), the Rockefeller Foundation and the World Bank, sent a petition to Edouard Sakiz asking him to reconsider the decision (see Exhibit 9.5 for the text of the petition). In addition, the directors of the International Federation of Gynecology and Obstetrics, which had organized the Rio Congress, sent a letter to Wolfgang Hilger, President of Hoechst. Apparently, in his reply, Hilger wrote that abortion was morally condemnable, and that the sale of RU 486 was against the firm's philosophy.

EXHIBIT 9.5

Text of the petition sent by the participants of the XII World Congress of Gynecology and Obstetrics to Roussel-Uclaf

We, the undersigned, participants of the XIIth World Congress of Gynecology and Obstetrics, deplore Roussel-Uclaf's decision to suspend the distribution of RU 486 (mifepristone), particularly in view of the recent approval of this product, considered safe and effective, by the French and Chinese government health authorities. Besides its use in early pregnancy termination, it has other potential therapeutic applications, including cancer treatment. We earnestly ask the company to deliver the license to the appropriate authority, in order to ensure women of the availability of this beneficial scientific advance.

9.2.3 The Government's order

Only a week after Roussel-Uclaf's top management had decided to withdraw RU 486 from the market, Claude Evin, France's Health Minister, invited Pierre Joly, Vice President of Roussel-Uclaf, to a meeting. Arguing 'in the interests of public health', he ordered the company to reverse its decision and start selling the product. The French Government's reasoning was straightforward. The sober 'communiqué' (for text, see Exhibit 9.6) that reported the meeting did not deal with the issue of a woman's right to choose; rather, it emphasized the law. The Minister stressed the legal right of women to undergo abortion, and the Government's authority to require companies to market drugs deemed to be in the public interest. He said that RU 486 should be sold to avoid the trauma and pain that surgical abortions cause women. Later, Evin made a comment to the press that was to become the slogan of pro-choice activists in the United States: 'RU 486 is the moral property of women.' Mademoiselle Euvrard now needed to consider the likely consequences of this command.

EXHIBIT 9.6

Official communiqué

October 28, 1988. 12 o'clock.

This morning, Claude Evin, Minister of Health, summoned Pierre Joly, Vice President of the Board of Directors of Roussel-Uclaf. On the 26th of October, this laboratory announced its decision to suspend the marketing of RU 486, even though after favourable notice from the special committee, the Health Minister had granted permission to place it on the market.

Monsieur Evin was surprised by the decision, as it was contrary to industrial policy up until this time. The minister called to mind that if such a decision was the laboratory's responsibility, it remained his duty to look after public health. The law of 1975 must be applied, and in this context, termination of pregnancy constitutes a right of the women in this country.

RU 486 is an advance since it does not require anaesthesia. The foreseen precautions to be taken in France for the release of this medicine (in registered centers only) offer, as the law demands, the utmost guarantees of safety.

The interest of public health being at stake, Mr Claude Evin requested that the Roussel-Uclaf laboratory resume distribution of RU 486, which (Mr Joly) has set out to do.

Source: *Le Monde*, October 31, 1988, p. 9. (Translation.)

9.3 THE HANDLING BY ROUSSEL-UCLAF OF A DOUBLE ETHICAL DILEMMA (C)

9.3.1 The French experience

On October 28, 1988, the French Government ordered Roussel-Uclaf to reverse its decision to suspend distribution of its abortive pill, RU 486, and to put it on the market. The order surprised the pharmaceutical firm; no one could recall an occasion when the Health Ministry had used its legal right to force a pharmaceutical firm to sell a product that it deemed to be in the interests of public health.

Catherine Euvrard, Communications Director of Roussel-Uclaf, analysed the situation in which the firm now found itself. The Ministry of Health, she thought, was legally empowered to give the order, under threat of taking away the licence of the product from the reluctant firm (in application of articles 37, 38 and following of the law of January 2, 1968 on patents). However, there was no certainty as to how the Government could oblige the laboratories to provide information on testing that only they possessed. Therefore, it would not have been easy for the Health Minister to enforce the order.

However, no one at Roussel even insinuated that the firm should refuse to abide by it. 'The Government has settled the issue; I do not see why I would search for legal quibbles to resist the order,' Pierre Joly told the press. Moreover, Dr Sakiz, Roussel-Uclaf's CEO, described the Health Minister's mandate as 'beautiful help'. Indeed, the Government's order was a great relief to the company.

The Confederation of Associations of Catholic Families declared they were outraged and described the Minister's intervention as a flagrant abuse of power. The committee 'Save the Unborn Children' said that this whole affair was a tragicomedy that discredited both Roussel-Uclaf and the French Government. Across the Atlantic, participants in the World Congress of Gynecology and Obstetrics applauded the determination and involvement of the French Government. Jose Pinotti, President of the International Federation of Gynecology and Obstetrics, stated: 'This courageous decision proves that the course of science cannot be blocked by political considerations.'

On December 7, 1988, Roussel-Uclaf's Board of Management decided on the policy for the commercialization of RU 486 abroad. A number of options were open to them. The option chosen was to consider France as a test market. 'It is, in effect, important', the Board said, 'to be able to judge from an adequate distance the satisfactory working and the viability of the distribution circuit, as well as the acceptability and the understanding of the product, by both doctors and patients.' While waiting for confirmation of the success of the drug, the Board decided not to make RU 486 available to foreign orthogenic centers. As a result, it decided the following:

- to withdraw the registration file submitted in Holland;
- to suspend the submissions that were about to be made in Great Britain and Sweden;
- to continue the clinical trials in progress, but not to accept new protocols for the indication of pregnancy termination;
- to continue studies into the product's other indications (cancer, endo-metriosis, obstetrics, etc.).

The many organizations that believed RU 486 constituted a major progress in reproductive medicine resented the overly-cautious – and slow – strategy of Roussel-Uclaf. For example, the International Planned Parenthood Federation passed, in November 1989, a resolution on RU 486 (see Exhibit 9.7).

EXHIBIT 9.7

Resolution the International Planned Parenthood Federation

Shortly after the Birth Control Trust Conference, the Central Council of the International Planned Parenthood Federation passed the following resolution on RU 486:

The Central Council of the IPPF, meeting in Ottawa, 5–11 November 1989, expresses its deep concern over the lack of progress in making the product RU 486 (mifepristone), a revolutionary breakthrough in fertility regulation, available to women in the world who could benefit greatly from using this drug.

Recognizing

1 The IPPF International Medical Advisory Panel (IMAP) statement which deplores the delays in allowing wider availability of RU 486 used in conjunction with prostaglandin analogues owing to restrictions not based on scientific or medical grounds;

2 Toxicological and clinical data already submitted have enabled RU 486 to be licensed in France, the country of manufacture. Further applied research is ongoing, including research sponsored by the World Health Organisation's Special Programme on Human Reproduction, for the continued assessment of safety and effectiveness of anti-progesterones; IMAP recommends that IPPF support the unique role which WHO can play in this area;

3 The October 1988 statement by the French Health Minister,

Claude Evin, asserting that the drug is the 'moral property' of women;

4   The resolution from participants at the 1988 XIIth World Congress of Gynaecology & Obstetrics in Rio de Janeiro, Brazil, urging wider access to the product;

5   The award in September 1989 of the US Albert Lasker Clinical Medical Research Award to Etienne-Emile Baulieu, for his role in developing RU 486.

6   The resolution passed by the October 1989 Birth Control Trust London Conference on RU 486, calling on the manufacturers Roussel-Uclaf to apply for a product licence to ensure the drug's availability in the UK;

7   That opposition to RU 486 comes from anti-choice groups, unrepresentative of majority opinion, and is based on political, not medical grounds.

The Central Council calls on the manufacturers Roussel-Uclaf and their parent company Hoechst to take immediate action to ensure world-wide availability of the drug and urges national licensing bodies and governmental agencies to prevent any unnecessary delay in allowing approval and use.

Source: *IPPF Medical Bulletin* (1989) 23(6), December.

A few months later, Doctor Baulieu received the 1989 Albert Lasker Award for Research in Clinical Medicine for his contribution to the knowledge of steroid hormones. The development of RU 486 was mentioned in the attribution of the award, presented in New York. As was to be expected, giving this prestigious award to Dr Baulieu provoked strong reactions and was followed by extensive press coverage.

After discussions on the price of the product, eventually set at FF256, Roussel-Uclaf started selling the pill in France at the beginning of 1990. (Before then, the product had been distributed free of charge.) Roussel had proposed a price of at least FF500, taking into account the high development costs of the product (not inferior to those incurred during the development of any other pharmaceutical product, like an antibiotic, for example) and the cost of alternative abortion methods. The French authorities proposed a price of less than FF100. Roussel-Uclaf decided not to insist on a high price because it feared being accused of wanting to make a profit out of abortion.

Today, RU 486 is being administered in France without any disruption and under strict controls ('as if it were morphine,' an executive has said). The laboratories have complete control over how many doses are administered, where they are administered (only in abortion clinics) and under what conditions.

In 1990, RU 486 was used in a quarter of the abortions performed in France. Fifty thousand patients used the drug to terminate unwanted pregnancies. The latest figures confirm the 96 per cent success rate that was attained when the drug was first tested in combination with prostaglandins. The French Social Security reimburses patients for 80 per cent of the total cost of the medical pregnancy termination (Arrêté Ministériel, February 26 1990).

Dr Sakiz has declared that, contrary to what the pill's foes anticipated, the number of abortions has not increased in France since RU 486 became available. This would be in accordance with Dr Baulieu's contention that abortion is neither more frequent when it is legal – the number of abortions in Eastern Europe actually diminished after abortion was legalized – nor is there a correlation between the 'easiness' of the abortion procedure and the number of abortions.

9.3.2 The situation in the rest of Europe in 1991

By mid-1990, Roussel-Uclaf decided it could move to selling RU 486 in other countries of Western Europe. Roussel-Uclaf's subsidiary in England started discussions with the British Health Minister to get his assurance that distribution circuits would be as efficient as they were in France, and that patients would also be required to sign a consent form in which they are informed that in case of failure, a surgical abortion is recommended. Once Roussel obtained a guarantee that it would be possible to meet all the requirements laid down by the laboratories, the firm filed an authorization demand. Holland and the Scandinavian countries should follow suit.

In the summer of 1990, RU 486 became a hot issue in Austria. The socialist Government became interested in having the abortive pill introduced into the country. A clinic went ahead and asked for a supply of 600 boxes in order to start using it immediately. Roussel-Uclaf refused.

In the Catholic countries of Southern Europe, the situation is on hold. Women's organizations and gynaecologists have shown some interest in the product, but no concrete steps have been taken to commercialize it. In Italy, RU 486 has produced considerable controversy. In 1989, Elena Marinucci, Undersecretary of State at the Health Ministry, asked Roussel Maestretti to present the product registration dossier because 'experience to date shows that it is the least traumatic and most economic way in which to terminate a pregnancy. Behind the 187,000 abortions in Italy every year lies the lack of any real education in matters of responsible procreation and contraception,' Ms Marinucci said. 'Unfortunately, recourse to abortion is a reality and it is to give women the chance to approach abortion in a less traumatic way that I have taken this initiative, of which the Minister has been informed.' Nevertheless, the Health Minister, Francesco de Lorenzo, appeared to have distanced himself from his undersecretary's move, saying that he did not oppose it but neither did he support it. 'I believe that it is not within our remit to ask a pharmaceutical company to begin the registration process for a drug. If a registration application is made, we will evaluate it with the usual technical and scientific objectivity. I am aware that this is a very sensitive case.' Mr de Lorenzo added that when the registration documentation was presented in Italy, he would set up a special ethical committee to examine the moral aspects of the product. Meanwhile, Catholics are preparing for some intense fighting.

Eastern Europe represents a market of enormous potential, of much greater importance than the US market. Moreover, in Eastern Europe, abortion is 'socially acceptable'. However, these countries cannot guarantee distribution circuits that would allow optimal control of the use of the product. Roussel executives have not yet found a solution to the possibility of black marketeering (profiting from the different prices at which the pill would be sold in Eastern and Western Europe), and fear that women's health will be put in peril through misuse of the product.

9.3.3 Possibilities in the Third World

China, which was the first country to approve the use of RU 486, never concluded an agreement with Roussel-Uclaf. The firm did not get an assurance that distribution circuits there would be effective enough. Ariel Mouttet explained that although testing in China has been impeccable, this testing has only been conducted in the major cities. However, China is mostly a rural country, and in the countryside inadequate facilities cannot ensure the safe distribution of the pill and its administration under close medical supervision. 'The Chinese authorities themselves recognize that, on a national scale, it would be impossible to monitor patients who take the pill,' she said.

However, the Chinese Government has recently made a proposal to the World Health Organization (WHO), which has an ongoing contract with Roussel-Uclaf for the testing and development of the pill in Third World countries. The Chinese suggest the implementation of a 'step-by-step' strategy; i.e., begin the use of the pill in Peking and other major cities, and move into other regions only when their control of distribution circuits is absolutely certain. WHO has not yet reacted to this proposal.

With regard to the distribution of RU 486 in other Third World countries, Roussel-Uclaf is waiting for WHO to take the initiative. WHO, in turn, is behaving cautiously, and awaiting further trials before recommending that governments of developing countries ask Roussel-Uclaf to supply the drug: it wants the pill to be 'discredit-proof'.

However, as said before, there are many obstacles to the approval of RU 486. For example, a Hoechst-Singapore spokesman has said that RU 486 would not be marketed in Singapore. Reportedly, there has been pressure on the Health Ministry from two Catholic groups to prevent the introduction of the drug there; tests carried out on the product by WHO and the national university hospital have been terminated. It is obvious that conditions in Third World countries must change significantly before they can meet the requirements set by Roussel-Uclaf for a medically safe and socially-non-disturbing use of the drug.

9.3.4 The situation in the US

Across the Atlantic, the situation is very delicate. The issue of RU 486 has been politicized; it even ranks first in many political agendas. And Roussel-Uclaf is a pharmaceutical firm. It sees itself as a scientific and technical organization and does not want to get involved in the political debate on abortion. Sakiz says: 'We had nothing to do with this discussion. We never said we are for abortion or we'd spread out the compound . . . We said, instead of using aspiration, if the woman wants, she can take three tablets, that's all.' But since many Americans do not see it that way, the company has thought it prudent to adopt a wait-and-see attitude. However, it does not anticipate compliance with the 'social approval' requisite that it has set in order to sell RU 486.

In addition, Roussel-Uclaf does not have access to prostaglandins in the US. Sakiz considers that RU 486 will have to be made available separately, as will prostaglandins, and then the two will have to be brought together. This would be a lengthy process. To start with, neither Schering nor Ono, the producers of prostaglandins, want to provoke the anger of the American pro-life lobby; thus, they remain reluctant to export the product to the United States.

Meanwhile, Roussel-Uclaf is feeling the growing pressure of American public opinion. Press coverage has been extensive. (See, for example, an editorial note in *The Washington Post* (Exhibit 9.8) and a page-one article in *The New York Times* (Exhibit 9.9)). Also boycott threats persist: abortion foes have pledged to boycott all products of Hoechst if the drug is exported from France. Executives of Roussel-Uclaf received Dr Willke on March 13, 1989, i.e. a few months after the French Government ordered the laboratories to resume sales of the pill. He insisted on the withdrawal of the drug.

EXHIBIT 9.8

A28 Saturday, February 17, 1990, The Washington Post

The Washington Post
An Independent Newspaper

In July 1988, in response primarily to AIDS sufferers who wanted to use foreign drugs that had been approved for sale here, the Food and Drug Administration issued guidelines to clarify this government's policy on importing small amounts of unlicensed medicine. The rules allow patients to bring in or have mailed to them, a three-month supply of unapproved drugs so long as the drugs are for personal use under the care of a doctor and not for commercial distribution of any kind. But 11 months later, the FDA issued another ruling specifically barring under any circumstances import of the new French pill RU 486 on grounds that it 'could pose a risk to the safety of the user.' This looks to us a lot more like a political decision than a scientific one. RU 486 is used in combination with prostaglandin to terminate pregnancies of less than seven weeks' duration, without surgery. Last year it was safely employed in one out of three abortions in France.

In theory, the FDA policy means that an American woman who is able to obtain the medicine in France cannot either mail it home or carry it into the United States in her purse. It will be confiscated, and she will run the risk of civil penalties. In practice, it hasn't happened yet. But the action of the Reagan administration FDA is illustrative of the political climate on abortion that prevailed in this country only a year ago. All kinds of untested and possibly worthless substances can be imported in small amounts by patients. But a pill that is effective, relatively inexpensive and that has been successfully used by tens of thousands of women in France cannot. Antiabortion forces want to block any product that might make that procedure less difficult. In 1988 they pressured the French manufacturer to suspend distribution temporarily. Population experts believe that the political climate in this country has adversely affected the distribution and commercial development of the product worldwide.

Now that climate is changing. The Supreme Court's decision in the *Webster* case last July has thrown abortion into the political arena and exposed the weakness of the abortion opponents' forces. This week, the French manufacturers of RU 486, apparently less intimidated than they were a year ago by threats of an organized international boycott, announced plans to market the pill in Britain, Holland and Scandinavia. The drug's developer, Dr. Etienne-Emile Baulieu of the University of Paris, said he is 'reasonably optimistic' that it will soon be available in the United States.

Scientists here are satisfied that RU 486 is safe and effective, and since extensive testing has already been done, FDA approval shouldn't take long once application is made. Neither this government nor the French manufacturer should let political consideration delay that process.

EXHIBIT 9.9

ABORTION POLITICS ARE SAID TO HINDER USE OF FRENCH PILL

BACKLASH IN US FEARED

Chemist Who Developed Drug Criticizes Distributor and World Health Agency

PARIS, July 27 – The French developer of a pill that induces abortion has asserted that worldwide distribution of the drug is being blocked by fears of American reprisals against its manufacturer and the World Health Organization.

The pill's developer, Etienne-Emile Baulieu, a 64-year-old biochemist, said that almost two years after the drug, known as RU 486, was approved by the French Government, the manufacturer, Roussel Uclaf, had so far decided only to expand its marketing to Britain, despite its demand from other countries.

'Scandinavia and perhaps the Netherlands will be next,' said Arielle Moullet, head of international marketing at Roussel Uclaf, adding that the company had so far not responded to expressions of interest in the pill by China and the Soviet Union. 'This is a step-by-step approach.'

Shifts in U.S. policy

But Dr Baulieu, who is a consultant to Roussel Uclaf, says the company's cautious approach to marketing the pill is a result of its fear of a backlash in the United States against its majority shareholder, the West German pharmaceutical company Hoechst.

Dr Baulieu also criticized the company for passing responsibility for international approval of the pill to the World Health Organization, which he said has withheld approval out of anxiety that the United States may retaliate by cutting contributions to its budget.

Dr Baulieu is looking for possible shifts in United States policy as a result of the abortion debate stirred by a 1989 abortion ruling by the United States Supreme Court, the retirement of Justice William J. Brennan Jr. from the Court and President Bush's nomination of Judge David H. Souter as successor.

'An indecent obstacle'

'I believe the key to the future of RU 486 lies in the United States,' the scientist said in an interview. 'We can't tell third-world countries to go to the WHO because we know it is not ready. It's a major obstacle, an indecent obstacle.'

He said that because of its simplicity, he was convinced that RU 486 could have a dramatic effect in reducing the number of illegal abortions and related maternal deaths and injuries throughout the third world. 'How can we ignore that 500 women die every day as a result of badly executed abortions?' he said.

The chemical method involves taking 600 milligrams of RU 486, followed 48 hours later by an injection or suppository of the hormone prostaglandin, which enhances the pill's effect and reduces the risk of hemorrhaging.

RU 486 can be taken as soon as pregnancy is confirmed, but it is not prescribed on suspicion of pregnancy. It is not supposed to be used after the 47th day after the last menstrual period.

Defending Roussel Uclaf's policy, Ms Moullet said the company had signed an agreement with the WHO giving the international group the right to recommend the use of RU 486 in countries dominated by public health systems. 'We don't expect to distribute in, say, China unless the WHO approves,' she said.

But she said: 'Dr. Baulieu is a scientist and not an industrialist. Hoechst has interests in the United States and cannot do any old thing. It can't close its eyes to this reality.'

Hoechst, which owns 54.5 per cent of Roussel Uclaf, last year had sales totaling $6.4 billion in North America, mainly the United States.

U.S. abortion debate

Although some small American pharmaceutical companies have offered to market RU 486 in the United States, Roussel Uclaf has turned down their proposals, apparently out of fear that antiabortion groups might organize a boycott of Hoechst in the United States.

'Selling in the United States is out of the question at the moment,' Ms Moullet said.

The United States Government has taken no position on the abortion pill, although President Bush has spoken out frequently against abortion in recent years. So far he has also not reversed decisions by the Reagan Administration to cut off funds to international organizations that support abortion.

Ms Moullet said that under those circumstances, it is natural for the future of RU 486 to be overshadowed by the American debate.

Things are pretty calm now

'One consequence is that negotiations with other countries, like the Soviet Union, have been neglected,' she said.

Roussel Uclaf's sensitivity to public opinion was apparent a month after the pill's approval by the French Government in September 1988, when threats and demonstrations prompted it and Hoechst to suspend distribution of RU 486. Two days later, the Government, which owns 36.25 per cent of Roussel Uclaf, ordered it to resume distribution.

But today, Roussel Uclaf seems delighted with the drug's rapid acceptance in France, where protests by anti-abortion and church groups have subsided. Some 4,000 doses per month are now being sold to the country's 793 authorized abortion clinics. 'Things are pretty calm now,' Ms Moullet said.

She said that between April 1988 and September 1989, 20,000 women were given the pill free of charge under a carefully monitored program that showed a success record of over 90 per cent. Through February this year, when agreement was reached with the Government on a $48 price for each dose of RU 486, another 14,000 used the drug without charge.

'From a psychological point of view, women seem very happy with the method,' said Dr Elizabeth Aubeny, who runs an abortion clinic at the Brussels Hospital in Paris. 'They take the pill themselves, they have hospital supervision, but they are not subject to physical manipulation at the hands of strangers.'

In developing its international strategy, Roussel Uclaf has drawn up what it calls five 'mandatory prerequisites' before marketing is approved. Abortion must be legal in the country in question, local public, medical, and political opinion must favor abortion, synthetic prostaglandin must be available locally, the distribution network must be strictly controlled, and patients should sign a consent form.

Ms Moullet said the United States currently failed to meet two of those prerequisites.

'Abortion is not an unchallenged right and synthetic prostaglandin is not on the market in the United States,' she noted. Synthetic prostaglandin is currently being tested in Western Europe as an antidote to hemorrhaging and bleeding ulcers.

Dr Baulieu said his main concern was the third world, where he said nearly 200,000 women die annually as a result of complications after self-induced abortions.

Moral duty and the Third World

'My personal view is that it is our duty to move ahead promptly in the developing world, not immediately selling, but researching how we can introduce the compound, taking into account the different situations in each country and each region,' he said. 'At present, things are so bad in the third world that anything that improves the situation is welcome. I think it is our moral duty to act.'

But he acknowledged that such a campaign was unlikely until the United States changed its policy, recalling that the United States suspended its contributions to the International Planned Parenthood Federation and the United Nations Fund for Population Activities on the grounds that in some cases they financed abortion clinics.

He said that while the WHO's Human Reproduction Unit is currently engaged in trials of RU 486, its director, Hirochi Nagashima, was reluctant to sponsor the pill's distribution. 'The money will be cut off if an RU 486 program comes under the WHO umbrella,' Dr Baulieu said.

Yet he insisted that he was not without hope. 'Nagashima's predecessor, Halfan Mahler of Austria, was also slow in recognizing the problem,' he said. 'Now he is President of the International Planned Parenthood Federation.'

by Alan Riding
The New York Times
Sunday, July 29, 1990

On December 7, 1989, Dr. Willke addressed a long letter to Wolfgang Hilger explaining the position of the International Right to Life Federation. In that letter, Willke held both Hoechst AG and Roussel-Uclaf directly responsible for the use of RU 486 as an abortifacient. He stated that Hoechst had been sending contradictory signals. On the one hand, Hoechst had attempted to distance itself from the abortion pill. Willke reported that in February 1988, Dr.

Victor Bauer wrote to him to state that his company 'will not become involved in (the abortion pill's) development, nor do we have any interest or intention whatsoever in marketing this compound.' But on the other hand, Willke went on, Hoechst officials failed to take positive steps to prevent RU 486 from being put back onto the market and then later participated in setting Roussel-Uclaf's current policy on using the abortion pill. Also, neither Roussel-Uclaf nor Hoechst challenged the legality of the Minister of Health's interpretation of French law.

Next, Willke explained the reasons for withdrawing RU 486:

- Killing unborn babies is morally wrong and ethically indefensible. 'Never in modern times, has the state granted to one citizen the absolute legal right to have another killed in order to solve their own personal, social, or economic problems. And yet, abortion does all of those,' he said;
- The pill poses serious risks to women. Willke emphasized that the drug could be dangerous to Third World women who often suffered from anemia, malnutrition, and other health problems. 'It borders on medical malpractice to send this death pill into the underdeveloped world.'
- Risk of foetal deformity. Willke offered as evidence the text of the consent release form that women who take RU 486 sign: 'I have been clearly warned that the child and/or I may be susceptible to risks, notably malformation of the foetus or the child.'
- Risk of psychological harm to women. He quoted studies that had identified a pattern of psychological problems, known as 'Post Abortion Syndrome'. Next, he underscored that the long-term effects of RU 486 were completely unknown.

Finally, Willke threatened that right-to-life advocates could approach Hoechst Celanese's large customers and request that they turn to alternative sources for their materials. And, more precisely, he enumerated some of Hoechst's and Roussel's products that would be the target of a boycott, if the firms did not decide to withdraw the product from the market.

Pressure from the pro-choice side is also important. (See Exhibit 9.10, an example of a campaign letter by the Feminist Majority Foundation.) In July 1990, a delegation made up of scientists and representatives of women's organizations went to Roussel-Uclaf's Paris headquarters with 400 kilos of petitions asking the firm to accelerate the process of making the product widely available in the US. Also in July 1990, 70 members of the US Congress, most of them Democrats, sent an open letter to Roussel-Uclaf urging the firm to allow American women to have access to the abortive pill.

(Barbara Boxer, Democratic Representative from California, took the initiative.)

EXHIBIT 9.10

Campaign for RU 486 and contraceptive research

CAMPAIGN FOR RU 486 and CONTRACEPTIVE RESEARCH
Don't Let American Women be Deprived of RU 486!

The women of America have the right to RU 486. And I want to do my part to see that this simple, safe, effective medication is not kept out of our country because of the intimidating tactics of the anti-abortion forces.

To help reduce the 1.6 million surgical abortions performed in America each year . . . and to show my support for RU 486 and more contraceptive research, I will do my part to support this bold, new campaign.

> I am sending a tax-deductible contribution to be used to help circulate more Petitions and to educate and mobilize the public as part of the Feminist Majority's **CAMPAIGN FOR RU 486 AND CONTRACEPTIVE RESEARCH**. I am enclosing by tax-deductible contribution in the amount of:
> $25 $35 * $100 $250   Other $_____

*We need many checks this size to make sure we have the resources to circulate petitions across America.

Please make your checks payable to the Feminist Majority Foundation and return to P.O. Box 96780, Washington, D.C. 20077. (If you prefer to charge, please see below.)

I would like to charge my tax-deductible contribution . . .

Check one to charge your remittance: MasterCard   VISA

Credit Card No. _____

Bank No.: _____   Expires: _____   Signature: _____

I have signed my petition and am returning it for presentation – along with tens of thousands more – to the chief executive officers of the pharmaceutical companies to show that the voice of women and men who support abortion rights will rally to support their bringing RU 486 into the United States.

DO NOT DETACH YOUR PETITION

Return it along with the Reply Memo above and we will detach and present it to the appropriate officials.

PETITION FOR RU 486

To: Edouard Sakiz, Chmn   To: Wolfgang Hilger
        Roussel Uclaf   Hoechst, A.G.
        Paris, France   Frankfurt, West Germany

WHEREAS . . . Roussel Uclaf holds the patent on RU 486, the new, safe, effective medication which could prevent millions of surgical abortions, and

WHEREAS . . . Your firms have been subjected to a vicious campaign of intimidation and threats of economic reprisal if you try to bring RU 486 into the United States; and,

WHEREAS . . . The vast majority of Americans –millions and millions of women who will benefit from RU 486 –have been silent up until now;

THEREFORE . . . I want you to know that you have my full support and encouragement to bring RU 486 into the United States and that I will do everything I can to counter – with my own voice and that of my friends and associates – those who attempt to threaten your firms.

_____   _____
Signature   Name (please print)

_____   _____
Street Address   City, State, Zip

Speak Up for RU 486!
Don't Let Them Keep It Away from American Women
The Feminist Majority Foundation
P.O. Box 96780
Washington, D.C. 20077

However, those Americans who could accelerate the process have remained reluctant to do so. Hoechst-Roussel Products Incorporated has already made it clear that it will not take the initiative for marketing the pill. Likewise, no other large firm has approached Roussel to get marketing rights, i.e. no one has requested the Food and Drug Administration's (FDA) approval for RU 486, which would anyway take several years.

Nevertheless, the FDA has already started to consider the possibility of the introduction of RU 486 in the United States. On June 14, 1990, the FDA's Fertility and Maternal Health Drugs Advisory Committee considered a just-released Institute of Medicine/National Research Council report on the state of contraceptive development in the US. RU 486 received its own heading in a chapter of the report. 'The report predicts that the introduction of RU 486 in the US for any purpose 'would be difficult because of widespread concern among medical scientists and pharmaceutical company executives about a conservative backlash against them, including the risk of economic boycott of manufacturers and distributors.' The report adds that the 'lack of strong public support' in the US 'has added to this climate of uncertainty' and has resulted in a lack of research on such compounds.' (FDC Reports, February 19, 1990, pp. 4–6)

Certainly, it would be a high-risk strategy for any firm to face the rage – and boycotting power – of the US pro-life lobby. Some American observers have speculated that Roussel-Uclaf will eventually licence RU 486 to a new company, created with venture capital for the sole purpose of marketing the drug in the United States. Several candidates have come forward. A boycott threat would be powerless against a single-product company, and the firm's lack of economic strength would make it less vulnerable to lawsuits. Nonetheless, Joseph Spielder, President of the Population Crisis Committee (Washington, DC), considers it unrealistic to believe that lawsuits would not also target the deep pockets of the French firm or of the giant Hoechst. In any event, Dr Sakiz and other managers do not agree with the idea of going through intermediaries, and believe that when the time is right, Roussel itself should market the product. 'At Roussel-Uclaf, we have mixed feelings about RU 486; we are both ashamed and proud of it,' Madame Mouttet explained.

Another Roussel executive has expressed the additional concern that the firm was caught in a dilemma with respect to liability risks. Liability suits, he said, could come from any side; they are not only a threat if the firm starts to market RU 486 in the United States. The most obvious tort suits could arrive if women fail to complete their treatment and babies are born with defects. On the other hand, if the firm does not make the pill available in the US, American lawyers may blame Roussel for not having done enough to avoid preventable injury or even death.

9.3.5 The future of RU 486

Step by step, RU 486 will probably make its way into Western Europe. The Western European market is limited, however, and, as pointed out previously, conditions in Eastern Europe and in the Third World are far from adequate for the safe use of the product. 'RU 486 is not an aspirin,' Madame Mouttet said. 'And our responsibility does not end with specifying its correct use. We will not let the product go where there will not be absolute control of its utilization.' With respect to the US, Roussel-Uclaf believes that Americans have to solve their internal disagreements; the laboratories will not get involved in America's political quarrels.

The future of RU 486, some believe, lies in its other uses. The drug has proved to be beneficial in therapeutic abortions, i.e., later in pregnancy, up to the third term, when a pregnancy must be ended because the foetus is significantly malformed or the health of the mother is at risk; it can also help to facilitate the expulsion of a foetus which has died in the uterus, and for the dilatation of the uterus neck in normal deliveries. The laboratories are ready to develop the product for these purposes.

Studies have further shown the beneficial effects of RU 486 in inducing labour at term, which may help to avoid some Cesarean deliveries; there is also some evidence that the drug can help to trigger lactation and to increase the volume of milk produced by the mother. However, Roussel-Uclaf has to await further trials before recommending the utilization of RU 486 for the last two purposes.

Finally, test-tube studies and clinical trials have indicated uses for RU 486 in fields other than reproduction. These include the treatment of breast cancer (cancers that bear progesterone receptors) and as a treatment for Cushing's syndrome (because of its function as a glucocorticoid antagonist).

However, it is not yet clear whether Roussel will be able to keep a tight control over the drug if its uses multiply. Neither does anyone know whether a 'stained' drug such as RU 486, already synonymous with abortifacient, will ever be accepted by all those who oppose it today, no matter how effective it might prove for other purposes.

10 *Starnes-Brenner Machine Tool Company – to bribe or not to bribe**

The Starnes-Brenner Machine Tool Company of Iowa City, Iowa, has a small one-man sales office headed by Frank Rothe in Latino, a major Latin-American country. Frank has been in Latino for about 10 years and is retiring this year; his replacement is Bill Hunsaker, one of Starnes-Brenner's top salesmen. Both will be in Latino for about eight months, during which time Frank will show Bill the ropes, introduce him to their principal customers, and, in general, prepare him to take over.

Frank has been very successful as a foreign representative in spite of his unique style and, at times, complete refusal to follow company policy when it doesn't suit him. The company hasn't really done much about his method of operation, although from time to time he has angered some top company men. As President McCaughey, who retired a couple of years ago, once remarked to a vice president who was complaining about Frank, 'If he's making money – and he is (more than any of the other foreign offices) – then leave the guy alone.' When McCaughey retired, the new chief immediately instituted organizational changes that gave more emphasis to the overseas operations, moving the company toward a truly world-wide operation into which a loner like Frank would probably not fit. In fact, one of the key reasons for selecting Bill as Frank's replacement, besides Bill's record as a top salesman, is Bill's capacity as an organization man. He understands the need for co-ordination among operations and will co-operate with the home office so the Latino office can be expanded and brought into the mainstream.

The company knows there is much to be learned from Frank, and Bill's job is to learn everything possible. The company certainly doesn't want to continue some of Frank's practices, but much of his knowledge is vital for continued, smooth operation. Today Starnes-Brenner's foreign sales account for about 25 per cent of the

* In Cateora, R. Philip (1993) *International Marketing*, Homewood, Illinois: Richard D. Irvin, pp. 666–669.

company's total profits, compared with about 5 per cent only 10 years ago.

The company is actually changing character, from being principally an exporter, without any real concern for continuous foreign market representation, to world-wide operations, where the foreign divisions are part of the total effort rather than a stepchild operation. In fact, Latino is one of the last operational divisions to be assimilated into the new organization. Rather than try to change Frank, the company has been waiting for him to retire before making any significant adjustments in their Latino operations.

Bill Hunsaker is 36 years old, with a wife and three children; he is a very good salesman and administrator, although he has had no foreign experience. He has the reputation of being fair, honest, and a straight shooter. Some, back at the home office, see his assignment as part of a grooming job for a top position, perhaps eventually the presidency. The Hunsakers are now settled in their new home after having been in Latino for about two weeks. Today is Bill's first day on the job.

When Bill arrived at the office, Frank was on his way to a local factory to inspect some Starnes-Brenner machines that had to have some adjustments made before being acceptable to the Latino government agency buying them. Bill joined Frank for the plant visit. Later, after the visit, we join the two at lunch.

Bill, tasting some chilli, remarks, 'Boy! This certainly isn't like the chilli we have in America.'

'No, it isn't, and there's another difference, too . . . the Latinos are Americans and nothing angers a Latino more than to have a "Gringo" refer to the United States as America as if to say that Latino isn't part of America also. The Latinos rightly consider their country as part of America (take a look at the map) and people from the United States are North Americans at best. So, for future reference, refer to home either as the United States, States, or North America, but, for gosh sakes, not just America. Not to change the subject, Bill, but could you see that any change had been made in those S-27s from the standard model?'

'No, they looked like the standard. Was there something out of whack when they arrived?'

'No, I couldn't see any problem – I suspect this is the best piece of sophisticated bribe-taking I've come across yet. Most of the time the Latinos are more "honest" about their *mordidas* than this.'

'What's a *mordida*?' Bill asks.

'You know, *kumshaw*, *dash*, *bustarella*, *mordida*; they are all the same: a little grease to expedite the action. *Mordida* is the local word for a slight offering or, if you prefer, bribe,' says Frank.

Bill quizzically responds, 'Do we pay bribes to get sales?'

'Oh, it depends on the situation but it's certainly something you have to be prepared to deal with.' 'Boy, what a greenhorn,' Frank thinks to himself, as he continues, 'Here's the story. When the S-27s arrived last January, we began uncrating them and right away the *jefe* engineer (a government official) – *jefe*, that's the head man in charge – began extra-careful examination and declared there was a vital defect in the machines; he claimed the machinery would be dangerous and thus unacceptable if it wasn't corrected. I looked it over but couldn't see anything wrong, so I agreed to have our staff engineer check all the machines and correct any flaws that might exist. Well, the *jefe* said there wasn't enough time to wait for an engineer to come from the States, that the machines could be adjusted locally, and we could pay him and he would make all the necessary arrangements. So, what do you do? No adjustment his way and there would be an order cancelled; and, maybe there was something out of line, those things have been known to happen. But for the life of me, I can't see that anything had been done since the machines were supposedly fixed. So, let's face it, we just paid a bribe, and a pretty darn big bribe at that – about $1,200 per machine. What makes it so aggravating is that that's the second one I've had to pay on this shipment.'

'The second?' asks Bill.

'Yeah, at the border, when we were transferring the machines to Latino trucks, it was hot and they were moving slow as molasses. It took them over an hour to transfer one machine to a Latino truck and we had 10 others to go. It seemed that every time I spoke to the dock boss about speeding things up, they just got slower. Finally, out of desperation. I slipped him a fistful of pesos and, sure enough, in the next three hours they had the whole thing loaded. Just one of the local customs of doing business. Generally, though, it comes at the lower level where wages don't cover living expenses too well.'

There is a pause and Bill asks, 'What does that do to our profits?'

'Runs them down, of course, but I look at it as just one of the many costs of doing business – I do my best not to pay, but when I have to, I do.'

Hesitantly, Bill replies, 'I don't like it, Frank, we've got good products, they're priced right, we give good service, and keep plenty of spare parts in the country, so why should we have to pay bribes? It's just no way to do business. You've already had to pay two bribes on one shipment: if you keep it up, the word's going to get around and you'll be paying at every level. Then all the profit goes out the window – you know, once you start, where do you stop? Besides that, where do we stand legally? The Foreign Bribery Act makes paying bribes like you've just paid illegal. I'd say the best policy is to never start; you might lose a few sales but let it be known that there are no bribes; we sell the best, service the best at fair prices, and that's all.'

'You mean the Foreign Corrupt Practices Act, don't you?' Frank asks, and continues, in an 'I'm-not-really-so-out-of-touch' tone of voice, 'Haven't some of the provisions of the Foreign Corrupt Practices Act been softened, somewhat?'

'Yes, you're right, the provisions on paying a *mordida* or grease have been softened, but paying the government official is still illegal, softening or not,' replies Bill.

'Oh boy!' Frank thinks to himself as he replies, 'Look, what I did was just peanuts as far as the Foreign Corrupt Practices Act goes. The people we pay off are small, and, granted we give good service, but we've only been doing it for the last year or so. Before that, I never knew when I was going to have equipment to sell. In fact, we only had products when there were surpluses stateside. I had to pay the right people to get sales, and besides, you're not back in the States any longer. Things are just done different here. You follow that policy and I guarantee that you'll have fewer sales because our competitors from Germany, Italy, and Japan will pay. Look, Bill, everybody does it here; it's a way of life and the costs are generally reflected in the markup and overhead. There is even a code of behaviour involved. We're not actually encouraging it to spread, just perpetuating an accepted way of doing business.'

Patiently and slightly condescendingly, Bill replies, 'I know, Frank, but wrong is wrong and we want to operate differently now. We hope to set up an operation here on a continuous basis: we plan to operate in Latino just like we do in the United States. Really expand our operation and make a long-range market commitment, grow with the country! And one of the first things we must avoid is unethical . . .'

Frank interrupts, 'But really, is it unethical? Everybody does it, the Latinos even pay *mordidas* to other Latinos; it's a fact of life – is it really unethical? I think that the circumstances that exist in a country justify and dictate the behaviour. Remember man, "When in Rome, do as the Romans do."'

Almost shouting, Bill blurts out, 'I can't buy that. We know that our management practices and techniques are our strongest point. Really all we have to differentiate us from the rest of our competition, Latino and others, is that we are better managed and, as far as I'm concerned, graft and other unethical behaviour have got to be cut out to create a healthy industry. In the long run, it should strengthen our position. We can't build our futures on illegal and unethical practices.'

Frank angrily replies, 'Look, it's done in the States all the time. What about the big dinners, drinks, and all the other hanky-panky that goes on? Not to mention PACs' (Political Action Committee) payments to congressmen, and all those high speaking fees certain congressmen get from special interests. How many congressmen have gone to jail or lost reelection on those kinds of things? What is that, if it isn't *mordida*, the North American way? The only difference is that instead of cash only, in the United States we pay in merchandise and cash.'

'That's really not the same and you know it. Besides, we certainly get a lot of business transacted during those dinners even if we are paying the bill.'

'Bull, the only difference is that here bribes go on in the open; they don't hide it or dress it in foolish ritual that fools no one. It goes on in the United States and everyone denies the existence of it. That's all the difference – in the United States we're just more hypocritical about it all.'

'Look,' Frank continues almost shouting, 'we are getting off on the wrong foot and we've got eight months to work together. Just keep your eyes and mind open and let's talk about it again in a couple of months when you've seen how the whole country operates: perhaps then you won't be so quick to judge it absolutely wrong.'

Frank, lowering his voice, says thoughtfully, 'I know it's hard to take; probably the most disturbing problem in underdeveloped countries is the matter of graft. And, frankly, we don't do much advance preparation so we can deal firmly with it. It bothered me at first; but then I figured it makes its economic contribution, too, since the payoff is as much a part of the economic process as a payroll. What's our real economic role, anyway, besides making a profit, of course? Are we developers of wealth, helping to push the country to greater economic growth, or are we missionaries? Or should we be both? I really don't know, but I don't think we can be both simultaneously, and my feeling is that, as the company prospers, as higher salaries are paid, and better standards of living are reached, we'll see better ethics. Until then, we've got to operate or leave, and if you are going to win the opposition over, you'd better join them and change them from within, not fight them.'

Before Bill could reply, a Latino friend of Frank's joined them and they changed the topic of conversation.

10.1 QUESTIONS

1 Is what Frank did ethical? Whose ethics? Latino's or the United States'?

2 Are Frank's two different payments legal under the Foreign Corrupt Practices Act as amended by the Omnibus Trade and Competitiveness Act of 1988?

3 Identify the types of payments made in the case; that is, are they lubrication, extortion, or subornation?

4 Frank seemed to imply that there is a similarity between what he was doing and what happens in the United States. Is there any difference? Explain.

5   Are there any legal differences between the money paid to the dock workers and the money paid the *jefe* (government official)? Any ethical differences?

6   Frank's attitude seems to imply that a foreigner must comply with all local customs, but some would say that one of the contributions made by US firms is to change local ways of doing business. Who is right?

7   Should Frank's behaviour have been any different had this not been a government contract?

8   If Frank shouldn't have paid the bribe, what should he have done, and what might have been the consequences?

9   What are the company interests in this problem?

10 Explain how this may be a good example of the SRC (self-reference criterion) at work.

11 Do you think Bill will make the grade in Latino? Why? What will it take?

12 How can an overseas manager be prepared to face this problem?

11 *Levi Strauss & Co.: global sourcing**

Levi Strauss & Co. has a heritage of conducting business in a manner that reflects its values. As we expand our sourcing base to more diverse cultures and countries, we must take special care in selecting business partners and countries whose practices are not incompatible with our values. Otherwise, our sourcing decisions have the potential of undermining this heritage, damaging the image of our brands and threatening our commercial success.

> Levi Strauss & Co.
> *Business Partner Terms*
> *of Engagement and*
> *Guidelines for Country*
> *Selection*

'If we really are an aspirational company, shouldn't we be in there trying to make a difference?' asked one member of the China Policy Group at Levi Strauss & Co. (LS&Co.), the world's largest brand-name apparel manufacturer. Another responded, 'We've got to be careful not to get into the wrong bed – we don't want to wake up with the fleas. There are some things we just can't be associated with – and still maintain our reputation.'

The China Policy Group (CPG) had been chartered in late 1992 by CEO Robert D. Haas and Vice President of Global Sourcing Peter A.

* Research Associate Jane Palley Katz prepared this case under the supervision of Professor Lynn Sharp Paine as the basis for class discussion rather than to illustrate either effective or ineffective handling of an administrative situation.

Jacobi specifically to consider whether LS&Co. should continue sourcing and purchasing fabric in China and whether it should make direct investments in marketing and manufacturing ventures there. The CPG had been asked to use the 'principled reasoning approach' to make a recommendation based on the company's ethical values and global sourcing guidelines. Announced in March 1992, these guidelines were part of a comprehensive set of sourcing standards widely acknowledged to be among the most far-reaching of any adopted by a US company (*The Economist* 1992). (See Exhibits 11.1 and 11.2.) The CPG would report its recommendation to the nine-member Executive Management Committee, LS&Co.'s most senior decision-making group, early in 1990.

EXHIBIT 11.1

Levi Strauss & Co., Global sourcing guidelines, business partner terms of engagement

Our concerns include the practices of individual business partners as well as the political and social issues in those countries where we might consider sourcing.

This defines Terms of Engagement which addresses issues that are substantially controllable by our individual business partners.

We have defined business partners as contractors and suppliers who provide labour and/or material (including fabric, sundries, chemicals and/or stones) utilized in the manufacture and finishing of our products.

1 **Environmental Requirements**
   We will only do business with partners who share our commitment to the environment. (Note: We intend this standard to be consistent with the approved language of Levi Strauss & Co.'s Environmental Action Group.)
2 **Ethical Standards**
   We will seek to identify and utilize business partners who aspire as individuals and in the conduct of their business to a set of ethical standards not incompatible with our own.
3 **Health & Safety**
   We will seek to identify and utilize business partners who provide workers with a safe and healthy work environment. Business partners who provide residential facilities for their workers must provide safe and healthy facilities.

4 **Legal Requirements**

We expect our business partners to be law abiding as individuals and to comply with legal requirements relevant to the conduct of their business.

5 **Employment Standards**

We will only do business with partners whose workers are in all cases present voluntarily, not put at risk of physical harm, fairly compensated, allowed the right of free association and not exploited in any way. In addition, the following specific guidelines will be followed.

■ **Wages and Benefits**

We will only do business with partners who provide wages and benefits that comply with any applicable law or match the prevailing local manufacturing or finishing industry practices. We will also favour business partners who share our commitment to contribute to the betterment of community conditions.

■ **Working Hours**

While permitting flexibility in scheduling, we will identify prevailing local work hours and seek business partners who do not exceed them except for appropriately compensated overtime. While we favour partners who utilize less than sixty-hour work weeks, we will not use contractors who, on a regularly scheduled basis, require in excess of a sixty-hour week. Employees should be allowed one day off in seven days.

■ **Child Labor**

Use of child labour is not permissible. 'Child' is defined as less than 14 years of age or younger than the compulsory age to be in school. We will not utilize partners who use child labour in any of their facilities. We support the development of legitimate workplace apprenticeship programmes for the educational benefit of younger people.

■ **Prison Labor/Forced Labor**

We will not knowingly utilize prison or forced labour in contracting or subcontracting relationships in the manufacture of our products. We will not knowingly utilize or purchase materials from a business partner utilizing prison or forced labour.

■ **Discrimination**

While we recognize and respect cultural differences, we believe that workers should be employed on the basis of their ability to do the job, rather than on the basis of personal characteristics or beliefs. We will favour business partners who share this value.

■ **Disciplinary Practices**
We will not utilize business partners who use corporal pun-
ishment or other forms of mental or physical coercion.
Source: Company document.

EXHIBIT 11.2

Levi Strauss & Co., global sourcing guidelines,
guidelines for country selection

The following country selection criteria address issues which
we believe are beyond the ability of individual business partners to control.

1 **Brand Image**
We will not initiate or renew contractual relationships in
countries where sourcing would have an adverse effect on
our global brand image.
2 **Health & Safety**
We will not initiate or renew contractual relationships in
locations where there is evidence that Company employees
or representatives would be exposed to unreasonable risk.
3 **Human Rights**
We should not initiate or renew contractual relationships in
countries where there are pervasive violations of basic
human rights.
4 **Legal Requirements**
We will not initiate or renew contractual relationships in
countries where the legal environment creates unreasonable
risk to our trademarks or to other important commercial
interests or seriously impedes our ability to implement these
guidelines.
5 **Political or Social Stability**
We will not initiate or renew contractual relationships in
countries where political or social turmoil unreasonably
threatens our commercial interests.
Source: Company document.

The CPG's leaders – Pete Jacobi, Lindsay Webbe, president of the
Asia Pacific Division; and Robert Dunn, vice president of Corporate
Affairs – had carefully identified and recruited nine others to join the
group. They sought individuals with relevant knowledge and a range
of perspectives informed by differences in experience, functional

area, race, and gender.[1] Elissa Sheridan, a specialist on loan from Corporate Affairs, prepared voluminous background reports to aid the discussion. Once formed, the CPG reviewed its membership, studied the background materials, and identified additional information needed for its work. The group also decided to try for a consensus recommendation while reserving to anyone who disagreed the right to submit a minority opinion.

11.1 COMPANY BACKGROUND

LS&Co. traced its roots to the 1850s, when a Bavarian-born immigrant, Levi Strauss, came to San Francisco from New York and joined his brother-in-law's dry goods business. The company achieved early success producing and selling sturdy canvas trousers, the first jeans, to the many miners who arrived during the gold rush. In 1873, Strauss adopted the idea, from a Nevada tailor, to rivet the pockets for added strength. The double-arcuate pattern sewn on the hip pockets, the oldest apparel trademark in the United States, was added the same year. By the last half of the twentieth century, 'Levi's®' had become synonymous with 'jeans,' while the spread of American popular culture – movies, television, and music – made the company's clothes a symbol of American values, sought after across the globe. Explained the vice president for Corporate Marketing, Levi's® jeans epitomized 'freedom, originality, youthfulness and the spirit of America' in markets world-wide (Janofsky 1994). They were even included in the Smithsonian Institute's permanent collection of the Smithsonian Institute, a museum of US history and culture located in Washington, DC.

For the first 100 years of its history, LS&Co. was a private company. Family members owned nearly all of its stock, with employees holding most of the remaining shares. In 1971, needing funds for expansion, the company went public, although the Haas family retained a significant amount of the stock, with some of its members opposing the move (HBO Case: 5).

During the early 1980s, in response to a decline in the US jeans market and a larger decline globally, LS&Co. closed 58 plants and laid off more than a third of its work force. In 1984, Robert D. Haas, the great-great-grandnephew of founder Levi Strauss, became president and chief executive officer, following in the footsteps of both his uncle, Peter Haas, and his father, Walter Haas Jr, who had previously served as president and chairman of the board, respectively, and as board members in 1993. In 1985, under Robert Haas's leadership, certain descendants of Levi Strauss's family repurchased publicly held shares for $50 a share a 42 per cent premium over the market price – or a total cost of $1.6 billion, at that time the biggest leveraged buyout in history (ibid.). In 1993, 95% of the company's stock was held by descendants of Levi Strauss and by certain non-family members of management. The remainder was held by the company's employee investment plans.

As the apparel industry became more competitive, with faster style changes and fewer, though larger, retail customers, LS&Co. reconceived itself from a manufacturer to a marketer. The company reorganized at the end of 1988, reducing layers of management and consolidating personnel, finance, and operations to advance its strategy of providing better and faster service to retail customers. Robert Haas became chairman of the board in 1989.

11.2   THE BUSINESS IN 1993

For 1992, LS&Co. recorded net earnings of $360 million on revenues of $5.6 billion, marking the sixth consecutive year of increased sales and earnings. (See Tables 11.1 and 11.2 for selected data on financial performance.) The company marketed products with the Levi's® brand name in more than 60 countries, using a variety of arrangements, including wholly owned and operated businesses, joint ventures, licensees, and distubutors. Production and distribution facilities were located in more than 20 countries. LS&Co. employed 25,000 people in the United States and 9,000 people overseas. About half of its hourly work force was represented by the Amalgamated Clothing and Textile Workers Union (ACTWU) and the International Ladies Garment Workers Union (ILGWU) (Swoboda 1992).

One estimate put the value of LS&Co., if publicly traded, at $55 billion (How 1993). When asked about the possibility of going public again, Tom Tusher, president and chief operating officer, replied, 'We have no reason to go public. Being private helps us focus on long-term strategies. We don't have to worry about quarter-to-quarter results all the time. And we can take more risks.' (Power 1992)

LS&Co. officials attributed the company's success of the late 1980s and early 1990s, in part, 'to sales of jeans and related products outside the United States, principally in Europe and the Asia-Pacific region' (*San Francisco Business Times* 1992). International sales had become a significant element of the business, accounting, in 1992, for 37 per cent of total revenues and 53 per cent of pretax profits. (See Table 11.3 for data on world-wide operations.) The company credited higher foreign profit margins to foreign consumers' willingness to pay for the perceived high quality of Levi's® clothing (Eckhouse 1993). Overseas, a pair of jeans sold for up to $60 to $100 – more than twice the average price in the United States. In some areas, a legal 'grey market' surfaced in which jeans were bought in bulk off the shelves of US retail stores, shipped to foreign countries, and sold in unauthorized outlets at cut-rate prices. The company estimated that the grey market cost it millions of dollars in sales each year and

Table 11.1 Levi Strauss Associates Inc. and subsidiaries, consolidated statements of income 1990–92 (dollars in thousands, except per-share data)

	Year Ended November 29, 1992[a]	*Year Ended November 24, 1991[a]*	*Year Ended November 25, 1990[a]*
Net sales	$5,570,290	$4,902,882	$4,247,150
Cost of goods sold	3,431,469	3,024,330	2,651,338
Gross profit	2,138,821	1,878,552	1,595,812
Marketing, general and administrative expenses	1,322,079	1,148,129	985,361
Stock option charge	157,964	–	–
Operating income	658,778	730,423	610,451
Interest expense	53,303	71,384	82,956
Other income, net	28,646	32,314	26,173
Income before taxes and extraordinary loss	634,121	691,353	553,668
Provision for taxes	271,673	324,812	288,753
Income before extraordinary loss	362,448	366,541	264,915
Extraordinary loss: Loss from early extinguishment of debt, net of applicable Income tax benefits[b]	(1,611)	(9,875)	(13,746)
Net Income	360,837	356,666	251,169
Dividends on preferred stock	1,895	11,570	7,899
Net income available for common stockholders	$358,942	$345,096	$243,270
Income per common share: Income before extraordinary loss	$6.94	$6.44	$4.28
Extraordinary loss	(.03)	(.18)	(.23)
Net income	$6.91	$6.26	$4.05
Average common shares outstanding	51,928,655	55,136,212	60,129,546

Source: LS&Co. Strauss Associates Inc., Form 10-K/A Amendment No. 1, July 30 1993.

[a] Fiscal year 1992 contained 53 weeks. Fiscal years 1991 and 1990 each contained 52 weeks. (see Note A on Table 11.2.)

[b] Applicable income tax benefits for fiscal years 1992, 1991, and 1990 are $947, $5,799, and $8,073, respectively.

Table 11.2 Levi Strauss Associates Inc., selected balance sheet data 1988–92

| | The Company Fiscal Year[a] | | | | |
	1992	1991	1990	1989	1988
	(Dollars in millions, except per-share data)				
Total assets	$2,880.7	$2,633.4	$2,389.9	$2,020.0	$1,933.4
Long-term debt and capital lease obligations	262.0	432.7	158.7	406.8	528.0
Redeemable Series A preferred stock	–	82.0	81.9	81.9	92.4
Employee Stock Purchase and Award Plan common stock	16.4	–	–	–	–
Stockholders' equity	768.2	558.3	641.3	394.5	333.3

Source: LS&Co. Strauss Associates Inc., Form 10–K/A Amendment No. 1, July 30 1993.

[a] Fiscal year 1992 contained 53 weeks and ended on November 29, 1992. Fiscal years 1991,1990,1989 and 1988 each contained 52 weeks and ended on November 24, 1991, November 25. 1990, November 26, 1989, and November 27, 1988, respectively.

damaged the image of its product. Noted a spokesperson for LS&Co., 'Our jeans are a premium product – and this damages their reputation and consumer confidence' (Davidson 1993).[2]

To protect its brand name, the company registered its trademark, Levi's®, in more than 150 countries, calling it 'the most recognized apparel brand and one of the most famous consumer brand names in the world.' (Levi Strauss & Co 1993) One study valued the Levi's® brand at $4.811 billion, the top apparel brand measured (the study also valued the Nike brand (sneakers) at $2.32 billion (*Financial World* 1993). Levi's® was the market leader in every country where the company sold jeans.

In general, LS&Co. manufactured goods in the countries or regions where they would be sold (Levi Strauss & Co. 1993). Throughout much of its history, almost all manufacturing occurred in its own facilities or through a small number of contractors in the United States. However, like most US apparel manufacturers, LS&Co. had moved an increased portion of its production to contract-manufacturers, many of them offshore, to cut costs (Kehoe 1993). (See Table 11.4 for a comparison of labour costs and hours in selected countries.) By 1993, contractor sourcing around the world accounted for about half the company's global production. Company officials estimated that 45 per cent of the LS&Co. apparel sold in the United States was made overseas, with 40 per cent coming from contractors in Asia, and 60 per cent from Central America, South

Table 11.3 Levi Strauss Associates Inc., US and non-US operations 1990–92 ($000s)

The following table presents information concerning US and non-US operations (all in the apparel industry).

	1992	*1991*	*1990*
Net sales to unaffiliated customers:			
United States	$3,482,927	$2,997,144	$2,560,662
Europe	1,367,783	1,209,428	1,032,404
Other non-US	719,580	696,310	654,084
	$5,570,290	$4,902,882	$4,247,150
Sales between operations:			
United States	$139,652	$111,742	$121,134
Europe	28	67	383
Other non-US	34,467	9,842	7,238
	$174,147	$121,651	$128,755
Total sales:			
United States	$3,622,579	$3,108,886	$2,681,796
Europe	1,367,811	1,209,495	1,032,787
Other non-US	754,047	706,152	661,322
Eliminations	(174,147)	(121,651)	(128,755)
	$5,570,290	$4,902,882	$4,247,150
Contribution to income before other charges			
United States	$460,218	$390,468	$312,697
Europe	362,174	334,220	255,954
Other non-US	151,644	137,359	136,468
	$974,036	$862,047	$745,119
Other charges:			
Corporate expenses, net	$128,648	$99,310	$108,495
Interest expense	53,303	71,384	82,956
Stock option charge	157,964	–	–
Income before taxes and extraordinary loss:	$634,121	$691,353	$553,668
Assets:			
United States	$1,480,527	$1,346,033	$1,251,537
Europe	491,491	400,197	376,780
Other non-US	273,355	317,284	272,549
Corporate	635,328	569,870	488,991
	$2,880,701	$2,633,384	$2,389,857

Source: Levi Strauss Associates Inc., Form 10–K/A Amendment No. 1, July 30, 1993.

Gains or losses resulting from certain foreign-currency hedge transactions are included in other expenses, net, and amounted to losses of $10.2 million. $19.7 million. and $18.3 million for 1992, 1991, and 1990, respectively.

Table 11.4 Labour costs and operator hours, production workers in the textile and apparel industries – selected countries 1993

Country	Hourly Labour Cost Textile (in US$)	Hourly Labour Cost Apparel (in US$)	Normal Equivalent Days Worked Textile (per operator per year)
North America			
United States	11.61	8.13	241
Canada	13.44	9.14	237
Mexico	2.93	1.08	285
European Community			
Denmark	21.32	17.29	226
France	16.49	14.84	233
East Germany[a]	14.17	11.90	231
West Germany[a]	20.50	17.22	232
Greece	7.13	5.85	231
Holland	20.82	15.41	207
Ireland	9.18	7.44	243
Portugal	3.70	3.03	246
United Kingdom	10.27	8.42	234
Other European Countries			
Austria	18.81	14.30	231
Czech Republic	1.43	1.25	223
Finland	11.86	9.25	236
Hungary	1.80	1.62	233
Slovakia	1.29	1.14	230
Switzerland	22.32	18.08	227
Near East			
Israel	7.20	6.54	244
Syria	1.12	0.84	275
Turkey	4.44	3.29	300
Africa			
Egypt	0.57	0.43	288
Mauritius	1.42	1.04	285
South Africa	1.64	1.12	302
Tanzania	0.22	0.18	239
Tunisia	2.97	1.54	232
Zambia	0.32	0.24	249
Zimbabwe	0.47	0.35	273
South America			
Argentina	2.47	1.85	268
Brazil	1.46	0.73	274
Peru	1.43	1.00	276
Uruguay	3.09	2.35	288
Venezuela	1.90	1.48	245
Asia and Pacific			
Australia	10.84	8.67	229
Bangladesh	0.23	0.16	250
Peoples Republic of China	0.36	0.25	306
Hong Kong	3.85	3.85	254
India	0.56	0.27	285
Indonesia	0.43	0.28	257
Japan	23.65	10.64	261
South Korea	3.66	2.71	312
Malaysia	1.18	0.77	261
Pakistan	0.44	0.27	310
Philippines	0.78	0.53	288
Singapore	3.56	3.06	284
Taiwan	5.76	4.61	251
Thailand	1.04	0.71	341
Vietnam	0.37	0.26	287

Source: Complied by casewriter based on data from Werner International Management Consultants, New York, New York.

[a] Designations East and West are used for economic purposes only.

America, and Mexico. Efforts were under way to consolidate and secure relationships with lone-term contractors world-wide.

The loss of domestic jobs in the apparel industry was an ongoing concern for both labour unions and the consuming and voting public. An official from the ILGWU estimated that, in 1992, the apparel industry employed 816,000 production workers, down from 1,079,000 in 1980 and substantially lower than the industry's largest workforce of 1,257,400, in 1973. The unemployment rate in the industry hovered around 11 per cent, about twice as high as for the nation as a whole.[3]

When in early 1990 LS&Co. closed a 1,115-employee plant in San Antonio, Texas, and moved production to contractors in Costa Rica, it gave 90 days' notice, continued employee medical insurance, contributed $100,000 to local agencies, and gave $340,000 to the city of San Antonio to fund additional services and retraining programmes for laid-off workers (Levering and Moskowitz 1993). Instead of praise for its handling of the situation, LS&Co. faced harsh public criticism, a class-action lawsuit, a boycott of its products, substantial bad publicity, and even a small demonstration in front of its San Francisco offices. Judy Belk, vice president of Community Affairs, remarked on the San Antonio experience, 'We were honest about what we were doing – work was going to be taken offshore – and we exceeded all the legal requirements in terms of severance. But the employees who were impacted did not think we were ethical in our attempts to make them whole.'

In 1993, achieving pre-eminent customer service was a top priority at LS&Co. Management knew that continuing success would require ongoing development of new products and improved processes for getting goods into retail outlets. Based on intensive research begun in 1991, the company was re-engineering the entire customer service supply chain, from the generation of new product ideas to the moment of purchase.

11.3 COMPANY PHILOSOPHY

LS&Co. was known for its longstanding commitment to employees and the communities where they lived and worked. The company's founder had served as a board member of the California School of the Deaf and established 28 scholarships at the University of California; after his death, the tradition of corporate citizenship continued. Following the great San Francisco earthquake and fire of 1906, LS&Co. continued to pay its employees, even though there was no work for some of them for six months. During the Great Depression, it kept its workers on the payroll to install hardwood floors. The company desegregated its plants in the southern United States 'before law or practice compelled them to do so' (HBO case: 7). In the 1970s, it set up the Community Affairs Department, which staffed the Levi Strauss Foundation and granted millions of dollars in its focus areas of AIDS, economic development, and social justice to institutions and groups in the communities it served (ibid: 6).

As LS&Co. contracted out more of its manufacturing, it also expanded its community affairs activities, recognizing that the new production arrangements did not extinguish its social responsibilities. In 1993, for example, it donated $127,000 toward maternal and child health care in Bangladesh, a valuable source of contract labour. The company received praise from the Amalgamated Clothing and Textile Workers Union, which represented its workers: 'In an industry noted for sweatshops and abuses of workers' rights, LS&Co. has earned a reputation as a good employer in the United States. Its labour relations are among "the best in the country"' (Kehoe 1993: 9).

Until the late 1980s, LS&Co. managers had viewed the company's community and employee responsibilities 'as something separate from how we ran the business.' Noted Robert Hass, 'We always talked about the "hard stuff" and the "soft stuff". The soft stuff was the company's commitment to our work force. And the hard stuff was what really mattered getting the pants out the door' (Howard 1990). That view changed as the business environment of the 1980s changed. Increasing competition, new technology, corporate restructurings, the globalization of enterprises, greater consumer choice, and a new generation entering the work force led Haas and other LS&Co. managers to conclude that the 'hard stuff and the soft stuff [were] becoming increasingly intertwined' (ibid: 134). Haas saw values as the link (ibid: 138). He explained:

> In a more volatile and dynamic business environment, the controls have to be conceptual. They can't be human anymore: Bob Haas telling people what to do. It's the ideas of a business that are controlling, not some manager with authority. Values provide a common language for aligning a company's leadership and its people.
>
> (ibid: 134)

LS&Co.'s top managers were convinced that values-based companies that honoured their social responsibilities would ultimately achieve greater competitive success. Believing that a company's reputation had become increasingly important to customers, investors, employees, regulators, and other stakeholders, management reasoned that there was 'not generally a conflict in the long term [between] doing good versus doing well' (Levi Strauss & Co. 1994). Noted Toni Wilson, manager of the company's ethics initiative, 'LS&Co. invites the whole person to the job . . . . Doing the right thing may cost in the short run, but in the long run it brings intangible benefits: trust, creativity, innovation. You can't buy trust, you have to earn it.'

In 1987, under Haas's leadership, LS&Co. adopted a Mission and Aspirations Statement to communicate 'where we wanted to go . . . [and] how we wanted to behave' (Sheff 1993). (See Exhibit 11.3.) Senior management defined the company's mission as 'responsible commercial success', which was operationalized as 'consistently meeting or exceeding the legal ethical, commercial and other expectations that society has of business'.[4] In 1991, LS&Co. introduced a values driven, principled approach to ethics, replacing its code of ethics (described by one manager as 'very proscriptive – rules and regulations in a big binder') with a more open-ended statement of core principles (see Exhibit 11.4). The company also articulated its environmental philosophy and principles (see Exhibit 11.5).

EXHIBIT 11.3

Mission statement and aspiration statement

Mission statement

The mission of Levi Strauss & Co. is to sustain responsible commercial success as a global marketing company of branded casual apparel. We must balance goals of superior profitability and return on investment, leadership market positions, and superior products and service. We will conduct our business ethically and demonstrate leadership in satisfying our responsibilities to our communities and to society. Our work environment will be safe and productive and characterized by fair treatment, teamwork, open communication, personal accountability and opportunities for growth and development.

Aspiration statement

We all want a company that our people are proud of and committed to, where all employees have an opportunity to contribute, learn, grow, and advance based on merit, not politics or background.

We want our people to feel respected, treated fairly, listened to, and involved.

Above all, we want satisfaction from accomplishments and friendships, balanced personal and professional lives, and to have fun in our endeavors.

When we describe the kind of LS&Co., we want in the future, what we are talking about is building on the foundation we have inherited affirming the best of our Company's traditions, closing gaps that may exist between principles and practices, and updating some of our values to reflect contemporary circumstances.

What type of leadership is necessary to make our Aspirations a Reality?

New behaviors

Leadership that exemplifies directness, openness to influence, commitment to the success of others, willingness to acknowledge our own contributions to problems, personal accountability, teamwork, and trust.

Not only must we model these behaviours but we must coach others to adopt them.

Diversity

Leadership that values a diverse work force (age, sex, ethnic group, etc.) at all levels of the organization, diversity in experience, and diversity in perspectives. We have committed to taking full advantage of the rich backgrounds and abilities of all our people and to promote a greater diversity in position of influence.

Differing points of view will be sought; diversity will be valued and honesty rewarded, not suppressed.

Recognition

Leadership that provides greater recognition – both financial and psychic – for individuals and teams that contribute to our success. Recognition must be given to all who contribute; those who create and innovate and also those who continually support the day-to-day business requirements.

Ethical management practices

Leadership that epitomizes the stated standards of ethical behaviour.

We must provide clarity about our expectations and must enforce these standards through the corporation.

Communications

Leadership that is clear about company, unit, and individual goals and performance.

People must know what is expected of them and receive timely, honest feedback on their performance and career aspirations.

Empowerment

Leadership that increases the authority and responsibility of those closest to our products and customers.

By actively pushing responsibility, trust, and recognition into the organization, we can harness and release the capabilities of all our people.
Source: Company document.

EXHIBIT 11.4

Levi Strauss & Co., code of ethics and ethical principles

Code of ethics

Levi Strauss & Co. has a long and distinguished history of ethical conduct and community involvement. Essentially, these are a reflection of the mutually-shared values of the founding families and of our employees.

Our ethical values are based on the following elements:

- A commitment to commercial success in terms broader than merely financial measures.
- A respect for our employees, suppliers, customers, consumers and stockholders.
- A commitment to conduct which is not only legal, but fair, and morally correct in a fundamental sense.
- Avoidance of not only real, but the appearance of conflict of interest.

From time to time the Company will publish specific guidelines, polices and procedures. However, the best test whether something is ethically correct is whether you would be prepared to present it to our senior management and board of directors as being consistent with our ethical traditions. If you have any uneasiness about an action you are about to take or which you see, you should discuss the action with your supervisor or management.

Ethical principles

Our ethical principles are the values that set the ground rules for all that we do as employees of Levi Strauss & Co. As we seek to achieve responsible commercial success, we will be challenged to balance these principles against each other, always mindful of our promise to shareholders that we will achieve responsible commercial success.

The ethical principles are:

Honesty: We will not say things that are false. We will never deliberately mislead. We will be as candid as possible, openly and freely sharing information, as appropriate to the relationship.

Promise-Keeping: We will go to great lengths to keep our commitments. We will not make promises that can't be kept and we will not make promises on behalf of the Company unless we have the authority to do so.

Fairness: We will create and follow a process and achieve outcomes that a reasonable person would call just, evenhanded and nonarbitrary.

Respect for Others: We will be open and direct in our communication and receptive to influence. We will honor and value the abilities and contributions of others, embracing the responsibility and accountability for our actions in this regard.

Compassion: We will maintain an awareness of the needs of others and act to meet those needs whenever possible. We will also minimize harm whenever possible. We will act in ways that are consistent with our commitment to social responsibility.

Integrity: We will live up to LS&Co.'s ethical principles; even when confronted by personal, professional and social risks, as well as economic pressures.
Source: Company document.

EXHIBIT 11.5

Levi Strauss & Co., environmental philosophy and guiding principles

Environmental philosophy

Consistent with Levi Strauss & Co.'s Mission and Aspirations, the Company will protect the environment wherever it is engaged in doing business. We will set high standards for responsible environmental stewardship and encourage our business partners to do the same. We will meet or exceed local practices, laws and Levi Strauss & Co. standards world-wide. In addition to our owned and operated facilities, we will also require our licensees, contractors and others who produce Levi Strauss & Co. products on our behalf to adhere to these standards. We will work diligently to safeguard the environment.

Guiding principles

Reduce, Reuse and Recycle: We will reduce and eliminate wastes from our business operations and ensure responsible disposal by supporting the 'Three Rs: reduce, reuse and recycle.'

Preservation of Non-Renewable Resources: We will reduce our dependence on non-renewable natural resources through the use of more effective technologies and recovery techniques.

Environmental Hazard Reduction: We will exercise high standards of care in the transportation, storage, use and disposal of chemicals. We will seek safe alternatives to hazardous chemicals to reduce their use and the potential for environmental harm.

Communications: We will communicate our environmental policies, programmes and actions to our employees, suppliers, customers, stockholders and the public.

Environmental Policy Assessment: We will continually assess and revise our policies, programmes and actions to ensure industry leadership as responsible environmental stewards.

Environmental Relationships: We will establish environmentally responsible relationships with licensees, contractors and others who produce Levi Strauss & Co. products on our behalf. We will also seek to influence our major suppliers who provide raw materials for our products to be responsible environmental stewards and to demonstrate a commitment as strong as our own.

Compliance Reviews: We will conduct ongoing reviews of our owned and operated facilities, licensees, contractors and others who produce Levi Strauss & Co. products on our behalf. We will use the results of these reviews to help us prioritize our environmental efforts and will report no less than annually on the status of these efforts.

Planning and Decision Making: We will consider our individual and corporate duties as responsible environmental stewards through the capital allocation process and in other business decisions. We will address both environmental issues as well as anticipate future issues.

Printed on 100% reclaimed LS&Co.'s [R] denim.

Source: Company document.

Though LS&Co.'s Executive Management Committee saw a strong link between good ethics and good business over the long run, they recognized that particular decisions could pose difficult dilemmas. Senior management made it clear that ethics was to be a ground rule, not just a factor in decision making, and that ethical values would take precedence over nonethical values. Moreover, conflicts between and among ethical principles were to be resolved through an ethical process. As the paradigm for all of its decision making, the company adopted the 'principled reasoning approach' (PRA), a thorough and explicit procedure that involved six discrete steps:

1   defining the problem;
2   agreeing on the principles to be satisfied;
3   identifying both high-impact and high-influence stakeholders and assessing their claims;
4   brainstorming possible solutions;
5   testing the consequences of chosen solutions;
6   developing an ethical process for implementing the solution.

LS&Co. managers agreed that this process could be extremely exacting and time consuming, and some favoured a more streamlined approach, especially for routine and medium-impact decisions. Yet most were convinced that understanding and applying the PRA was worth the effort. Bob Dunn explained,

> If there is anyone with a moral claim on the outcome [of a decision], their views have to be clear and present. The principled reasoning approach insists that we identify the ethical issues, the people who are affected, the possible solutions, and the ways to minimize harm. At the beginning, people are frustrated with the process, but at the end they feel it serves us well. It prevents the pressure of the moment, of personal involvement from getting in the way. Over time, people do it more naturally.

To support the new thinking and increase the organization's ability to do the right thing, LS&Co. managers developed a three-part core curriculum with a week of leadership training, four days of diversity training, and three days of ethics training, which introduced participants to the PRA Management modified the criteria for performance evaluations, which were linked to compensation, basing a significant portion of the evaluation on adherence to aspirations and the rest on meeting business goals.

11.4   GLOBAL SOURCING GUIDELINES

In September 1991, after several managers expressed misgivings about the business practices employed by some of LS&Co.'s overseas contractors, top management set up a 12-person Sourcing Guidelines Working Group (SGWG) to determine what standards the company should expect of its contractors world-wide. Dunn explained, 'As we expanded our operations to more diverse cultures and countries, we felt that we needed to set standards to ensure that our products were being made in a manner consistent with our values, that would not be damaging to our brand image' (Kehoe 1993: 9). In looking at both internal and external stakeholders, this senior-level, cross-functional working group would consider the full range of sourcing issues that could affect the company's assets, people, or products. As Dunn noted, they would in many cases be developing a vocabulary for issues previously left to individual discretion.

LS&Co.'s actions coincided with a rising public focus on the issue of supplier standards.

> Scrutiny by labour unions, activists and socially conscious investors is forcing importers to monitor not just their foreign subsidiaries but their far-flung networks of independent suppliers – and their suppliers' suppliers as well . . . Socially conscious investors and mainstream religious groups promote the positive message that companies should extend their own high standards to all their business partners. Environmentalists and other activists tend toward the more direct pressure that comes from naming names. Union officials are taking a more investigative approach to locate human rights and other violations, including schemes in which foreign manufacturers, especially in China, circumvent US textile quotas by misidentifying the country in which their goods were made.
>
> (McCormack and Levinson 1993)

Some US companies benefiting from questionable labour practices abroad had been targeted on television shows, such as NBC's news magazine Dateline. At the same time, marketers were beginning to pay more attention to consumers who based their purchasing decisions, at least in part, on ethical concerns. Termed 'vigilante consumers' by one British consultant, such consumers were interested not only in the products or services they bought but also 'in the behaviour of the company behind the brand and the way the product or service is developed' (Dickenson 1993). Dunn agreed that consumers were increasingly 'sensitive to goods being made under conditions that are not consistent with U.S. values and fairness'.

11.4.1 The Saipan incident

LS&Co.'s sourcing initiative proved timely. The SGWG approved a set of guidelines in December 1991. In February 1992, before the guidelines were ratified by management, the media turned a spotlight on a company supplier in Saipan, a US territory in the western Pacific, accused of paying workers substandard wages and forcing them to work long hours in fenced and guarded factories. In a suit filed four months earlier in October 1991, the US Department of Labor charged that five garment manufacturers owned and operated by the Tan family recruited workers from China – mosty non-English-speaking women in their late teens and early twenties – and then seized their passports and kept them in padlocked and guarded barracks and factories for the duration of their employment contract. The government's investigation, which had begun in 1990, found that Tan employees worked up to 11 hours a day, seven days a week, for as little as $1.65 an hour, well below Saipan's minimum wage of $2.15 (*The Economist* 1992). The companies were cited also for deducting between $270 and $365 a month from workers' pay for room and board, 'management fees', and other expenses (Reuters 1991).

Saipan manufacturers, such as the Tans, were allowed to ship their goods to the United States, labelled 'Made in the USA', without quota limits or duty. They were exempt from the US minimum wage, but were legally required to comply with all other US labour laws. According to government estimates, the Tan operations manufactured garments worth $100 million to be sold by U.S. clothing companies in the United States under brand names such as Perry Ellis, Eddie Bauer, Chaps Sportswear, Christian Dior, and Van Heusen, as well as private labels (Swoboda 1992).

When queried by LS&Co. managers in San Francisco in late 1991, Tan officials denied the charges and downplayed their seriousness. The media stories prompted LS&Co. to take a closer look. Within 48 hours, of the February broadcast, LS&Co. suspended new business with the Tans and sent a team to investigate. As a result of the investigation, LS&Co. cancelled its contract with the Tan family, incurring several hundred thousand dollars in contract penalties. Although LS&Co. investigators found the media's allegations of 'slave labour' to be unwarranted, the Tan's practices did not conform to the company's new guidelines.

Later in May 1992, as part of a consent decree with the Labor Department, the five Tan companies agreed to pay $9 million in back pay and damages to contract employees who had worked for them from 1988 to 1992. Under the decree, in which the companies neither admitted nor denied breaking the law, they agreed to be monitored for four years (*BNA International Business Daily* 1992). According to Dunn, LS&Co.'s soon-to-be-ratified sourcing guidelines were 'the best insurance policy we could have' to deal with the situation. Noted another manager, 'If anyone doubted the need for guidelines, this convinced them.'

11.4.2 Guidelines announced

In March 1992, LS&Co. publicly announced its new global sourcing guidelines, which established standards in the areas of worker health and safety, employment practices, ethics, the environment, and human rights. Recognizing that some matters were under the control of individual contractors, whereas others were not, the SGWG had developed the guidelines in two parts: the **Business Partner Terms of Engagement** (see Exhibit 11.1) and the **Guidelines for Country Selection** (see Exhibit 11.2).

LS&Co. officials expected the standards, which were intended to be visionary and strategic, as well as practical to result in higher production costs in 1993, affecting both 1993 net income and gross profit (Levi Strauss Associates Inc. 1993). Noted Dunn, 'Sourcing decisions that emphasize cost to the exclusion of all other factors will not best serve our long-term business interest . . . . Sometimes it costs a little more in the short term, but it really is possible to have your cake and eat it too' (*Apparel Industry Magazine* 1993).

LS&Co. began an intensive communications programme to inform employees and contractors world-wide about the guidelines. According to Sabrina Johnson, a corporate communications manager, the company took care to explain the reasoning behind the guidelines and to convey its willingness to co-operate with contractors in meeting them. Merchandisers, who were responsible for negotiating with and selecting contractors, received special briefings. Senior management indicated the possibility of 'margin relief' for merchandisers whose bonuses might suffer if sourcing cost increases were necessary to meet the guidelines.

(a) Business partner terms of engagement

To implement the Business Partner Terms of Engagement, management sent audit teams to inspect the facilities of all the company's contractors. Training for these teams became a top priority. Richard Woo, at the time Community Affairs manager for the Asia Pacific region, was involved in designing and delivering the first training programme, which was held in Singapore for employees from 13 Asian nations. Recalling that some managers wondered whether LS&Co. was imposing Western values on the rest of the world, Woo noted the challenge of 'calibrating what was happening on the factory floor with the written standards', especially in differing cultural contexts. After refinement, the training programme and audit instruments were introduced around the world.

Inspection teams visited more than 700 facilities in 60 countries.

LS&Co. managers focused initially on sewing and finishing contractors and planned later to look at suppliers of fabric, sundries (e.g., buttons, thread), and chemicals. The auditors found 70 per cent of the contractors to be in compliance. Another 25 per cent, found lacking, made significant improvements in bathrooms, emergency exits, ventilation, and wastewater treatment equipment as a result of LS&Co.'s review. About five per cent were dropped because of poor personnel practices, child labour, health and safety conditions, and trademark or other violations.

The sourcing guidelines introduced new factors into the process for selecting contractors, who had previously been chosen on the basis of price, quality, and delivery time from the pool of firms with available quota.[5] With adoption of the guidelines, LS&Co. began to require that potential contractors satisfy the Business Partner Terms of Engagement and the company's environmental principles, in addition to meeting the traditional selection criteria. LS&Co. sought long-term relationships and offered contractors large-volume orders and technical advice. Many contractors liked to have LS&Co. as a customer and took pride in their ability to meet the company's demanding quality standards. Having LS&Co. on a contractor's 'résumé' could help attract new business. At the same time, contractors resisted becoming too dependent on LS&Co. and claimed they could not make as much money on LS&Co. contracts as on some others.

Recognizing that certain improvements, particularly environmental ones, could be costly, LS&Co. sometimes accepted higher prices or offered contractors generous timetables, loans, and volume guarantees. However, contractors slow to upgrade their practices were reminded that LS&Co. would have to discontinue the relationship if changes were not made by the agreed-on deadline. In some instances, LS&Co. took extra steps to help contractors meet the guidelines. In Bangladesh, for example, two contractors employing underage workers agreed to send them to school – with pay – after LS&Co. offered to cover the cost of their books, tuition, and uniforms. The contractors agreed to rehire the children wishing to return when they turned 14. In both instances, the children represented less than two per cent of the contractor's 200-person workforce.

Though a few contractors balked at making improvements, most were quite receptive. According to Y. S. Chan, manager of the Hong Kong branch of LS&Co.'s Asian sourcing organization

> Most contractors don't mind spending money to make the improvements we recommend, since we try to be fair and reasonable, and we make it clear that we would like to work together . . . . We don't force things . . . . There are different ways to establish mutual understanding.

One approach was to show contractors video clips from television documentaries exposing shoddy conditions. A manager involved in training LS&Co. inspection teams around the world found that 'regardless of whether they agreed with the media coverage or not, they understood [the relationship between the guidelines and the brand]'.

Iain Lyon, vice president of Offshore Sourcing and, later, a member of the CPG, recalled his apprehension at the guidelines initiative. 'This was America interfering with another country's business,' he remembered thinking. But Lyon, English by birth, changed his mind after seeing the specifics of the company's approach and 'how quickly contractors see the point and want to do the right thing' He added, 'It's hard for anyone to say it's wrong to open up the fire exits, stop polluting, or give children an education.' A relative newcomer to the company, Lyon found LS&Co.'s approach refreshing. He noted, 'The vast majority [of sourcing managers outside LS&Co.] don't give a damn . . . Taking maximum advantage of contractors seems okay because they are foreigners. Getting away from that has been a great relief to me.'

(b) Guidelines for Country Selection

Administering the LS&Co. Guidelines for Country Selection required an assessment of every country in which LS&Co. did business. The first evaluations concentrated on countries suspected of being in violation. In mid-1992, LS&Co. decided to withdraw its business from Burma, cancelling contracts to buy 850,000 trousers and shirts annually, because, 'under current circumstances, it is not possible to do business without directly supporting the military government and its pervasive human-rights violations' (Billenness 1993). Run by a military junta that had taken power in 1962, Burma was ranked by the human-rights watchdog Freedom House as one of the 12 most repressive regimes in the world (Maclean 1993). The military continued to rule in defiance of a 1990 election that gave 60 per cent of the vote and 82 per cent of the parliamentary seats to the National League for Democracy (NLD) party of Daw Aung San Suu Kyi, the recipient of the 1991 Nobel Peace Prize who had been held under house arrest since July 1989. In its 1993 report, the US State Department called the human rights situation in Burma 'deplorable', noting:

> Arbitrary detentions and compulsory labor persisted, as did harsh treatment and torture of detainees. Freedom of speech, the press, assembly and association remained nonexistent . . . . Over 25% of the NLD winners [in 1990] had either resigned under pressure, fled into exile, been disqualified after conviction on political charges, or died.

(Department of State 1993)

Human rights groups reported the systematic rape, torture, and murder of Burmese and minority peoples, forcing 300,000 refugees into Bangladesh and 80,000 into Thailand (*The Boston Globe* 1993). The military was charged with 'selling off natural resources at a rapid rate with little concern for the environmental impact, including destruction of rain forests' (Bertsch 1993)

The decision to withdraw from Burma was fairly uncontroversial within LS&Co., though some managers, such as Lyon, felt mixed emotions. Said Lyon, 'I have no sympathy for the Burmese government at all . . . [but] it was a shame because of the impact on the people . . . The operators in Burma were university graduates – we were the best job in town. When we left, I felt badly for them.'

11.4.3 The China situation

When the China Policy Group began its work in late 1992, LS&Co.'s presence in China was small. Though the company had been sourcing in China since 1986, sales remained 'minuscule' since Levi's® clothing was not mass marketed there. In early 1991, LS&Co. managers had decided in the '11th hour' of negotiations to forgo a China joint venture to produce clothes for sale in local markets after discovering that the venture would be responsible for enforcing China's one-child-per-family policy. In many parts of China, the work group was still the central organizing fact of life – where citizens received medical care and women registered their chosen form of birth control. Employers could be required to fine or dock the pay of workers who had second children. Some worker groups, it was reported, used physical force to 'encourage' abortions and sterilization, even though such tactics were unlawful. Although support for the government's birth control policy was widespread in China, many LS&Co. managers found it abhorrent to risk involvement in family planning at this level. Operational concerns added to the troublesome nature of the venture.

Senior management put the China issue on hold, waiting until the company fully implemented its new principled reasoning approach (PRA) and global sourcing strategy. At that point, wrote the president of LS&Co.'s Asia-Pacific division, the company would be better prepared 'to address the human rights issues in a full, responsible, [and] effective way'. Meanwhile, LS&Co. made no direct investment in China, although Asia managers continued to investigate and hoped to enter the market at some time in the future. By 1993, some of LS&Co.'s low-priced jeans competitors were beginning to become popular in China.

As for sourcing in China, LS&Co. purchased, either directly or indirectly through contractors, a large quantity of sundries (buttons, thread, and labels) and about eight million yards of fabric in China, which was increasingly popular as a site for fabric mills relocating from other parts of Asia.[6] The company also sourced about five million items of clothing (called 'units'), totalling about $50 million, from Chinese sewing and laundry contractors (Carlton 1993). More than half the units sourced in China were finished in Hong Kong and shipped to the United States with a 'Made in Hong Kong' label as part of Hong Kong's legal quota.[7]

Any change in LS&Co.'s China stance would be felt most directly by employees in the Hong Kong branch of the company's Asian sourcing organization. Responsible for all Hong Kong and China sourcing, the 120-person office arranged for a total of 20 million to 22 million units from about 20 contractors in 1992. The Hong Kong branch was confident there would be no problem finding satisfactory contractors if LS&Co. expanded its China presence. In fact, the company's Chinese contractors were doing well under the Business Partner Terms of Engagement – better even than contractors in some other parts of Asia with whom LS&Co. had very successful relationships.

However, withdrawing from China was another matter. Even though China represented only about 10 per cent of LS&Co.'s total Asian contracting (and two per cent of world-wide contracting), it would not be easy to find alternative contractors with available quota at reasonable prices. In most Asian countries, the largest part of the quota was held by a few large contractors, with the remainder spread among many small ones. Moving production would mean increasing the number of contractors, sacrificing scale economies, and increasing auditing costs. Also, shifting production to other locations would add to the cost and complexity of transportation. (Items sourced in China could be transported relatively easily to Hong Kong, the preferred port for shipping to the United States.) Employment opportunities in the Hong Kong office would very likely diminish. It was estimated that moving production to other parts of Asia over a three-year period would raise costs between four per cent and 10 per cent, depending on the country.

11.4.4 Business conditions

In contrast to LS&Co., many companies were rushing to establish an early foothold in China. Economic liberalization of the Chinese economy and a shift toward free markets which had begun in the late 1970s ushered in a period of rapid growth, estimated at more than 10 per cent a year (*The Wall Street Journal* 1993). With retail sales rising an average of 15 per cent per year since 1979 (Goll and Ono 1993) and a potential market of more than one billion customers, a US Treasury Department official predicted that 'China will soon have the world's second-biggest economy' (Barnathan *et al.* 1993: 43).

Procter & Gamble, Johnson & Johnson, and H.J. Heinz were among the firms adding production facilities in 1993. Coca-Cola

Co. Chairman Roberto C. Goizueta announced a deal to add 10 bottling plants to increase the total to 22, noting that the Chinese market had 'virtually limitless long-term potential' (Engardio *et al.* 1993). Total US investment was expected to increase to $5 billion in 1993, up from less than $0.5 billion in 1990; US exports rose from $5 billion to $9 billion during the same period (Barnathan *et al.* 1993: 43). In 1992, US imports from China totalled $26 billion, mostly consumer goods such as clothing, shoes, and toys (Southerland 1993a). One commentator noted,

> If you don't take the dive into China you may be missing the biggest sales opportunity of your generation. It could take years for your investment to bear fruit, but right now while the market's still immature – may well be the time to make the jump. China may pitch into convulsions tomorrow, but that will always be a risk. And remember, that's also what people were saying about Japan in the 1950s.
>
> (*Wall Street Journal* 1993)

John B. Wing, the chairman of Wing-Merrill, a US energy company with a $2 billion contract to build a power plant in Henan province, agreed: 'China is going to be a big global player, and if Americans aren't part of it, we are fools' (Engardio *et al.* 1993).

The apparel and textile industry was particularly active in China. With shipments totalling $7.3 billion a year, China was the largest supplier of textiles and apparel to the United States, accounting for 20 to 25 per cent of US textile and apparel sales (Skidmore 1994). The removal of trade quotas for Chinese-made apparel (likely to occur if China were admitted to GATT), would most certainly boost China's share even more.

11.4.5 Challenges

Nevertheless, China still posed difficulties for business. Outmoded infrastructure and tariffs meant it was difficult and expensive to transport goods across its vast distances. Though large, the China market was hardly unified; tastes and buying power varied greatly by region, and distribution systems were chaotic or nonexistent. Furthermore, economic growth had been accompanied by inflation and sharp rises in stock prices and property values, adding to the cost of doing business and the expense of stationing American workers in major Chinese cities. Restrictions on imports and currency convertibility created other problems. And, the threat of political instability was always present (*Wall Street Journal* 1993). China experts consulted by the CPG advised that the death of Deng Xiao Ping, China's then 88-year-old leader, could be followed by a period of chaos, probably with increased repression, social unrest, and anti-foreign sentiment. A coup or another 'Cultural Revolution' could not be ruled out.

The CPG learned that foreign companies operating in China were under increasing pressure to accept government-backed Communist party representation on their boards and faced intensified levels of government inspections and audits. Though government-supported party organizing in the workplace was common, union organizing was illegal. Since 1989, companies' authority to hire, fire, and compensate employees as they wished had become more limited. The wages payable by joint ventures were capped at 150 per cent of the amount paid by state owned enterprises. To secure greater control over the workplace, some companies had chosen to establish wholly owned enterprises rather than joint ventures. Companies taking the joint venture route favoured partnerships with private companies, collectively owned companies, or local government entities rather than national or provincial government entities.

The Chinese legal system remained a concern. Business laws and their enforcement lagged behind economic development, and the country still ran on power politics and personal relationships. Corruption was a problem, and public officials sometimes accepted bribes (*Wall Street Journal* 1993). Laws and rules were vague and arbitrarily enforced. In the apparel industry, manufacturers were allowed to use false country-of-origin labels to avoid US quotas (Maggs 1991). If caught by US Customs, these mislabelled goods were deducted from China's quota, reducing the quota amount that remained and potentially jeopardizing US companies' ability to take delivery on contracted items. The Chinese government lacked clear policies on foreign investment, though officials eagerly courted foreign capital and technology. Withdrawal from joint ventures posed particular problems for foreign firms because dissolution required the Chinese partner's consent. Unable to secure such consent, some Western companies had been forced to abandon the assets of their ventures.

Protection of intellectual property, nonexistent under Communist ideology, was a particular worry for many American businesses. Copyright and patent protection had existed on paper since 1979, but, according to the US Embassy, 'procedures for enforcement were still unclear'. Legislation implementing trademark laws was not passed until 1987. The US government called China 'the single largest pirator of US copyrights' and estimated the cost to American companies at $400 million in 1991 (Auerbach 1992). In 1992, US customs made 104 seizures of counterfeit merchandise worth $456 million in China, second only to its seizures of $585 million in goods from South Korea (Lucas 1993).[8] In January 1992, under pressure from the US government, China agreed to improve protection of intellectual property by extending patent protection on chemicals and pharmaceuticals to 20 years, joining international copyright conventions, and agreeing to protect all existing copyrights on computers, software, books, and recordings. However, later that year, some companies still complained about a lack of 'follow up' (Dunne 1992). LS&Co.'s legal department could find no reports of successful actions for trademark infringement in China.

As of May 1992, LS&Co. had seized nearly two million pairs of counterfeit '501' jeans produced in China with 'Made in the USA' labels. Most were destined for Europe, where they would fetch high prices. According to David Saenz, LS&Co.'s director of Corporate Security, few consumers could detect that the blue jeans did not meet Levi's® standards. He noted also that the Chinese authorities had been co-operative in investigating reports of false labelling (Maggs 1991). However, the authorities' effectiveness was limited by China's size and the fragmentation of political power. In 1993, the problem of counterfeit jeans from China persisted; it remained unclear how aggressive US and Chinese officials would be in trying to shut down factories making such goods (Dayle 1993).

11.4.6 Human rights

The CPG learned that leading human rights organizations considered China's human rights record among the worst in the world. Using the 1948 Universal Declaration of Human Rights as a benchmark, organizations such as the United Nations, Human Rights Watch, and Amnesty International, found human rights violations in China to be severe and persistent (see Exhibit 11.6).[9] Freedom House, for example, included China among the countries where political rights and civil liberties were absent or virtually nonexistent in 1992.[10] Since the Tiananmen Square attack on pro-democracy students in June 1989, the Chinese Communist Party had continued its harsh practices with the backing of its military and other security forces. According to the US State Department, China's human rights practices fell 'far short of internationally accepted norms'.[11]

EXHIBIT 11.6

Universal Declaration of Human Rights
... the **General Assembly** *proclaims* this **Universal Declaration** of Human Rights as a common standard of achievement for all people and all nations, to the end that every individual and every organ of society, keeping this Declaration constantly in mind, shall strive by teaching and education to promote respect

for these rights and freedoms and by progressive measures, national and international, to secure their universal and effective recognition and observance,. . . .

Article 1	All human beings are born free and equal in dignity and rights. They are endowed with reason and conscience and should act towards one another in a spirit of brotherhood.
Article 2	Everyone is entitled to all the rights and freedoms set forth in this Declaration, without distinction of any kind, such as race, colour, sex, language, religion, political or other opinion, national or social origin, property, birth or other status.
Article 3	Everyone has the right to life, liberty and security of person.
Article 4	No one shall be held in slavery or servitude; . . . .
Article 5	No one shall be subjected to torture or to cruel, inhuman or degrading treatment or punishment.
Article 6	Everyone has the right to recognition everywhere as a person before the law.
Article 7	All are equal before the law and are entitled without any discrimination to equal protection of the law . . . .
Article 8	Everyone has the right to an effective remedy by the competent national tribunals for acts violating the fundamental fights granted him by the Constitution or by law.
Article 9	No one shall be subjected to arbitrary arrest, detention or exile.
Article 10	Everyone is entitled in full equality to a fair and public hearing by an independent and impartial tribunal.
Article 11	Everyone charged with a penal offense has the right to be presumed innocent until proved guilty according to law in a public trial at which he has had all the guarantees necessary for his defence . . . .
Article 12	No one shall be subjected to arbitrary interference with his privacy, family, home or correspondence . . . .
Article 13	(1) Everyone has the right to freedom of movement and residence within the borders of each State. (2) Everyone has the right to leave any country, including his own, and to return to his country
Article 14	(1) Everyone has the right to seek and enjoy in other countries asylum from persecution. .
Article 15	(1) Everyone has the right to a nationality . . . .

Article 16 (1) Men and women of full age, without any limitation due to race, nationality or religion, have the
right to marry and to found a family . . . .

Article 17 (1) Everyone has the right to own property alone as
well as in association with others.
(2) No one shall be arbitrarily deprived of his
property.

Article 18 Everyone has the right to freedom of thought, conscience and religion; . . . .

Article 19 Everyone has the right to freedom of opinion and
expression; . . . .

Article 20 (1) Everyone has the right to freedom of peaceful
assembly and association . . . .

Article 21 (1) Everyone has the right to take part in the government of his country, directly or through freely
chosen representatives.

Article 22 Everyone, as a member of society, has the right to
social security and is entitled to realization, . . . of
the economic, social and cultural rights indispensable for his dignity . . .

Article 23 (1) Everyone has the right to work, to free choice of
employment, to just and favourable conditions of
work and to protection against unemployment.
(2) Everyone, without any discrimination, has the
right to equal pay for equal work.
(3) Everyone has the right to just and favourable
remuneration ensuring for himself and his family an
existence worthy of human dignity . . . .
(4) Everyone has the right to form and to join trade
unions . . . .

Article 24 Everyone has the right to rest and leisure, including
reasonable limitation of working hours and periodic
holidays with pay.

Article 25 (1) Everyone has the right to a standard of living
adequate for the health and well-being of himself
and of his family, ...

Article 26 (1) Everyone has the right to education . . . .

Article 27 (1) Everyone has the right to freely participate in
the cultural life of the community, ...

Article 28 Everyone is entitled to a social and international
order in which the rights and freedoms set forth in
this Declaration can be fully realized

Article 29 (1) Everyone has duties to the community . . . .

Article 30 Nothing in this Declaration may be interpreted as
implying for any State, group or person any right to
engage in any activity or to perform any act aimed

> at the destruction of any of the rights and freedoms
> set forth herein.
>
> Adopted by the United Nations General Assembly, December
> 10, 1948.

(a) Legal process

The State Department did note some 'modest progress' in resolving a few individual human rights cases and reported that 'rigid ideological controls reimposed after June 1989 were beginning to ease'.[12] However, there had never been a comprehensive public accounting of those detained after the Tiananmen demonstrations, and trials of dissidents, religious figures, and other political offenders continued. These trials often violated China's own legal principles, as well as international standards of due process and fair-trial procedures: trials were conducted rapidly, often in secret by judges, police, and prosecution working together, defendants had limited access to legal counsel; and many were threatened with a harsher sentence if they did not 'show the right attitude' and confess. The country's security apparatus was responsible for numerous instances of arbitrary arrest, detention without formal legal proceedings, maltreatment, and torture. Furthermore, there were no independent Chinese organizations that publicly monitored human rights conditions, and authorities made it clear that they would not allow the existence of such groups.

(b) Expression and association

Although guaranteed by the Chinese Constitution, freedom of expression and association were severely restricted. Some well-known dissidents were not permitted to travel abroad. The press and academic institutions were tightly controlled and the authorities extensively monitored personal and family life. Freedom of religion, also constitutionally guaranteed, became increasingly difficult in the 1990s, with government crackdowns on Christian, Buddhist, and Muslim religious groups that refused to practice their faith through government-supervised bodies particularly in Tibet and Mongolia, where cultural and religious groups were intertwined with forces for independence. Though laws existed to protect minorities and women, in practice, discrimination based on sex, religion and ethnicity continued in the areas of housing, jobs, and education.

(c) Prison labour

Although China had mostly ended its traditional use of massive forced labour to build public facilities, there was still some reliance on 'mobilized' workers for security forces and public works. More-over, imprisonment usually involved forced labour in prison or in the *laogai* ('reform through labour'), a network of government 'reeducation' camps where political and other offenders were compelled to work for little or no pay in tiring and often dangerous conditions. It was difficult to estimate accurately the extent of forced-labour production. A news article reported that one such prison facility consisted of 850 textile looms capable of producing sweaters worth 'hundreds of millions of dollars' annually, all for export (Barnathan 1991/2). Chinese authorities valued prison labour production at about $500 million in 1990, not including output from the *laogai*. In 1991, the US State Department found 'substantial evidence' that China was exporting products produced with forced labour (Southerland 1993b). Since imports of products made by convict labour were prohibited under the Hawley-Smoot Tariff Act of 1930, the US government responded by barring specific Chinese products known to be produced with prison labour from entry into the country.

In August 1992, the US State Department and China's Ministry of Foreign Affairs signed an agreement prohibiting forced-labour exports and permitting the United States to inspect certain facilities to ensure compliance with the agreement (ibid). Nonetheless, press accounts indicated that neither the suppliers in question nor the Chinese authorities could always be relied on to monitor abuses. Peter Yeo, an aide to the US House of Representatives Subcommittee on Trade and the Environment, cautioned, 'Don't trust your suppliers to tell the truth' (Veverka 1993). Harry Wu, a research fellow at the Hoover Institute, Stanford University, claimed, 'You can get a guarantee from the Chinese government. No trouble at all. But these people lie' (ibid). And, in 1993, the US Customs Department reported that the Chinese government had denied members of the US Embassy access to all or parts of five factories, in violation of the earlier agreement. Monitoring difficulties were compounded because forced-labour exports were 'often falsely labeled, mixed with other products and sold through intermediaries', according to the Customs Department's memorandum (Southerland 1993b).

(d) The concept of human rights

The Chinese government rejected reports made by the US State Department, Amnesty International, and Asia Watch on its human rights violations.

> Despite the [Chinese] Government's adherence to the United Nations Charter, which mandates respect for and promotion of human rights, Chinese officials do not accept the principle that human rights are universal. They argue that each nation has its own

concept of human rights, grounded in its political, economic, and social system and its historical, religious, and cultural background. Officials no longer dismiss all discussion of human rights as interference in the country's internal affairs, but remain reluctant to accept criticism of China's human rights situation by other nations or international organizations.

(*Country Reports on Human Rights Practices for 1992*: 549)

However, Chinese officials had begun to promote academic study and discussion of concepts of human rights. Chinese research institutes organized centres and symposia on the subject and sent a group to France, Sweden, and the United Kingdom to study human rights practices there. The US State Department believed that these activities were motivated by the Chinese government's desire to improve its image abroad and strengthen its ability to respond to criticism of its human rights record.

(e) Engage or withdraw

Thus, China presented a thorny problem; many considered it 'the proverbial test case' (Orentlicher and Gelatt 1993: 98). It was a country both 'marred by systematic violations of fundamental rights, and at the same time . . . in massive need of support in reaching its development and modernization goals' (ibid: 69). Human rights activists were divided as to whether socially responsible corporations should 'remain and act as a progressive force or divest and withdraw' (Billenness and Simpson 1992: 11). Those advocating divestment argued that 'economic growth and trade will merely finance a corrupt Communist elite' (ibid.: 12) and that the Chinese government would use the presence of reputable companies 'to boost its image and maintain its grip on power' (ibid.). Concerned that economic liberalization would not necessarily lead to political liberation, they argued that development and growth in Southern China's special economic zones had not been accompanied by human rights advances. Advocates for a presence in China believed that foreign corporations that were 'actively engaged' with the Chinese economy were 'helping to create power structures outside the government and state industries' (ibid.). They stressed the dangers of isolating China, arguing that constructive engagement could contribute to human rights improvements. In South China, they said, people had become free to start their own businesses, to change jobs at will, and to talk and travel.

(f) Code-of-conduct bill

Several human rights groups favoured a federal 'code-of-conduct bill' under discussion in Washington. The bill asked companies with a significant presence in China to 'adhere to a basic set of human rights principles, on a "best efforts' basis"'.[13] Under the proposal, US businesses would extend the same minimum rights protection to foreign employees that they provided to their US workers, such as protection against discrimination based on religious or political beliefs, gender, or ethnic background They would not allow their premises to be used for human rights violations in, for example, compulsory indoctrination programmes. And they would try to use their influence to end human rights abuses – for example, in raising before Chinese public officials cases of individuals detained because of their political views. Compliance would be voluntary (ibid.: 110). The only requirements would be that the US parents (a) register with the Secretary of State and indicate whether they would implement the principles; and (b) report annually on their China operation's adherence to the code.

(g) MFN debate

As LS&Co.'s CPG conducted its deliberations, China watchers were beginning to speculate on whether the United States would renew China's most-favored-nation (MFN) trade status when it expired, in June 1993. MFN status, which entitled China to the same tariff treatment accorded normal US trading partners (the lowest available), had been conferred yearly, on China since the 1970s. But, in 1993, the debate on Capitol Hill was expected to be fractious, with the substantial US trade deficit with China – $18.2 billion in 1992 – affected by the outcome.

The Clinton administration was thought to favour continuing China's MFN status, but with conditions attached, such as changes in China's coercive family-planning programme and its alleged missile sales to Pakistan, as well as overall progress in human rights. The Democrats in Congress planned to move for legislation that would apply lowest tariffs only to products produced by private firms which accounted for about half of US imports from China – while imposing higher tariffs on those made in state ventures. Some business research groups opposed attaching any conditions to MFN status, fearing Chinese retaliation could jeopardize up to 171,000 American jobs (Dunne 1993). Michael Bonsignore, chairman and chief executive of Honeywell, believed there were better ways to encourage human rights in China, noting: 'The Chinese do not respond terribly well to ultimatums' (Osland 1993).

(h) Company experience

Despite conditions in China, none of the US companies consulted by the CPG had taken steps to become informed about or to address human rights issues related to their business activities.

11.5   THE DECISION

CPG members had met five times for a total of 19 days between November 1992 and February 1993. They had heard directly from a wide range of internal and external stakeholders, along with outside sources knowledgeable about the China situation. They included a former prisoner in China, a former head of the US–China Business Council, and several China experts, as well as representatives of human rights organizations, the US government, Chinese pro-democracy groups, US labour unions, and other companies doing business in China. With the information and insights gained from these sources, the CPG was reviewing the company's global sourcing guidelines and working through the steps of the principled reasoning approach (PRA). Soon the group would have to settle on its recommendation to LS&Co.'s Executive Management Committee.

11.6   NOTES

[1] Members were drawn from Human Resources, Levi Strauss International, Legal, Global Sourcing, the Asian Pacific Division, and Corporate Affairs.

[2] Levi also feared that US retailers, in clearing their shelves to grey-market buyers, might be unable to offer the full selection to regular customers. As a result, it raised US prices to 'narrow the gap' and ask US retailers to limit the number of jeans sold to each shopper.

[3] Dr Herman Starobin, research director, International Ladies Garment Workers Union, AFI-CIO, statement before the US House of Representatives Ways and Means Committee, September 15, 1993.

[4] The LS&Co. definition of 'responsible commercial success' was adapted from the work of Professor Archie B. Carroll, a management professor specializing in corporate responsibility at the University of Georgia.

[5] The United States limited apparel and textile imports through quotas permitted by the Multifiber Arrangement (MFA) under the auspices of the General Agreement on Tariffs and Trade (GATT). The MFA allowed the United States to set quotas, either by imposing them unilaterally or, more commonly, by negotiating bilateral agreements with other nations. Most Asian countries, including China, had an agreement with the United States which established that country's quota by product type and fibre content – men's cotton pants, men's noncotton pants, and so on. These agreements had some flexibility: there were usually provisions for category shifting, for borrowing against next years quota, and for increasing the quota each year. Each government had the right to administer and divide that country's quota among local contractors on whatever basis they desired. Most countries distributed

quota based on past shipping record; those contractors who had shipped large quantities in the past were most likely to get assigned large quota again, so as to minimize the risk of not shipping all allowable quota. Under serious consideration in 1993 was a proposal to phase out all textile and apparel quotas for GATT signatories over a 10-year period.

[6] Levi did not contract directly with fabric mills for fabric purchases. Instead, the mill generally contracted with the sewing firm, which in turn, contracted with Levi.

[7] This system or 'outward processing,' which was entirely legal, permitted apparel companies to take advantage of Hong Kong's large quota, while substantially bypassing its expensive wage rates.

[8] Officials believed that merchandise seized at customs represented only a fraction of all counterfeit goods because only a small portion of all imports were examined. As in the instances of mislabelled goods, the amounts seized were deducted from China's quota.

[9] For 1992, China appeared on the 'worst country' lists prepared by Freedom House, the World Human Rights Guide, and the United Nations Commission on Human Rights.

[10] Other countries on the list were Afghanistan, Burma, Cuba, Equatorial Guinea, Haiti, Iraq, North Korea, Libya, Somalia, Sudan, Syria, and Vietnam.

[11] For a catalogue of human rights practices in China, see, for example, *Country Reports on Human Rights Practices for 1992*, pp. 540–54.

[12] *Country Reports on Human Rights Practices for 1992*, p. 540.

[13] In 1991, then-Congressman John Miller (R-Washington) introduced code-of-conduct legislation, which was never enacted – see Orentlicher and Gelatt 1993: 82–3.

11.7   REFERENCES

Apparel Industry Magazine (1993) Apparel makers can do well by doing the right thing, September, pp. 108–10.

Auerbach, S. (1992) China, U.S. reach trade accord; Beijing agrees to curb piracy of product, safeguarded material. *The Washington Post*, January 17, p. A24 ff.

Barnathan, J. (1991/2) It's time to put screws to China's gulag.' *Business Week*, December 30, January 6, p. 52 ff.

Barnathan, J., Curry, L. and Ullmann, O., (1993) Behind the Great Wall. *Business Week*, October 25, p. 43.

Bertsch, K. (1993) Coalition for withdrawal from Burma intensifies shareholder campaign. *IRRC News for Investors*, Social Issues Service, November, p. 5.

Billenness, S. (1993) Burma: a new issue for social investors. *Franklin's Insight Investing for a Better World*, Franklin Research and Development Corporation, October 15.

Billenness, S. and Simpson, K. (1992) Thinking globally: study of international corporate responsibility. *Franklin's Insight: The Advisory Letter for Concerned Investors*, Franklin Research and Development Corporation, September.

Boston Globe (1993) From South Africa to Burma, October 18, p. 12.

BNA International Business Daily (1992) Five Saipan garment manufacturers to pay $9 million to settle FLSA suit, May 26.

Carlton, J. (1993) Ties with China will be curbed by Levi Strauss. *Wall Street Journal*, May 4, p. A3 ff.

Davidson, R. (1993) Levi Strauss sees red over jeans grey market. Reuters, September 10.

Dayle, J. (1993) U.S. crackdown on bogus Levi's; smuggling ring accused of plot to import jeans made in China. *San Francisco Chronicle*, November 13, p. A17 ff.

Department of State (1993) *Country Reports on Human Rights Practices for 1992*. Report Submitted to the Committee on Foreign Relations, US Senate, and the Committee on Foreign Affairs, US House of Representatives, by the Department of State, 103rd Congress, 1st Session, February p. 523.

Dickenson, N. (1993) Consumers get ethical with choices. *South China Morning Post*, May 29, supplement.

Dunne, N. (1992) Patent pirates still dodging the rules: U.S. complaints over enforcement of anti-counterfeiting measures. *Financial Times*, December 3, p. 6 ff.

Dunne, N. (1993) Clinton's $7 billion dilemma on China: linking human rights to trade could backfire. *Financial Times* May 20, p. 5 ff.

Eckhouse, J. (1993) Record profit as Levi's sales top $5 billion. *San Francisco Chronicle*, March 2, p. D2.

Economist (1992) A stitch in time, June 6, (1992) pp. 27 ff.

Engardio, P., Curry, L. and Barnathan, J. (1993) China fever strikes again. *Business Week*, March 29, p. 46 ff.

Financial World, (1993) Brands, September 1, 1993, p. 41.

Goll, S.D. and Ono, Y. (1993) Consuming Passions. *The Wall Street Journal*, December 10, p. R15.

HBO, Case No. 391–189, Levi Strauss & Co. and the AIDS Crisis.

How, K. (1993) The finance lowdown on 25 big private firms. *San Francisco Chronicle*, September 23, p. D2 ff.

Howard, R. (1990) Values make the company. *Harvard Business Review*, September–October, p. 134.

Janofsky, M. (1994) Whether it's bluejeans or mini-motors or power plants . . .: Levi Strauss, American symbol with a cause. *New York Times*, January 3, p. C4 ff.

Kehoe, L. (1993) Bold fashion statement Levi Strauss's decision not to invest in China. *Financial Times*, May 8, pp. 9 ff.

Levering, R. and Moskowitz, M. (1993) *The 100 Best Companies to Work for in America* New York: Doubleday, pp. 501–2.

Levi Strauss & Co. (1993) *Fact Sheet*, company document, May.

Levi Strauss & Co. (1994) *Going Global*, company document, January 31, p. 11.

Levi Strauss Associates Inc. (1993) *Form 10–K/A Amendment No. 1*, July 30, p. 3.

Lucas, L. (1993) U.S. brings war against copiers from H.K. *South China Morning Post*, January 6, 1993, p. 3 ff.

Maclean, J.N. (1993) Abuses in Burma stir questions of conscience. *Chicago Tribune*, October 25, Business, p. 3. ff.

Maggs, J. (1991) Levi's gets the blues after explosion of fakes hits the market. *Journal of Commerce*, December 29, p. B8 ff.

McCormack, J. and Levinson, M. (1993) The supply police. *Newsweek*, February 15, pp. 48 ff.

Orentlicher, D.F. and Gelatt, T.A. (1993) Public law, private actors: the impact of human rights on business investors in China. *Northwestern Journal of International Law and Business* (Fall).

Osland, J.J. (1993) High stakes in China. *Star Tribune*, May 21, pp. 1D ff.

Power, G. (1992) Levi's plan to sew up Europe growth aided by rise of 42% in yearly profits. *San Francisco Chronicle*, February 20, pp. B1 ff.

Reuters (1991) U.S. alleges illegal treatment of garment workers in Saipan, October 1.

San Francisco Business Times (1992) Apparel business unwrinkled by retailing slump, May 22, pp. 5 ff.

Sheff, D. (1993) Mr. Blue Jeans. *San Francisco Focus*, October p. 128.

Skidmore, D. (1994) U.S. penalizes China over illegal trade. *Boston Globe*, January 7, p. 59.

Southerland, D. (1993a) China purchases nearly $1 billion in US goods; recent buying spree turned a bid to preserve trade status. *Washington Post*, April 13, pp. A23 ff.

Southerland, D. (1993b) China said to still use forced labor.' *Washington Post*, May 19, pp. F3 ff.

Swoboda, F. (1992) Levi Strauss to drop suppliers violating its worker rights rules. *Washington Post*, March 13, pp. D1 ff.

Wall Street Journal (1993) China Supplement, December 10, p. R1.

Veverka, M. (1993) China syndrome: firms struggle on rights issue. *Crain's Chicago Business*, July 5, pp. 3 ff.

12 *Audi of America Inc.**

12.1 INTRODUCTION

On March 19, 1986, the Center for Auto Safety, a Washington-based group founded by consumer activist Ralph Nader, and the New York state attorney general submitted a petition to the National Highway Traffic Safety Administration (NHTSA) claiming that 1978–86 Audi 5000s equipped with automatic transmission were unsafe and demanding that they be recalled. A number of incidents involving injury and death had been reported in which Audi 5000s had surged out of control when the drivers shifted from park to drive or reverse. Unintended acceleration problems had been reported on other cars but not nearly as often as with the Audi 5000. The Audi, like many other European cars, placed the brake and gas pedals closer together than in many American designs so that a driver could move faster between pedals in high-speed emergencies. It was not, however, immediately clear that this was the cause of the problem.

12.1.1 The recall

In July 1986, Audi of America Inc. agreed to recall 132,000 1984–86 models to replace the idle stabilization valve and to relocate the brake and gas pedals. Audi management subsequently decided that installing a shift lock, which required the driver to depress the brake before shifting into gear, would be preferable. The cost of the recall to Audi was estimated at $25 million.

---

* This case was prepared by Professor John A. Quelch as the basis for class discussion rather than to illustrate either effective or ineffective handling of an administrative situation.

By January 1987, Audi had installed the shift lock in 70,000 cars. In that month, Audi decided to recall another 120,000 Audi 5000s sold between 1978 and 1983 for the same retrofit. Unfortunately for Audi, unintended acceleration incidents began to be reported on cars equipped with the shift locks. By May 1987, the Center for Auto Safety recorded the toll taken by unintended acceleration of Audi 5000s at 1,700 incidents, 1,500 accidents, over 400 injuries and seven deaths. In addition to product liability suits filed by victims of unintended acceleration, a class action suit seeking compensation from Audi was initiated on behalf of existing Audi owners whose cars' resale values were depressed by the problem.

12.1.2 Sales impact

The unintended acceleration problem had a devastating effect on Audi sales. In 1985, Audi of America enjoyed record sales of 74,000 units. In 1986, sales dropped to 60,000. The rate of decline accelerated following coverage of the Audi safety problem in November, 1986, on the CBS Show, *60 Minutes*. Audi management complained that reports of unintended acceleration increased dramatically following the broadcast. In January 1987, sales fell to 1,439, or 3.5 units per dealer, from 2,072 the previous year.

By March, Audi management faced a 248-day supply of 5000 models compared to a normal inventory of 60–65 days. Hence, Audi announced a $5,000 rebate from April 1 to June 30, 1987, on the purchase or lease of any 5000 series model. The rebate represented a 23 per cent discount off the dealer list price. Close to 120,000 coupons were mailed; 18,000 cars were sold or leased under the programme. An Audi survey showed that only six per cent of coupon recipients would have bought a car had the rebate been $4,000.

In the absence of the promotion, Audi of America sold only 41,300 vehicles in 1987 despite a new advertising campaign launched in the summer with a spending level double that in 1986. In addition, Audi introduced the more aerodynamically styled Audi 80 and 90 to replace the Audi 4000 series, a small and less expensive companion line to the 5000. World-wide Audi sales rose 14 per cent in 1987 despite the problem in the United States which accounted for only six per cent of the total.

12.1.3 The value assurance plan

January 1988 sales were only half those in January 1987. The new Audi 80s and 90s were not selling as well as had been expected. Audi management believed that consumer concern over the resale value of new Audis was restraining sales. They, therefore, conceived and launched in February 1988 a value assurance plan on all Audi 80s, 90s and 5000s.

Under the plan, Audi promised to refund the difference between any new Audi's resale value and the resale value of comparable models sold by BMW, Mercedes-Benz and Volvo. The Audi had to be resold between two and four years of the purchase date, and the value would be determined by the National Automobile Dealers Association (NADA) used car guide. A hypothetical example was cited in a February 1988 issue of *Automotive News*: assume a 1988 model Audi sold three years after the date of purchase was worth, on average, 56 per cent of its $25,000 value. If the average price of the designated competitive models was 60 per cent of their original prices, there would be a difference of four per cent in resale value. Audi would then multiply the $25,000 purchase price by four per cent – an equation worth $1,000 to the owner. Under the programme, the Audi 80 and 90 were considered comparable to the Mercedes Benz 190-E, BMW 325i, and Volvo 740. The Audi 5000S and Quattro were lined up against the Mercedes 269-F, BMW 528e and the Volvo 760 GLE. The Audi 5000 CS Turbo and Turbo Quattro were compared with the Mercedes 300-E, BMW 535I and Volvo 760 GLE Turbo.

12.1.4 The 1988 rebate

The value assurance plan had a positive but limited impact on retail sales. Frequent media reports on the progress of lawsuits filed against the company by victims of unintended acceleration did not help. Audi management looked forward to September when the 5000 series would be replaced by the new Audi 100 and 200 models that were already sold in Europe. Meanwhile, 1988 sales were still running at only half those in 1987.

Hence, Audi management conceived a second rebate programme whereby 400,000 certificates were mailed to current and former Audi owners offering a $4,000 rebate on those Audi 5000s with automatic transmissions still in stock. These vehicles carried a dealer sticker price of $22,180. The rebate offer was good from May 1 to August 31. An existing $2,500 per unit dealer incentive on remaining Audi 5000s was curtailed in favour of the consumer promotion.

It soon became apparent that only 5,500 qualified vehicles were available at Audi dealerships. In June 1988, Costa N. Kensington filed a $76 million class action suit claiming that the Audi promotion represented bait-and-switch advertising with the intent of selling Audi 80s and 90s which, at the time, carried a $2,000 per unit dealer incentive. Mr. Kensington stated: 'It is clear that the plan was not intended to benefit Audi customers but to jump-start sluggish sales of Audi's newly introduced automobiles.'

Federal Trade Commission regulations required a retailer to have 'a sufficient quantity of the advertised product to meet reasonably anticipated demands unless the advertisement clearly and adequately discloses that the supply is limited.' Audi officials pointed to a sentence on the back of the rebate coupon that read 'The availability of eligible vehicles is limited.' Attorney-general offices in Pennsylvania and Connecticut contended that this warning was inadequate because it did not specify the average number of cars at each dealership.

The Wall Street Journal reported on June 22 1988, that Audi executives had told their dealers to expect 24,000 interested buyers to visit showrooms as a result of the offer. Responding to a question regarding the gap between supply and demand of the Audi 5000, Audi's general sales manager, Joe Tate, said that the company's projection of 24,000 was inflated in order to generate enthusiasm among dealers and corporate members. 'If anything,' he said, 'we have pulled a bait-and-switch in the minds of our dealers. We may have hyped our numbers to excite a retail organization . . . so we could be certain to sell out the 5000s we had left. It was an attempt to build their confidence.' In a memo dated May 2 1988, Tate told the dealers that the programme had been devised 'to present attractive purchase alternatives' to coupon holders 'who discover that the new 80 and 90 series vehicles may be a better solution to their driving needs.' In the company newsletter of the same month, Tate expanded on the company's intentions pointing out that 'Hopefully we can send some of the excess (Audi) 5000 customers toward the 80 and 90 line. What we're trying to do is jump-start Audi sales.'

Separately, Dick Mugg, president of Audi America, commented: 'In the past, I expected total commitment from the dealer to the product. Now I realize that is a totally unfair expectation. The industry has changed over the years – and probably for the better. We're no different from Procter and Gamble. We've got to earn shelf space; we've got to earn dealer share of mind every day.'

Having already suffered allegations of mechanical failure, Audi shuddered at the prospect of a marketing plan which would compound criticism. An unidentified Audi executive commented: 'It's frightening to think that just after we've enraged customers with the whole sudden-acceleration issue, we can come back with something that could be construed as bait-and-switch and cause another whole public relations blow up.'

12.1.5 Future plans

Audi executives were concerned that their plans for launching the Audi 100 and 200 in August 1988, might be derailed by the accusations of bait-and-switch. In addition, Audi of America faced over 100 product liability suits and the class action suit faced by Audi owners seeking compensation for the loss in resale value of their cars had yet to be resolved. Management planned to launch a new programme called the Audi Advantage programme that covered almost all normal maintenance and repairs for three years or 50,000 miles on any new

Audi. Free roadside assistance was also included. Audi's agency had proposed an advertising campaign that claimed: 'Audi introduces a better car to own. And a better way to own a car.'

12.2   SOURCES

Automotive News (1988) Audi 5000 carries discount of $4,000, April 18.

Kahn, H. (1988) Audi tries to settle class suit. *Automotive News*, June 13.

Kumar Naj, A. (1987) Audi of America agrees to recall 5000 model cars. *Wall Street Journal*, January 16, p. 2.

Schwartz, B.A. (1988) Audi agrees to give owners of its 5000 rebate toward future Audi purchases. *Wall Street Journal*, June 8.

Schwartz, B.A. (1988) VW's Audi unit in the U.S. draws fire over controversial incentive programs. *Wall Street Journal*, June 22, p. 7.

Sundstrom, G. (1988) NHTSA won't end Audi probe. *Automotive News*, June 27.

Versical, D. (1987) An anatomy. *Automotive News*, May 4.

Versical, D. (1988a) Audi guarantees resale, offers dealer rebate. *Automotive News*, February 15.

Versical, D. (1988b) Mugg–Audi healer. *Automotive News*, May 30.

—PART III
Readings in international marketing ethics

13 Ethics and working with the Japanese: the entrepreneur and the 'elite course'*

Ernest Grundling

It has been widely acknowledged in recent years that American companies need to do a better job of adapting themselves to the Japanese market. Indeed, this is a favourite theme of Japanese executives and government officials when they discuss the trade imbalance, and many Americans will agree that they are at least partly right. But just what more effective 'adaptation' might mean in concrete terms is not always as clear, and sometimes the truth is not pleasant. One nitty-gritty area that has produced a great deal of ill will on both sides of the Pacific is that of business ethics.

The problem of when and how to adapt to different ethical standards is best approached by examining two sets of issues: those faced by Americans doing business in Japan, and those encountered by Japanese working with Americans. Comparative ethics is not an area which lends itself to scientific objectivity. It is hard to find objective indicators for moral outrage – that is, the feeling that you and yours have been abused or taken advantage of through foul play. (The one exception to this is the cases which wind up in court; some of these will be mentioned later on.) My presumption is that Americans and Japanese each have their ethical strengths and shortcomings, and that neither has the exclusive right to set up standards by which they may judge the other. The remarks below are based primarily on my own exposure to dozens of different companies and situations. I try here to present the hard truth – actual cases that represent all-too-common ethical disputes – and to speak plainly in the hope that this will lead to better mutual understanding and accommodation among Americans and Japanese.

13.1　AMERICANS IN JAPAN

13.1.1　Case #1

Mr Davidson, a US businessman who owns his own import/export firm, went to Tokyo representing an American client. The client is a small, high-tech manufacturer of various innovative products; the product that Mr Davidson was attempting to market for his client was a precision measuring device. In Tokyo, Mr Davidson contacted a Japanese trading company and set up a meeting. The Japanese firm was enthusiastic about the product and offered to look into the prospects for marketing it.

Soon a small order was placed from Japan; Mr Davidson and his client were very pleased. Unfortunately, there were no further orders that year. Repeated inquiries from Mr Davidson produced only vague responses. The next year another small order was placed, but once again this was to be the entire year's business. Mr Davidson made a second trip to Japan, and in a meeting with the trading firm he was assured that future prospects were bright and that it was only necessary to be patient. Mr Davidson could not be entirely unhappy because this was an expensive piece of equipment and he received a good commission even for a limited order. Although he felt that the Japanese market prospects were much brighter than sales to date reflected, he decided to go along with his Japanese partners for one more year.

Early in the third year, Mr Davidson received a letter from the Japanese trading company which abruptly terminated their marketing agreement. The letter cited changed market conditions, the expenses of large-scale marketing, and so on. However, soon Mr Davidson received an angry call from his American client, who informed him that a Japanese firm associated with the trading company had begun to manufacture and sell a device very similar to theirs. Further inquiries from Mr Davidson to Tokyo received no response.

Issue: not in the family

Among the many cases that I have seen and heard about, it appears that the US companies that most often experience rough treatment in the Japanese market are small vendors like Mr Davidson and his client who have not yet established any strong 'family' connection within the Japanese marketplace. Being both small and in a position of selling rather than buying means that they are at a disadvantage from the start in an acutely hierarchy-conscious society. Not having the protective umbrella of a strong tie-in with an established Japanese partner or customer further renders them fair game until such a connection – and the accepted social niche that it implies – is established.

Generalizations are obviously dangerous here and can never be more than partly true. Nor is the phenomenon of callous behaviour towards non-family members by any means unique to Japan. One client remarked that the Japanese attitude toward outsiders reminded him of his upbringing in an isolated part of the United States. Anthropologist Marshall Sahlins observes, 'There is a tendency for morality . . . to be sectorally organized in (traditional) societies. The norms are characteristically relative and situational rather than absolute and universal' (Sahlins 1972).

For foreigners doing business in Japan, it makes a great deal of difference whether they are perceived as being *uchi* (inside the company or home) or *soto* (outside). The old Japanese saying, '*Hito o mitara dorobo to omoe,*' can be translated roughly as, 'When you see a stranger, regard him as a thief.'

This leads to a paradoxical challenge for Americans who want to do business in Japan: they must build relationships and trust with a potential Japanese partner and yet exercise great caution until those relationships are secure. At a 1989 conference in San Francisco that dealt with US/Japan partnerships in the computer and software areas, speaker after speaker emphasized how crucial it is to do exhaustive homework on any joint venture prospect and to initiate contacts, whenever possible, through reliable, competent intermediaries.

13.1.2 Case #2

Mr Takahashi, a Japanese manager for a large American company, described the troubles his firm is having in bringing its products into Japan. The formulas for their sophisticated products are quite advanced, and involve proprietary information. According to Japanese law, these formulas must be registered exactly, but the company refuses to do so for fear that confidential information will be leaked to Japanese competitors (such events have apparently occurred in the past). Thus, a formula which has been registered, let's call it formula A, may be different in some respects from the range of products which are in fact brought into Japan under its name, say AA, AB, and AC.

Although the letter of the law is strict, and government officials will interpret it very rigidly when describing it in principle, the actual checking procedures are often not so strict, and the techniques used are not necessarily sophisticated enough to differentiate, for example, between formula A and formula AA. Moreover, if you begin to ask in detail about how to best comply with the regulations without disclosing essential proprietary information, one governmental department refers you to another, which refers you back to the first, which then might remark, 'Well, if *they* say it's okay, then . . .'

The Japanese competitors of the American company, according to Mr Takahashi, are importing similar products. They, too, for various reasons, are technically in violation of the registration laws. However, their employees are in regular contact with the government officials, whom they have known for years. If a violation is found in one of their products, a letter of apology is quickly sent from a high-ranking official of the company, and then that specific product is no longer imported. (In other words, they will no longer bring in, for instance, AA, but will continue with AB and AC, and perhaps even a new AAA.) In actual practice, a mere section chief might write the letter of apology, using the company president's name if the matter is serious enough.

As Mr Takahashi observed, these circumstances place his American employer at a competitive disadvantage. This particular US company is one of America's oldest and most conservative and prides itself on being a good corporate citizen. While its Japanese competition is energetically importing not only AA, AB, and AC, but AXYZ, and so on, the American company is reluctant to stray too far from the established formula. The company's president back at US headquarters takes letters of apology seriously and directs his Japan staff to avoid potential problems. Talking to the firm's lawyers only makes matters worse, because they foresee significant legal exposure whenever the law is not followed to the letter. In Mr Takahashi's view, his own company's stance, while in a sense admirable, is overly stiff and inflexible – not fully adapted to the 'real life' complexities of the Japanese business environment.

Issue: grey areas

Veteran expatriates in Japan and executives of American companies like Mr Takahashi's will describe as one of their greatest frustrations the many grey areas in Japan's laws. William Best, head of the distribution subcommittee at the American Chamber of Commerce in Japan, says, 'A number of vague regulations have created barriers for American enterprises operating in Japan . . . Japan has too many gray zones' (Inoue 1989).

The laws themselves, their arbitrary interpretation or non-enforcement by government bureaucrats, and/or the readiness of Japanese firms to exploit or even violate them, all seem from the American perspective to work to the advantage of local competitors. One of the best known recent examples was the legal catch-22 whereby foreign companies that wanted to bid on major Japanese public-works projects were required to have prior Japan experience in order to bid. A different case, this time of seemingly arbitrary enforcement, was the discovery by Merck Japan Ltd. that it would take at least eighteen months to obtain a licence to import a pharmaceutical raw material that Japanese competitors have been producing in bulk for years (ibid.). And lest one think that the energetic exploitation of vague and unevenly enforced laws is confined to the case detailed above, it is only necessary to turn to Japan's freewheeling securities industry. Knowledgeable observers claim that lax regulation there supports the common practice of boosting sales by making unwritten guarantees of profits to corporate customers and concealing this practice through the filing of false business reports.

The Japanese custom of giving gifts (including cash on numerous occasions) can make many grey areas look even greyer. The sensational Recruit scandal, which tarred virtually the entire front rank of leaders in Japan's ruling Liberal Democratic Party, focused international attention on enormous corporate donations made to politicians or their aides in a brazen attempt to curry favour. Perhaps the most striking fact about these donations, however, was that they were seldom illegal, but merely 'unseemly' in the eyes of an increasingly attentive Japanese press and public.

Awkward situations may be faced by US businessmen in Japan who are setting up a new distribution network, arranging special events, or even seeking medical care from a top physician within Japan's national health system. Sometimes a gift may genuinely represent a mere token of one's appreciation (as one customarily says in Japanese when presenting it), but other times the cash in the envelope is a lot more important than the envelope. The lavish entertainment expected by customers in Japan can be chalked up to relationship-building, yet at the same time those who have received Japanese-style red carpet treatment testify to a sense of tightening strings of obligation and may express doubts about their host's motives.

Americans in Japan who encounter one of the multitude of grey areas have at least two options, and sometimes both of these are pursued simultaneously. The first is to attempt to emulate local practices in so far as they do not place the company in violation of US laws. Hiring former government ministry officials to improve communication with the regulators, joining trade associations, setting up special expense account allowances for entertainment, creating a 'gift pool' to which expatriate employees and visiting executives donate gifts received – these are all measures that American corporations have implemented in good conscience to better fit into this world of grey. The second option is to make a frontal assault on the particular regulation or practice in question, often through the US Embassy's Commercial Section, and perhaps, as a final resort, through government to government trade negotiations. This latter course of action raises the stakes considerably; it almost invariably leads to heightened tensions, and it may or may not produce meaningful results.

13.2 THE JAPANESE AND US BUSINESS

13.2.1 Case #3

A Japanese trading company executive in New York complained bitterly about an event that for him confirmed the poor ethics of an American employee. This individual, he said, had been with the trading company for three years and was beginning to win the trust and respect of his Japanese colleagues. He was even invited to attend a series of vital strategic meetings held at the company's US head-quarters. But shortly after attending these meetings the American left the company and joined a competing firm.

It was particularly galling to this Japanese executive that, if such an employee had already been making plans to leave, he would compound his disloyalty by attending these meetings and walking off with vital strategic information. Such a man, the executive said vehemently, would not be hired by another company in the same industry in Japan, and he should certainly not be trusted with any significant responsibility.

Issue: loyalty

The ethical primacy in Japan of loyalty to one's working group is confirmed by the reaction to other cases which have been inter-preted quite differently in the West. Clyde Prestowitz, whose insight and respect for the Japanese is often overlooked amidst the charges of 'Japan bashing', makes a very interesting observation about the Hitachi-IBM spy incident, in which an FBI sting opera-tion caught Hitachi employees in the act of obtaining proprietary IBM documents.

The American consultant for Hitachi, William Palyn, who first tipped off the FBI, was seen in a positive light by Americans for upholding principle at his own personal expense. In the Japanese press, on the contrary, he was portrayed as having dishonorably violated a human bond and betrayed those who had placed their trust in his loyalty: 'In Japan it was Hitachi, not IBM, that was seen as the aggrieved party' (Prestowitz 1988).

Unfortunately, the perceived failure of American employees to live up to Japanese ethical standards in this area can produce a negative spiral of self-confirming expectations. Forewarned by a litany of similar stories, Japanese managers in the US are under-standably cautious about sharing inside information with employees whose long-term loyalty to the company might be in question. As one such manager said to me recently, 'Many of them are just using us to get a few years of experience with a Japanese company, and then they'll go off to work elsewhere.' This attitude tends to substantiate the fears of those very employees that they will not be granted any real authority, making them still more likely to seek other employment, and thus the cycle is perpetuated.

Japanese companies here are confronted with the difficult imperative to build loyalty – in spite of past disappointments – by creating an upward spiral of increasing mutual trust, shared information and responsibility, and employee stability. Figures released by MITI show that in Japanese-related companies in the US, 85 per cent of the CEOs and 68 per cent of the executives are from Japan; the comparable figure for American CEOs in Japan is approximately 20 per cent. The director of the Japanese Overseas Enterprises Association puts the matter simply: 'Head offices should entrust more decision making to the overseas affiliates and subsidiaries. They would be better able to relate to local concerns' (Ogihara 1988/9).

Akio Morita has been criticized for his co-authorship of *The Japan That Can Say No*. However, anyone who reads the book carefully will recognize that it includes excellent suggestions for Japanese managers in the US who want to create a dedicated, loyal workforce and be welcomed in the communities where they live: offer employees a combination of training opportunities and job security, be personally accessible, join the PTA, contribute to local charities, and set an example of modest living and hard work (Morita and Ishihara 1989a, b).

13.2.2 Case #4

The US marketing office of a leading-edge American computer maker announced that a new product line would be available to the company's Japanese customers in October of 1988. But one month before the announced date, there was a four-month postponement to February 1989. Later, the date was pushed back again to mid-1989. At last word, the mid-1989 deadline, too, had passed and the schedule was still uncertain.

The Japanese president of the company's subsidiary in Japan described in no uncertain terms how damaging this series of events had been to the reputation and morale of his company and its Japanese sales staff. The only way that his sales force had been able to blunt the displeasure of established customers had been for them to actually recommend the use of competitors' products. One key sales manager, and a good friend of the president, was so ashamed and humiliated at having to go back to the customer repeatedly to apologize that he finally left the company.

Issue: commitments

Overly optimistic product schedules are a fact of life for American and Japanese companies alike in competitive markets where the technology is changing quickly. What often seems to get Americans in trouble in this area is that they fail to communicate with sufficient care and frequency. There is a perpetual cat and mouse game in Japan between customer and vendor, where a 'commitment' is ardently sought by each and usually given only with a high degree of certainty.

Americans tend to stumble unwittingly into this game and are perceived, sometimes not without wilful misinterpretation, as too readily making commitments which they then cannot keep. (The converse result, where the American side misreads the vaguely positive but non-committal signals of the Japanese, is better known.) The game becomes deadly serious once a specific commitment is made, as it is then a point of honour to deliver, or at the very least to do one's absolute best and to keep the other party constantly informed of any progress or changes.

The Japanese antidote to unmet commitments is an immediate, sincere, unqualified apology, but this is a serum whose efficacy decreases with use; broken commitments in Japan soon lead to a judgement of unreliability and ultimately to expulsion and ostracism from the group. The sales manager who left his company in a sense anticipated such a reaction and preserved whatever honour remained to him by sacrificing his own job. Some skilled Japanese salesmen in other, similar firms have been able to turn their American employer's unmet commitments to their advantage by evoking a sympathetic reaction: 'Well, it must be tough for you to work for a foreign company; just don't let it happen again.' Yet this tactic, too, only works for so long.

From the standpoint of almost any Japanese company employee with purchasing authority, it is a risk to buy from a foreign supplier that may or may not understand the local definition of 'commitment'. Not only will he have to turn a deaf ear to the fraternal pleas of long-time associates from within the same commercial family who want to supply the product, but he must shoulder the blame if the supplier fails to deliver as promised. The failures of American companies to meet commitments have become legendary within the Japanese rumour mill, just as Japanese bureaucratic shenanigans are played up in the US media. It is particularly the leading Japanese exporters, prompted by outside demands for reciprocity and threats of retaliation, who are swallowing their doubts and taking the 'risks'. The US company's reputation for quality and reliability, a manufacturing site in Japan, sought-after technology, continuity of personnel in key positions – factors such as these help to overcome the worries of prospective Japanese customers about relying on commitments made by potentially unreliable outsiders.

Although out of respect for the confidentiality of friends and clients I have made some modifications in the four cases given above, they are all none the less quite real, and I encounter similar events on a daily basis in my work. They are not intended to imply, for example, that Americans never prey upon small Japanese companies (T. Boone Pickens has made the mistake of trying to rustle a junior affiliate of the Toyota family). Nor do they mean that people in the US are incapable of strong and enduring loyalty to their employers. But I believe that these cases do represent common 'types' of ethical misunderstandings between Americans and Japanese.

13.3   COURT CASES

The types of ethical confrontations which I have illustrated are confirmed by disputes that have appeared in US and Japanese courts. Several of the most widely publicized cases of the last decade brought by Americans against Japanese can be seen as further variations on the theme of 'not in the family'. They include:

- The public as well as formal legal opposition of the small American manufacturer Fusion Systems Corp. against Mitsubishi Electric Corp. for what it claims to be predatory violations of its patents.
- The suits of two former high-level NEC Electronics, Inc. executives against their employer for, among other things, violation of assurances that they would have significant management authority.
- The sex discrimination case, resolved by a multi-million dollar settlement in 1987, of thirteen female clerical workers against Sumitomo Corp. of America.

Whether these American complaints are against predatory competitive practices, allegedly false promises of membership and authority, or second class status within a given organization, they are all directed against some perceived form of Japanese family exclusivity.

It is only fair to point out that Japanese executives familiar with these cases have their own point of view. They observe that American companies and workers don't see the big picture and have an unrealistic time frame for advancement within the Japanese system. Qualified candidates for promotion are hard to find – many US workers lack even the most basic knowledge of English, math, or geography. And Americans, they say, will forgo sustained effort or compromise and prematurely resort to acrimonious public lawsuits even though problems could be settled more amicably.

On the other hand, a court case still pending in Japan that has garnered considerable negative publicity there has been portrayed as a classic tale of 'broken commitment'. This case stems from the withdrawal of the venerable *Reader's Digest* from the Japanese market. As far as *Reader's Digest* is concerned, the company gave Japan its best shot: during its 24 years as a wholly-owned subsidiary, *Reader's Digest* Japan had only 11 profitable years, and underwent numerous reorganizations; circulation dropped from 1.5 million in 1949 to a final figure of 400,000 in 1985. 'We tried to make it work, we were hopeful . . . but there was no foreseeable improvement,' a *Reader's Digest* spokesman told me. From the standpoint of the company's headquarters in the US, the closure of its Japan subsidiary was an eminently sensible business decision.

The company's union and segments of the Japanese press, on the other hand, portrayed the parent company as being guilty of neglect and abandonment in the face of unswerving loyalty. Indeed, one gets a sense from some of their comments that the company is guilty of a crime akin to child abandonment, and should be branded with the same moral invective that Americans would heap on a father or mother who leaves their infant on someone else's doorstep. The disgruntled Japanese labour union went so far as to place op-ed ads in the *New York Times* saying that 'they are a company that dumped its Japanese readers and its own employees' and that the company's behaviour was 'unfair', 'unscrupulous', 'irresponsible', that it acted 'without warning' – the charges go on and on (Carter 1987; *The New York Times* 1986)[1].

13.4   EXPLANATION – US VS THEM THEORIES

The ethical differences which I have outlined are commonly explained in terms of dualistic sets of attributes:

Japanese

- group-orientation
- case-by-case (depending on the relationship)
- administrative guidance, go-betweens

Americans

- self-orientation
- principles
- laws and legal remedies

Such dichotomies have long held explanatory value, and social commentators will no doubt continue to make reference to them. But in light of rapid changes in Japan and in the US, I believe that we must begin to consider their limitations and the many counter-trends which they do not explain.

How about, for example, the celebrated 'group-orientation' of the Japanese? Recently there have been startling developments in Japan's private sector which have attracted little popular attention in the US, perhaps because they are so commonplace in our own country. There is a strong and accelerating trend among Japanese companies to recruit mid-career workers away from their competitors, and many of these workers willingly leave their former employers for more pay, better opportunities for advancement, and so on. Although this phenomenon has existed to some degree for many years, it has begun to take on significant proportions: a recent survey indicates that about one fourth of the present white collar work force has changed jobs within the last three years; 65 per cent of 1,474 large Japanese companies polled use mid-career recruitment. In fact, mid-career hiring is now being practised by a number of what have traditionally been Japan's most conservative banking and insurance institutions (Nagashima 1990; Berger 1990).[2]

The term, self-orientation, on the other hand, is not particularly helpful in explaining the successes that certain Japanese manufacturing concerns in the US have had in recruiting and retaining long-term employees. One can cite a growing cadre of American workers in Japanese companies, most especially in rural areas, who work well together in Japanese-style teams, are highly motivated, have perhaps even received training in Japan, and who could end up spending their entire working career at the same company if present circumstances continue.

The Japanese government has made considerable efforts to supplement a 'case-by-case' approach and the traditional practice of 'administrative guidance' with more transparent principles and legal remedies. One can point, for example, to Japan's new insider trading law and the efforts of the Finance Ministry to implement it. In a separate case, the Fair Trade Commission reacted swiftly some months ago to charges that low ball bids in the computer industry lock out foreign competition; it launched an investigation which has led to rare public rebukes of at least two prestigious companies by MITI. These efforts may represent in part simply a reluctant response to foreign demands, but it is worth remembering that foreign pressure has functioned historically in Japan as a rationale and a catalyst for reforms with strong internal backing.

American companies in Japan, too, are learning how to constructively coexist with the government ministries and to resolve disputes through 'go-betweens' when necessary. Companies that have paid their dues and created their own network of business and government relations in Japan – IBM, Coca-Cola, and Procter & Gamble, for example – have found that the Japanese market can be a profitable place for insiders.

13.5 INTERLOCKING IDEALS – AN ALTERNATIVE EXPLANATION

Thus, simple dichotomies no longer provide an adequate explanatory framework for US/Japan relations, if indeed they ever did. The real fabric of our world is more alive and intensely interconnected. Our countries have dynamic cultural systems which shape our development, explain us to ourselves, provide a vision of the future, and are constantly being reshaped by human ingenuity and fresh exigencies. Our cultures exert strong transformative pressures on each other through exchanges in almost every conceivable cultural field: economics, politics, language, the media, art, scholarship. (A case in point is the latest turn in our government to government negotiations: both countries have presented lists of fundamental structural reforms which the other must undertake in order to resolve trade issues.)

We are each other's severest critics and greatest impetus to economic, social, and cultural change. For this reason 'creativity', a treasured American asset, can also become a rallying-point for Japanese industry; at the same time, the highest-ranking US government official in Japan has seriously suggested changes in American antitrust law to permit more Japanese-style co-operation between companies in certain areas (Tatsuno 1990; Armacost 1989).

Rather than neat dichotomies, then, it is more accurate to envision sets of contrasting cultural ideals embedded within a vast, interlocking web. We are different; we are the same; we overlap; they are our distant reflection. Japan is an echo of each American's lost home country, the elusive refinement and cultural sophistication that we always seem to lack, our work ethic, our great enemy and friend risen harrowingly from the ashes. America, for Japan, is openness, freedom from narrow spaces and tiresome social obligations, a fascinating, repulsive paragon of the fertile, the mixed, the impure, of the chaotic social decay that it seeks to drive out from its own tidy islands.

13.5.1 The entrepreneur and the elite course

The ideals of our respective cultures, I think, somehow capture and portray for us our primary values and aspirations. It is, moreover, at least partly on this symbolic level that ethical assumptions are formed. Ideals are important, even if they are also elusive and difficult to analyse. Two pivotal, linked ideals which I would suggest to help explain our ethical differences are the *Entrepreneur* and the *Elite Course*.

The entrepreneur is easily recognized by most Americans. He or she (because this is America) is someone who has the vision, the guts, and the drive to start a company, and is tough and flexible enough to keep it going.

If you work for a big company and you have a bright idea that no one will listen to, you have a choice: take the safe route and bury your dreams or step out on your own. There is nothing wrong with moving on if that's what it takes to make your idea work. The fault lies rather with the company that is not able to accommodate the restless, creative, entrepreneurial spirit. Harnessing creative entrepreneurship is the guiding theme behind much of contemporary American management training and corporate models like 3M's 'champion' system. 'Go for it', Americans say, and their cultural heroes are those who have done just that, whether they were a Thomas Edison or George Eastman in the past or a present-day Steven Jobs or Bill Gates.

The Japanese expression 'Elite Course' (originally borrowed from English and pronounced 'Eriito Coosu' in Japanese) focuses less on certain individuals than it does on a type of group member and a 'way' of doing things. The course includes graduation from one of the best schools and lifetime employment at a prestigious large company, or, for the very best candidates, in a government ministry. Gradually, through systematic training and rotation between the various key company departments, possibly even including a stint (but not too long) at an overseas subsidiary, one gains vital experience. Balanced judgement, thoroughness, and above all a good human network are valued qualities. With experience comes not only good business sense but also sensitivity to nuance and human subtleties; the ability to read the emotions of colleagues and customers requires what the Japanese call *kan* (finely-honed intuition).[3]

At the peak of the Japanese bureaucratic and corporate world are many such men (and they still almost invariably are men): experienced, savvy, quietly proud, and utterly dedicated to their particular institution. It is a roll call of elite government ministries and conglomerates, and not necessarily individuals, which comes to mind: The Ministry of Finance, MITI, the Ministry of Foreign Affairs, Mitsubishi, Mitsui, Sumitomo, Sanwa, Dai-lchi Kangyo.

13.5.2 Dialogue among 'natives'

Understanding cultures as many-sided, interlocking systems without rigid dichotomies permits us to acknowledge that America has its Ivy League version of the Elite Course and Japan has its own sophisticated forms of entrepreneurship.[4] At the same time, it is unrealistic to suppose that the complexity and interdependence of our societies precludes all distinctions. The extraordinary dominance of Tokyo University graduates in Japanese government and business – about half of the post-war prime ministers, for example, are graduates of this one university – finds no equivalent in the United States. Nor is the seething, restless brew of small, independent, high-tech start-ups present in California or on Route 128 in Massachusetts yet to be found in Japan. And if we succumb to the temptation to minimize differences, how can we account for the deep sense of ethical violation that we are still able to engender in each other?

It seems to me that the deeply entrepreneurial cast of US social life and imagination may help to explain why Americans' first loyalty is to themselves and their ideas. Broken commitments are usually not intended, but are rather a regrettable fact of life when mobility and change are taken for granted; the fixation of US business negotiations on detailed legalisms and written contracts is an attempt to slow this moving target.

The Elite Course is commonly pursued by an individual Japanese within a single institutional family, and this institution has its place within a larger hierarchical pyramid where movement of both institutions and individuals is restricted. Given these facts, it is not surprising that ethics should have an inwardly-focused, centripetal alignment, and that extreme measures are justified in defence of one's institutional household and career path. 'Grey' administrative guidance from on high by government bureaucracies can be accepted and properly interpreted because so much else is clear: the place of the individual, of his company, and of the bureaucratic elite.

Although I do not feel that this kind of explanation of our ethical differences is complete or likely to meet with universal agreement, it does seem to me worthwhile for both sides to examine more closely the values, images, and assumptions that jostle for pre-eminence in our minds. Ideals like those of the Entrepreneur and Elite Course may be so close to the heart of our ethical choices that we take them for granted, and we are thus all the quicker to brand the other person as a scoundrel when he fails to measure up.

The very assumption that the way to solve problems is to 'explain' and to engage in 'dialogue' is perhaps itself more American than Japanese. Nevertheless, in a world where no single country can legitimately lay claim to economic and cultural superiority, it is vital to recognize along with the anthropologists that 'we are all natives now', to stop calling each other names, and to try to figure out how to deal with the differences that persist (Geertz 1983: 151).

13.6   TOWARDS A FULLER VISION – THE MIRROR ON OUR WALL

Part of the challenge of ethical misunderstandings between the US and Japan lies in the fact that each country has to overcome its own greatest contemporary social weakness to succeed in terms of the other's ethical standards. 'Their' ideals must to a certain degree become 'ours', not just to make money in their country but to right our own social evils.

Americans – champions of personal freedom, rights, and mobility, as well as of the assimilation of different cultures – suffer from the assorted consequences of attenuated family structure. Yet in order to succeed in Japan, it is precisely the artful give and take of the extended family that we must practise. This includes certain responsibilities to nurture and uphold loyalties and to fulfil commitments that are integral to a productive constellation of relationships in Japan. Careful, long-term planning and a substantial investment is required to build dedicated, skilled human resources and a faithful customer base. Excessive legalism is generally an unproductive short-cut that must be supplanted by an accumulation of mutual trust and reasonable, good-faith solutions.

On the other hand, the Japanese – masters of the tightly structured, hardworking village, be it agricultural or corporate – need to learn how to open up the village and its family structure to include Caucasians, blacks, Koreans, women managers, creative eccentricity, and the enthusiastic ideal of service to a wider humanity. Takako Doi, leader of the main opposition party in Japan, recently described her country as an economic giant but a human rights midget. Internationalization, a contemporary buzzword in Japan, is more than learning English, driving a BMW, or travelling abroad on a carefully planned group tour. It is knowing the *gaijin* (literally, 'outside person', the Japanese word for foreigner) as a full-fledged friend and associate, a fellow human being. It is also being able to trace a clear path from the periphery of the village to the warm core of the family and being willing to walk that path together.

The only way to account not only for the typical issues enumerated above – family exclusivity, grey areas, loyalty, commitment – but also for countertrends and future directions is to acknowledge that Americans and Japanese alike are capable of recognizing their weaknesses and modifying their ideals, especially when faced with dire economic and political pressures. Countless American entrepreneurs are now eagerly in search of Japanese partners; whether a significant number of them can ever become honoured family members is still hard to predict. Elements of the many-sided Japanese bureaucracy, representing the pinnacle of the Elite Course and much of the brain power behind Japan's export machine, are also, ironically, at the forefront of legal reforms and other important steps toward internationalization.

Mike Mansfield, former US Ambassador to Japan, is famous for characterizing America's connection with Japan as its 'most important bilateral relationship bar none'. One can certainly justify such a statement on the basis of the size of our respective economies, the pace of technological innovation, and the weight of political decisions made by the two countries. But there is more to it than this.

The unsettling truth that lies behind Mr Mansfield's observation is that the US/Japan relationship is a profound test of human good will, and of our capacities to stretch our understanding and adapt to the 'other'. I have enumerated crucial ethical differences, concrete steps which have been or could be taken by both sides, certain theoretical tools for understanding, and general prescriptions towards mutual accommodation. But nobody ever said it would be easy. This is the test that our crucial bilateral relationship can least afford to fail.

13.7   NOTES

[1]   The former Editor-in-Chief of Reader's Digest Japan has written a detailed account in Japanese of the subsidiary's demise, pointing out errors by both union and management, see Ko Shioya (1986).

[2]   There is also an interesting series of articles in a special edition of the Japanese magazine *Kin'yu zaisei jijo* (October 1989) entitled, 'Jinzai no jidai' ga kite' ('The Age of Human Resources Has Come'). In this series, for example, a personnel manager of a prestigious financial institution cites his company's plan for mid-career hires to eventually number at least 20 per cent of all employees, up from zero as recently as six years ago.

[3]   Other writers have adopted the term 'Elite Course', including, for example, Thomas Rohlen and Robert Frager in Lewis Austin, ea., *Japan: The Paradox of Progress*, New Haven, CT: Yale University Press, 1976, p. 264.

[4]   See, for example, Tatsuno's (1990) discussion of Japanese intra-preneurs' and the considerable efforts of Japan's government and commercial enterprises to fill out what Tatsuno calls the 'mandala of creativity'.

13.8   REFERENCES

Armacost, M., US Ambassador to Japan (1989) We know what we need to do, and we will do it! *The Journal of the American Chamber of Commerce in Japan* (September 1989), pp. 49–60.

Berger, M. (1990) *The San Francisco Chronicle*, March 19, pp. C1, C10.

Carter, J.M. (1987) Translating the Japanese market. *Adweek*, February 28, p. 26.

Geertz, C. (1983) *Local Knowledge: Further Essays in Interpretive Anthropology*, New York, NY: Basic Books, Inc.

Inoue, Y. (1989) Ministries rapped for excessive 'guidance'. *The Japan Economic Journal*, December 2, pp. 1, 6.

Morita, A. and Ishihara, S. (1989a) The Japan that can say no, *U.S. Congressional Record*, November 14.

Morita, A. and Ishihara, S. (1989b) *'NO'* to ieru Nihon, Tokyo: Kobunsha.

Nagashima, H. (1990) *The Japan Times*, February 28.

Ogihara, M. (1988/9) MITI: Japan firms overseas slow to adopt local customs. *The Japan Economic Journal*, December 31, January 7, p. 5.

Prestowitz, C. (1988) *Trading Places. How We Allowed Japan to Take the Lead*, New York, NY: Basic Books, Inc., p. 87.

Sahlins, M. (1972) *Stone Age Economics*, New York, NY: Aldine Publishers, p. 199.

Shioya, K. (1986) *Riidai noshi* (A Requiem for Reader's Digest), Tokyo: Simul Press, Inc.

Tatsuno, S. (1990) *Created in Japan: From Imitators to World-Class Innovators*, New York, NY: Harper and Row.

The New York Times (1986) Op-ed page, December 29.

14 *Corporate policy and the ethics of competitor intelligence gathering**

Lynn Sharp Paine

Competitor intelligence, information that helps managers understand their competitors, is highly valued in today's marketplace. Firms, large and small, are taking a more systematic approach to competitor intelligence collection. At the same time, information crimes and litigation over information disputes appear to be on the rise, and survey data show widespread approval of unethical and questionable intelligence-gathering methods. Despite these developments, few corporations address the ethics of intelligence gathering in their corporate codes of conduct. Neither managers nor management educators have paid sufficient attention to this topic. From a review of questionable intelligence-gathering practices reported in various literatures, the author identifies some important ethical principles to help managers draw the line between legitimate and illegitimate methods of information acquisition. The chapter also discusses the costs of failure to heed these principles and suggests steps managers can take to provide ethical leadership in this area.

14.1 CORPORATE POLICY AND THE ETHICS OF COMPETITOR INTELLIGENCE GATHERING

Top management's ethical leadership role requires continuing attention to the changing nature of the market-place. New businesses and business practices often raise novel ethical questions and introduce new areas of ethical vulnerability. Interpreting or reinterpreting ethical standards in the light of the changing business environment, alerting employees to the new ethical issues and pressures they may face, and providing guidance and institutional structures that support appropriate responses are important aspects of the manager's role.

* Reprinted from the *Journal of Business Ethics*, 10 (1991), pp. 423–36. Corporate policy and the ethics of competitor intelligence gathering, L. Sharp Paine, with kind permission from Kluwer Academic Publishers.

The purpose of this paper is to highlight the need for management to address the ethics of competitor intelligence gathering. Recent developments in the business environment have generated increasing interest in competitor intelligence, information that helps managers understand their competitors. Although information about rival firms has always been a valued and sought-after commodity, competitor intelligence gathering has only recently begun to be systematized and legitimated as a business function. While understanding the competition is an important part of running a business, there are ethical limits on the types of competitor information that may be acquired; on the methods that may be employed to acquire it; and on the purposes for which it may be used. To date, however, few managers or management educators have addressed the ethics of intelligence gathering.

This chapter will focus primarily on methods of acquiring competitor information. Separating legitimate from illegitimate approaches to information acquisition is, in practice, the central ethical issue for intelligence-gathering specialists. Although important questions surround the issue of what types of information, if any, should be treated as private or confidential to a firm, and thus off-limits for intelligence gatherers, these questions can in practice be minimized, although not eliminated, by respecting certain ethical principles in the selection of acquisition techniques. By examining some questionable but commonly used intelligence-gathering practices, this chapter will identify the ethical principles at issue; discuss the risks of failure to respect these principles; and suggest steps managers can take to encourage ethically sound intelligence-gathering activities.

14.1.1 Growth of competitor intelligence gathering

Evidence of the growth of interest in competitor intelligence is abundant. A 1985 study which looked at the intelligence-gathering budgets of twenty-five Fortune 500 companies found that all had increased substantially over the preceding five-year period (Information Data Search, Inc. 1986). Five years earlier, one-third of the companies had not had intelligence-gathering departments at all. Respondents to a 1986 study of 50 firms anticipated a dramatic increase in their intelligence-gathering budgets and almost all foresaw rapid growth in the staff assigned to intelligence gathering over the succeeding five-year period (ibid.: 6). The findings of a recent Conference Board study of more than 300 US firms were similar. Nearly all respondents said that monitoring competitors' activities is important and more than two-thirds expect their monitoring efforts to increase (Sutton 1988). The trend is not confined to the United States. British companies, too, are increasingly setting up systems to collect competitor intelligence (The Fuld & Company Letter 1989). The Japanese reputation for careful intelligence gathering is well-established.

In-house formalization of the intelligence-gathering function has been accompanied by the growth of consulting firms specializing in competitor information collection (Tucker 1986). Some consultants have prospered by offering seminars for employees of smaller companies that cannot afford separate intelligence-gathering departments.[1] Data bases, newsletters, and self-help books have proliferated as well. National membership in the Society of Competitor Intelligence Professionals has grown to nearly 900 in its first three years.[2]

Although the value of competitor intelligence has long been appreciated, it appears that systematic efforts to collect it are on the increase.[3] This is understandable, given the sheer proliferation of available information and the advantages that can flow from knowing what rivals are up to.[4] Knowledge about rival firms' strategies, research and development efforts, products, customers, expansion plans, workforce, costs, pricing, and so on can translate into competitive advantages for the short, if not the long, terms.[5]

14.1.2 The darker side

There is, however, a darker side to the growth of intelligence gathering. It is reflected in the use of ethically questionable techniques for collecting information, the increase in trade-secret litigation and information crimes, and the increase in the resources devoted to corporate security. One expert on trade-secret law estimates that court rulings on theft and misappropriation of information have increased fourfold over the past decade to more than 200 a year and that the actual problem of information misappropriation is at least ten times as large.[6] Another reports a surge in information crimes.[7] The American Society for Industrial Security, which includes both outside consultants and in-house security groups, was reported in 1986 to have 24,000 members and to be gaining 5,000 new members a year (Haas 1986).

Explanations for the increase in information disputes are varied. Some commentators point to the rising costs of research and development associated with today's advanced technology. It is simply cheaper to get ideas from a competitor than to invest in research.[8] Other commentators point to the inadequacy of law in the face of advancing technology: the law is just not keeping up.[9] Still others suggest that the increase in information disputes is simply a reflection of the sheer increase in the volume of information now available through information technology. While there may be some truth to all these explanations, it is doubtful that all the turmoil can be laid at the door of developing technology. Many well-documented information disputes have arisen over questionable intelligence-gathering practices unrelated to modern information technology in industries that are decidedly low-tech. Trash surveillance in the casket industry,

(Johnson 1987) cookie recipe espionage in the food industry,[10] and employee piracy in the car rental business,[11] for example, have all given rise to information litigation.

Moreover, a close look at information quarrels in high-technology industries shows that they frequently involve intelligence about marketing strategies or costs and pricing rather than new technologies. Charges which resulted from the 'Ill Wind' investigations of the defence industry, for instance, centre on the bribery of public officials to obtain information about competitors' bids (Carrington and Pound 1988). Similarly, marketing information was at issue in the dispute that arose when an advertising agency seeking the business of software manufacturer Microsoft hired account executives who had worked on the account of Microsoft's main rival, Lotus Development Corporation, at a competing agency. In a letter to Microsoft, the agency touted its access to information about Lotus: 'You see, the reason we know so much about Lotus is that some of our newest employees just spent the past year and a half working on the Lotus business at another agency. So they are intimately acquainted with Lotus' thoughts about Microsoft . . .'[12]

These examples, and others described in the press and recent court decisions, show that the increase in information litigation cannot be explained solely by increasingly complex and costly technology. The increase also reflects the growing use of questionable techniques to gain access to ordinary business information generated by or about competing firms. The use of these techniques may evidence a general decline in ethical standards or a decline in resourcefulness and creativity. It may also be a by-product of increased competition and the competitor orientation of current thinking about business strategy.[13]

14.1.3 Ethics and the competitor orientation of strategy

Within the competitive strategy framework, competitor information and analysis are essential to strategy formulation. There is nothing inherently wrong with such an approach to business strategy. Indeed, much can be said for it from the point of view of efficiency. However, the approach raises broad ethical questions about ideals of competition and the spirit in which it is undertaken, as well as more specific questions about the methods and limits of information acquisition.

Traditionally, the highest and best form of competition was thought to reflect a striving for excellence by each competitor. Interfering with a rival's efforts, or even taking advantage of his weaknesses, was regarded as a departure from this ideal. Motivated by a vision of excellence, each competitor was thought to be engaged in an independent, constructive and positive effort to attain the objective in question. As Adam Smith said, 'in the race for wealth . . . [a person] may run as hard as he can, and strain every nerve and every muscle, in order to outstrip all his competitors. But if he should jostle, or throw down any of them . . . it is a violation of fair play (Smith 1976). The traditional view is reflected in the common law of unfair competition and in antitrust law, both of which prohibit certain business tactics whose motive is to drive out competition.

The traditional ideal recognizes a fine but important distinction between using competitor information constructively to guide strategy formulation and using it destructively to undo the competition. This distinction is largely a matter of the attitude or spirit in which economic rivalry is undertaken rather than its results. Contrary to the traditional ideal, much current thinking recommends explicit consideration of how best to undermine the competition. Some of the tactics recommended by competitive strategy specialists directly conflict with the ideal and would very likely violate competition law.[14]

To the extent that firms adopt the competitor orientation of current thinking about strategy, their need for information about their competitors increases. Along with new incentives for employees to gather competitor information come new pressures and opportunities for unethical conduct. As competitor analysis becomes the order of the day and the premium on competitor information rises, management can expect the use of questionable intelligence-gathering tactics to spread unless ethical limits are articulated and widely understood.

14.1.4 Questionable methods of acquiring intelligence

While surveys have examined people's willingness to engage in specific questionable practices, and at least one author has provided a list of ethical and unethical intelligence-gathering techniques, the ethical principles at issue in this area have not generally been made explicit.[15] However, a review of studies of questionable practices, judicial opinions, news reports, popular articles, and the writings of intelligence-gathering experts, reveals that the most prevalent methods of questionable intelligence gathering fall into three broad ethical categories:

1   those involving deceit or some form of misrepresentation;
2   those involving attempts to influence the judgement of persons entrusted with confidential information, particularly the offering of inducements to reveal information;
3   those involving covert or unconsented-to surveillance.

Norms prohibiting practices in these categories appear to be weaker than norms prohibiting theft of documents and other tangible property, a fourth category of ethically problematic intelligence gathering.

In contrast to intelligence gathering which relies on information that firms have disclosed to public authorities or to the general public or which is available through open and above-board inquiry, questionable techniques are generally employed to obtain information which the firm has not disclosed, is not obligated to disclose, and probably would not be willing to disclose publicly. But most of these techniques would be objectionable – whatever type of information they elicited – because they offend common standards of morality calling for honesty, respect for relationships of trust and confidence, and respect for privacy. While stating these principles does not resolve difficult and disputed questions concerning their interpretation and application, some of which are discussed below, understanding the principles can contribute to clearer thinking about the factors distinguishing legitimate from illegitimate practice.

Several indicators point to the use of techniques that violate or call into question these principles.

(a) Misrepresentation

Opinion research indicates that many employees say their companies condone, and they themselves approve of, the use of various forms of misrepresentation to gather competitor intelligence (Cohen and Czepiec 1988). For example, 45.9 per cent of the respondents to a questionnaire administered to 451 participants in seminars on intelligence gathering approved of getting information by posing as a graduate student working on a thesis (ibid.: 200–1). A striking 85.6 per cent of the respondents believe their competitors would use this method of intelligence gathering.

The same study found that 46.8 per cent felt comfortable posing as a private research firm and that 38.4 per cent approved of posing as a job-seeking college student. The study showed a close correspondence between respondents' level of approval for various practices and their perceptions of their employers' approval. The study concluded that practitioners seem to align their views of what is acceptable with what they perceive to be company standards, although the authors were not sure who influenced whom (ibid.: 202).

The use of misrepresentation can take many forms: conducting phony job interviews (Flax 1984), hiring students to gather intelligence under the guise of doing academic work (Ansberry 1988), posing as a potential joint venturer, supplier or customer.[16] The prevalence of phony interviews has led at least one marketing manager to remind his people that 'a job interview may be a total sham, a way to get intelligence' (Sutton 1988: 15). The victims of deceit may be rival firms, themselves, their suppliers and customers, or other parties with access to valuable information.

In a recently litigated case, a marketing manager and his firm were found liable for damages incurred by a competitor that had revealed confidential information to the manager and another employee when they posed as a potential customer.[17] The marketing manager, whose branch office was failing to meet its sales quotas and who personally was failing to meet his own quotas, arranged to have a new hire who had not yet joined the firm pose as a potential customer for the competitor's software. The manager attended the software presentation as a friend and consultant of the supposed customer, but without identifying himself or his employer. As a result of the misrepresentation, the pair were given a detailed demonstration of the software, in-depth answers to their questions, and access to the competitor's sales manual. They made unauthorized copies of critical information in the manual and successfully developed a competitive software program within a short period of time. In testimony reported in the court's opinion, the marketing manager referred to himself as a 'scoundrel', but explained that market pressures had led him to this tactic.

(b) Improper influence

A second category of questionable techniques centres on attempting to influence potential informants in ways that undermine their judgement or sense of obligation to protect confidentiality or to act in their employer's best interests. Frequently, the attempt involves offering inducements or the possibility of certain advantages to those who may be able to provide valuable information. In its crudest form, this technique is bribery, the offering of something of value in exchange for the breach of a fiduciary duty. In the recent Pentagon scandals, consultants to defence contractors offered large sums of money to government officials in exchange for revealing information they were as fiduciaries legally obliged to protect. In more subtle cases not involving legal obligations of confidentiality, the inducement may work to compromise the potential informant's judgement. The source may decide to reveal information which is not, strictly speaking, confidential, but whose revelation is contrary to the employer's interests.

The inducement to disclose need not be cash; it may be a better job. The hiring of a rival's employee to gain access to confidential information appears to be a widely used and approved intelligence-gathering technique. Surveys conducted in 1974 (Wall 1974: 32–4), 1976 (Brenner and Molander 1977: 57), and 1988 (*Advertising Age* 1988: 88) all found that many executives would use the practice. Fifty-one per cent of the smaller companies and 37 per cent of the larger ones surveyed in 1974 said they expected employees hired from competitors to contribute all they knew to the new job, including the competitor's trade secrets (Wall 1974: 38). And the Conference Board found that nearly half the respondents to its 1988 survey regard former employees of competitors as a very or fairly important source of information (Sutton 1988: 19). About half the executives responding to the 1976 study said they would try to hire a rival's employee to learn about an important scientific discovery that could substantially reduce profits during the coming year (Brenner and Molander 1977: 57).

In 1988, *Advertising Age* asked its readers whether it was ethical to hire an account supervisor from a competitor in order to gain information about the competitor's client. Seventy-three per cent of the 157 professionals responding – advertisers, agency personnel, media people, consultants, and 'others' – said the practice was ethical (*Advertising Age* 1988). The Center for Communications posed the same hypothetical to professors and students of marketing. Fifty-nine per cent of the 626 students responding said the practice was ethical, and 70 per cent said they would do it.[18]

The hiring of employees with access to valuable competitor information has been the subject of numerous recent lawsuits and threatened lawsuits. When Wendy's International decided to substitute Coke products for Pepsi products in its restaurants, Pepsi threatened to sue Coke for pirating executives to gain information about Pepsi's contract and programmes with Wendy's and for tampering with contractual relationships (*Washington Post* 1986). Similar issues have arisen in litigation between Johns-Manville and Guardian Industries,[19] Avis and Hertz (Lewin 1984), and AT&T and MCI (*Business Week* 1986: 122–3).

Sometimes the inducement to reveal valuable information is not an actual job, but the possibility of a job or some other commercial advantage. As reported in *Fortune*, Marriott recently hired a headhunter to gather competitor information from regional managers of five competing economy-hotel chains. The managers were told the truth: that no jobs were available at the time of the interview but that Marriott might have jobs in the future (Dumaine 1988: 76).[20]

These sorts of inducements are designed to give competitors' employees incentives to talk. Some of the more subtle uses of this technique do not introduce new incentives for disclosure but play on the existence of relationships of dependence or on natural human propensities. Customers, for example, may be willing to reveal confidential information about a competitor in order to maintain an advantageous supply relationship. Conversely, a competitor's supplier may talk if he thinks it will lead to new business. A competitor's technical people may divulge sensitive information in the course of describing their achievements at scientific meetings, particularly if they are asked the right questions in the right way (see Flax 1984: 31). Plying a competitor's employee with drinks at a trade meeting, a technique approved of by nearly 60 per cent of the respondents to a survey mentioned earlier, is yet another way of undermining the judgement of a potential source (Cohen and Czepiec 1988: 200–2).[21]

These techniques are ethically problematic because they involve attempts to undermine relationships of trust and confidence. In many cases, the information-seeker deliberately creates a conflict of interest in the hope that self-interest will overcome the potential informant's sense of obligation to protect his employer's confidential information or to act on his behalf. One must assume that the offering of valuable inducements reflects the fact, or at least the information-seeker's belief, that the information is not publicly available and can only be acquired, or can be acquired more cheaply, by attempting to induce a breach of confidence or to otherwise influence the judgement of those acting on behalf of the rival firm.

Part of the effectiveness of these inducements is explained by employees' uncertainty about what information may and may not be disclosed. While most firms treat some information as freely available to the public and other information as strictly confidential, there is a great deal of information that could be quite valuable to a competitor and whose confidentiality status is ambiguous in the minds of many employees, suppliers, and customers. For example, a firm may regard certain information shared with a supplier as confidential while the supplier sees it as public knowledge. The annals of trade secret litigation contain many examples of this sort of discrepancy. Indeed, there may be in-house discrepancies about what information is confidential and what may be revealed. The use of disclosure incentives in these cases may be the decisive influence tipping the potential informant's judgement in the direction of disclosure.

Ethical judgements about particular intelligence-gathering practices in this category are complicated by these same uncertainties. Still, legitimate questions about the scope of employees' obligations of confidentiality do not remove the moral difficulty that attaches to offering inducements deliberately intended to undermine a person's judgement or sense of obligation.

(c) Covert surveillance

Covert surveillance, another category of ethically problematic intelligence gathering, includes electronic espionage as well as other unconsented-to forms of observation such as eavesdropping and aerial photography. This category, perhaps the most difficult to define, raises questions about the legitimate scope of corporate privacy. When covert surveillance involves trespass or theft of tangible property, there is a convenient legal label for condemning it. But when it involves eavesdropping in public places or observation from afar using sophisticated technology, the wrong is most readily described as a violation of corporate privacy. Although the prevailing view is that corporations have no legal right to privacy, the idea persists that businesses and their employees should be able to assume they will not be observed or listened to in certain situations.[22]

The techniques of covert surveillance are varied. They range from planting a spy in a competitor's operation – a technique which also involves deception and perhaps inducing actual employees to violate duties of confidentiality – to strategic eavesdropping in the bar and grill favoured by a competitor's employees.[23] A widely discussed case of covert surveillance which resulted in an award of damages for the target company involved aerial photography of an unfinished manufacturing plant.[24] Clever gadgets of various types are available to assist covert observation: binoculars that hear conversations up to five blocks away, a spray that exposes the content of envelopes, a gadget that can read computer screens some two blocks away by picking up radio waves emitted by the machine (*Fortune* 1988). Inspecting the competition's trash is another type of unconsented-to surveillance that has received attention in the press and has been litigated in at least one case.[25]

Covert observation, like misrepresentation and improper influence, is yet another way to obtain information which a rival does not wish to divulge. Ethical assessments of various forms of undisclosed observation may be controversial since privacy expectations are quite variable, as are judgements about the legitimacy of those expectations.

Covert observation in or from public places is especially problematic. For example, it may be possible to ascertain the volume of product that competitors are shipping by observing from public property the number of tractor-trailers leaving the plant's loading bays and by noting the size of the product in relation to the size of the trailers.[26] Opinions vary about the legitimacy of this practice. One might say that the firm has consented to observation by not putting a fence around the property. And yet, just as it is unseemly to peer through an open window into the neighbours' living room while walking down the sidewalk, we may think observation an invasion of the firm's privacy.

Likewise, we may raise eyebrows at the Japanese practice of employing students surreptitiously to record the conversations of competitors' employees as they commute to work on the train, and at the same time wonder why employees would discuss sensitive matters in such crowded public places.[27]

(d) Unsolicited intelligence

The questions raised by covert surveillance are closely related to those raised by the receipt of unsolicited information. Disgruntled former employees of rival firms have been known to offer highly confidential technical information as well as more general information to competitors. Two recently litigated cases involved disputes about valuable information acquired as a result of a rival's mistake. In one case, a coded customer list was inadvertently left in the memory of a computer which was purchased at an auction by a competitor. The rival gained access to the code-word from an unwitting computer operator.[28] In another case, a dealer list was accidentally left in the store of a dealer who later became a competitor.[29]

There is no question of deceit or improper influence in these cases. The ethical question centres on whether unsolicited or inadvertently revealed information should be respected as private to the competitor. If intelligence gathering is governed by respect for the competitors' voluntary disclosure decisions, then information acquired through accident or mistake, or a former employee's breach of fiduciary duty, should not be examined and utilized. Indeed, this is the view reflected in the Uniform Trade Secrets Act.[30] Some courts and commentators, however, have taken the position that privacy is forfeited if information is accidentally revealed.[31]

The forfeiture view has some plausibility when disclosure is the result of a rival firm's carelessness. It is not unreasonable to expect a firm to suffer some loss if it acts carelessly. The view has less merit, however, when a third party, such as a supplier, inadvertently discloses a rival's valuable information. Still, in a survey discussed earlier, nearly half the marketing professionals questioned said it would be ethical to use information acquired as the result of a supplier's mistake (*Advertising Age* 1988). In the survey vignette, a marketing professional is accidentally given slides prepared for a direct competitor's final presentation in a competition in which both are participating. Having examined the slides before returning them to the embarrassed employee of the slide supply house, the marketer must decide whether to use the information to alter his presentation to attack the competitor's recommended strategy.

Marketing students were more guarded than the professionals about the propriety of using the information, but nearly two-thirds said they would use it, despite their ethical judgement to the contrary. While 73 per cent said that it would be unethical to use the information, only 31 per cent said they would refrain from doing so.[32]

14.1.5 The death of corporate guidance

Despite the growing importance of intelligence gathering and the occurrence of unethical and questionable practices, top management has not yet faced the issue squarely. Only a handful of corporations offer employees practical guidance on intelligence gathering in their codes of conduct or ethics policies.[33] While codes of conduct are not the only, or even the most important, index of a corporation's ethical standards, they do provide some indication of ethical issues thought by the code's authors to merit attention.[34]

Among approximately 480 non-confidential corporate codes of conduct on file at The Ethics Resource Center, Inc.,[35] and the Defense Industry Initiative Clearing House in Washington, D.C.,[36] only five could reasonably be expected to be useful to an employee looking for ethical guidance on intelligence gathering.[37] These five codes make explicit mention of general governing principles and provide specific illustrations of their application. They mention acquisition methods that are to be avoided, kinds of information that are off bounds, and in some cases, objectives that are improper. For instance, one code explains that 'improper means include industrial espionage, inducing a competitor's personnel to disclose confidential information, and any other means that are not open and aboveboard.'[38] However, none of the five explicitly addresses all four types of ethically problematic practice discussed above.

Another 19 codes provide little practical guidance but at least alert employees that intelligence gathering is an area of ethical vulnerability. These codes typically contain a conclusory statement or general principle cautioning employees about improperly seeking proprietary information of a competitor or admonishing them to ensure that data collection is proper and legal. However, the codes offer little or no advice as to what specific practices are improper or illegal.

Thirteen other codes contain one or two provisions prohibiting specific practices such as industrial espionage, using confidential information of former employers, or mishandling government information. These narrowly drawn provisions, however, are not backed by general principles which could be helpful in thinking about other intelligence-gathering practices. Six companies warn employees not to accept the confidential or proprietary information of others. Although relevant for intelligence gathering, these provisions appear to address the problem of unsolicited submissions of confidential information of others rather than deliberately undertaken data collection.[39]

The code of ethics adopted by the Society of Competitor Intelligence Professionals in 1987 targets two areas for specific mention.[40] It requires intelligence professionals to make full disclosure of their identity and organization prior to interviews and to respect requests for the confidentiality of information. Otherwise, the code's provisions express general commitments to acting ethically, legally, and in accordance with the policies of the professional's employer.

Top management is not alone in neglecting the ethics of intelligence gathering. In the Conference Board's ethics survey of 300 companies world-wide, intelligence gathering was not included among the list of topics posing ethical issues for business (Berenbeim 1987). Only slightly more than one quarter of the respondents to a survey on ethics education in accredited United States graduate and undergraduate business programmes say they cover intelligence gathering (Paine 1988).[41]

14.1.6 Explaining corporate silence

Corporate failure to provide guidance may reflect an assumption that intelligence gathering is adequately covered by the corporation's commitment to honesty, integrity or legal compliance. Many company codes begin by asserting that the firm's business is to be conducted in accordance with the highest standards of law and ethics. Quite apart from evidence that much intelligence gathering is not conducted according to the highest standards of law and ethics, such highly general statements are of little practical value when the requirements of law and ethics are unclear to employees or when they conflict with other corporate demands.

Compliance with conclusory general standards like these depends on employees' abilities to recognize when legal and ethical principles might be relevant to their work and to interpret the relevant principles in the particular context at hand. It is quite implausible, however, to assume that employees are familiar with the general principles of law governing confidential information or with their interpretation in the courts. Variation in ethical sensibilities and intellectual capacities, coupled with legitimate disagreement about the ethical status of certain practices, require that management provide more specific guidance. It may be too much to expect the average employee under pressure to collect information to make the connection between the company's policy of conducting business ethically and the particular intelligence-gathering practices he may consider, especially if the company's evaluation system favours the practices.

An alternative explanation for corporate failure to address the ethics of intelligence gathering is management's desire not to hamstring its intelligence operations. By remaining silent, management can perhaps benefit from questionable practices without explicitly condoning them. This is a risky policy, as well as a costly one in the long run. It also violates management's responsibility to alert employees engaged in intelligence gathering to the legal and ethical risks associated with their job. Few employees engage willingly and without reservation in legally questionable activities for their employers. But if management does not address the ethics of intelligence gathering, employees may unwittingly find themselves in legal difficulty.

14.1.7 Risks of corporate silence

The most immediate risk of neglecting to address the ethics of intelligence gathering is the risk of litigation invited by the use of questionable practices. Under the general principles of trade secret law, intelligence gathering may be actionable if it involves misrepresentation, theft, bribery, breach or inducement of a breach of a duty to maintain secrecy, espionage, or other improper means.[42] Although liability is limited to cases involving acquisition of trade secrets, the definition of 'trade secret' is quite broad in many jurisdictions and quite vague in others.

In some jurisdictions, for example, a trade secret must be 'continuously used in one's business.'[43] Thus, the date of a new policy or information about a particular proposed event or a key executive's health problems would not qualify. In other jurisdictions, information need only afford a competitive advantage and be subject to reasonable efforts to maintain its secrecy to qualify as a trade secret. While manufacturing methods, processes, and chemical formulations are generally accorded trade secret status, other types of information have received different treatment in different courts. Customer lists, marketing plans, bidding procedures, identities of suppliers, and operations information, for example, have been protected in some cases but not in others.[44]

Given jurisdictional variation and the uncertainty surrounding interpretation of trade secret principles, it is difficult to know precisely what information enjoys legal protection and what does not. Moreover, the outcome of trade secret cases seems to be influenced by the court's analytical starting point. In theory, liability for misappropriation of a trade secret depends on finding both that the information in question is a trade secret and that it was acquired by improper means. However, one commentator has observed that protection is less likely if the court's inquiry focuses on the trade secret question than if it focuses on the means of acquisition. It seems that courts are reluctant to deny trade secret protection if they find the use of 'improper means' to gather information (Spanner 1984).

'Improper means' is, itself, a somewhat indefinite and expanding category. The well-known case of *duPont v. Christopher* shows that courts are willing to go beyond the standard legal classifications of prohibited means in finding liability.[45] The question in the case, a novel one under Texas law, was whether aerial photography was an 'improper means' of discovering trade secrets. The Christophers had taken aerial photographs of a duPont plant which, because it was still under construction, was exposed to view from above. Analysis of the photographs revealed a secret, but unpatented, process for producing methanol which duPont contended was a trade secret. Even though aerial photography did not fall within the usual legal categories of 'improper means', the court held that, under the circumstances, it was improper. The court reasoned that it would be unfair to permit a rival to reap the benefits of the process developed by duPont and that it would be unreasonable to expect companies to protect themselves against espionage of this sort.

The legal picture is further complicated by the possibility of other theories of recovery, such as inducing a breach of fiduciary duty or breach of confidence. Even if information gathered from an informant is not protected as a trade secret, legal action for inducing a breach of confidence may be possible. Thus, information about the impending appointment of a key executive, although treated as confidential within the firm, might not count as a trade secret. Still, someone who revealed that information might be in violation of a duty of confidentiality.

As a practical matter, the risks of litigation and legal liability can best be minimized by avoiding intelligence-gathering activities in the ethically problematic categories discussed above: misrepresentation, improper influence, unconsented-to surveillance, and theft. Admittedly, the threat of legal reprisal for engaging in these practices may be minimal in certain situations. Victims of unethical practices may not know they are being targeted, or they may lack evidence to prove their case in a court of law. Moreover, the law does not provide a remedy for every violation of ethics. If the victim of misrepresentation is not individually harmed, for example, he will have no legal recourse against the intelligence gatherer. And even if substantially harmed, the victim may have no remedy if the information acquired does not qualify as a trade secret or if the target firm has not taken adequate steps to protect the information in question.

From a management perspective, however, it is quite impractical to instruct employees to fine-tune their use of questionable practices on the basis of the legal risk in particular situations. Not only is it difficult to undertake an objective assessment of legal risk when under everyday performance pressures, but the legal risk of using unethical practices depends on consequences which are difficult, if not impossible, to anticipate in advance: the kind of information that will be obtained, the use to which it will be put, the harm that the target will suffer, the adequacy of the target's security measures, the likelihood of discovery, and the evidentiary strength of the target's case. What is known in advance is that certain types of practices, namely, those involving misrepresentation, theft, improper influence, and covert surveillance, can provide the necessary foundation for legal liability. Even from the narrow perspective of legal costs, there is a good case for instructing employees to avoid questionable practices altogether rather than attempt to assess the fine points of legal risk.

14.1.8 Increasing security needs

More costly, perhaps, than the litigation and liability risks involved in the use of questionable practices are the increased security needs these practices generate over the long term. Every user of unethical practices must recognize his contribution to a general climate of distrust and suspicion. In so far as individuals are more likely to engage in unethical conduct when they believe their rivals are doing so, unethical intelligence gathering contributes further to the general deterioration of ethical expectations. As the recent growth of interest in information security illustrates, declining ethical expectations translate into intensified programmes for self-protection.[46]

Firms that expect to be subjected to intelligence gathering through covert surveillance, deceit, and various forms of improper influence – especially when legal recourse is unavailable or uncertain – will take steps to protect themselves. They will tighten information security by building walls, installing security systems, purchasing sophisticated counter-intelligence technology, and instituting management techniques to reduce the risks of information leakage. Although some degree of self-protection is necessary and desirable, security can become a dominant consideration and a drain on resources.

Besides their out-of-pocket cost, security activities often introduce operational inefficiencies and stifle creativity. Avoiding the use of the telephone and restricting access to information to employees who demonstrate a 'need to know' impose obvious impediments to the exchange of information vital to co-operation within the firm. When researchers, for instance, are denied information about the projects they are working on and about how their work relates to the work of others, they are cut off from stimuli to creativity and useful innovation.

Employee morale and public confidence may also be at stake. Information systems designed to ensure that employees do not know enough to hurt the firm if they depart, like the dissemination of information on a 'need to know' basis, proceed from a premise of distrust which can undermine employee morale. Even more clearly, information protection programmes encourage an attitude of distrust toward outsiders. Employees are trained to be suspicious of public inquiries and to be wary of talking to or co-operating with outsiders who do not have security clearances. Over-restrictions on public access to information and excessive corporate secrecy generate public suspicion and hostility.

Although questionable intelligence-gathering practices may offer short-term advantages, they contribute, over the longer term, to a climate of distrust and the need for costly expenditures to tighten information security. These expenditures represent a diversion of management resources from more productive activities. Moreover, it is doubtful that firms can effectively protect their own valuable information if they encourage or tolerate loose ethical standards in acquiring competitor information. As the 1985 Hallcrest Report on private security in America concluded from studies of employee theft, '[E]ffective proprietary security programs . . . must emanate from a . . . strong sense of organizational ethics in all levels of the organization' (Cunningham and Taylor 1985).

14.1.9 Suggestions for managers

There are compelling reasons for management to address the ethics of competitor intelligence gathering. In the absence of clearly communicated standards of propriety in this field, as in others, some employees will be uncertain about what is expected of them. They may feel that management expects them to engage in acts of misrepresentation, improper influence, and covert surveillance in order to gain information. Or they may be unsure what conduct constitutes misrepresentation, improper influence, or covert surveillance. As found in one study discussed earlier, there is a close correspondence between the intelligence-gathering practices employees find acceptable and those they perceive to be in line with company standards (Cohen and Czepiec 1988: 202). It also appears that employees are more willing to engage in questionable practices if they believe their competitors are doing so (ibid.). Given the general prevalence of questionable and unethical practices, it is risky for management to remain silent on the ethics of intelligence gathering.

There are various steps managers can take to discourage ethically questionable intelligence-gathering practices. The first is to work toward developing a shared commitment to the ethical standards that should govern intelligence gathering. Essential to this process is involvement of employees, particularly those active in the intelligence function, to promote open discussion of the opportunities and pressures encountered in the field as well as discussion of the 'grey areas' where the requirements of ethics may be unclear.

Managers may choose to create a written code or other document to express the governing standards and to provide guidance on their application, but more important than such documentation is sustaining a commitment to these standards in practice. Various activities beyond the initial process of developing standards may be useful in building and sustaining a commitment to these standards in practice. Various activities beyond the initial process of developing standards may be useful in building and sustaining commitment: monitoring the pressures and grey areas employees encounter and providing a forum for discussing them; including ethics in orientation and training for all intelligence personnel; encouraging managers to ask employees about the ethical questions they encounter and to be responsive when employees raise such questions.

For such effort to be taken seriously, however, it is critical that performance evaluation and, more generally, the firm's system of rewards and incentives, be compatible with the ethical standards espoused. Employees who govern their activities by the standards should not be penalized for doing so; nor should employees be rewarded for successes achieved at the expense of ethics. An evaluation and reward system that ignores the ethical dimensions of performance can breed cynicism and outright hostility to well-intentioned efforts to promote ethical practices unless there is a strong culture of ethical commitment already in place.

14.2   CONCLUSION

Managers who remain silent or fail to incorporate their 'official' ethics policies into day-to-day management practice run the risk that they, their employees, and their firms will be involved in costly litigation over questionable intelligence-gathering tactics. More important, they jeopardize their own information security and run the risk of contributing further to the increasing demand for information protection. This demand represents a costly diversion of resources from the positive and creative aspects of doing business, a drag on innovation, and an impediment to good public relations. By supporting a competitive system which respects the principles of common morality and the right of rivals not to divulge certain information, management supports its own vitality and the vitality of the competitive system.

14.3   ACKNOWLEDGEMENTS

An earlier version of this paper was presented at the European Business Ethics Network conference held in Barcelona in September 1989. The author is grateful to members of that group for their criticisms and suggestions. She also wishes to thank Professor J. Ron Fox for his detailed comments on a version of the paper and Gary Edwards, Executive Director of The Ethics Resource Center, for discussions of intelligence-gathering practices and for making the Center's resources available for research. In addition, the staff at the Defense Industry Initiative Clearing House were most helpful.

14.4   NOTES

[1]   Small firm interest in competitor intelligence is described in Robichaux (1989).

[2]   Information provided by the Society of Competitor Intelligence Professionals in Washington, DC.

[3]   The current growth of interest appears to be the continuation of a trend. See Wall (1974).

[4]   Intelligence gathering stories with happy endings can be found in many news articles. See, e.g., Dumaine (1988).

[5]   The 1988 Conference Board study reports the types of competitor information considered most useful by executives. Sutton (1988: 16).

[6]   Roger Milgrim, author of *12 Business Organizations*, Milgrim on Trade Secrets (1988), quoted in *Business Week* (1986: 120).

7 The surge in information crimes is noted by Donn B. Parker of SRI International as reported in Sutton (1988).

8 See judge's introductory comments in *Fortune Personnel Agency of Ft. Lauderdale, Inc. v. Sun Tech Inc. of South Florida*, 423 So. 2d 545 (Fla. Dist. Ct. App. 1982): 'As the cost of research and development increase the theft of trade secrets becomes a lucrative, although somewhat immoral, alternative to the expenditure of one's own funds.'

9 See, e.g., *Business Week* (1986: 120).

10 Nabisco, Keebler, and Frito-Lay were all accused of stealing cookie secrets from Procter & Gamble's Duncan Hines. Neiman (1984).

11 A dispute between Hertz and Avis arose when the president of Hertz departed to become head of Avis. See Lewin (1984).

12 Quoted in Putka (1987). See also Horton (1987).

13 See, e.g., Porter (1985).

14 The antitrust law implications of tactics recommended by Porter in his *Competitive Strategy and Competitive Advantage* are discussed in Fried and Oviart (1989).

15 For lists of ethical and unethical techniques, see Johnson and Maguire (1988).

16 In a 1987 lawsuit, Service Corp. International alleged that Hillenbrand Industries had posed as a prospective supplier in order to deceive Service Corp. into divulging confidential information. 'Service Corp. Is Suing Hillenbrand, Alleges Theft of Trade Secrets,' *Wall St. Journal* (March 4, 1987), p. 7.

17 *Continental Data Systems, Inc. v. Exxon Corporation*, 638 F. Supp. 432 (E.D. Pa. 1986). In addition to actual damages, the court awarded the competitor punitive damages. The court found that it would be unfair to permit the firm to use its formal written 'policies' to avoid corporate liability where the evidence allowed the jury to infer that these formal 'policies' were not the actual operational understanding at the branch in question.

18 The results noted here are available from the Center for Communications, a non-profit educational organization located in New York, New York.

19 *Johns-Manville Corp. v. Guardian Industries Corp.*, 586 F. Supp. 1034, 1075 (E.D. Mich. 1983), aff'd., 770 F. 2d 178 (Fed. Cir. 1985).

20 According to the article, Marriott eventually hired five or so of the competition's managers.

21 See also Beltramini (1986).

22 For a general discussion, see Allen (1987).

23 Both practices are described in Flax (1984) pp. 28, 32.

24 *E.I. duPont deNemours v. Christopher*, 431 F. 2d. 1012 (5th Cir. 1970), *cert. denied*, 400 U.S. 1024 (1971).

25   *Tennant Co. v. Advance Machine Co.*, 355 N.W. 2d 720 (Ct. App. Minn. 1984). The appeals court upheld a verdict awarding compensatory and punitive damages to Tennant, the victim of trash surveillance. Under California law, said the court, 'an owner retains a reasonable expectation of privacy in the contents of a dumpster "until the trash has lost its identity and meaning by becoming part of a large conglomeration of trash elsewhere."' Tennant had disposed of its documents in sealed trash bags put into a covered dumpster used only by Tennant. For another example of trash surveillance, see Johnson, 'The Case of Marc Feith'.

26   Discussed in Flax (1984).

27   This practice is described in Sutton (1988).

28   *Defiance Button Mach. Co. v. C & C Metal Products*, 759 F. 2d 1053 (2d Cir. 1985).

29   *Fisher Stoves, Inc. v. All Nighter Stove Works*, 626 F. 2d 193 (1st Cir. 1980).

30   *Uniform Trade Secrets Act With 1985 Amendments*, sec. 1(2)(ii)(c), in Uniform Laws Annotated, vol. 14 (1980 with 1988 Pocket Part).

31   *Fisher Stoves; Defiance Button.* See also *Kewanee Oil Co. v. Bicron Corp.*, 416 U.S. 470, 476 (1973) ('A trade secret law . . . does not offer protection against discovery by fair and honest means, such as by . . . accidental disclosure . . .').

32   Survey results received from the Center for Communication, New York, New York.

33   This research was conducted in March–April 1989. It is quite possible that many corporations do not include intelligence-gathering in their company-wide code of conduct, but instead provide employees in the most relevant areas, marketing for example, with ethical guidance in the form of a specific policy statement on intelligence gathering. I have not attempted to locate specific policy statements beyond those available in the collections assembled by The Ethics Resource Center and the Defense Industry Initiative Clearing House, both described in notes below.

34   As illustrated in the *Continental Data Systems* case, discussed in note 17, above, written codes do not always reflect the actual operational understanding of a firm's employees.

35   The Ethics Resource Center, Inc., is a non-profit educational organization in Washington, DC. Its library contains corporate codes of conduct gathered over the past seven years in the course of four major research studies involving Fortune 500 companies, major defence contractors, and most recently a varied sample of 2000 American corporations. Besides those involved in these studies, other companies interested in furthering the Center's research efforts have also contributed codes.

36   The Defense Industry Initiative Clearing House has on file the

codes of conduct of some forty-five defence contractors. All these contractors are signatories of the Defense Industry Initiatives on Business Ethics and Conduct, a voluntary industry effort undertaken in 1986 in response to the report of President Reagan's Blue Ribbon Commission on Defense Management, better-known as the 'Packard Commission.'

[37] Another study of ethics policies gathered from 67 Fortune 500 companies found only one that covered intelligence gathering. See Hite *et al.* (1988).

[38] Hewlett Packard Co., *Standards of Business Conduct*.

[39] For a discussion, see Seidel (1984).

[40] The code is available through the Society of Competitor Intelligence Professionals in Washington, D.C.

[41] Among M.B.A. programme respondents, 32 per cent cover intelligence gathering. Only 23 per cent of the responding undergraduate programmes discuss the ethics of intelligence gathering.

[42] *Uniform Trade Secrets Act.* Sec. 1(1).

[43] The requirement of continuous use was written into the Restatement of Torts (First), but is not part of the Uniform Trade Secrets Act definition of a trade secret.

[44] For a readable discussion of treatment of different types of information, see Spanner (1984).

[45] *E.I. duPont deNemours v. Christopher*, 431 F. 2d 1012 (5th Cir. 1970), *cert. denied*, 400 U.S. 1024 (1971).

[46] The 1985 Hallcrest Report documents the growth of employment and expenditures for private security, including information security, in the 1970s and projects continuing growth in security-related sectors of the economy. The report's authors link this growth with increased crime in the workplace and with increased awareness and fear of crime. See Cunningham and Taylor (1985).

14.5 REFERENCES

Advertising Age (1988) Industry ethics are alive, April 18, p. 88.

Allen, A.L. (1987) Rethinking the rule against corporate privacy rights: some conceptual quandaries for the commonn law. *John Marshall Law Review*, 20, Summer, p. 607.

Ansberry, C. (1988) For these M.B.A.'s class became exercise in corporate espionage. *Wall Street Journal*, March 22, p. 37.

Beltramini, R.F. (1986) Ethics and the use of competitive information acquisition strategies. *Journal of Business Ethics*, 5, pp. 307–11.

Berenbeim, R.E. (1987) *Corporate Ethics*, Conference Board Research Report No. 900 (The Conference Board, Inc.), p. 4.

Brenner, S.N. and Molander, A. (1977) Is the ethics of business changing? *Harvard Business Review*, January–February.

Business Week (1986) Information thieves are now corporate enemy no. 1, May 5.

Carrington, T. and Pound, E.T. (1988) Pushing defense firms to compete, Pentagon harms buying system. *Wall Street Journal,* June 27, p. 1.

Cohen, W. and Czepiec, H. (1988) The role of ethics in gathering corporate intelligence. *Journal of Business Ethics,* 7, pp. 199–203.

Cunningham, W.C. and Taylor, H. (1985) *Private Security and Police in America,* The Hallcrest Report, Portland, Oregon: Chancellor Press, pp. 105–16.

Dumaine, B (1988) Corporate spies snoop to conquer. *Fortune,* November 7.

Flax, S. (1984) How to snoop on your competitors. *Fortune,* May 14, p. 31.

Fortune (1988) New ways to battle corporate spooks, November 7, p. 72.

Fried, V.H. and Oviart, B.M. (1989) Michael Porter's missing chapter. The risk of antitrust violations. *The Academy of Management Executive III,* No. 1, pp. 49–56.

Fuld & Company Letter (1989) Competitor intelligence: present & growing in UK. Summer, p. 1.

Haas, A.D. (1986) Corporate cloak and dagger. *Amtrak Express,* October/November, pp. 19–20.

Hite, R.E., Bellizzi, J.C.A. and Fraser, A. (1988) A content analysis of ethical policy statements regarding marketing activities. *Journal of Business Ethics,* 7, p. 771.

Horton, C. (1987) Ethics at issue in Lotus case. *Advertising Age,* December 21, p. 6.

Information Data Search, Inc. (1986) *Corporate Intelligence Gathering, 1985 and 1986 Surveys,* Cambridge, MA, p. 24.

Johnson, R. (1987) The case of Marc Feith shows corporate spies aren't just high-tech. *Wall Street Journal,* January 9, p. 1.

Johnson, W. and Maguire, J. (1988) *Who's Stealing Your Business? How to Identify and Prevent Business Espionage,* New York: AMACOM, pp. 12–15.

Lewin, T. (1984) Putting a lid on corporate secrets. *New York Times,* April 1, section 3, front page.

Neiman, J. (1984) Cookie makers deny swiping P&G secrets, *Adverising Age,* June 25, p. 2.

Paine, L.S. (1988) *Ethics Education in American Business Schools,* a Report of the Ethics Resource Center, Inc., Washington, DC, February 1988, pp. 16–17.

Porter, M. (1985) *Competitve Advantage: Creating and Sustaining Superior Performance,* New York Free Press.

Putka, G. (1987) Lotus gets order barring ad agency from telling secrets. *Wall Street Journal,* December 14, p. 16.

Robichaux, M. (1989) Competitor intelligence: a grapevine to rivals' secrets. *Wall Street Journal*, April 12, p. B2, vol. 3.

Seidel, A.H. (1984) Handling unsolicited submission of trade secrets. *The Practical Lawyer*, 30, March, pp. 43–52.

Smith, A. (1976) *The Theory of Moral Sentiments*, Il.ii.2.2 (first published 1759), Oxford: Oxford University Press, p. 83.

Spanner, R.A. (1984) *Who Owns Innovation?* Homewood, IL: Dow-Jones-Irwin.

Sutton, H. (1988) *Competitive Intelligence*, Conference Board Report No. 913, The Conference Board, Inc., New York, pp. 6–7.

Tucker, E. (1986) Corporate gumshoes spy on competitors. *Washington Post*, March 30, p. F1.

Wall, J.L. (1974) What the competition is doing: your need to know. *Harvard Business Review*, November–December.

Washington Post (1986) Pepsi to sue Coke over Wendy's, November 13, p. E1.

15 *Ethical attitudes to bribery and extortion*

Jack Mahoney

Bribery is a source of considerable concern in many quarters of the globe, as events and scandals in various countries in the last twenty years have shown. Reasons for its common ethical condemnation are examined, as well as attempts made by international agencies to outlaw the practice. A distinction is drawn between bribery and extortion, and conditions are explored under which payment of extortion may be considered morally justifiable. However, situations of social change or transition call for particular resistance to practices of bribery and extortion. Such resistance requires governments and businesses to take all possible practical measures within their respective spheres of influence. It also often calls for a considerable degree of moral courage on the part of individual managers.

15.1 ETHICAL ATTITUDES TO BRIBERY AND EXTORTION

Among the topics suggested for treatment at this international conference by its organizers, that of managerial responses to corruption, presents considerable intellectual, as well as ethical and moral, challenges. In responding, then, with great pleasure to the invitation to address the conference, I intend to explore one particular expression of corruption by offering some reflections on Ethical Attitudes to Bribery and Extortion. I propose first to review various approaches to bribery and the reasons why it is judged to be unethical in principle and calls for international action; then to consider whether an ethically meaningful distinction can be drawn between bribery and extortion and under what conditions; and finally to review what steps might be taken by governments, businesses, and managers faced with the prospect of bribery and extortion in varying situations.

I understand bribery to be the providing of an inducement to influence an official improperly in the exercise of their duties. Not only is it a topic which greatly concerns business people who are interested in the ethical conduct of business; modern business history contains no lack of national and international bribery scandals to keep the subject also before the public eye. In my own country of Great Britain, the death last July of T. Dan Smith recalled for many people what amounted to a national crisis in the 1970s over the disclosures and trials of Smith and his co-conspirator, the architect and public building contractor, John Poulson, whose 'systematic web of corruption' involved bribery at every level of British society and led to a Royal Commission and the resulting requirement for Members of Parliament to list their business interests (Fitzwalter and Taylor 1981: 216).

In those years, of course, it was the tidal waves of bribery scandals in the USA which seized the world's shocked headlines. As the Watergate investigations into domestic political payments by major corporations began also to uncover large overseas bribes, it became evident that considerably more was at stake for US business than re-electing President Nixon. So much so that when the US Government invited voluntary disclosures from American corporations, the consequence was, as Clinard noted in his 1990 study of *Corporate Corruption*, that

> more than 450 large U.S. corporations, mostly Fortune 500s, ultimately disclosed to the Securities and Exchange Commission during the late 1970s and early 1980s illegal or questionable payments abroad, totaling more than $1 billion and paid either as direct bribes to foreign government officials or through foreign corporate 'sales agents'.
>
> (Clinard 1990: 121; Kline 1985: 24)

The tentacles of US overseas bribery spread throughout the globe at the time, and to countries as far apart as Japan, the Middle East, and The Netherlands, rocking the political structure of several countries (Noonan 1984: 652–80). Yet it was by no means the only cause for concern at the time about bribery in the world of business. In Hong Kong also the 1970s saw major steps being taken to cope with the problem by the introduction in 1971 of the Prevention of Bribery Ordinance, to be followed three years later by the establishment of the Independent Commission Against Corruption (ICAC). On that period an interesting commentary was offered in January of this year by the Chief Secretary, Mrs Anson Chan, when she observed in the debate in the legislative council to review the ICAC's powers and accountability (26.1.94) that 'When the ICAC was established twenty years ago, Hong Kong was very different from what it is today. In the 60s and early 70s . . . the community was in danger of becoming resigned to corruption. Today things are very different. Our community demands and expects clean government. Far from being resigned to corruption, it now shows a high degree of intolerance of corruption' (cf Lee 1981).

Italy too is a country where, as we are increasingly learning today, bribery has been systemic for decades. The corruption scandals first broke in Milan in early 1992, and the increasing revelations of bribery throughout many sectors of Italian society, including its major political parties and its major business companies, do not yet appear to have exhausted the uncovering of what the *Economist* described as 'the rot . . . in the pillars of Italy's establishment' (*Economist* 1993).

Depressing as the apparently widespread incidence of bribery in business is, nevertheless there is also some ground for encouragement in recognizing that influential parties in at least some major societies are not prepared to countenance it, and that they take determined steps to counter its presence, as in Hong Kong in the 1970s and Italy today. Of course, the major step was taken in the USA, with the passing in 1977 of the Foreign Corrupt Practices Act (FCPA) to prohibit American corporations from offering or making payments to officials of foreign governments (Donaldson 1989: 31). Nor was the USA alone in its aim to influence the international scene in commercial bribery. Various world-wide bodies also began to attempt to control the phenomenon, as we shall see, and all this local and internationally concerted action to combat the practice naturally leads into a consideration of why there should be such universal condemnation, at least in theory, of the offering and accepting of bribes.

Commercial bribery can be faulted ethically on three general grounds: as being bad for business; bad for the participants; and bad for the society in which it occurs. The arguments against bribery as being bad for business are headed by the consideration that in seeking unfair advantage over others the practice undermines the whole philosophy of the market as a system in which success depends on the notion of fair competition. The leading business ethicist De George sums it up: 'Bribery is a way of getting preferential treatment' (De George 1993: 104). Moreover, by its bid for a virtual monopoly it can result in the inefficiencies which are widely recognized as characteristic of monopolies (Velasquez 1992: 196). As Nobel Laureate Gary S. Becker observed, bribery usually does considerable damage, including the extracting of monopoly prices and misusing time and resources which could be better used to produce useful goods and services (Becker 1994: 8).

Again, by its need to cultivate secrecy, bribery introduces a note of public surmise and suspicion about various transactions, driving out certainty from exchanges, and at the same time deceiving investors as to the true state of the market. By diverting negotiations away from being product-related to being determined by the size of the bribe, 'it seriously distorts the decision-making process' (Moody-Stuart 1993: 27), ignoring product quality, satisfaction and often safety, and also often increasing costs and thus adversely influencing production.

Bribery can also have harmful consequences for those actively involved in the transaction. Not only does it involve stealing from their owners and possibly violating company policy as well as the law, with the danger of blackmail and the continual risk of detection, shame and punishment; the colluding in dishonesty and the conspiring to defraud also constitute a fundamental breach of trust and dereliction of duty.

Finally, bribery is regarded as on various grounds harmful to the society in which it takes place. There is the economic loss of taxes on the money and activities which can be involved. Another is noted by Shleifer and Vishny in their suggestion that 'many poor countries would rather spend their limited resources on infrastructure projects and defense, where corruption opportunities are abundant, than on education and health, where they are much more limited' (Shleifer and Vishny 1993: 19; cf Moody-Stuart 1993: 28–30). More generally, the lying, dishonesty, and other crimes entailed in promoting or covering up a culture of bribery are not only profoundly dispiriting to a citizenry in simple human terms of the collective quality of social life. Bribery and extortion are particularly harmful to the poor in any society, who cannot afford the additional costs to be paid to obtain simple justice (*The Economist* 1988). For the practice can become addictive for the individual and contagious to others. It was not without reason that George Moody-Stuart wrote, from a lifetime's experience of business, of 'the invasive cancer of grand corruption' (Moody-Stuart 1993: 3). And even on a more petty scale, the practice can easily become endemic and provide a breeding ground for other antisocial practices, so tainting many other expressions of social life and intercourse.

One particular expression of bribery which is considered especially harmful to a society is that resorted to by multinational or transnational corporations in Third World or less-developed countries. In his study of multinational corporations, Feld observes (Feld 1980: 1–3) that during the 1970s MNCs with their immense economic power and financial muscle became increasingly a subject of controversy. In the developing world such disquiet was compounded by the ability of MNCs at times to engage in large-scale bribery often to the disadvantage of local enterprises. As one Director of Exxon summed up the reputation of the MNC, it was

> viewed by some as an intruder in foreign countries, even an arm of domination by its home country. Others view it as an outsider even at home, dangerously lacking the legitimacy that comes with having a firm place among purely national institutions
>
> (Coolidge 1977: 29)

In the circumstances it was not surprising that in the 1970s LDCs in particular were eager for steps to be taken at an international level to curb the power and activities of MNCs by aiming to introduce agreed codes of conduct for them. The best known attempt was that undertaken by the United Nations Economic and Social Council, beginning in 1972, which set up a Commission on Transnational Corporations to produce an agreed code of conduct on how MNCs should behave in host countries and also how they should be treated by host governments. In 1976 the Council set up an Ad Hoc Inter-governmental Working Group to consider the Problem of Corrupt Practices, and in 1978 this produced a draft International Agreement on Illicit Payments. This draft (pare 20) required MNCs to

> refrain, in their transactions, from the offering, promising or giving of any payment or other advantage to or for the benefit of a public official as consideration for performing or refraining from the performance of his duties in connection with those transactions.
>
> (UN Code 1988: 32–3)

It further required MNCs to maintain accurate records of payments made by them to any public official or intermediary, and to make these records available on request to the competent authorities of the countries in which they operate (UN Code 1988: 33). In the event, the Agreement was not, however, accepted by the UN General Assembly, and there matters have remained.

Another international approach to regulating the conduct of MNCs in relation to bribes is to be found in the activities of the Organization for Economic Cooperation and Development (OECD) in the dis-charge of its role to develop international co-operation among indus-trialized countries. In June 1976 the OECD Conference of Foreign Ministers adopted a set of Guidelines for Multinational Enterprises (Feld 1980: 108), which stipulated that 'Enterprises should . . . 7. not render – and they should not be solicited or expected to render – any bribe or other improper benefit, direct or indirect, to any public servant or holder of public office' (Feld 1980: 164).

The OECD guidelines had the merit, as Feld points out (ibid.: 116), of being 'the first major statement by the industrialized countries of the world about their expectations regarding the future behaviour of MNCs everywhere.' However, the OECD has still not secured com-plete agreement among the twenty-four participating nations on the means to deter companies from making illicit payments for overseas contracts and to punish those which are apprehended. The US cam-paign to have other countries follow its own lead in outlawing over-seas bribes and to cease allowing them to be tax-deductible at home came to a head in April this year at a meeting of the OECD working party on illicit payments. It seems likely, however, that the recom-mendation to be put to finance ministers for ratification this month (June 1994) will reflect the alternative preference of other OECD countries, including Britain and Japan, that each country should carry out a national review and take appropriate local steps as it sees fit (Waterhouse 1994).

On such illicit payments a much fuller statement than that of the OECD came from the International Chamber of Commerce, whose 1977 Report on Extortion and Bribery in Business Transactions (ICC 1977; Kline 1985: 92–3) was the most detailed international treatment of the subject, no doubt because, as Feld observed, 'The ICC, as a nongovernmental organization, had the least obstacles to overcome' (Feld 1980: 108). The Report's explicit concern was 'to set forth the cooperative action that should be taken by governments and enterprises to combat bribery and extortion in business transactions' (ICC 1977: 6). Addressing governments in the first instance and having in mind the aim of international harmonization of standards, the Report called on each government (Part II, 1) to introduce, review or perfect its statutes

> to ensure that they effectively prohibit, within its territorial jurisdiction, all aspects of both the giving and the taking of bribes, including promises and solicitation of bribes, as well as so-called facilitating payments to expedite the performance of functions which government officials have a duty to perform.

The ICC was also able, as the world business organization, to admonish the international business community that it had 'a corresponding responsibility to make its own contribution towards the effective elimination of extortion and bribery' by self-regulation in international trade. To that end it presented for business enterprises a set of Rules of Conduct to Combat Extortion and Bribery, which were more stringent than those legally imposed in many countries, but it expressed the hope that the spirit of the Rules of Conduct would be faithfully followed by 'all business enterprises, whether international or domestic' (Part III, Introduction).

With the ICC Rules of Conduct, then, we have moved from exclusive concentration on multinational corporations and the need or the wish to control their behaviour in various countries around the globe, to consider regulation against bribery and extortion on the part of all national governments and business enterprises. Moreover, they provide a useful introduction to an ethical analysis of the whole issue, on which we may now embark. More than one commentator, for instance, on the US FCPA notes that its proscribing of bribes abroad does not include 'facilitating payments' to minor government officials, or in more colloquial terms 'grease' injected into the bureaucratic system in order to lubricate it and ensure its smooth running (De George 1993: 103). As Jacoby, Nehemkis and Eells point out, 'foreign political payments are made more frequently to induce government employees to perform their official duties than for any other purpose' (Jacoby *et al*. 1977: 113). In other words, a basic distinction which can cast light on various degrees of moral responsibility involved in engaging in bribery is that between bribing someone to do what they ought to be doing in any case in the line of duty, and on the other hand bribing someone to use their position or power to do what they ought not to do. The distinction does not occur explicitly in the ICC Rules, but it is implied in the Rules' recommendations to governments to criminalize 'so-called facilitating payments to expedite the performance of functions which government officials have a duty to perform' (ICC 1977: II.1).

Paying bribes just to get normal business expectations fulfilled is what appears to worry many, if not most, ordinary business people who are attempting to run their business with integrity along ordinary decent lines. And certainly the other form of bribery, inducing people to do what is inherently unethical, such as breaking the law, turning a blind eye to defects, condoning tax avoidance or permitting exploitation, appears much more reprehensible conduct than surreptitiously paying people to do their duty. Noonan (1984: 688) captures the essential ethical distinction when he refers to paying bribes for 'the proper performance of a task not its perversion'.

Of even more ethical significance, however, is the further distinction to which this points the way, that between bribery and extortion. For no one would pay a bribe to ensure normal service unless they were being in some way coerced to do so. As the ICC observes,

> public opinion has sometimes tended to assume that corruption is generally initiated by enterprises . . . . The truth is that much bribery is in fact the response to extortion. Enterprises have too often had the experience, in many countries, of having to choose between giving in to extortion or not doing business.
>
> (ICC 1977: I)

Noonan (Noonan 1984: 89,149) traces back to Roman law and early Christianity a juridical and ethical distinction between the free offering of a bribe and being compelled to pay extortion (cf Jacoby *et al*. 1977: 90). The distinction is not always clear-cut and is 'frequently blurred' in reality (ibid.: 154). Nor does it imply that the payment of bribes is criminal while the payment of extortion is necessarily exempt from criminal proceedings (ibid.: 176; Noonan 1984: 579–80). Nevertheless, if the handing over of extortion money is essentially compulsory and is aimed at dissuading someone from inflicting or threatening unjustified harm or damage, either by commission or omission, then the payment of extortion can have a degree of ethical justification which would not apply to the voluntary offer of a bribe. For paying extortion is akin to 'justifiably buying off harassment, paying a kind of ransom' (Noonan 1984: 638) simply in order to go about one's ordinary and legitimate business without fear or hindrance (cf Velasquez 1992: 196). As De George observes, somewhat grudgingly in my view, 'the coercion mitigates to some extent the culpability of the victim.' Yet he also notes that payment serves to reinforce the practice. 'It acquiesces in evil rather than resisting it. At best it may be the lesser of two evils' (De George 1993: 198 n.19; 126). As Noonan also warns, 'the excuse of paying off harassment cannot be invoked in a merely individual situation; the damage to the common good is too great' (Noonan 1984: 695).

If paying extortion in business is to be on occasion ethically justified, on what conditions might this be the case? I suggest that there are four conditions, all of which need to be fulfilled. The first would be that unless one pays extortion there is simply no practical possibility of going about one's business. One is faced with a climate of extortion, or socially deep-rooted practices of being overtly or subtly bullied into submission in a manner akin to the protection rackets which flourished in Chicago earlier this century and, if reports are true, which are present in parts of Northern Ireland today. A second condition would be that the purpose of the payment is to persuade the extortioner to desist or refrain from doing something wrong, that is, from unjustifiably doing or threatening damage. A third ethical condition is that the business which one wishes to conduct is lawful and legitimate, and of benefit not only to its immediate participants but also to stakeholders and notably to the economy and society in which it is conducted. Indeed, this positive benefit of a business to society is the countervailing factor which balances or outweighs the social ill of contributing to the continuance of a practice of extortion. Finally, if one is seeking to do business by surrendering to so socially harmful a practice, then a fourth ethical condition of doing so is to do all in one's power at the same time to combat that practice.

The bribery required as a condition of doing normal business may be due to explicit demands or expectations. It may more subtly result from an inherently unjust market characterized by inequality of access and unfairness in distribution, as has been alleged with regard to modern Russia, where trying to work within such an unethical system can justify taking counter-measures which would not otherwise be ethically acceptable (cf Filatov 1994: 12). Yet the case which I have outlined for apparently colluding in wrongdoing by paying extortion under certain well-defined circumstances is not unique. In a wider perspective, there are illuminating parallels between doing business in a society characterized by extortion and doing business in a society, for example, which depends on apartheid, as in South Africa until recently, or doing business in or with a country where there is widespread violation of human rights or a corrupt regime or appalling labour conditions. Such regrettable situations pose the more general ethical question whether one can ever be justified in doing business in or with a society which contains certain features which one considers unethical or with which one is reluctant to be associated, yet which one cannot ignore.

Is the ethical stance either to avoid all such societies – an almost impossible undertaking – or to deal with them and share their guilt by collusion or at least by association? Or is there a middle way? One lesson which can be learned from the debate over trading with South Africa is that there can be more than one ethical answer to that and similar questions (cf Williams 1986). The adoption of the Sullivan Code by companies doing business in South Africa indicated that, while the general ethical strategy was to abolish apartheid, there was nevertheless more than one ethical tactic to bring that about. One could either express concerted disapproval from a distance to pressurize the economy and the government by withdrawal, or one could be present in the country trading and at the same time undermining the foundations of apartheid from the inside.

It seems possible, then, to formulate a general ethical principle which can apply to a climate of extortion just as much as to a climate of apartheid or dictatorship or human rights violation: that one can be ethically justified in working in a culture which has certain unethical features, but only on condition that they are unavoidable, at least for the time being, that one is operating for good business and social reasons, and that one is also working to change those unethical features of the culture.

How much can, or should, be done by individual companies to work at changing the climate of extortion in any particular culture then depends on two circumstances: one relating to the power of the company to influence the situation; and the other relating to how much the prevailing social situation can in fact be changed. Clearly, the larger and more powerful a company is, and the more it is likely to profit from trading even when submitting to extortion, the greater is its ethical responsibility to use its power, influence and profits to remedy the situation, either by refusing to succumb to extortion, or by exposing would-be extortioners or by pressing government to take effective measures against them. Even companies which are not giants on the commercial scene are not powerless, however, if they can combine their forces to pressurize or work with government. As De George observed,

official complaints by groups of American companies have changed the practice of bribery in some countries, and collective or industry-wide efforts have proved to be more effective than efforts by individual firms to oppose a pattern of bribery solicitation.

(De George 1993: 14)

The other circumstance which affects the moral responsibility of companies to work to combat a climate of extortion depends on how socially entrenched the practice is in the country in question. It is here that one tends to meet a mood of moral fatalism, in the frequently expressed view that extortion is too deep-rooted as a way of life to be significantly diminished, far less uprooted, from a particular society. If this were true, and extortion was literally an irremovable feature of business life in any society, then companies would be exonerated from wasting their resources in attempting to do the impossible, and moral fatalism would appear to win the day. Yet it may be that there are scenarios where a commercial and political renaissance in a country can provide grounds for giving the lie to moral fatalism, or where a society is undergoing or facing a process of transition where the social stakes for the future are so high as to provide an immensely powerful ethical incentive and determination to combat the spread or the further consolidation of extortion.

What has been happening in Italy recently, for example, was well described by *Business Week* in March this year (28.3.94) in its statement that 'since a political hack was caught red-handed with $5,000 in bribes two years ago in Milan, a steamrolling anti-corruption investigation has smashed an entire political regime – and way of life – to bits.' In the estimation of the *Economist* the same week (26.3.94), 'close to 5,000 businessmen and politicians have been arrested on corruption charges over the past two years.' One early result of this 'clean hands' Italian judicial campaign was the issuing in May 1993 of a new 'code of business ethics' by Italy's biggest private company, FIAT, which was being accused of widespread and long-lasting payment of bribes to Italy's various political parties. This set out required behaviour for all the group's employees towards government officials, political parties and civil servants to avoid any form of bribery or kickbacks involving the public sector 'even as a result of illegal pressure' (*Financial Times* 12.5.93). And this idea of illegal pressure was spelled out in self-justifying detail the following week in the statement of the group chairman of Olivetti, Carlo De Benedetti, providing magistrates with information about the L20bn (£8.5m) in bribes which his company had paid to political parties over the years. As he explained, 'the pressure from the parties and their representatives in the state entities reached an impressive crescendo . . . of menaces and extortion to become in the last few years nothing short of racketeering' (Graham 1993).

Whether Italian business has been the unwilling victim of extortion by the major political forces in the country, as the chairman of Olivetti claimed, or whether, on the contrary, the business leaders were often all too ready accomplices, as accused politicians alleged (Graham 1993), the case can be made that in the past co-operating in extortion in Italy was less ethically reprehensible for a company than straightforward bribing, and that it could have been justified on the conditions which I have just outlined. However, now that the rot has been uncovered and a massive cleanup operation is under way, the overriding ethical consideration for any company is not now to acquiesce fatalistically in the old order, but on the contrary to throw its weight behind the movement for change and to contribute to the continuing momentum and completion of that social revolution.

It may be that the progressive exposure of endemic political and business corruption in Italy was made easier by the collapse of the Soviet Union and the end of any need for a united front to support anti-Communist political and business forces in Italy. At any rate, the disintegration of the Soviet hegemony in central and eastern Europe has certainly led to a major transition stage for business there, with enormous future stakes which make it imperative not to surrender to a climate of corruption and systematic extortion. In a recent study on 'Unethical Business Behaviour in Post-Communist Russia' Professor Alexander Filatov analyses the origins and trends in such behaviour, and he diagnoses the current transitional situation as characterized by instability, uncertainty and conflict. It is not therefore surprising if he concludes that 'many experienced Western businessmen know that in order to operate in such distorted market conditions their strategies . . . must be pursued without any reference to ethical considerations that govern within fairer economic structures' (Filatov 1994: 11–12). At street level there are also alarming indications in Russia of local economies being effectively controlled by 'mafia chiefs who [impose] gangster-style levies on private kiosks and businesses' (Binyon 1993). In the Ukraine one leading young entrepreneur finds that his biggest running costs are paying corrupt local bureaucrats for government 'licences' and paying interior ministry troops to guard his many pavement kiosks from local gangs (*Economist* 1994b). On the former Eastern bloc as a whole, the Czech economist, Marie Bohata, reports that 'the decline in morale threatening former communist countries has been very disturbing . . . . Corruption, financial deals and 'agreed' auctions, in many cases with foreign capital participation, have been growing' (Bohatá 1994: 91).

The European Bank for Reconstruction and Development, in the words of its recent President, Jacques Atali, is all too aware of the need to restructure such economies and of the price which will have to be paid for failure to do so: 'the black market, bribery and corruption' (Atali 1993: 114). All of these observations serve only to confirm the statement made in 1992 by the Director of the US Office of Government Ethics, Stephen Potts, that 'the single greatest threat to the emerging democracies of Eastern Europe and the former Soviet Union is corruption.' They also reinforce his strong admonition to American companies doing business there not to offer bribes and kickbacks to corrupt officials or intermediaries, precisely because such actions may hinder the development of the fragile democracies (Singer 1992: 1).

If it is true, then, that surrendering to extortion is less justifiable in a socially volatile and improving situation, as in Italy, or during an all-important period of transition, as in central and east Europe, then perhaps a similar conclusion can be drawn with regard to Hong Kong in the light of the major change in its relationship with China which it is preparing to undergo in 1997.

The observation of the Chief Secretary early this year which I have already mentioned, that the Hong Kong community now shows a high degree of intolerance of corruption, appears borne out by a survey conducted in August 1991 among Hong Kong managers and reported in the *Hong Kong Manager* last summer, which concluded that 'Hong Kong managers . . . have positive opinions of the ethical and social responsiveness of their organizations and feel the organizations they worked for are favourably perceived by others' (Migliore *et al.* 1993: 20). Reassuring as such perceptions about the ethical quality of Hong Kong business are for the present, they nevertheless appear to coexist alongside serious anxieties concerning mainland Chinese companies or individuals. Such was the situation reported from Hong Kong last November by Simon Holberton of *The Financial Times* (Holberton 1993), referring to the recent ICAC finding that corrupt business practices may represent three to five per cent of the cost of doing business in China, a factor which respondents nevertheless claimed was bearable and not a disincentive to doing business there.

Such anxieties, it appears, can only increase as Hong Kong companies become even more involved with its largest trading partner, and Chinese firms increasingly arrive in Hong Kong. It is expressed baldly in *The Other Hong Kong Report for 1993* edited by Choi Po-king and Ho Lok-sang, which claims to identify 'a perception that corruption will worsen in the run-up to 1997' and which refers to 'the business community's concerns for the difference between anti-bribery regulations in Hong Kong and China' (Po-king and Lok-sang 1993: 66, 68). Given that, as *The Economist* has also recently observed (1994a), 'Hong Kongers are increasingly worried about the contagious nature of Chinese business practices', it is not surprising that the focus of the activities of the Independent Commission Against Corruption has shifted from investigating government malpractice to concentrate increasingly on the private sector.

Yet it can also be noted that it is not only honest people in Hong Kong who are concerned about the future ethical quality of business. In March of this year the Chinese Prime Minister, Li Peng, described corruption as 'a matter of life and death' for China, and 'the abuse of power for personal gain, graft and bribery' as behaviour which must be 'punished unsparingly' (Poole 1994). As one writer reports the situation, since last autumn the Chinese government has been campaigning against corruption and business fraud, including bribery, as a serious threat to the Communist party. In so doing it has also been responding to popular ethical anger and revulsion: 'ordinary Chinese citizens are increasingly disgruntled about petty graft; an anticorruption hotline set up by the Supreme People's Procuratorate has been swamped with calls' (Poole 1994).

If, then, there are certain social situations of revolution or transition in which it is particularly incumbent on business to work for the common good, and to decline to acquiesce in a culture of extortion continuing or becoming entrenched, it then becomes all the more important for governments as well as businesses to take all possible effective steps to combat bribery and extortion within their sphere of influence. Governments can usefully begin by criminalizing the practice and by denying the legitimacy of custom as a justification or mitigation, as was done by the Hong Kong Prevention of Bribery Ordinance (cap. 201, 19). Reference to a de facto acceptance of the practice in various societies, which is so regularly appealed to by outsiders, may be sometimes discounted as a need to find an excuse for business failure and partly identified as exaggerated and self-fulfilling rumours, as was noted some years ago by the *Economist* (1988). Yet, in this connection governments can also usefully take positive steps to educate the public on the social and economic damages inflicted by all forms of corruption, as exemplified by Hong Kong's Announcements in the Public Interest to the general public, including new immigrants from China, and as described in the 1992 Annual Report of the ICAC (ICAC 1992).

More specific and practical steps also can and need to be taken at national and international levels, in accordance with what the ICC Guidelines called 'the political will and the administrative machinery' (ICC 1977: I.a). Such steps include anything which, in the words of Husted (Husted 1994: 25), will make bribery 'prohibitively expensive', whether this be in financial terms or in any other human or corporate terms. This includes the establishment or strengthening of national background institutions to promote the rule of law and its protection of human rights (cf De George 1993: 144); intergovernment co-operation and harmonization, as well as appropriate provision for extradition; procedures for regularly disclosing details of relations between public officials and commercial agents; independent review of the award of government contracts, which should not be left to individuals (Jacoby *et al.* 1977: 245); the requirement of an anti-bribery clause in all major contracts; strict enforcement of auditing legislation; and transparency in the payment of political contributions at least by requiring public record of such payments and public accounting of their receipt. Since bureaucracy can be a labyrinth, especially for strangers, governments should put their own houses in order by radically simplifying regulations in order to diminish the need to resort to bribery and to cut down opportunities for exacting extortion (cf Shleifer and Vishny 1993: 5). Provision should be made for an adequate salary structure for public officials which will attract suitable candidates and obviate their need to supplement their income by bribery; there should be strict limitation and regular supervision of the discretionary authority of minor officials (Jacoby *et al.* 1977: 244–5), frequent transfer of officials and agents to prevent long-term relationships being developed, and conflict of interest laws preventing official association or relations with suppliers (Husted 1994: 25). Finally, government should ensure effective prosecution and appropriate penalties, including imprisonment, for convicted companies, top executives and chairmen and regular publication of the relevant information; and should also encourage freedom of expression in the press and other public media of communication (cf *The Economist* 1988).

So far as businesses themselves are concerned, self-regulating structures can be introduced and regularly reviewed comparable to many of those enumerated for government. What now appears indispensable are explicit codes of conduct, which, in the words of the ICC, 'may usefully include examples and should enjoin employees or agents who find themselves subjected to any forms of extortion or bribery immediately to report the same to senior management' (ICC Code 1977: art 10). But in the case of bribery, as in all other business malpractices, it is absolutely essential that codes of conduct have teeth, and that infringement is immediately and publicly penalized. Other possible procedures to delimit bribery and extortion include annual signed statements by CEOs (Moody-Stuart 1993: 59) and all employees; more non-executive directors who are truly independent, who are given an explicit ethics remit and who form audit committees along the lines of the recent UK Cadbury Report on Corporate Governance; a policy that middlemen should receive remuneration which is strictly commensurate with their detailed services and which is not to be shared with others as bribes or transferred outside the country as accommodation payments (cf Kline 1985: 133–4); the refusal to countenance 'off the books' or secret accounts; and strict compliance with the letter and spirit of local laws.

The goal of such governmental and corporate structures and procedures is to lessen the pressures on companies and individuals and to decrease the occasions for wrongdoing, thus making it that much easier for them to resist temptations or solicitations to bribe. In the same context it will be interesting to follow the fortunes of a new body, Transparency International, which was founded last year for the express purpose of forming a coalition against corruption in international business transactions, particularly in evolving or developing countries. TI is based in Berlin with many national chapters in the process of being established, and among the means to which it is committed is the creation of what it terms national 'islands of integrity,' where honest business practices are encouraged, honest businesses are attracted and companies which bribe, or attempt to bribe, are exposed and penalised (Transparency International Newsletter 1994).

All these and other aids and supports to promote and protect ordinary decent business dealings without recourse to bribery and extortion are surely valuable. Yet ultimately there can be no substitute for personal self-regulation, or the individual manager's own integrity as he or she goes about their business. At the end of his classic history and analysis of bribery, Noonan concludes, 'Human beings do not engage in such acts without affecting their characters, their view of themselves, their integrity' (Noonan 1984: 700). Whether one agrees with so sweeping a judgement or not, the subject of the ethics of bribery and extortion cannot be adequately covered without some concluding remarks on the need for personal business integrity, and particularly, where bribery and extortion are concerned, on the need for the personal quality and the exercise of moral courage.

I began this chapter by observing that the subject of bribery and extortion was one which offered considerable intellectual, ethical and moral challenges; and so far we have been concerned with the first two, the intellectual challenge of analysing and understanding the practice and varieties of bribery, and the ethical challenge of evaluating bribery and extortion in terms of whether and why they are wrong. It remains, however, to consider briefly the moral challenge which follows from these intellectual and ethical analyses, namely, the challenge of actually deciding whether or not to behave in accordance with one's intellectual and ethical conclusions about bribery and extortion.

For most practical purposes, the two terms 'ethical' and 'moral' are synonymous, one deriving from Greek and the other from Latin to refer to the same characteristics of some forms of human behaviour. It is also possible to consider 'ethics' as the more academic term of the two, used to describe the scientific and systematic analysis of various ways of behaving and to deliver a theoretical verdict on them, as we have been doing with reference to bribery and extortion. However, coping with bribery and extortion in business calls for considerably more than intellectual analysis of the issues involved, and a good deal more than just arriving at a judgement in principle on the ethical quality of such behaviour. It also involves personally acting on that analysis and that judgement in particular situations, and facing up in practice to what can thus be properly called the moral challenge of matching one's actions to one's ethical principles.

This is where recent work in ethics to recover the classical notion of moral virtue has much to contribute to our subject, concerned as it is with the character of individuals and their integrity. Such moral integrity directed at actually behaving ethically implies the notion of a certain moral wholeness of character and a moral loyalty to one's principles. De George remarks that 'integrity requires that one have developed ethical views to which one adheres' (De George 1994: 4). In addition to this, however, the idea can often also include an element of moral courage to follow through in putting these ideas into action.

This idea of moral courage as a necessary personal resource for individuals seeking to behave ethically in business was first popularized by O'Toole in his 1985 study of Vanguard Management in a chapter entitled 'Moral Courage: The Sine Qua Non of Greatness' (O'Toole 1985: 340–371), although he did little more than illustrate it as the leadership quality of taking a public stand on controverted social issues. The subject is usefully deployed in a little more detail by De George in the context of international business, especially when he observes that 'moral courage is central to acting ethically in difficult situations' (De George 1993: 111; cf 22). Recognizing this traditional philosophical insight into the nature of moral courage can be of particular help to individuals when faced with the pressure of having to decide on occasion whether or not to have recourse to bribes or to succumb to extortion.

Courage in the face of difficulties and dangers is commonly seen as the capacity to cope with the fear which such situations can arouse in us. In his study, *The Anatomy of Courage* (Moran 1945), Winston Churchill's physician, Lord Moran, defined fear as 'the response of the instinct of self-preservation to danger,' and courage as 'will-power' to handle that instinctive reaction. As such, it may not, of course, necessarily be moral courage. A fraudster may well have the courage to overcome the fear of being caught out; or a cat burglar may need to acquire the courage to overcome a fear of heights. What makes the difference between merely physical or psychological courage and moral courage is when the action which it is feared will lead to unpleasant consequences is itself a moral action, such as telling the truth, or keeping a promise or resisting various pressures to do something one knows or believes to be unethical. In this context it was instructive to read the forthright verdict of *The Economist* (14.11.92) on the explanations given for the conduct of some members of the British government in the Churchill Matrix mess, that 'nine-tenths of the explanation boils down to cowardice', that is, to the absence of moral courage.

Moral courage, then, appears to be the capacity to do what one judges is ethically called for in spite of one's perception of the dangers and difficulties involved. As such it is an almost routine requirement on the part of people engaged in ethical business. Yet such moral courage to withstand fear seems especially required in situations where the instinct for survival, whether personal or corporate, can exert very considerable pressure on the individual to remove that fear by simply having recourse to bribery or extortion. In such cases to succumb to offering and receiving bribes is to court the lowest standards of human social intercourse. To exact their contribution is to poison the wells of human and business relationships. To decline or refuse to be associated with bribery, and particularly with routine extortion, can call for the exercise of moral courage to an impressive degree. Yet sometimes the conduct of ethical business calls for no less.

15.2 ACKNOWLEDGEMENTS

A previous version of this paper has been published in *Proceedings of the Inaugural Conference of the Centre for the Study of Business Values*, University of Hong Kong, June 1–June 3, 1994, Hong Kong, pp. 244–256.

15.3 REFERENCES

Atali, J. (1993) The ethics of European transition. *Business Ethics. A European Review*, 2(3), pp. 111, 116.

Becker, G.S. (1994) To root out corruption, boot out big government. *Business Week*, 31 January.

Binyon, M. (1993) Capitalism gone wild, *The Times*, 5 October 1993.

Bohatá, M. (1994) Ethics in the Czech transformation process. *Business Ethics. A European Review*, 3(2), pp. 86–92.

Clinard, M.B. (1990) *Corporate Corruption. The Abuse of Power*, New York, Praeger.

Coolidge, P., Spina, G.C. and Wallace, D., Jr. (eds) (1977) *The OECD Guidelines for Multinational Enterprises: A Business Appraisal*, Georgetown University Institute for International and Foreign Trade Law, Washington, DC.

De George, R.T. (1993) *Competing with Integrity in International Business*, Oxford: Oxford University Press.

De George, R.T. (1994) International business ethics. *Business Ethics Quarterly*, 4(1), pp. 1–9.

Donaldson, T. (1989) *The Ethics of International Business*, Oxford, Oxford University Press.

Economist (1988) Business bribes, 19 November.

Economist (1993) Cosí fan tutti, 23 October.

Economist (1994a) Hong Kong, 29 January.

Economist (1994b) Geller the seller, 19 February.

Feld, W.J. (1980) *Multinational Corporations and U.N. Politics. The Quest for Codes of Conduct*, New York: Pergamon Press.

Filatov, A. (1994) Unethical business behavior in post-Communist

Russia: origins and trends. *Business Ethics Quarterly*, 4(1), pp. 11–15.

Financial Times (1993) Bribery alleged in construction contracts. Japanese provincial governor held, 28 September.

Fitzwalter, R. and Taylor, D. (1981) *Web of Corruption. The Story of John Poulson and T. Dan Smith*, London: Granada.

Graham, R. (1993) Buck stops at De Benedetti, *Financial Times*, 18 May.

Holberton, S. (1993) Anti-corruption official sacked in Hong Kong. *Financial Times*, 11 November.

Husted, B.W. (1994) Honor among thieves: a transaction-cost interpretation of corruption in Third World countries, *Business Ethics Quarterly*, 4(1), pp. 17–27.

ICAC (1992) *Annual Report* by the Commissioner of the Independent Commission Against Corruption, Hong Kong: Government Printer.

International Chamber of Commerce (1977) *Extortion and Bribery in Business Transactions*, Paris: International Chamber of Commerce.

Jacoby, N.H., Nehemkis, P. and Eells, R. (1977) *Bribery and Extortion in World Business. A Study of Corporate Political Payments Abroad*, New York: Macmillan.

Kline, J.M. (1985) *International Codes and Multinational Business. Setting Guidelines for International Business Operations*, Westport, CT: Quorum.

Lee, R.P. (ed.) (1981) *Corruption and its Control in Hong Kong. Situations Up to the Late Seventies*, Hong Kong: Chinese University Press.

Migliore, H.R., Martin, R.T., Stevens, R.E. and Loudon, D.L. (1993) Hong Kong managers: a survey of corporate culture. *Hong Kong Manager*, July/August.

Moody-Stuart, G. (1993) *Grand Corruption in Third World Development*, York: Quacks.

Moran, Lord (1945) *The Anatomy of Courage*, London: Constable.

Noonan, J.T., Jr. (1984) *Bribes*, New York: Macmillan.

O'Toole, J. (1985) *Vanguard Management: Redesigning the Corporate Future*, New York: Doubleday.

Po-king, C. and Lok-sang, H. (1993) *The Other Hong Kong Report 1993*, Hong Kong: The Chinese University Press.

Poole, T. (1994) Greasing the dragon, *Independent on Sunday*, 3 April.

Shleifer, A. and Vishny, R.W. (1993) *Corruption*, Working paper No. 4372, May, National Bureau of Economic Research, Cambridge, MA.

Singer, A.W. (1992) Is corruption a threat to the new-born democracies of Eastern Europe? *Ethikos* 6(1), New York: Mamaroneck.

Transparency International Newsletter (1994) Transparency International, Berlin, March.

The United Nations Centre on Transnational Corporations (1988) *The United Nations Code of Conduct on Transnational Corporations*, London: Graham & Trotman.

Velasquez, M.G. [1982] (1992) *Business Ethics. Concepts and Cases*, Englewood Cliffs, NJ: Prentice-Hall.

Waterhouse, R. (1994) Britain spurns US over bribes. *Independent on Sunday*, 3 April.

Williams, O.F. (1986) *The Apartheid Crisis: How We Can Do Justice in a Land of Violence*, San Francisco: Harper & Row.

16 *The influence of country and industry on ethical perceptions of senior executives in the US and Europe**

Bodo B. Schlegelmilch and Diana C. Robertson

This chapter reports the results of a large-scale survey among senior executives in the US, the UK, Germany, and Austria. The research provides empirical evidence on the variation of perceptions of ethical issues by country and type of firm. Our findings suggest that country and industry type have significant effects, both with regard to identification of ethical problems and the comprehensiveness of written ethics policies and ethics training.

16.1 THE INFLUENCE OF COUNTRY AND INDUSTRY ON ETHICAL PERCEPTIONS OF SENIOR EXECUTIVES IN THE US AND EUROPE

Attention to the field of business ethics by both managers and researchers has increased dramatically over the past five years. For ethical issues in international business, scholars have indeed engaged in considerable theoretical work on questions such as cultural relativism (Freeman and Gilbert 1988), the obligations of multinational companies operating in other countries (Donaldson 1989), and the need for global ethical systems (Buller, Kohls and Anderson 1991).

Empirical research is sparse, however, although the need for such cross-national research is increasingly recognized (Vitell, Nwachukwu and Barnes 1993; Wines and Napier 1992). During the past ten years, for example, the *Journal of International Business Studies* published only two empirical papers specifically devoted to aspects of

---

* Reproduced from the *Journal of International Business Studies*, 1995, 26(4), pp. 859–81, with permission.

international business ethics. Langlois and Schlegelmilch (1990) focused on corporate codes of ethics; and Dubinsky, Jolson, Kotabe, and Lim (1991) used vignettes to investigate ethical perceptions of industrial sales people in the United States, Japan and South Korea. Even in one of the specialized journals of the field, the *Journal of Business Ethics*, less than five per cent of the articles published between 1988 and 1992 involve cross-national empirical research (Robertson 1993). Consequently, the research base remains extremely fragmented and provides little guidance to international managers, who often must develop their own understanding of ethics in international markets.

The present study attempts to redress, in part, the lack of empirical evidence in international business ethics. Specifically, it uses a large-scale survey of senior executives in the US, the UK, Germany, and Austria to investigate whether:

- the perceptions of the importance of ethical issues vary by country, by industry, and/or by interaction between the two;
- the issues that managers perceive to be important are the same issues that are emphasized in their company codes and ethics training.

16.2 THEORETICAL BACKGROUND AND HYPOTHESIS DEVELOPMENT

Discussion is ongoing as to the meaning and interpretation of business ethics in different countries (Ciulla 1991; Mahoney and Vallance 1992; van Luijk 1990; Vogel 1992). Some scholars contend that organizational issues are similar everywhere. They suggest this similarity is due to comparable missions and use of common technology (Hickson, Hinings, McMillan and Schwitter 1974; Miller 1987). Other management studies document the existence of country differences in managerial values and attitudes (England 1978; Hofstede 1993; Kanter 1991; Kelley, Whatley and Worthley 1987; Maurice, Sorge and Warner 1980). Parallel to these findings, previous ethics studies have documented country differences in attitudes toward ethical issues (Becker and Fritzsche 1987b; Izraeli 1988; Tse, Lee, Vertinsky and Werhung 1988).

It is our expectation that perception of ethical issues varies by country and can be linked to differences in country ideology. Such country differences are relevant to the development of ethical theory. Knowledge of country differences could also guide firms and other organizations in the development of transnational codes of ethics, not in the sense of providing 'moral authority', but by alerting the individuals writing codes to the salience of issues in different countries (Frederick 1991; Rowan and Campbell 1983).

Although interest in ethical issues should not be limited to Western countries, we chose to study the UK, the US, Germany, and Austria because their firms are more likely to adopt formal ethics initiatives, such as written codes of ethics (Langlois and Schlegelmilch 1990). In addition, we expected that the form of capitalism in the US and the UK, which is very different from the German and Austrian model (Lodge 1990; Thurow 1992), would result in differing perceptions of ethical issues among managers in the four countries. The intersection of the co-authors' interests and countries of background also had an impact on country selection.

In the following sections we will first discuss the most important variations in the ways business ethics is understood in the US, UK, and Germany. (To our knowledge business ethics in Austria has hardly been pursued in the literature.) Next, we will establish the basis for our hypotheses about country differences. Finally, we will discuss possible effects of industry on the perception of ethical issues and on ethical practices, as well as the relationship between perceptions of ethical issues and the inclusion of these issues in corporate codes of ethics and training.

16.2.1 Ethical perspectives relating to country ideology

A useful distinction can be made between individual and group decision-making on ethical issues and, consequently, responsibility for the outcome of decisions resting either with the individual or the group. This is consistent with a more general individualistic-communitarian ideology of nations. Lodge (1990) characterizes the US as the most individualistic of capitalist countries and Germany as more communitarian than the UK. Hofstede (1980; 1993) ranks fifty countries on individualism versus collectivism, finding that the US ranks first on individualism, the UK ranks third, Germany is fifteenth, and Austria eighteenth. (Although Vitell *et al.* (1993) present testable propositions for all four major cultural dimensions identified by Hofstede (1976, 1980), the individualism dimension is best supported in the business ethics literature discussed below.)

Vogel (1992) states that 'Americans tend to emphasize the role of the individual as the most critical source of ethical values, while in other capitalist nations relatively more emphasis is placed on the corporation as the locus of ethical guidance' (p. 44). He cites as one point of evidence the requirement of US business ethics cases that the individual must decide what is right or wrong based on his or her own value system. In addition, the trend in the US is toward legal protection of the individual whistleblower, whereas very few European laws offer such protection. Van Luijk (1990) agrees that business ethics in the US is distinctive to a culture in which individualism is revered. Emphasis is placed on individual businesspeople making decisions about what is right and wrong. In Germany there is a greater emphasis on consensual ethics or 'communicative ethics' (van Luijk

1990). Decisions lie not with the individual but with the moral community. Similarly, Austrian business decision-making is consensual (März & Szecsi 1981), which may extend to decision-making about ethical issues as well. Business ethics in Germany has been characterized as most concerned with relationships between economics and society, not relationships between the individual employee and the firm (Ciulla 1991; Steinmann and Löhr 1992).

These country differences in ethical perspectives lead to our first hypothesis:

■ H1 Managers' perceptions of ethical issues will vary by country.

(This hypothesis is developed into further, more specific detail following our discussion of the results of a factor analysis in the next section.)

16.2.2 Industry differences

Management research acknowledges considerable differences across industries in the issues faced by firms (Gordon 1991). An expectation of our study is that industry will have an impact on the perception of ethical issues. Our expectations follow an integrative social contracts approach outlined by Donaldson and Dunfee (1994). They argue that members of numerous localized communities (such as industries) will consent to the terms of specific 'micro' social contracts. These communities are 'capable of establishing norms of ethical behaviour for themselves' (p. 13). We reason that industries may well constitute communities in which ethical norms evolve. However, most studies of ethics in corporations have not specified how ethical issues may vary by industry (see, for example, Center for Business Ethics 1986, 1992; Webley 1992). An exception is the work of Chatov (1980; 1982) who found differences in issues emphasized in corporate codes of ethics in a number of different industries. Similarly, a more recent study by Beneish and Chatov (1993) found that 'codes emphasize operational rather than symbolic issues and that their content varies across firms to reflect interests logically related to major industry groups' (p. 5). Thus, we hypothesize:

■ H2 Managers' perceptions of ethical issues will vary by industry.

Furthermore, we expect country and industry effects to interact. This expectation is based on the observation that the perception of ethical issues is very sensitive to specific contexts (Donaldson and Dunfee 1994; Jackall 1988).

■ H3 Country and industry will interact to affect managers' perceptions of ethical issues.

16.2.3 Ethics policy and training

We also expect that ethical issues perceived to be important will be the ones that are addressed in written ethics policies or codes and in employee training, and that there will be country and industry differences in ethical issues addressed in corporate policy and training.

- ■ H4   The ethical issues perceived to be important by managers will be addressed in written ethics policies or codes and in employee training.
- ■ H5   Ethical issues addressed in corporate codes and training will vary by country.
- ■ H6   Ethical issues addressed in corporate codes and training will vary by industry.

We know, for example, that 93 per cent of Fortune 1000 survey respondent companies have implemented codes of ethics (Center for Business Ethics 1992), that 90 per cent of US business schools teach a course on business ethics (*The Economist* 1993), and that business ethics has been a growth industry for academics and consultants over the past decade. Similarly, Webley (1992) reports that 71 per cent of the companies responding to his survey of the 400 largest UK companies have adopted corporate codes. In the UK, corporate interest in ethics (Ryan 1994; Schlegelmilch and Houston 1989), the teaching of business ethics (Mahoney and Vallance 1992), and academic study of business ethics have increased dramatically.

Although Germany has also witnessed an increased interest in the topic of business ethics on the part of academics (Hansen 1988; Steinmann and Oppenrieder 1985; Steinmann and Lohr 1989; Schlegelmilch 1990), there remains considerable scepticism among German businesspeople about business ethics, particularly the notion that ethics and profitability are compatible (Vogel 1992). Furthermore, van Luijk (1990) points out that Europeans are generally less optimistic about the effectiveness of corporate codes of ethics than are Americans.

16.3   METHODOLOGY AND DEVELOPMENT OF FURTHER HYPOTHESES

Data on perceptions of ethical issues as constituting a problem were collected from respondents in all four countries and factor analysed. This factor analysis then formed the basis for formulating hypotheses about country differences. Thus, we will first discuss the methodology employed and then present our hypotheses.

In the US, mail questionnaires were sent to a stratified sample of 2000 CEOs of companies, varying in size and drawn from six industries (see below). Dun and Bradstreet's *Million Dollar Directory* served as the sampling frame. Mailing of the questionnaires was followed up by phone calls in order to maximize response. A total of 711 managers completed and returned the mail questionnaires, constituting a response rate of 35.6 per cent. The questionnaire elicits detailed information about corporate ethics programmes, as well as respondents' perceptions about ethical issues.

In Europe, mail questionnaires identical to those used in the US were sent to 1,481 UK, 1,098 German, and 368 Austrian companies. To make the samples as representative as possible, they were stratified to reflect the industry structure in each country.[1] (The questionnaire was translated into German and independently back-translated into English to check for consistency.) The sampling frame used for Britain and Germany was *Major Companies in Europe*. Austria is not included in this directory and *Goldener Trend* served as the basis for the selection of Austrian firms. Given the relative size of industrial activity in the US and the three European countries, the sample size for the latter may appear unduly large. However, the sampling decision was made in anticipation of two potential problems that would reduce response rates in the European sample, namely the use of a printed rather than a computerized address base which tends to include a much higher proportion of 'invalid' and out-of-date addresses, and the fact that budget limitations did not permit telephone follow-ups in Europe.

The samples in all four countries are comprised of firms in the following industries: agriculture, manufacturing, communications, wholesale and retail trade, finance and insurance, and other services. These industries were selected to represent a range of business functions and thus a correlative range of potential business ethics issues. Size of company ranged from firms with under 1,000 employees (11.7 per cent) to those with over 50,000 employees (4.9 per cent) with most firms in the 2,500 to 9,999 size range (45.7 per cent). Analysis of the job titles of the respondents showed that the large majority of questionnaires were, indeed, completed by the CEOs themselves. However, some questionnaires were passed to other senior managers in the company identified as having responsibility for implementing ethics programmes. These typically held job titles such as Deputy Chairman or Head of Human Resources. The responses broken down by industry and country are presented in Table 16.1. A comparison with the proportion in the original mailing shows a good overall match between the intended and obtained sample, except for agriculture, which is underrepresented in all countries, and retail and wholesale, which is underrepresented in the UK.

As expected, the response rate in Europe was considerably lower than that in the US. The unadjusted response rate was seven per cent in the UK, six per cent in Germany, and 10 per cent in Austria. However, discussions with list brokers indicate that in printed

Table 16.1 Response by industry and country

	US		UK		Germany		Austria	
Industry Group	No.	Pct.	No.	Pct.	No.	Pct.	No.	Pct.
Agriculture	74	10.4	10	9.8	5	7.7	4	10.8
Manufacturing	201	28.3	53	52.0	37	56.9	15	40.5
Communication	110	15.5	5	4.9	4	6.2	3	8.1
Retail & Wholesale	130	18.3	4	3.9	5	7.7	8	21.6
Finance & Insurance	91	12.8	14	13.7	7	10.8	4	10.8
Other Services	93	13.1	14	13.7	6	9.2	2	5.4
Missing	12	1.7	2	2.0	1	1.5	1	2.7
Total	711	100.0	102	100.0	65	100.0	37	100.0

directories approximately 20 per cent of the entries on the list become invalid each year. Thus, in dealing with a list that is three years old, the assumption is that only 51.2 per cent of the questionnaires will reach the targeted individual. Therefore, we consider the adjusted rate of response to be 14 per cent in the UK, 12 per cent in Germany, and 10 per cent in Austria (Austria's directory was only one year old).

The lower response rate in Europe is further attributable to lack of telephone follow-ups due to a shortage of resources to conduct call-backs. However, the variation in response rate would be of greater concern if the study was documenting the incidence of corporate codes of ethics, in which case those companies that respond would be expected to be those with codes of ethics. Instead, the study is comparing managerial perceptions of ethical issues and comparing the content of the codes of companies that did respond.

The study elicited responses to 26 statements designed to explore the relative importance of key ethical issues in the respondents' organizations. These issues originally were formulated from experience in working with US firms in the development of ethics policies and, more generally, were based on the ethical issues faced by the firms (Ethics Resource Center 1990). These items are similar to those found in European codes of ethics (Langlois and Schlegelmilch 1990). Examples include 'abuse of expense accounts', 'bribery', and 'employee theft'. The responses to these statements were measured on ten-point scales, ranging from 'not a problem' to a 'major problem'.

Rather than formulating hypotheses about each of the 26 issues, we decided to base our hypotheses on the underlying dimensions inherent in the set of ethical issues. To this end, a factor analysis (Nunnally

1978) was conducted and its appropriateness was assessed by the Bartlett test of sphericity[2] and the Kaiser-Meyer-Olkin measure of sampling adequacy.[3] To determine the number of factors extracted, we used eigenvalue >1 and a visual examination of the scree test. While the eigenvalue indicated an extraction of seven factors, the scree test flattened out after five factors. Based on the latter and supported by the fact that the computed *alpha* reliabilities (Cronbach 1971) of the variables with the highest loading on each factor (bold) only reached .51 and .58 for factors six and seven respectively, we ignored the last two factors in establishing our hypotheses.[4]

Table 16.2 shows the results of the factor analysis based on the entire European and US sample and illustrates that the dimensions possess a high degree of face validity.[5]

Explaining 28 per cent of the variance, the first factor represents an employee conduct dimension, loading on variables such as 'receiving excessive gifts', 'giving excessive gifts', 'kickbacks', 'bribery', and 'abuse of expense accounts'. Factor 2 reflects the inappropriate use of information, showing high loadings on variables which relate to obtaining or misusing proprietary information. The high loadings on Factor 3 relate to personnel issues such as 'drug and alcohol abuse' or 'discrimination'. Factors 4 and 5 load on conceptually similar issues. However, Factor 4 appears to represent primarily central and foreign government relationships, while Factor 5 centres on political contributions and activities at the local level. We therefore labelled this factor 'political and local involvement' (Factor 5).

As a further preliminary step before establishing our hypotheses about country differences, we pooled the German and Austrian sub-samples. The rationale behind this decision was the lack of variation across responses from these two countries in virtually all variables included in the questionnaire.[6] (This was established by conducting F-tests of sample variances together with subsequent t-tests.) For the set of variables analysed in the present study, these tests did not reveal a single significant difference between the German and Austrian subsets. Based on the factor analysis, further hypotheses about country differences follow.

Our initial discussion of the dimensions of individualistic decision-making and reliance on the codification of ethical imperatives (which are most likely to characterize the US, followed by the UK, then Germany and Austria) suggests that US managers will place more emphasis on ethical issues related to the control of employee behaviour. Ciulla (1991) characterizes the UK as having stronger 'cultural restraints' than the US. In her view this accounts at least partially for the relative lack of enthusiasm of British firms for codes of ethics. 'In a more homogeneous society with a stronger class consciousness, ethical behavior tends to be imbedded in roles and articulated in virtues related to those roles' (p. 74). Similarly, Becker and Fritszche

Table 16.2 Rotated factor matrix and factor loadings of major ethical issues

	Factors				
	1	2	3	4	5
Employee Conduct					
Gifts and entertainment (receiving)	**.79**	.22	.19	.01	.17
Kickbacks	**.78**	−.04	.17	.30	.04
Gifts and entertainment (giving)	**.70**	.27	.09	.15	.25
Bribery	**.66**	.01	.07	.44	−.03
Abuse of expense accounts	**.51**	.24	.41	.02	.05
Misuse of company assets	**.49**	.19	.44	−.01	.23
Use of Information					
Misuse of proprietary information	.12	**.84**	.12	.07	.06
Misuse of sensitive information (belonging to others)	.14	**.84**	.15	.14	.03
Methods of gathering competitor's information	.08	**.69**	.06	.25	−.04
Conflicts of interest	.24	**.54**	.15	−.10	.35
Insider trading	.10	**.40**	.11	.06	.39
Personnel Issues					
Drug and alcohol abuse	.10	.15	**.81**	.12	.09
Employee theft	.32	.04	**.76**	−.05	−.04
Discrimination	.07	.13	**.74**	.09	.20
Inaccuracy of books and records	.19	.10	**.41**	.16	.26
Central and Foreign Government Relations					
Inaccurate time charging to government	.16	.13	.06	**.80**	.04
Improper relations with foreign government representatives	.05	.10	.09	**.78**	.11
Improper relations with central government representatives	.30	.14	.00	**.65**	.51
Political and Local Involvement					
Political contributions	.12	.06	.15	.17	**.75**
Relations with local communities	.06	−.02	.14	.03	**.69**
Improper relations with local government representatives	.34	.10	.01	.47	**.59**

Table 16.2 *Continued*

	Factors				
	1	*2*	*3*	*4*	*5*
Eigenvalue	7.28	2.20	1.95	1.83	1.28
% of variance	28.0	8.5	7.5	7.0	4.9
Cronbach's *alpha*	.84	.80	.75	.77	.67

(1987a) found that German managers were sceptical about the effectiveness of codes of ethics.

In the US, business ethicists have focused a great deal of attention on topics such as employee whistleblowing that relate to the ethical decision-making of individual businesspeople (Bowie 1982; DeGeorge 1986). A cross-national study found that US managers are significantly more likely than German managers to indicate that they would blow the whistle in response to a hypothetical vignette (Becker and Fritzsche 1987b).

Additional arguments for the expectation that the US will emphasize employee behaviour stem from Cressey and Moore (1983), who report that US codes of ethics give 'a disproportionate degree of attention' to controlling conduct directed against the firm (p. 58), and Mathews (1988: 61), who found that large US companies are more concerned with 'conduct against the firm or specific illegal activity – such as bribery – on behalf of the firm than with product safety and quality, environmental affairs, and other issues directly related to consumers'. Corporate codes may fail to consider the importance of the individual employee ethics documented by Gilbert (1991) and Derry (1991). As such, corporate guidelines may be excessively represented in anomic organizations (Cohen 1993) and appear to be formulated as a socially acceptable means of control of employee behaviour (Weaver 1993).

■ H1a   US managers will be more concerned with controlling employee behaviour than will UK, German and Austrian managers.

Individual employees have the potential to use information either to further the goals of the firm or to undermine them. Factor 2 contains some items in which employee misuse of information would run contrary to the best interests of the firm and for which, arguably, control of individual behaviour is needed. For the reasons cited above, the US is hypothesized to be the most concerned with this control over employee behaviour. Furthermore, business ethicists in the US have conducted considerable research on the ethics of corporate information (Beltramini 1986; Paine 1991).

A possible competing hypothesis states that because German firms are more likely than US, UK and French firms to emphasize innovation and technology in their corporate codes of ethics (Langlois and Schlegelmilch 1990), German and Austrian firms would be the most protective of corporate information. However, corporate codes in Germany are not focused on the protection of technology; instead, they present innovation and the use of technology as a value to be pursued by the firm and its employees. Given that individualistic societies are much more protective of company rights to technology and information than countries with a communitarian ideology (Lodge and Vogel 1987), we hypothesize:

- H1b   US managers will be more concerned with ethical issues associated with controlling employee use of corporate information than will UK, German and Austrian managers.

The individualistic nature of the ethical concerns comprising our 'personnel issues' factor (drug and alcohol abuse, employee theft, and discrimination) suggests that US managers will be most focused on these issues. Mathison (1993) reports that US executives are more tolerant than European executives of corporate drug testing, a finding that may indicate a greater concern on the part of US executives about potential employee drug abuse. The issues of discrimination, drug and alcohol abuse, and employee theft are well-documented problems in US corporations (Lasher and Grashof 1993; Murphy 1993).

- H1c   US managers will be more concerned with ethical issues of employee drug and alcohol abuse, employee theft, and discrimination than will UK, German and Austrian managers.

The extent of government involvement in business also varies among the four countries. Thurow (1992) characterizes US history as one of adversarial relations between government and the private sector. Similarly, Langlois and Schlegelmilch (1990: 530) find that US corporate documents reveal 'an underlying mistrust of government intervention in the private sector'. In Germany and Austria, on the other hand, government and industry have had to work closely together (van Luijk 1990). For example, partnerships between Germany's central government and industry are common in steel, oil, shipbuilding, automobiles, and electronics (Allen 1987).

Our expectation is that the more individualistic nature of US society will result in greater acknowledgment of relationships with government officials as an ethical issue. Lodge (1990) argues that an individualistic society stresses the individual over the community, and its government tends to have a limited role in business. Business activity takes place in a free market, and government regulates business only to achieve objectives that the market cannot meet. By contrast, in a communitarian society government is important in achieving consensus about the future direction of the community. Our expectation is supported by Langlois and Schlegelmilch (1990) who found that the vast majority of US firms refer to relations with the US government in their codes, whereas a small percentage of European firms include the topic of government relations.

Budde *et al.* (1982) found that British executives on the whole were more supportive than German managers of the need for government intervention in business. However, other studies have found support for an Anglo-Saxon view that governments should not intervene in the market process except where it is necessary to protect individual and corporate rights, and that Europeans perceive themselves as more tolerant than Americans of government intervention in social issues (O'Neil 1986).

- H1d   US managers will be more concerned about relationships with government officials as ethical issues than will UK, German and Austrian managers.

In addition, corporate involvement in the political process and in the local community is more likely to take place in Germany and Austria than in the US and the UK. Regional governments in Germany are a major source of power, and work to foster educational and industrial policy favourable to firms in their region (Allen 1987); German and Austrian political systems are similar (von Riekhoff and Neuhold 1993). Individuals tend to be more politically active than in the US and UK.

- H1e   US and UK managers will be less concerned about political and local involvement as ethical issues than will German and Austrian managers.

16.4 RESULTS

Both country and industry were hypothesized to affect managerial perception of ethical issues (H1 and H2). These hypotheses were tested (while controlling for size) through an analysis of covariance. Specifically, the five factors were used instead of the original variables, and we initially adjusted for the effect of company size and then assessed the effects of country and industry. The results of this analysis are presented in Table 16.3.

Our findings confirm our expectation that both country and industry have a strong influence on the perception of ethical issues (and that firm size does not). The country effect is significant in three of the five factors and the industry effect is significant in four of the five

Table 16.3 Covariance statistics based on factors

	Effects			
	Covariate	*A*	*B*	*(A*B)*
Dependent	*Size of Company*	*Country*	*Industry*	*Interaction*
Factor 1: Gifts & Entertainment				
F-Ratio	.072	1.192	4.447	.996
Significance	.788	.304	.001	.445
Factor 2: Use of Information				
F-Ratio	.918	2.357	2.084	1.025
Significance	.338	.096	.066	.420
Factor 3: Personnel Issues				
F-Ratio	11.034	60.935	1.814	.614
Significance	.001	.001	.108	.802
Factor 4: Central & Foreign Government Relationships				
F-Ratio	1.751	1.718	5.038	.716
Significance	.186	.180	.001	.710
Factor 5: Politics & Local Relationships				
F-Ratio	2.571	2.894	8.552	1.199
Significance	.109	.056	.001	.289

factors. In contrast, there is no significant country-industry interaction effect, i.e. no evidence that particular country/industry combinations produce different effects than do each of the variables alone, and H3 is not supported.

Although the above analyses identify which ethical issues are affected by country, industry, or both, they do not describe the *direction* and *magnitude* of the differences. Therefore, multiple classification analyses were carried out, yielding the deviations from the overall mean for each of the country and industry sub-samples (see Appendix 16.A). Contrast tests then allowed the comparison of individual means where overall differences are significant.[7]

16.4.1 Country differences

We now turn to the specific country difference hypotheses established earlier in the chapter. H1a predicted that US managers would be more concerned with ethical issues surrounding the control of employee conduct than UK, German and Austrian managers (Factor 1). Our results indicate that the US managers are not significantly more likely to identify these as ethical issues, so that H1 is not supported. H1b made a prediction similar to that of H1a; in the case of H1b, controlling behaviour has to do with employee behaviour in regard to information (Factor 2). We found that the US managers are indeed significantly more likely than European managers to identify these as ethical issues of concern, thus providing support for H1b.

Significant differences are found in personnel issues (Factor 3), and H1c is supported because US managers are far more likely than UK and German and Austrian managers to identify personnel issues as ethical issues of concern. H1d predicted that US managers would be most concerned with the ethics of government relations (Factor 4). No significant differences are found. H1e predicted that German and Austrian managers would be more likely to express concern about political and local involvement (Factor 5), and this hypothesis is supported.

Our results suggest that country patterns of identification of ethical issues of concern are not as distinct as we had hypothesized. For example, the hypotheses that would seem to be the most closely related in that they both include the issue of employee control of behaviour, H1a and H1b, do not share significant results.

16.4.2 Industry differences

Our expectations led us to predict that industry would have an impact on the issues identified (H2). This was confirmed by our multiple classification analysis, showing that the perception of ethical issues varies strongly with the type of industry. Among the more notable differences are the comparably larger concern about 'employee conduct' (Factor 1) in wholesaling and retailing, and the greater concern about 'central and foreign government relations' (Factor 4) within agriculture and manufacturing. While most of these differences would be expected (e.g., the importance of 'insider trading' in finance), others (e.g., the lack of attention to 'central and foreign government relations' (Factor 4) in the communications sector) are more difficult to explain. The only area where no significant industry effects could be observed was 'personnel issues' (Factor 3).

16.4.3 Formulation of ethics policies and training

Shifting the focus to the formulation of ethics policies and training, initially two new variables were computed. They represent a count of the ethical issues a company addresses in its written policy and training and are expressed as a proportion of the total number of potential policy/training items listed in the questionnaire. Our findings indicate that companies tend to address substantially more ethical issues in written policy statements (mean = 36 per cent) than in training (mean = 5 per cent). Moreover, it is worth noting that 108 companies (14 per cent) do not address any of the listed ethical issues in written policy statements, and 534 (67 per cent) do not address any of the issues in employee training.

To test our hypotheses that different countries and industries will have different ethical issues included in their written ethics policies and in ethics training, two analyses of covariance were conducted. The design of these analyses specifies the proportion of ethical issues addressed in written policies and in training as dependent variables and treats the company size *together* with the five factors representing the perception of ethical problems as covariates. The rationale is that not only company size but also the perception of ethical issues potentially influence the formulation of ethics policies and training. The country and industry measures are again treated as main effects with a design introducing the covariates prior to the main effects. The results of the two analyses are presented in Table 16.4.

Country and industry effects are highly significant, reiterating the importance of these variables, supporting H5 and H6. No significant interaction effect could be observed between country and industry. The direction and magnitude of the country and industry-specific influences were again determined with multiple classification analyses (Appendix 16.B) and subsequent contrast tests permitted the comparison of individual means where overall differences are significant.[8] Interestingly, the results provide no support for H4 in that the perception of ethical problems appears to have *no* significant bearing on the proportion of ethical issues addressed either in written policies or training. In terms of written policies, the results show that the US and the UK are rather similar to each other and considerably different from the German and Austrian subsample. With regard to training, the results again point towards the US and UK aligning in relationship to Germany and Austria; however, the magnitude of this difference is not as pronounced as it is in regard to written policies. Looking at the influence of industry, the multiple classification analysis illustrates that manufacturing and agriculture are addressing a relatively higher proportion of issues in their written policies, while service industries address comparatively more issues in training.

16.5 DISCUSSION

Our results indicate that the US (the most individualistic of the countries) is most likely to stand alone and the European countries to align. Vogel (1992) has characterized business ethics in the US as shaped by the 'tradition of individualism'. Furthermore, as the European Union becomes more solidified, European alignment on ethical issues may be expected to follow.

The most striking country difference occurs for personnel issues, with the United States managers much more likely than the United Kingdom or German and Austrian managers to perceive personnel issues as ethical issues. This finding is consistent with that of Langlois and Schlegelmilch (1990) who reported that US firms tended to emphasize concepts of employee fairness and equity and focused on

Table 16.4 Covariance statistics: written policies and training

Dependent	Covariates	F-Ratio (Sign.)	Effects	F-Ratio (Sign.)	Interaction	F-Ratio (Sign.)
Proportion of Ethical Issues Addressed in Written Policies	Size of Company	.041 (.839)	Country	8.263 (.001)	Country × Industry	1.269 (.244)
	Employee Conduct	.024 (.877)	Industry	4.040 (.001)		
	Use of Information	2.190 (.139)				
	Personnel Issues	.124 (.724)				
	Central and Foreign Gov't Relationships	1.228 (.268)				
	Political and Local Involvement	.814 (.367)				
Proportion of Ethical Issues Addressed in Training	Size of Company	.052 (.820)	Country	2.965 (.052)	Country × Industry	0.977 (.462)
	Employee Conduct	.017 (.896)	Industry	1.876 (.097)		
	Use of Information	1.063 (.303)				
	Personnel Issues	.027 (.870)				
	Central and Foreign Gov't Relationships	1.163 (.281)				
	Political and Local Involvement	1.755 (.186)				

the 'quality of company policy towards employees', while European firms were more likely to stress 'employee responsiveness to company activities'.

In addition, US managers are significantly more likely to perceive that employee use of information constitutes an ethical issue. On the other hand, German and Austrian managers are significantly more likely to consider political and local involvement an ethical issue of concern. Such involvement is likely to take place at the firm level, as well as at the individual employee level, and thus would be consistent with a communitarian perspective. The lack of difference on the employee conduct dimension is particularly surprising because other studies show that US corporations are 'rules-minded' about formulating guidelines for employee ethical behaviour (Cressey and Moore 1983; Mathews 1988). In fact, the UK is ahead of the US on this factor. One possible explanation to be tested in future research is that more recent US corporate codes of ethics have tended to be concerned with employees, but in a protective rather than a restrictive manner.

The US demonstrates the most concern and the UK the least about central and government relationships (Factor 4), although country differences are not significant. We had expected that the least concern with government relationships would characterize the most communitarian society. However, the UK has a long tradition of government involvement in industry, and despite recent privatization initiatives, has close government-corporate relationships (Budde et al. 1982). Budde et al. report that British executives were significantly more supportive of 'appropriate government intervention in the business world' than were German executives.

Four out of the five factors show significant industry differences. The exception is the personnel issues factor, suggesting that these are common to all industries. Most of the industry differences are not surprising. However, the profile of political and local involvement is puzzling in that it is not immediately obvious why the communications and finance and insurance industries would have the greatest concern and wholesale and retail industries the least. Similarly, in looking at industry differences for the individual variables, we note, for example, that the issue of drug and alcohol abuse varies significantly with the communications industry having the most concern, whereas the finance and insurance industries do not. Companies in the manufacturing industry may be more inclined to drug test and therefore less inclined to report this as an ethical issue.

Given the country and industry differences found, from a managerial perspective, it appears to be a mistake to expect all corporate ethics policies to look alike. Careful thought should be given to tailoring the policy to the particular firm, industry and country. Large multinational firms operating in a number of countries need to consider the general applicability of a code of ethics or ethics training that was developed in the country in which the firm's headquarters is located. If ethical concerns differ by country, then imposing a set of standards developed for one country on another country may be counterproductive. Similarly, expatriates working for multinational firms need to be aware that their own perception of ethical issues may not match that of their native fellow employees.

However, our results should not be interpreted as supportive of a cultural relativism argument. The fact that there are country differences in approaches to ethical issues does not necessarily mean that there should be country differences in ethical principles, nor that it is impossible to formulate universal ethical principles. What 'is' should not be the determinant of what 'ought to be'. Donaldson (1991: 50) points to the counterproductive and sceptical nature of cultural relativism in that it 'declares morality to be defined exclusively in terms of cultural norms'. We agree with Donaldson that empirical research to identify such norms can make pronouncements only on cultural practice, not on moral theory. A full discussion of cultural relativism is outside the scope of the present study (see Freeman and Gilbert 1988, for an excellent criticism of theories of cultural relativism).

This research is exploratory, and the generalizability of our findings is consequently uncertain. The low rates of response in the European sample suggest that we need to be particularly cautious about our results. However, our study leads to at least three avenues that appear promising for future research. First, and most obvious, the study should be repeated in other nations to explore the generalizability of the results. It would be especially interesting to study countries such as Japan and China which are highly communitarian, but have adopted very few corporate ethics initiatives such as ethics codes and training. One may even focus on subcultures within countries, recognizing that these may have distinctive approaches to ethical issues.

Second, future research could concentrate on discovering the ethical issues that are salient in other countries and the ways in which corporations are addressing those issues. One possible approach would be to link stakeholder theory to ethical issues. Identification of the most relevant stakeholder groups in each country should prove revealing about which ethical issues managers perceive to be important.

Finally, the findings demonstrate considerable similarities between the US and UK on written ethics policies and training. In other words, the ethical issues in the two countries may be different, but the corporate response in terms of ethics initiatives is similar. Future studies could investigate diffusion patterns of corporate ethics practices among countries. Ciulla (1991) has argued that Europeans are beginning to adopt codes of ethics because managers are increasingly dealing with a pluralism of values within their firms similar to the pluralism found in US companies. This still does not explain why the ethical issues European managers identify are different from those of concern to US managers. Our discovery of a European alignment on these issues needs to be explored further.

16.6   NOTES

[1] The four countries analysed operate slightly different SIC (Standard Industrial Classification) systems. To facilitate comparison, the US categories were adopted.

[2] The Bartlett test of sphericity tests the hypothesis that the correlation matrix is an identity matrix. If this hypothesis cannot be rejected, factor analysis is not appropriate for the data set.

[3] The Kaiser-Meyer-Olkin (KMO) measure of sampling adequacy compares the magnitudes of the observed correlation coefficients with the magnitudes of the partial correlation coefficients. If the value of the KMO statistic is low (less than .60), the use of factor analysis is not recommended.

[4] Since the US sample was so much larger than the sample drawn from the European countries, we also re-ran the factor analysis five times with successive random samples of the US respondents in order to achieve roughly equal subsample sizes for the European countries and the US. These analyses confirmed the stability of the factor structure obtained when all US cases were processed.

[5] To test for possible country-specific influences on the resulting factor dimensions, separate factor analyses were conducted for the country subsamples and a number of factor comparison indicators were computed, notably the root mean square (RMS), the coefficient of congruence (CC), and the Pearson Correlation coefficient (r) (Levine 1977). While, overall, similar factor structures emerged, the results indicate no total congruence. However, in interpreting these findings, some caution is called for in the light of the ratio between the analysed variables and the total number of cases in the European subsamples.

[6] A high degree of congruency in the attitudes of German and Austrian managers has also been observed in different fields (e.g. Müller 1991: 136–9) and lends support to our findings.

[7] The ANCOVA design had to be changed in order to conduct multiple classification analyses. This did not have a substantial impact on the results; all significant findings remained significant and additional significant relationships were found. SPSS/PC$^+$ also does not permit the direct calculation of contrast tests (cf. SPSS/PC$^+$ V2.0 Base Manual, p. B-169). Thus, to check for statistically significant differences between the country and industry subsam-

ples, the covariate (company size) was regressed against the response variables to isolate the residuals as follows:

$$Residuals = Response\ Variable - b_o - b_1 x_1 - b_2 x_2 - b_n x_n$$

The obtained residuals were subsequently included in the SPSS/ PC$^+$ ONEWAY procedure which permits multiple comparisons (such as Scheffé, LSD, etc.).

[8] Changing the ANCOVA design (see Note 7) to facilitate a multiple classification analysis again reiterates the stability of the results, i.e. this had no effect on either the significance of size, industry or country. The factors used as covariates also remained relatively stable, with the exception of 'central and foreign government relations', which become significant in the analysis of written policies.

16.7   REFERENCES

Allen, C.S. (1987) Germany: competing communitarianisms, in G.C. Lodge and E.F. Vogel (eds), *Ideology and National Competitiveness*, Boston, MA: Harvard University Press.

Becker, H. and Fritzsche, D.J. (1987a) Business ethics: a cross-cultural comparison of managers' attitudes. *Journal of Business Ethics*, 6(4), pp. 289–95.

Becker, H. and Fritzsche, D.J. (1987b) A comparison of the ethical behavior of American, French and German managers. *Columbia Journal of World Business*, 22(4), pp. 87–95.

Beltramini, R.F. (1986) Ethics and the use of competitive information acquisition strategies. *Journal of Business Ethics*, 5(4), pp. 307–11.

Beneish, M.D. and Chatov, R. (1993) Corporate codes of conduct: economic determinants and legal implications for independent auditors. *Journal of Accounting and Public Policy*, 12, pp. 3–35.

Bowie, N. (1982) *Business Ethics*, Englewood Cliffs, NJ: Prentice-Hall.

Budde, A., Child, J., Francis, A. and Kieser, A. (1982) Corporate goals, managerial objectives, and organizational structures in British and West German companies. *Organization Studies*, 3(1), pp. 1–32.

Buller, P.F., Kohls, J.J. and Anderson, K.S. (1991) The challenge of global ethics. *Journal of Business Ethics*, 10(10), pp. 767–76.

Center for Business Ethics (1986) Are corporations institutionalizing ethics? *Journal of Business Ethics*, 5(2), pp. 85–91.

Center for Business Ethics (1992) Instilling ethical values in large corporations. *Journal of Business Ethics*, 11(11), pp. 863–67.

Chatov, R. (1980) What corporate ethics statements say. *California Management Review*, 22(4), pp. 20–9.

Chatov, R. (1982) Corporate conduct codes: operational or symbolic? Paper presented to the Academy of Management, New York.

Ciulla, J.B. (1991) Why is business talking about ethics? Reflections on foreign conversations. *California Management Review*, Fall, pp. 67–86.

Cohen, D.V. (1993) Creating and maintaining ethical work climates: anomie in the workplace and implications for managing change, *Business Ethics Quarterly*, 3(4), pp. 343–58.

Cressey, D.R. and Moore, C.A. (1983) Managerial values and corporate codes of ethics. *California Management Review*, 25(4), pp. 53–77.

Cronbach, L.J. (1971) Test validation, in R.L. Thorndike (ed.), *Educational measurement* (2nd edn), pp. 443–507. Washington, DC: American Council on Education.

De George, R. (1986) *Business Ethics* (2nd edn), New York: Macmillan.

Derry, R. (1991) Institutionalizing ethical motivation: reflections on Goodpaster's agenda, in R.E. Freeman (ed.), *Business Ethics: The State of the Art*, New York: Oxford University Press.

Donaldson, T. (1989) *The Ethics of International Business*, New York: Oxford University Press.

Donaldson, T. (1991) Just business abroad. *Responsive Community*, 1(4), pp. 48–55.

Donaldson, T. and Dunfee, T.W. (1994) Towards a unified conception of business ethics: integrative social contracts theory. *Academy of Management Review*, 19(2), pp. 252–84.

Dubinsky, AJ., Jolson, M.A., Kotabe, M. and Lim, C.U. (1991) A cross-national investigation of industrial salespeople's ethical perceptions. *Journal of International Business Studies*, 22(4), pp. 651–70.

Economist (1993) How to be ethical, and still come top. June 5, p. 71.

England, G.W. (1978) Managers and their value systems: a five-country comparative study. *Columbia Journal of World Business*, 13(2), pp. 35–44.

Ethics Resource Center (1990) *Ethics Policies and Programs in American Business*, Washington, DC: ERC.

Frederick, W.C. (1991) The moral authority of transnational corporate codes. *Journal of Business Ethics*, 10(3), pp. 165–77.

Freeman, R.E. and Gilbert, D.R. (1988) *Corporate Strategy and the Search for Ethics*, Englewood Cliffs, NJ: Prentice-Hall.

Gilbert, D.R. (1991) Respect for persons, management theory, and business ethics, in R.E. Freeman (ed.), *Business Ethics: The State of the Art*, New York: Oxford University Press.

Gordon, G.G. (1991) Industry determinants of organizational culture. *Academy of Management Review*, 16(2), pp. 396–415.

Hansen, U. (1988) Marketing und soziale Verantwortung. *Die Betriebswirtschaft*, 48, pp. 711–21.

Hickson, D.J., Hinings, C.R., McMillan, C.J. and Schwitter, J.R. (1974) The culture-free context of organization structure: a trinational comparison. *Sociology*, 8, pp. 58–80.

Hofstede, G. (1976) Nationality and espoused values of managers. *Journal of Applied Psychology*, 61(2), pp. 148–55.

Hofstede, G. (1980) *Culture's Consequences*, Beverly Hills, CA: Sage.

Hofstede, G. (1993) Cultural constraints in management theories. *Academy of Management Executive*, 7(1), pp. 81–94.

Izraeli, D. (1988) Ethical beliefs and behaviour among managers: a cross-cultural perspective. *Journal of Business Ethics*, 7(4), pp. 263–71.

Jackall, R. (1988) *Moral Mazes*, New York: Oxford University Press.

Kanter, R.M. (1991) Transcending business boundaries: 12,000 world managers view change. *Harvard Business Review*, May–June, pp. 151–64.

Kelley, L., Whatley, A. and Worthley, R. (1987) Assessing the effects of culture on managerial attitudes: a three culture test. *Journal of International Business Studies*, 18(2), pp. 17–31.

Langlois, C.C. and Schlegelmilch, B.B. (1990) Do corporate codes of ethics reflect national character? Evidence from Europe and the United States. *Journal of International Business Studies*, 21(4), pp. 519–39.

Lasher, H.J. and Grashof, J.F. (1993) Substance abuse in small business: business owner perceptions and reactions. *Journal of Small Business Management*, 31(1), pp. 63–75.

Levine, M.S. (1977) *Canonical Analysis and Factor Comparison*, Beverly Hills, CA: Sage Publications.

Lodge, G.C. (1990) *Perestroika for America*, Boston, MA: Harvard University Press.

Lodge, G.C. and Vogel, E.F. (eds) (1987) *Ideology and National Competitiveness*, Boston, MA: Harvard University Press.

Mahoney, J. and Vallance, E. (1992) *Business Ethics in a New Europe*, Dordrecht/Boston/London: Kluwer Academic Press.

März, E. and Szecsi, M. (1981) Austria's economic development, 1945–1978, in K. Steiner (ed.), *Modern Austria*, pp. 123–40. Palo Alto, CA: SPOSS.

Mathews, M.C. (1988) *Strategic Intervention in Organizations: Resolving Ethical Dilemmas*. Newbury Park, CA: Sage.

Mathison, D.L. (1993) European and American executive values. *Business Ethics. A European Review*, 2(2), pp. 97–100.

Maurice, M., Sorge, A. and Warner, M. (1980) Societal differences in organizing manufacturing units: a comparison of France, West Germany and Great Britain. *Organization Studies*, 1(1), pp. 59–86.

Miller, G.A. (1987) Meta-analysis and the culture-free hypothesis. *Organization Studies*, 8(4), pp. 309–25.

Müller, S. (1991) *Die Psyche des Managers als Determinante des Exporterfolges*. Stuttgart, Germany: Verlag für Wissenschaft und Forschung.

Murphy, K.R. (1993) *Honesty in the Workplace*, Belmont, CA: Brooks/Cole.

Nunnally, J.C. (1978) *Psychometric Theory* (2nd edn), New York: McGraw-Hill.

O'Neil, R. (1986) Corporate social responsibility and business ethics: a European perspective. *International Journal of Social Economics*, 13(10), pp. 64–76.

Paine, L.S. (1991) Corporate policy and the ethics of competitive intelligence gathering. *Journal of Business Ethics*, 10(6), pp. 423–36.

Robertson, D.C. (1993) Empiricism in business ethics: suggested research directions. *Journal of Business Ethics*, 12, pp. 585–99.

Rowan, R.L. and Campbell, D.C. (1983) The attempt to regulate industrial relations through international codes of conduct. *Columbia Journal of World Business*, 18(2), pp. 64–72.

Ryan, L.V. (1994) Ethics codes in British companies. *Business Ethics. A European Review*, 3(1), pp. 54–64.

Schlegelmilch, B.B. (1990) Die Kodifizierung ethischer Grundsätze in europäischen Unternehmen: eine empirische Untersuchung. *Die Betriebswirtschaft*, 3, pp. 365–74.

Schlegelmilch, B.B. and Houston, J.E. (1989) Corporate codes of ethics in large UK companies: an empirical investigation of use, content and attitudes. *European Journal of Marketing*, 23(6), pp. 7–24.

Steinmann, H. and Löhr, A. (1989) *Unternehmensethik*, Stuttgart, Germany: Poeschel Verlag.

Steinmann, H. and Löhr, A. (1992) A survey of business ethics in Germany. *Business Ethics: A European Review*, 1(2), pp. 139–41.

Steinmann, H. and Oppenrieder, B. (1985) Brauchen wir eine Unternehmensethik? *Die Betriebswirtschaft*, 45, pp. 170–83.

Thurow, L. (1992) *Head to Head: The Coming Economic Battle Among Japan, Europe, and America*, New York: William Morrow.

Tse, D.K., Lee, K., Vertinsky, I. and Werhung, D.A. (1988) Does culture matter? A cross-cultural study of executives' choice, decisiveness, and risk adjustment in international marketing. *Journal of Marketing*, 52(4), pp. 81–95.

van Luijk, H.J.L. (1990) Recent developments in European business ethics. *Journal of Business Ethics*, 9(7), pp. 537–44.

Vitell, S.J., Nwachukwu, S.L. and Barnes, J.H. (1993) The effects of culture on ethical decision-making: An application of Hofstede's typology. *Journal of Business Ethics*, 12(10), pp. 753–60.

Vogel, D. (1992) The globalization of business ethics: why America remains distinctive. *California Management Review*, 35(1), pp. 30–49.

von Riekhoff, H. and Neuhold, H. (1993) *Unequal Partners: A Comparative Analysis of Relations between Austria and the Federal Republic of Germany and between Canada and the United States*, Boulder, CO: Westview Press.

Weaver, G.R. (1993) Corporate codes of ethics: purpose; process and content issues. *Business and Society*, 32(1), pp. 44–58.

Webley, S. (1992) *Business Ethics, Company Values and Codes: Current Best Practice in the United Kingdom*, London: Institute of Business Ethics.

Wines, W.A. and Napier, N.K. (1992) Toward an understanding of cross-cultural ethics: a tentative model. *Journal of Business Ethics*, 11(11), pp. 831–41.

APPENDIX 16.A MULTIPLE CLASSIFICATION ANALYSIS

Variables and Effects		Deviations from Grand Mean		
		Unadjusted	Adjusted for Independents	Adjusted for Independents and Covariate
Factor 1: Employee Conduct (Grand Mean = −.003)				
1 United States	(a)	.03	.01	.01
2 United Kingdom		.00	.08	.07
3 Germany/Austria		−.18	−.15	−.16
1 Agriculture	(b)	−.01	−.01	.00
2 Manufacturing		−.12	−.12	−.12
3 Communications		−.09	−.09	−.09
4 Wholesale, Retail		.42	.42	.42
5 Finance, Insurance		.11	−.11	−.11
6 Services		−.03	−.04	−.03
Factor 2: Use of Information (Grand Mean = −.004)				
1 United States	(c)	.04	.05	.05
2 United Kingdom		.00	−.05	−.04
3 Germany/Austria		−.23	−.25	−.24
1 Agriculture	(d)	−.20	−.21	−.21
2 Manufacturing		.05	.09	.09
3 Communications		−.13	−.15	−.16
4 Wholesale, Retail		−.07	−.09	−.09
5 Finance, Insurance		.19	.18	.18
6 Services		.10	.08	.08

		Deviations from Grand Mean		
Variables and Effects		Unadjusted	Adjusted for Independents	Adjusted for Independents and Covariate
Factor 3: Personnel Issues (Grand Mean = .009)				
1 United States	(e)	.26	.25	.25
2 United Kingdom		−.72	−.68	−.68
3 Germany/Austria		−.87	−.84	−.84
1 Agriculture	(f)	.10	.07	.07
2 Manufacturing		−.26	−.07	−.07
3 Communications		.25	.11	.11
4 Wholesale, Retail		.21	.09	.09
5 Finance, Insurance		−.17	−.22	−.22
6 Services		.17	.10	.10
Factor 4: Central and Foreign Government Relations (Grand Mean = −.007)				
1 United States	(g)	.02	.04	.05
2 United Kingdom		−.05	−.13	−.15
3 Germany/Austria		−.05	−.11	−.13
1 Agriculture	(h)	.42	.41	.42
2 Manufacturing		.11	.15	.14
3 Communications		−.16	−.18	−.18
4 Wholesale, Retail		−.15	−.17	−.17
5 Finance, Insurance		−.21	−.22	−.22
6 Services		−.05	−.07	−.06
Factor 5: Political and Local Involvement (Grand Mean = −.017)				
1 United States	(i)	−.02	−.03	−.03
2 United Kingdom		−.10	−.06	−.08
3 Germany/Austria		.24	.28	.25
1 Agriculture	(j)	.00	.00	.00
2 Manufacturing		−.10	−.12	−.13
3 Communications		.34	.36	.36
4 Wholesale, Retail		−.35	−.35	−.34
5 Finance, Insurance		.35	.36	.37
6 Services		−.08	−.07	−.06

Scheffé Procedure at .05 level

(a) not significant
(b) Group 4 vs. 2, 3, 5
(c) not significant
(d) not significant
(e) Group 1 vs. 2, 3

(f) Group 2 vs. 3, 4, 6
(g) not significant
(h) Group 1 vs. 3, 4, 5
(i) Group 1 vs. 3
(j) Group 3 vs. 2, 4
    Group 5 vs. 2, 4

APPENDIX 16.B MULTIPLE CLASSIFICATION ANALYSIS

Variables and Effects		*Deviations from Grand Mean*		
		Unadjusted	*Adjusted for Independents*	*Adjusted for Independents and Covariate*
Proportion of Ethical Issues Addressed in Written Policies (Grand Mean = 36.22)				
United States	(a)	.84	1.53	1.80
United Kingdom		4.40	1.99	1.41
Germany/Austria		−9.88	−11.69	−12.81
Agriculture	(b)	.92	.84	1.97
Manufacturing		5.07	6.03	6.29
Communications		.76	.09	−.64
Wholesale, Retail		−2.97	−3.33	−2.77
Finance, Insurance		−5.60	−6.02	−7.47
Services		−4.88	−5.52	−5.55
Proportion of Ethical Issues Addressed in Training (Grand Mean = 5.54)				
United States	(c)	−.07	−.15	−.26
United Kingdom		−2.12	−1.85	−1.63
Germany/Austria		2.62	2.90	3.31
Agriculture	(d)	−.47	−.50	−.91
Manufacturing		−.87	−.90	−1.00
Communications		−1.72	−1.72	−1.45
Wholesale, Retail		.96	.89	.72
Finance, Insurance		−.03	.05	.58
Services		3.70	3.81	3.81

Scheffé Procedure at p< .05
  (a) Group 3 vs. 1,2
  (b) not significant
  (c) not significant
  (d) not significant

17 *International marketing of organs for transplantation*

Robert S. Tancer

As the technology for organ transplantation continues to improve and procedures become more accessible on a world-wide level, the inadequate supply of suitable organs creates situations which violate established legal and ethical norms. Pressures to commercialize the process continue to build, raising such difficult questions as increasing the supply of organs, the quality of care for both donor and recipient, paying for organs, and equitable access to the supply of available organs for those in need. Various approaches are being utilized to resolve these problems on the local or national levels, but these have not been successful because organ transplantation technology is available on a global level. It is the attempt of this chapter to review various national approaches and urge consideration of an international regime to control standards for organ transplants that will maintain high health standards, assure equitable distribution, and share the latest and most effective technology.

17.1 INTERNATIONAL MARKETING OF ORGANS FOR TRANSPLANTATION

17.1.1 Introduction

A recent visitor to China reported that she had been cautioned about using public restrooms because of rumours that people were sometimes murdered at these locations so that their organs could be removed for use in transplant surgery in local hospitals; a civil judge in Chile was advised by his superiors to scrutinize any foreign adoptions because it is rumoured that children are murdered for their organs; a Colombian medical school is under indictment by local authorities because the neighbors complain about the staff killing the nearby homeless to obtain organs for its transplant programme.[1]

These unrelated cases reflect a universal phenomenon: the growing market for organs suitable for transplantation. Comparable examples often appear in the press and are a result of the world-wide situation where transplant technology is rapidly surpassing the number of available organs. Any environment where the demand exceeds the supply, and particularly when the demand encompasses life or death situations, is bound to produce issues often outside the legal or ethical norms of a given society. One such issue in the area of organ transplants is that of marketing. How are organs transferred from donors to recipients? In traditional marketing terms we are comfortable with the idea of the exchange of goods for money. This simplistic formula, common for centuries in the sale of goods, is not usually acceptable in the world of organ transplants where there is a long tradition prohibiting the sale of organs and exclusive reliance on the view that organs must be donated. Thus the historical rationale from the perspective of the donor, and one reinforced by laws and ethical standards, is that of altruism rather than profit. Scarcity of organs and extreme poverty in many developing countries raises questions as to the wisdom of maintaining this traditional view. The organ transplant process, really the marketing of organs, involves three discrete steps, each of which raises ethical issues of its own: the harvesting of the organs themselves (from whom and under what condition), the acquisition of the organs (donation or sale) and, finally, allocation of the organs (who will receive the scarce organs).

It is the purpose of this chapter to consider each of these issues and evaluate some selective solutions. In recent years much has been written on the subject of organ transplants either at the clinical or national levels. The clinical materials may be found largely in medical journals and are beyond the scope of this discussion. The national literature treats the subject either from a legal or ethical point of view, but only in terms of specific country solutions. This paper will attempt to examine these legal and ethical issues from a comparative perspective. Obviously space does not permit consideration of every country but it is believed that the sampling is sufficiently diverse to reach global conclusions. Internationally the issues remain the same, but solutions are often different, based on diverse cultural, legal and ethical differences among countries, religions and cultures. Although medical practice and its attending technology may be universal, acceptance and participation in the organ transplant process does vary greatly from group to group and country to country. It is therefore interesting to examine some of the distinct issues in an effort to harmonize our own practices.

17.1.2 Issues

(a) Harvesting organs

Acquisition of organs suitable for transplantation is the logical beginning. Two situations exist: the harvesting of an organ or part of it from a living person (living donor), currently possible in the case of kidney or liver transplants. Working with a living donor raises relatively simple questions – the relationship, if any, between the parties, and in the absence of any such relationship, payment. In those situations where organs are for sale from unknown donors, implementation problems regarding standards and criteria affecting both donors and beneficiaries arise. Harvesting an organ from a deceased donor (cadaveric donation) is the more common practice for other kinds of transplants. Harvesting from a cadaver raises special problems of timing and consent.

Cadaveric donations (CD) raise the immediate problem of when is the appropriate time to remove the organ. There are multiple considerations ranging from one extreme such as when an individual is dead to when the organ must be harvested to assure its greatest viability. These concerns are not necessarily mutually exclusive. The prevailing standard for organ harvesting is that of brain death, a condition of irreversible coma that does not respond to any known therapy (Churchill and Pinkuss 1990). This definition has replaced the more traditional view of heart or lung death. For organ transplantations, a beating heart, even if kept beating artificially, is considered optimum for harvesting. Removal of organs from a non-heart-beating body may affect their quality (US General Accounting Office 1993).

Although brain death is the common accepted criterium, Japan has resisted the concept due to cultural factors which place the gut (or belly) as the 'master organ'. Some other Japanese attitudes toward transplantation are also influenced by the Buddhist tradition that it is not natural to remove an organ from a body when the heart is still beating, and a greater distrust of doctors than exists in many other societies (Akatsu 1990). The Japanese attitude is shifting toward greater acceptance of brain death as the demand for organs increases. Organs removed from brain dead donors were accepted for transplantation by the bioethics committee of the medical school at Osaka University as of August 1990 (Yamauchi 1990).

The most controversial issue in the transplant process, however, is that of consent. It is standard practice to obtain some form of consent from the donor prior to death, or from the next of kin following death. In Mexico the regulations governing organs transplants provide a ranking of those able to grant consent beginning with the spouse and ending with designated public officials (*NORMA* 1988). The form of consent will vary from jurisdiction to jurisdiction, but the essential purpose remains the same: to assure that the deceased or his next of kin agreed to the procedure, and that the organ was not taken from the body of the deceased unknowingly. Consent may be granted in writing, with or without the attestation of a witness, or orally, usually in the presence of two witnesses. As with other juridicial acts where consent is required, the prospective donor's legal capacity to grant consent will be at issue and is subjected to familiar legal norms.

Thus a minor will not be allowed to grant consent because he is unable to enter into a contract without the consent of his parents or guardian. Most legislation empowers an 'adult' as one able to grant consent or sometimes actual ages are specified, usually 18 or 21.

Even though it may not be required legally, the next of kin will be consulted even if the deceased has granted unequivocal prior consent. The system leaves much to be desired because obtaining consent from the next of kin is often awkward in the period prior to or immediately following death. Often the next of kin will refuse to grant consent despite the prior expressed wishes of the deceased. In such cases the hospital or attending physician will usually respect the wishes of the next of kin. This process, particularly when the next of kin is not immediately available, can cause delays which render the organs unsuitable for transplantation.

In the United States many states have adopted the Uniform Anatomical Gift Act[2] which enables a prospective donor to make a gift of his organs either through a will or other written document. It is common practice for a potential donor to make a sworn affidavit to this effect at the motor vehicle bureau for recording on his or her driver's licence. This practice of obtaining consent and noting it on a document that the potential donor carries with him is gaining acceptance. Proposed legislation in Chile provides that a person may specify his consent or objection to being an organ donor on his identity card (*cédula*) (Reseña Legislative 1990).

'Required request' laws have also been enacted in a large number of states within the United States providing that health care personnel seek organs from potential donors and their families in suitable situations. The legal profession has been asked to help increase the organ pool by reviewing organ donations with clients in an appropriate context (McCormick 1992).

In an effort to increase the supply of usable organs, many European countries have enacted legislation that assumes that any brain dead adult has consented to be an organ donor unless he has advised to the contrary. These laws are often characterized as granting 'implied' or 'presumed' consent. Such a law has been in effect in France since 1976, and it is credited, in part, to the fact that more transplants take place in France per million population than in any other country in Europe (Bader 1992). In the former East Germany a comparable law existed but did not allow for opposition as in France. Transplant legislation in Germany exists on the state level with many of the states of former West Germany favouring expressed consent of the deceased to or from the next of kin (Tuffs 1991). Belgium is said to have increased its organ recovery rate by 117 per cent during the first two years of its implied consent law (US General Accounting Office 1993: 62).

In the United States the presumed consent approach has not

enjoyed much favour. Ethical considerations seem to favour express consent from the donor or at least the next of kin. Health care professionals are reluctant to harvest organs without either or both of these (ibid.). Obviously the threat of malpractice litigation has greatly influenced attitudes in the United States.

One of the more interesting and innovative consent laws can be found in the Human Organ Transplant Act (HOTA) in Singapore, passed in 1987. Under this law all legally competent adults who are accident victims are presumed to have consented to be kidney donors unless they have indicated prior dissent. Muslims, a significant minority in Singapore, are assumed to dissent on religious grounds. As an incentive to participate in the programme HOTA gives priority to individuals who have accepted the law and later need organ transplants. This practice raises ethical questions under the concept of equitable access.

(b) Selling organs

Traditionally the sale of organs has been prohibited and is illegal.[3] This view is logical since the rationalization of transplantation technology is based on the concept of a voluntary donation, motivated by the altruism of the donor, which enables a beneficiary to live or improve the quality of life through the gift of the decedent. Moreover, the organs of the decedent live on in the body of the recipient.

The volunteer tradition in the development of organ transplantation legislation is so strong that early legislation reads like a treatise on the law of gifts. In the Canadian provinces of Ontario and Alberta, the law is named *'Human Tissue Gift Act'*; *inter-vivos* gifts are distinguished from post mortem gifts for transplant purposes (Revised statutes of Ontario and Alberta 1980). In the United States a donor is defined as '. . . an individual who makes a **gift** of all or part of his body' (emphasis supplied)[4] and in the Latin Amerian countries, the process is always one of *donación*.

Due to the ever growing demand for additional organs, by the late 1980s a minority of writers began challenging the assumption that it was unethical to receive any form of payment for organs (Haansmann 1989; Kittur *et al.* 1991; Zoler 1990). The discussion distinguished between payment for cadaveric organs and payment to live donors. In the case of the former, suggestions have varied from death benefit payments to the next of kin to cover burial costs and other final expenses of the deceased (Kittur *et al.* 1991: 1443), to reducing the cost of health insurance to a prospective donor (Haansmann 1989: 63), and even to providing medical care to the family of the deceased in government hospitals. The latter approach has actually been incorporated into the Singapore law which provides payment of 50 per cent of medical expenses incurred at government hospitals for a five year period to the families of the donors (Teo 1991).

These approaches vary both as to whom and by whom payment is made. Opinion is unanimous that payment, if made, should come from a neutral source rather than from participating physicians or hospital staff. Such payors might be the United Network for Organ Sharing (UNOS), the entity responsible for administering the national organ procurement and allocation system in the United States (US General Accounting Office 1993: 2), or a health insurance company (Haansmann 1989: 63). The issue has become so acute that in 1992 the National Kidney Foundation undertook a poll of two thousand people throughout the United States asking their opinion about some form of payment (Khanna 1992).

Payment to live donors remains controversial, but raises the added question that the donors, often poor and living in the developing world, are asked to provide organs for individuals living in the developed world. In addition to the entire question of payment, securing organs from live donors in developing countries raises new issues related to the medical standards of harvesting, the quality of care offered both the donor and recipient, care of the organ from the time of harvesting to transplantation, and the medical environment for the transplant, assuming the transplant surgery takes place at or near the site where the organ has been harvested. All of these variables affect the success or failure of the outcome.

A recent study considers the outcome of 130 persons from the United Arab Emirates (UAE) who travelled to Bombay, India for kidney transplants from living unrelated donors. The results were not very satisfactory. Eight died in Bombay, and of the 122 who returned to the UAE, 24 died within the first year following transplantation (Salahudeen *et al.* 1990). This high percentage of deaths was caused by infections, poor patient education as to self-medication and the dangers of immunosuppression, quality of medical facilities in Bombay and, finally, the quality of the blood or the organs used in the transplants (ibid.: 728–9). The high death rates were also the result of giving transplants to patients unfit for the procedure. The authors conclude that the Bombay activity was manifest by 'rampant commercialism . . . the whole enterprise is predicated on profit for the transplanters and brokers, with invariable exploitation of the donors and recipients' (ibid.: 735).

With the possibility of exploitation of the donor so great, efforts have been made in certain countries to control or restrict the sale of organs by living donors. As of July 1992, Egypt restricts the sale of kidneys from living donors to relatives and prohibits sales to third parties (Hedges 1992). In Britain a physician recently lost his licence and two of his colleagues were sanctioned by the professional conduct committee of The General Medical Council for participating in a scheme of buying kidneys in Turkey for unrelated kidney transplants (Dyer 1990). Physicians in both Egypt and India are concerned about the number of individuals in their own countries who are suffering from renal failure and would benefit from kidney transplants. They see the solution in establishing organ banks and setting up appropriate procedures for obtaining kidneys from cadavers (Hedges and Hazarika 1992).

As we have seen, traditional concern over the question of organ sales is generally expressed in prohibiting payment to the living donor or the next of kin of the deceased. A related issue has surfaced in the United States – the cost of the organ to the recipient. Although the donor or his estate may not be paid, the recipient, or more likely his third party payor, is required to make a significant payment to the hospital where the transplant occurs. Costs for the organs have been increasing over the years. Currently it is estimated that between nine per cent and 31 per cent of the total cost for the transplant is the result of organ acquisition. These variables can be explained, in part, in terms of harvesting and preservng the organ itself, and the attendant costs based on specific environmental factors. The cost of kidney transplants has increased 12.9 per cent since 1983, while heart and liver transplants have escalated 64.1 per cent and 61.8 per cent respectively during the same period (Evans 1993).

Determining a fair cost for an organ is difficult. Any attempt must include three factors: expenses, charges, and amounts paid by the third party payor. Obviously with wide fluctuations in these costs questions will arise as to calculating the cost and why the donor or his estate has not benefited from the process while everyone else in the process has. These difficult questions recently emerged in an authoritative fashion by R.W. Evans, Ph.D., of the Mayo Clinic in an article in the June 23/30 issue of the *JAMA*. Dr Evans concludes that there is no proper accounting system which reflects real costs, net costs, nor has any effort been made to standardize charges from one facility to another. Without some form of control or uniform fee schedule, charges of abuse will emerge that could undermine the entire transplant process (ibid.: 3116).

(c) Allocating organs

The final major issue in organ transplants occurs over the question of allocation. What criteria exists to determine who is entitled to an organ? As with the question of consent and sale, organ allocation is an issue because of the limited availability of organs in relation to demand. In the United States this problem was recognized in the National Organ Transplant Act, one of whose goals was the equitable distribution of organs. The Act contemplated the creation of an Organ Procurement and Transplantation Network made up of organ procurement organizations (OPOs) operating on a regional basis throughout the United States. In 1986 the Secretary of Health and Human Services (HHS) granted the United Network for Organ Sharing (UNOS) a contract to implement the Network.

In carrying out its mandate, UNOS has developed a series of point systems per specific organ on the basis of which it makes organs available. In the case of kidneys, highest priority is given to patients with a six-antigen match regardless of geographic location. A six-antigen match means that there is a perfect or apparently perfect match of antigens between donor and recipient (US General Accounting Office 1993: 46). Following this determination priority is established as follows (ibid.: 46–7):

- time – beginning at the time the patient is placed in the UNOS computer;
- quality of match – decreasing points awarded for antigen mismatches;
- highly sensitized – patients who show a preliminary negative cross-match, i.e. the beneficiary is less likely to reject the organ;
- blood type – blood type O kidneys are transplanted into blood group O recipients (except when the six-antigen match takes place);
- medical urgency – this issue is not a factor for UNOS and is determined by the local physicians;
- pediatric recipients – children from 0–5 years old are granted a priority, and those between six and 10 a lesser priority.

Comparable procedures are in place for heart and liver transplants (ibid.: 47–8).

In a recent review of the implementation of the UNOS allocation system the GAO found that the system does not work as it should due to failure to comply with existing allocation policies and abuses within the system (ibid.: 44). The approval of multiple waiting lists by UNOS permits patients on such lists to increase their chances of receiving a transplant in relation to a patient on a single list (Childress 1989). Another abuse that has been noted and not wholly under the control of UNOS goes back to the creation of the waiting list or, even more basic, who should be included on it. A recent discussion raised the question of whether foetuses should be included on the waiting lists. The new UNOS policy of not placing foetuses on the waiting lists until 32 weeks gestation has been approved in a recent *JAMA* article reviewing the subject (Michaels *et al.* 1993). Since UNOS allocation is based on the existing list it receives and, more often than not, UNOS does not prepare the list nor is it privvy to the priorities used in a given hospital, dialysis unit or OPO, it appears to be necessary to standardize these practices or extend UNOS authority to question lists it receives. It has been noted that wealthy white males receive a higher percentage of organs than women or other minorities. Unequal access to waiting lists may also be linked to the patient's ability to pay. Since some organ transplants are considered experimental by insurance companies and thus not eligible for coverage, patients requiring such procedures must often cover the costs themselves. When they are unable to do so, their opportunity to receive a transplant disappers.

The issue of medical urgency is also a matter beyond the control of UNOS and raises difficult questions. Although there is perhaps a natural tendency to provide an organ to the sickest patient, or one on the waiting list the longest time, such a patient is not always the optimum choice as the one to receive the greatest benefit from the transplant. Obviously the attitude and commitment of the attending physician to a given patient in a life or death situation will often influence the allocation of an organ without regard to his location on a waiting list. OPOs and hospitals are continuously involved with the screening process, both as to desirable characteristics of donors and recipients. Considerations will invariably include such factors as the general health and age of the participants. Some transplant centres will not, for example, undertake heart transplant surgery on any patient older than sixty, although exceptions are often made for older individuals in otherwise excellent health. The recent case of providing sixty-one year old William Casey, then governor or Pennsylvania, with a heart and liver transplant at the University of Pittsburgh only hours after the diagnosis was made raised the issue of fairness in the national press (Alexander and Baker 1993). Explanations to the contrary, many felt this was but another example of better health care for the wealthy and prominent. A study undertaken by the National Center for Health Statistics published in *The New England Journal of Medicine* on July 8, 1993 seems to confirm that overall wealthier people live longer than poorer ones (Pear 1993).

(d) A global perspective

Abundant organ transplant literature is available on the national level which reflects varying levels of success. As valuable as this material may be, its national focus obscures the fact that the issues and solutions raised by organ transplantation must be considered globally. Specific national solutions may establish rational procedures in a given country, but with the ease of international travel and the increasing accessibility of organ transplant technology, inequitable results often occur. Perhaps of even greater concern than the equities involved are the risks inherent in the present system where desperately ill recipients increase their medical risks by going to foreign countries where transplant procedures may be carried out under less than optimum circumstances.

Although it is an over-simplification, and perhaps even an

offensive comparison to some, organs have certain similarities to other internationally traded commodities and their use and allocation must be regulated through a world-wide system to assure a maximum benefit to the largest number. Even in the United States, with its sophisticated and carefully thought out UNOS system, inequality exists. The growing scarcity of organs and the economic gap between the Third World and the developed world as to availability of organs increases the likelihood of abuse and exploitation. Therefore we will have to look forward to some world-wide system of organ harvesting and transplantation that will consider such factors as health standards for both donor and recipient and fairness in the allocation system. Implementing a universal system of this kind is a long range goal and it is likely we will see it achieved through regional arrangements before a truly global system becomes possible.

Efforts in this direction have begun in a limited fashion exemplified by the permissible exchange of organs that exists between Canada and the United States (Fuenzalida-Puelma 1990). The European Community recognizes this need for international standards and the Ad Hoc Committee for Bioethics, the *Comité ad-Hoc de Bioéthique* (CAHBI), under a mandate from the Council of Europe to prepare a European Convention on Bioethics, has determined that the subject of 'organ transplant and use of human substances' is one of 'urgency'. CAHBI has noted that transplantation has been subject '. . . to serious abuse which had occurred in the recent past and which had shown that national regulations in this field could be circumvented at the international level so long as there were no corresponding international rules' (Byk 1993: 15). It is interesting to note that CAHBI's focus of concern in the area of organ transplantation is with the issues of consent and the 'commercial trafficking in organs' (ibid.: 16).

For Latin America one comprehensive study exists covering the area on a country-to-country basis. Inadequacies in various national legislation are noted, but there is no hemispheric approach suggested. Rather the article calls for guidelines to be promulgated by the World Health Organization, but only on a national basis (Fuenzalida-Puelma 1990: 433).

As regional groups work toward harmonization as a first step in establishing universal guidelines, the following areas, in addition to the three issues considered earlier in this paper, will have to be considered. These are:

(i) International sharing

National barriers will have to be eliminated. The source of available organs will have to be made available on a regional or world-wide basis, looking beyond national boundaries. For such a system to gain acceptance health requirements for donors and priorities for recipients will have to be established. For a truly 'sharing' system to work reciprocity will have to be assured to overcome the already surfacing economic nationalism which prohibits the international sharing of organs (e.g. Colombia) (ibid.) and proposed legislation in the United States that would virtually prohibit foreigners from receiving organ transplants (McCartney 1993). Under the proposed legislation foreign emergency recipients would, for all practical purposes, be ineligible, while other candidates would be placed on a second tier waiting list which would not be reached until all Americans on the primary list had received an organ. There is an inherent conflict between international sharing of organs and restricting organ transplant surgery to nationals. No sovereign nation would agree to share its organs while its citizens were denied new organs in the receiving country.

(ii) International borders

Once the concept of international sharing of organs is accepted, national laws will have to recognize the logical conclusions of this practice. Immigration and customs laws will have to be modified to facilitate the movement of health care professionals crossing national borders to harvest and preserve organs. Similarly, medical teams will have to be granted rapid entry and be permitted to carry out their activities without concern for transportation of the organs themselves. They will have to be subjected to minimum inspection and delays to ensure that they will not lose their viability.

Even if an international regime were established, national self interest would require countries to maintain some control over the movement and activities of these individuals within their territories. The European Community in its far reaching concept allowing for the Free Movement of Persons, Services and Capital provides a model in that member states can restrict entry to protect 'public policy, public security and public health'.[5] These terms have been interpreted narrowly and thus suggest a direction for a solution to the problem of globalization of organ transplants.

17.2   CONCLUSION

This chapter has demonstrated the diverse issues and solutions toward organ transplants on a global level. Health care delivery is undergoing dramatic changes throughout the world and the importance of marketing health care has been recognized as a means in improving its quality. The growing world-wide acceptance of health maintenance organizations (HMOs) to replace corrupt, inefficient government-run health care systems has demonstrated how the use of marketing can create competition, resulting in better quality and

lower costs for consumers. This lesson should not be lost in the area
of organ transplants where international marketing can assist in producing standardization as well as quality for both donors and recipient. As we inevitably move towards some form of payment system for
the benefit of the donor the marketing of organs becomes increasingly
more important.

17.3 NOTES

[1] Anecdotal information related by Thunderbird students to the
author.
[2] See particularly Section 4. Manner of executing anatomical gifts,
1968.
[3] See, for example, *Ley 30/1979, de 27 de Octobre. Sobre extración y
transplante de órganos*, Article 2, Spain.
[4] Uniform Anatomical Gift Act 1968, Section 1(c).
[5] Treaty establishing the European Economic Community, 298
UNTS 11. Article 48.

17.4 REFERENCES

Akatsu, H. (1990) The heart, the gut, and brain death in Japan (brain
death standards). *The Hastings Center Report.* March/April, 20,
p. 3.

Alexander, K.L. and Baker, S. (1993) Governor Casey's timely
transplant, *Business Week*, June 28, p. 40.

Bader, J.M. (1992) France: Transnational transplants. *The Lancet.*
July 1, 1992, 340, p. 108.

Byk, C. (1993) The European convention on bioethics. *Journal of
Medical Ethics*, 19, p. 15.

Childress, J.F. (1989) Ethical criteria for procuring and distributing
organs for transplantation, *Journal of Health, Politics, Policy and
Law*, Spring 14(1), pp. 107.

Churchill, L.R., and Pinkuss, R.L.B. (1990) The use of anencephalic
organs: historical and ethics dimensions (from infants). *Milbank Q.*
68, pp. 150–151.

Dyer, Clare Editorial. (1990) *British Medical Journal*, 300, pp.
961–962.

Evans, R.W. (1993) Organ procurement expenditures and the role of
financial incentives. *Journal of the American Medical Association*,
269, pp. 3113–18.

Fuenzalida-Puelma, H.L. (1990) Organ transplantation: the Latin
American legislative response. *Bulletin of PAHO*, 24(4), pp. 433.

Haansmann, H. (1989) The economics and ethics of markets for
human organs. *Journal of Health, Politics, Policy and Law.*
Spring, 14, p. 57.

Hedges, C. (1992) Egyptian doctors limit kidney transplants. *The New York Times International*, January 23, Section A, p. 5.

Hedges, C. and Hazarika, S. (1992) India debates ethics of buying transplant kidneys. *The New York Times*, August 17, Section A, p. 20.

Khanna, P.M. (1992) Scarcity of organs for transplant sparks a move to legalize financial incentives. *Wall Street Journal*, September 8, Section B, p. 1.

Kittur, D.S., *et al.* (1991) Incentives for organ donation? *The Lancet*, December, 338, p. 1441–1443.

McCartney, S. (1993) Law may allow few transplants for foreigners. *Wall Street Jounal*, June 30, Section B, p. 1.

McCormick, B. (1992) Medicine, law urged to focus more on organ donations. *American Medical News*, September 7, 35, pp. 8–9.

Michaels, M.G., Frader, J., and Armitage, J. (1993) Ethical considerations in listing fetuses as candidates for neonatal heart transplantation (Commentary), *Journal of the American Medical Association*, January 20, 269, pp. 401.

NORMA (1988) Tecnica numero 323 para la disposición de órganos y tejídos de seres humanos con fines terapeúticos, September 22, Art. 13.

Pear, R. (1993) Wide health gap linked to income is reported in U.S. *The New York Times*, July 8, p. 1.

Reseña Legislative (1990) Protector de ley sobre transplantes de órganos y otras piezas anatómicas. September 13, 20, p. 33.

Salahudeen, A.K. *et al.* (1990) High mortality among recipients of bought living-unrelated donor kidneys. *The Lancet*, 335, pp. 725–729.

Teo, B. (1991) Organs for transplantation: the Singapore experience. *The Hastings Center Report*, November–December, 21, pp. 10–14.

Tuffs, A. (1991) Germany: Calls for unified transplantation law (organ transplantation). *The Lancet*, June 8, 337, pp. 1403.

United States General Accounting Office (1993) Organ transplants: Increased Effort Needed to Boost Supply and Ensure Equitable Distribtion of Organs. Washington, DC. April. Publication GAO/HRD-93-56, P. 63.

Yamauchi, M. (1990) Transportation in Japan. *British Medical Journal*, September 15, 301, p. 508.

Zoler, M. L. (1990) Cash reward for organ. *Medical World News*, August, 31, p. 23.

18 Ethics, pricing and the pharmaceutical industry*

Richard A. Spinello

This chapter explores the ethical obligations of pharmaceutical companies to charge fair prices for essential medicines. The moral issue at
stake here is distributive justice. Rawls' framework is especially
germane since it underlines the material benefits everyone deserves
as Kantian persons and the need for an egalitarian approach for the
distribution of society's essential commodities such as health care.
This concern for distributive justice should be a critical factor in the
equation of variables used to set prices for pharmaceuticals.

18.1 ETHICS, PRICING, AND THE PHARMACEUTICAL INDUSTRY

18.1.1 Introduction

A perennial ethical question for the pharmaceutical industry has been
the aggressive pricing policies pursued by most large drug companies. Criticism has intensified in recent years over the high cost of
new conventional ethical drugs and the steep rise in prices for many
drugs already on the market. One result of this public clamour is that
the pricing structure of this industry has once again come under
intense scrutiny by government agencies, Congress, and the media.

The claim is often advanced that these high prices and the resultant
profits are unethical and unreasonable. It is alleged that pharmaceutical companies could easily deliver less expensive products without
sacrificing research and development. It is quite difficult to assess,
however, what constitutes an unethical price or an unreasonable
profit. Where does one draw the line in these nebulous areas? I will
consider these questions as they relate to the pharmaceutical industry
with the understanding that the normative conclusions reached in this
analysis might be applicable to other industries which market essential consumer products. My primary axis of discussion, however, will

---

* Reproduced from *Journal of Business Ethics*, 1992, 11: pp. 617–626.

be the pharmaceutical industry where the issue of pricing is especially complex and controversial.

18.1.2 The problem

Beyond any doubt, instances of questionable and excessive drug prices abound. Azidothymide or AZT is one of the most prominent and widely cited examples. This effective medicine is used for treating complications from AIDS. The Burroughs-Wellcome Company has been at the centre of a spirited controversy over this drug for establishing such a high price – AZT treatment often costs as much as $6,500 a year, which is prohibitively expensive for many AIDS patients, particularly those with inadequate insurance coverage. The company has steadfastly refused to explicate how it arrived at this premium pricing level but industry observers suggest that this important drug was priced to be about the same as expensive cancer therapy (Holzman 1988).[1] In dealing with its various constituencies Burroughs has relied on two key arguments to justify this price: high research and development cost and the threat of obsolescence. Burroughs maintains that in order to recoup its oppressively high research and development costs for this medication it has no choice but to charge a price in the range of $6,500 per year. The company also defends its pricing policy by noting that proceeds from the sale of AZT will be used to finance other drugs for AIDS which are more effective than present treatments. Of course, if there is a superior second generation of the AZT medication, the drug will soon become obsolete. Moreover, once the patient expires, generic competition could erode the drug's current market share. Hence the need to generate substantial profits very quickly.

The lack of more reasonable prices for drugs such as AZT can be attributed to the functioning of the American free market and the oligopolistic nature of the drug industry. Prices in other countries are often much lower since they are the result of a negotiation process between drug companies and their host governments. For example, the average price of Roche Products' Valium is $9.70 in the United States but $3.60 elsewhere. Most European governments determine pricing levels by bargaining with pharmaceutical companies. The end result is that these prices cover companies' manufacturing and distribution costs and to much lesser extent research and development costs. But since these companies pass on such costs to their customers in the United States, they can still make a reasonable profit at these lower price levels (Kolam 1991).

Thus, there are many inequities in the distribution of pharmaceutical products. Within the United States certain medicines are simply inaccessible for many people due to the industry's pricing scheme. High drug prices have the most negative impact on the elderly and the chronically ill. The elderly, for example, are usually forced to pay for their prescription drugs, since Medicare does not cover their drug costs unless they are in a hospital. In addition the American consumer ends up subsidizing lower drug prices for other countries in which medicine is often available at much lower prices. As a result many of the industry's most vocal critics contend that the only solution to this injustice is government regulation, perhaps in the form of the European model.

But the major pharmaceutical companies strongly resist any form of regulation as a serious threat to the stability of their powerful industry. This industry has consistently put forward the same arguments for high prices as those advanced by Burroughs. These focus on the premise that premium prices are justified due to the excessive costs of developing new drugs. This rationale is based on the most fundamental principle of free market economies: high risk deserves high rewards. Beyond question, there are great risks involved in researching and developing new drugs especially since such a small percentage make it through the long and costly process. Moreover, even if a drug is a commercial success, there is always the impending threat of product liability problems and expensive law suits. Finally, the industry maintains that earnings received from breakthrough drugs such as AZT are necessary to stimulate future research and compensate for many commercially unsuccessful drugs.

Regardless of the merit of these arguments, the superior financial performance of the pharmaceutical industry in recent years is beyond dispute. In studies which compare the performance of various US industries the pharmaceutical industry has consistently been the leader in several important categories such as return on sales, return on assets, and return on common equity. For example, the drug industry currently boasts a return on sales of 20 per cent. Also, its return on common equity of 31.9 per cent compares quite favourably with the average return of 11.7 per cent and is the highest of all the industry groups tracked by *Business Week* (1991). These figures reveal that at least according to some criteria drug companies and their stockholders are receiving substantial returns for the risks they take.

18.1.3 Ethical questions

The behaviour of Burroughs and the tendency of most drug companies to charge premium prices for breakthrough medicines raises serious moral issues which defy easy answers and simple solutions. As Clarence Walton observed, 'no other area of managerial activity is more difficult to depict accurately, assess fairly, and prescribe realistically in terms of morality than the domain of price' (Walton 1969: 209). This difficulty is compounded in the pharmaceutical industry due to the complications involved in ascertaining the true cost of production.

To be sure, every business is certainly enticed to a reasonable profit as a reward to its investors and a guarantee of long-term stability. But the difficulty is judging a reasonable profit level. When, if ever, do profits become 'unreasonable'? It is even more problematic to determine if that profit is 'unethical', specially if it is the result of premium prices.

Obviously, the issue of ethical or fair pricing assumes much greater significance when the product or service in question is not a luxury item but an essential one such as medicine. Few are concerned about the ethics of pricing a BMW or a waterfront condo in Florida. But the matter is quite different when dealing with vital commodities like food, medicine, clothing, housing, and education. Each of these goods has a major impact on our basic well-being and our ability to achieve any genuine self-fulfilment. Given the importance of these products in the lives of all human beings, one must consider how equitably they are priced since pricing will determine their general availability. Along these lines several key questions must be raised. Should free market, competitive forces determine the price of 'essential' goods such as pharmaceuticals? Is it morally wrong to charge exceptionally high prices even if the market is willing to pay that price? Is it ethical to profit excessively at the expense of human suffering? Finally, how can we even begin to define what constitutes reasonable profits?

Also, the issue of pricing must be considered in the context of the pharmaceutical industry's lofty performance guidelines for return on assets, return on common equity, and so forth. On what authority are such targets chosen over other goals such as the widest possible distribution of some breakthrough pharmaceutical that can save lives or improve the quality of life? Pharmaceutical companies would undoubtedly contend that this authority emanates from the expectations of shareholders and other key stakeholders such as members of the financial community. In addition, these targets are a result of careful strategic planning that focuses on long-term goals.

But a key question persistently intrudes here. Should other viewpoints be considered? Should the concerns and needs of the sick be taken into account, especially in light of the fact that they have such an enormous stake in these issues? In other words, as with many business decisions, there appear to be stark tradeoffs between superior financial performance versus humane empathy and fairness. Should corporations consider the 'human cost' of their objectives for excellent performance? And what role if any, should fairness or justice play in pricing decisions? It is only by probing these difficult and complex questions that we can make progress in establishing reasonable norms for the pricing of pharmaceuticals.

18.1.4 Free market vs regulation

Of course, many would question the validity of basing drug prices on anything other than pure economic factors. Milton Friedman and his followers have argued persuasively that the only social responsibility of business is to increase profits. According to this 'free market. philosophy, the responsible course of action is to charge whatever price the market will accept. Thus, if the market will support an annual price of $8,000 a year for a drug such as AZT, that should be the end of the matter. Managers who fail to price in a fashion that will maximize profits are shirking their primary fiduciary duty to stockholders. Therefore if executives in the pharmaceutical industry refrained from raising prices for a social objective, they would be unfairly imposing a tax on shareholders. When managers go beyond economic and financial data in their decisions they become political agents with a social agenda. This is regarded by Friedman as a pernicious state of affairs which will undermine the very foundations of our free society, 'since managers lack the wisdom and ability to resolve complex social problems such as the equitable distribution of pharmaceutical products' (Friedman 1979: 90).

One problem with this narrow view of corporate responsibility is that it fails to appreciate that corporate decisions often have a powerful social impact. The strategic decisions of large organizations 'inevitably involve social as well as economic consequences, inextricably intertwined' (Mintzberg 1989: 173). Thus such firms are social agents whether they like it or not. It is virtually impossible to maintain neutrality on these issues and aspire to some sort of apolitical status. The point for the pharmaceutical industry and the matter of pricing seems clear enough. The refusal to take 'non-economic' criteria into account when setting prices is itself a moral and social decision which inevitably affects society. Companies have a choice – either they can explicitly consider the social consequences of their decisions or they can be blind to those consequences, deliberately ignoring them until the damage is perceived and an angry public raises its voice in protest.

If companies do choose, however, to be attentive and responsible social agents they must begin to cultivate a broader view of their environment and their obligations. To begin with, they must treat those affected by their decisions as people with an important stake in those decisions. This stakeholder model, which has become quite popular with many executives, allows corporations to link strategic decisions such as pricing with social and ethical concerns. By recognizing the legitimacy of its stakeholders such as consumers and employees, managers will better appreciate all the negative as well as positive consequences of their decisions. Moreover, an honest stakeholder analysis will compel them to explore the financial and human implications of those decisions. This will enable corporations to become more responsible social agents, since explicit attention will be given to the social dimension of their various strategic decisions.

Quite simply, then, the assumption that corporations are pure economic agents represents a facile approach to this issue. Hence the free market philosophy of Friedman offers little guidance for reaching a solution to the dilemma of fair pricing in the pharmaceutical industry. At the other extreme we find the solution offered by a framework of government regulations, but this too seems to be fraught with difficulties. Obviously, there would be severe practical and procedural problems if an attempt were made to directly regulate drug prices through a government agency such as the FDA. To begin with, there is the problem of exclusive trademark and patent rights. If the investment supporting these patented drugs is treated as a cost, firms would be able to raise prices by increasing these costs, and this would open the door for all sorts of abuses. Similar problems would arise with the regulated pricing of generic drugs. If, for example, generic drug prices were based on an industry wide basis, the price would most likely be determined by calculating the industry's average cost. Inefficient firms with above average costs, however, would fail to make a profit at this price and would be forced to withdraw from the market. As these firms exit, competition is diminished, and in the long run fewer players will probably mean higher costs and higher prices. Indeed, the problem with any regulatory solution is that it provides no real incentives for efficiency and cost controls. Hence relying exclusively on cumbersome government regulations to solve the problem of high drug prices seems completely unfeasible.

Given the inadequacy of regulating prices or letting them be determined by the marketplace, the only viable means of realizing fair pricing appears to be some form of self-regulation. According to Goodpaster and Matthews, the most effective solution to this and most other moral dilemmas is one 'that permits or encourages corporations to exercise independent, non-economic judgment over matters that face them in their short- and long-term plans and operations' (1989: 161). In other words, the burden of morality and social responsibility does not lie in the marketplace or in the hand of government regulation but falls directly on the corporation and its managers.

Companies aspiring to such moral and social responsibility will adopt *the moral point of view*, which commits one to view positively the interest of others, including various stakeholder groups. Moreover, the moral point of view assigns primacy to virtues such as justice, integrity, and respect. Thus, the virtuous corporation is analogous to the virtuous person – each exhibits these moral qualities and acts according to the principle that the single-minded pursuit of one's own selfish interests is a violation of moral standards and an offence to the community. The moral point of view also assumes that both the corporation and the individual thrive in an environment of co-operative interaction which can only be realized when one turns from a narrow self-interest to a wiser interest in others.

18.1.5 Pricing policies and justice

This brings us back to the specific moral question of fair pricing policies for the pharmaceutical industry. The moral issue at stake here concerns justice and, more precisely, distributive justice. As we have remarked, justice has always been considered a primary virtue and thus it is an indispensable component of the moral point of view. According to Aristotle, justice 'is not a part of virtue but the whole of excellence or virtue' (1962: 114). Thus, there can be no virtue without justice. This implies that if corporations are serious about assimilating the moral point of view and exercising their capacity for responsible behaviour, they must strive to be just in their dealings with both their internal and external constituencies. Moreover, traditional discussions on justice in the works of philosophers such as Aristotle, Hume, Mill, and Rawls have emphasized distributive justice, which is concerned with the fair distribution of society's benefits and burdens. This seems especially relevant to the matter of ethical pricing policies.

Corporations which control the distribution of essential products such as ethical drugs like AZT can be just or unjust in the way they distribute these products. When premium prices are charged for such goods an artificial scarcity is created, and thus gives rise to the question of how equitably this scarce resource is being allocated. The consequence of a premium pricing strategy whose objective is to garner high profits would appear to be an inequitable distribution pattern. As we have seen, due to the expensiveness of AZT and similar drugs they are often not available to the poor and lower middle class unless their insurance plans cover this expense or they can somehow secure government assistance which has not been readily forthcoming. However, if this distribution pattern can be considered unjust, what determines a just distribution policy?

There are, of course, many conceptions of distributive justice which would enable us to answer this question. Some stress individual merit (each according to his ability) while others are more egalitarian and stress an equal distribution of society's goods and services. Given a wide array of different theories on justice, where does the manager turn for some guidance and straightforward insights?

One of the most popular and plausible conceptions of justice is advanced by John Rawls in his well known work, *A Theory of Justice*. A thorough treatment of this complex and prolix work is beyond the scope of this essay. However, a concise summary of Rawls' work should reveal its applicability to the problem of fair pricing. Rawls' conception of justice, which is predicated on the Kantian idea of personhood, properly emphasizes the equal worth and universal dignity of all persons. All rational persons have a dual capacity: they possess the ability to develop a rational plan to pursue their own conception of the good life along with the ability to respect this same capacity of self-determination in others. This Kantian ideal underlies the choice of the two principles of justice in the original position. Furthermore, this choice is based on the assumption that the 'protection of Kantain self-determination for all persons depends on certain formal guarantees – the equal rights and liberties of democratic citizenship – plus guaranteed access to certain material resources' (Doppelt 1989: 278). In short, the essence of justice as fairness means that persons are entitled to an extensive system of liberties *and* basic material goods.

Unlike pure egalitarian theories, however, Rawls stipulates that inequities are consistent with his conception of justice so long as they are compatible with universal respect for Kantian personhood. This implies that such inequities should not be tolerated if they interfere with the basic rights, liberties, and material benefits all deserve as Kantian persons capable of rational self-determination. In other words, Rawls espouses the detachment of the distribution of primary social goods from one's merit and ability because these goods are absolutely essential for our self-determination and self-fulfilment as rational persons. These primary goods include 'rights and liberties, opportunities and power, income and wealth' (Rawls 1971: 92). Whatever one's plan or conception of the good life, these goods are the necessary means to realize that plan, and hence everyone would prefer more rather than less primary goods. Their unequal distribution in a just society should only be allowed if such a distribution would benefit directly the least advantaged of that society (the difference principle).

The key element in Rawls' theory for our purposes is the notion that there are material benefits everyone deserves as Kantian persons. The exercise of one's capacity for free self-determination requires a certain level of material well-being and not just the guarantee of abstract and formal rights such as freedom of expression and equal opportunity. Thus the primary social goods involve some material goods, like income and wealth. To a certain extent health care (including medicine) should be considered as one of the primary social goods since it is obviously necessary for the pursuit of one's rational life plan. Therefore, the distribution of health care should not be contingent upon ability and merit. Also it would be untenable to justify an inequitable distribution of this good by means of Rawls' difference principle. It is difficult to imagine a scenario in which the unequal distribution of health care in our society would be more beneficial to the least advantaged than a more equal distribution which would assure all consumers access to hospital care, medical treatment, medicines, and so forth. If we assume that the least advantaged (a group which Rawls never clearly defines) are the indigent who are also suffering from certain ailments, there is no advantage to any inequity in the distribution of health care. Unlike other primary goods such as income and wealth it cannot be distributed in such a way that a greater share for certain groups will benefit the least advantaged. In short this is a zero sum game – if a person is deprived of medical treatment or pharmaceutical products due to premium pricing policies that person has lost a critical opportunity to save his life, cure a disease, reduce suffering, and so on.

Thus, at least according to this Rawlsian view of justice with its Kantian underpinnings, there seems to be little room for the unequal distribution of a vital commodity such as health care in a just society. It follows, then, that the just pharmaceutical corporation must be far more diligent and consider very carefully the implications of pricing policies for an equitable distribution of its products. The alternative is government intervention in this process, and as we have seen, this has the potential to yield gross inefficiencies and ultimately be self-defeating. If these corporations charge premium prices and garner excessive profits from their pharmaceutical products, the end result will be the deprivation of these goods for certain classes of people. Such a pricing pattern systematically worsens the situation of the least advantaged in society, violates the respect due them as Kantian persons, and seriously impairs their capacity for free self-determination.

It should be emphasized, however, that this concern for justice does not imply that pharmaceutical companies should become charities by distributing these drugs free of charge or at prices so low they must sustain meagre profits or even losses. To be sure, their survival, long-term stability, and ongoing research are also vital to society and can only be guaranteed through substantial profits. Thus, the demand for justice which I have articulated must be balanced with the need to realize key economic objectives which guarantee the long-term stability of this industry. As Kenneth Goodpaster notes, 'the responsible organization aims at congruence between its moral and nonmoral aspirations' (1984: 309). In other words, it does not see goals of justice and economic viability as mutually exclusive, but will attempt to manage the joint achievement of both objectives.

We are arguing, then, that pharmaceutical companies should seek to balance their legitimate concern for profit and return on investment with an equal consideration of the crucial importance of distributive justice. There must be an explicit recognition that for the afflicted certain pharmaceutical products are critical for one's well-being; hence they are as important as any primary social good and are deserved by every member of society. As a result these products should be distributed on the widest possible basis, but in a way that permits companies to realize a realistic and reasonable level of profitability.

It is, of course, quite difficult to define a 'reasonable level of profitability'. In many respects the definition of 'reasonable' is the crux of the matter here. Unfortunately, as outsiders to the operations of drug companies we are ill prepared to judge whether development costs for certain drugs are inflated or truly necessary. As a result, these corporations must be trusted to arrive at their own definition of a reasonable profit, given the level of legitimate costs involved in researching and developing the drug in question. But we can look to some case histories for meaningful examples that would serve as a guide to a more general definition. One of the most famous controversies over drug prices concerned the Hoffman-LaRoche corporation and the United Kingdom in which the government's Monopoly Commission alleged that Hoffman-LaRoche was charging excessive prices for Valium and Librium in order to subsidize its research and preserve its monopoly position. In the course of the prolonged deliberations between the British government and the company reasonable profits were defined as 'profits no higher than is necessary to obtain the "desired" performance of industry from the point of view of the economy as a whole' (Matthews *et al.* 1985).[4] In general, then, under normal circumstances reasonable profits for a particular product should be consistent with the average return for the industry. Exceptions might be made to this rule of average returns if the rises and costs of development are inordinately and unavoidably high.

Thus, based on this Rawlsian ideal of justice I propose the following thesis regarding ethical pricing for pharmaceutical companies: for those drugs which are truly essential the just corporation will aim to charge prices that will assure the widest possible distribution of these products consistent with a reasonable level of profitability. In other words, these companies will seek to minimize the deprivation of material benefits which are needed by all persons for their self-realization by imposing restraints on their egocentric interests in premium prices and excessive profits. Since only some pharmaceutical products can be considered as truly 'essential', it remains to be seen which of those products should be subject to the imperative of justice. Moreover, we must present some sort of methodology for reaching this determination.

18.1.6 A tentative model for evaluating the role of justice in pricing decisions

As we have observed, for companies producing essential goods such as pharmaceuticals, the moral imperative of justice is one element in a complex equation that includes the need for profit, a respectable return on investment, and many other factors. Obviously some drugs are far more important than others and hence the issue of their just distribution must be weighted much more heavily than it would be for other medicines. The weight given to the concern for distributive justice in this equation will be directly proportionate to some measurement of how critical this drug is to patients. For pharmaceutical products this can be determined by considering the nature of the illness, the efficacy of the particular product, the availability of low-price substitutes, and so forth. The framework in Exhibit 18.1 includes the key questions for determining the importance of a pharmaceutical product for society. The way in which these questions are answered will determine the role which should be played by the demands of distributive justice in the pricing equation.

EXHIBIT 18.1

Questions for considering the relative importance of a pharmaceutical product

- What is the nature of the malady? Is it life threatening or physically and/or mentally disruptive? Does it deprive the afflicted of their physical or mental well-being (e.g., schizophrenia) or is it more of an inconvenience (e.g. baldness)?
- Do patients have other options? Is there any other therapeutic recourse? Is this medication a last resort for the illness in question?
- Are there other drugs available for similar effectiveness and if so how affordable are these drugs?
- At the planned pricing level will people likely be deprived of treatment?
- How 'experimental' is this drug considered to be? What is the likelihood that government agencies and insurance companies will offer assistance so that it can be afforded by everyone who needs it?
- Who is the likely end-user of the drug? The chronically ill? The elderly? Special consideration should be given to these groups who bear the biggest burden of high drug prices.

This brief framework serves as a general guide for pharmaceutical managers, which will enable them to discern how essential the product is, the likelihood of its affordability, and the probability of government assistance for the indigent. The more critical the product and the less likely it will be affordable to certain segments of society, the more prominent should be the consideration given to distributive justice in pricing policy deliberations. Justice cannot be the exclusive concern in these deliberations, but must be given its proportionate weight depending upon the way in which the questions in this framework are addressed. Thus, as pricing decisions duly consider factors such as production and promotion costs, etc. they should also take into account the element of distributive justice. Clearly, however, drugs that are less important for society because they deal with less serious ailments should not be subject to the same demands of justice as those for diseases which are truly life threatening or debilitating. Hence drug companies should have much more flexibility in pricing medicines for these less critical ailments.

18.1.7 A collaborative approach

There is no doubt that pharmaceutical executives would raise many objections to the proposal on fair pricing which I am advocating. Thus, despite their concern about these issues the likelihood of any significant change is probably quite slim. Unfortunately, the premium pricing policy of these companies is perpetuated by industry-wide peer pressure for above average returns and the quasi-monopoly status of certain brand name drugs. Also, if a company unilaterally sought to distribute some of its products more equitably, it would probably find itself in an anomalous position in the drug industry with no followers. In the face of this threat it is difficult to envision one of the pharmaceutical companies taking the initiative and complying with Rawls' distribution criterion, even if there is some concession that in principle this is the right thing to do. Hence the current impasse which many argue can only be overcome by decisive intervention and regulation, perhaps in the form of 'European style' controls of drug prices.

Although these arguments have some merit, they should not interfere with a proper ethical resolution to the intractable dilemma of high returns versus accessibility and a reasonable pricing scheme. Of course the apprehension that following the right course of action will jeopardize one's competitive position is quite common and is frequently brought forth to justify all sorts of corporate inaction and indifference on ethical matters. It is a variation of the traditional but jaded claim that ethics cannot be reconciled with economics.

As I have been at pains to insist here, however, ethical values can be integrated with economic success. But in order to accomplish this it is necessary to transcend traditional thinking which posits a sharp dichotomy between morality and the economic criteria of success. As Laura Nash and others have argued, this 'bottom line' mentality erects many barriers between managers and the marketplace. An exclusive and relentless focus on profit, continued growth, and increased market share tends to shut off much of the legitimate feedback from customers. For example, the demise of the automobile industry in the 1970s and 1980s can partially be attributed to Detroit's narrow focus on these criteria and its unwillingness to listen to its customers.

On the other hand, when the focus shifts from pure economic measures of success to the relationship between corporations and their customers, the prevailing concerns become value creation and mutual benefit (Nash 1990: 91–4). In other words, mutual benefit is the essence of a sound business relationship, and this is achieved by delivering created value. When we consider the problem of pricing from this perspective it becomes clear that an essential part of value creation in the pharmaceutical industry is the provision of medicines to those who need them at a fair and reasonable price. Moreover, listening to the concerns of its customers and various other constituencies on this matter is also an important aspect of value creation and a key to long-term success. Thus, by adopting a framework that centres on mutually beneficial relationships and value creation, pharmaceutical executives will come to realize that pricing is not a remote ethical problem that can be dismissed by invoking the principle of free market economics. Rather, it is a grave business problem which impedes these corporations from delivering value and impairs the critical relationship with their customers.

But even if the companies in question accept this line of reasoning, how should they proceed? A unilateral action might be well intentioned but it will probably not settle this acute industry-wide problem. Instead, the optimal solution must follow a more complicated path that entails a collaboration effort in which the major firms work with government agencies such as the FDA to develop a tenable pricing framework that addresses the social costs of high prices. Both the industry and government share responsibility for dealing with this problem given the community's need for reasonably priced medicine. Also, as I have argued previously, if government regulators act independently they will not have access to the information and specialized competence necessary to make the most effective decisions. A collaborative approach, on the other hand, will ensure that the community will be well-served and it will also preserve the level playing field for all the firms involved. It will also allow these companies to retain control of the pricing process and avoid the intricate problems associated with explicit price controls of any sort.

18.2 FINAL OBSERVATIONS

Let me now summarize and conclude. My aim has been to attempt an ethical analysis of pricing in the pharmaceutical industry in order to make some normative recommendations. This analysis might also be applied to other industries which are in the business of supplying essential commodities. I have argued that if these pharmaceutical companies seek to be responsible and adopt the moral point of view, they must practise the primary virtue of justice. No person can be considered virtuous and moral if he or she is unjust, and the same can be said for the corporation. Although there are several conflicting notions of distributive justice, the conception delineated by John Rawls seems both compelling and practically feasible. It is grounded in a Kantian view of the person which stresses the need for both abstract rights and concrete material resources for one's rational self-determination.

I have argued with some insistence that an essential commodity such as health care is analogous to the primary social goals considered by Rawls since it is so crucial for one's self-determination. Hence its distribution should not be contingent on one's abilities and standing in the community. Thus pharmaceutical firms must be prepared to impose some restraints on profits for the sake of distributive justice. The alternative is a more comprehensive involvement of government in this process which will lead to cumbersome pricing regulations that are likely to be ineffectual in the long run.

Given the importance of profitability and the long-term stability of these companies, however, justice cannot be their exclusive concern. Rather, the imperative of justice must be balanced with the need to realize key financial objectives. I am simply arguing that these objectives should not be pursued to the exclusion of justice, which must be responsibly and fairly factored into the pricing equation. Moreover, the weight given to justice in that equation will depend on how critical the product is and this depends on the nature of the illness, the availability of substitutes, and so forth.

I have also pointed out that since this is such an entrenched and complex industry-wide problem, it cannot be resolved by any unilateral policy changes by a particular firm. Rather, the major producers must act in concert in collaboration with the government in order to ensure a fair pricing scheme.

This analysis does not by any means eliminate the frustrations regarding ethical pricing which were cited earlier by Walton. I can offer no definitive, quantitative formulae or comprehensive criteria to assure that pricing in this industry will always be fair and just. As with most moral decisions, much will depend on the individual judgement and moral sensitivity of the managers making those decisions. But if managers are sincere in their quest for the primary virtue of justice, the general guidelines proposed here will offer some modest assistance for this foray into the uncharted territory of fair pricing. It seems beyond doubt that responsible and fair pricing in the pharmaceutical industry is a serious moral imperative, since for so many consumers it is a matter of well-being or infirmity and perhaps even life or death.

I consider once again the wisdom of Aristotle on this topic of justice. In the Nicomachean he writes that 'we call those things "just" which produce and preserve happiness for the social and political community' (1962: 113). If corporations respond to the demands of justice for the sake of the common good, it will help promote the elusive goal of a just community and a greater harmony between the corporation and its many concerned stakeholders.

18.3 NOTES

[1] For more recent data on drug prices see *The New York Times* (1990) Maker of Schizophrenia Drug Bows to Pressure to Cut Costs, (December 6), pp. Al and D3.

18.4 REFERENCES

Aristotle (1962) *Nicomachean Ethics*, trans. by M. Oswald, Indianapolis: Library of Liberal Arts, Bobbs Merrill Company, Inc.

Business Week (1991) Corporate scorecard, March 18, pp. 52ff.

Doppelt, G. (1989) Beyond liberalism and communitarianism towards a critical theory of social justice. *Philosophy and Social Criticism* 14 (3/4).

Friedman, M. (1979) The social responsibility of business is to increase profit, in T. Beauchamp and N. Bowie (eds), *Ethical Theory and Business*, Englewood Cliffs, NJ: Prentice Hall.

Goodpaster, K. (1984) The concept of corporate responsibility, in T. Regan (ed.), *Just Business New Introductory Essay in Business Ethics*, New York: Random House.

Goodpaster, K. and Matthews, J. (1989) Can a corporation have a conscience, in K. Andrews (ed.), *Ethics in Practice*, Boston, MA: Harvard Business School Press.

Holzman, D. (1988) New wonder drugs at what price? *Insight*, March 21, pp. 54–5.

Kolam, G. (1991) Why drugs cost more in US. *The New York Times*, May 24, p. D3.

Matthews, J., Goodpaster, K. and Nash, L. (eds) (1985) F. Hoffman-LaRoche and Company AG, Harvard Business School Case Study, in *Policies and Persons*, New York, NY: McGraw Hill Book Company.

Mintzberg, H. (1989) The case for corporate social responsibility, in A. Iannone (ed.), *Contemporary Moral Controversies, in Business*, New York: Oxford University Press.

Nash, L. (1990) *Good Intentions Aside: A Manager's Guide to Resolving Ethical Problems*, Cambridge, MA: Harvard Business School Press.

Rawls, J. (1971) *A Theory of Justice*, Cambridge, MA: Harvard University Press.

Walton, C. (1969) *Ethos and the Executive*, Englewood Cliffs, NJ: Prentice Hall, Inc.

19 Do corporate codes of ethics reflect national character? Evidence from Europe and the United States*

*Catherine C. Langlois and
Bodo B. Schlegelmilch*

This chapter analyses the usage and contents of corporate codes of ethics. The results from a sample of 600 large European companies are contrasted with findings reported for similar US firms. The comparison reveals that significantly fewer European than US firms adopted codes of ethics. In Europe, the large majority of codes have been introduced only very recently and there are indications that codes made their way into Europe via subsidiaries of US firms. However, there are striking differences in content between US and European codes of ethics pointing to the existence of a distinctly European approach to codifying ethics.

19.1 DO CORPORATE CODES OF ETHICS REFLECT NATIONAL CHARACTER?
EVIDENCE FROM EUROPE AND THE UNITED STATES

In the United States, business ethics is the focus of a growing literature. Several book-length and a number of shorter bibliographies attempt to keep pace with the well over 50 books and countless articles that are written on the subject (Donald 1986; Bond 1984; Center for Business Ethics 1982). Some scholarly journals, including the *Journal of Business Ethics* and the *Business & Professional Ethics Journal* are exclusively devoted to ethics. A wide range of subjects is covered, including such diverse areas as economic justice (e.g. Rawls 1971; Nozick 1974), social responsibility of business (e.g. Friedman 1970; Stone 1975), conceptual models of ethical and unethical behaviour in

* Reprinted from the *Journal of International Business Studies*, 1990, 21(4), pp. 519–39, with permission.

organizations (e.g. Bommer *et al.* 1987) ethical decision-making in marketing (e.g. Ferrell and Gresham 1985), corporate morality and conscience (e.g. Goodpaster and Matthews 1982), whistle-blowing (e.g. James 1984) and the integration of ethics into the teaching of business schools (e.g. Dunfee and Robertson 1988) to name but a few. Codes of ethics, the subject of this paper, has been discussed by the Center for Business Ethics (1986), Bowie (1979) and the Foundation of the Southwestern Graduate School of Banking (1980).

In contrast, business ethics has received much less attention in the European literature, where articles on the topics are few and far between. There are, however, some notable exceptions, such as contributions by Melrose-Woodman and Kverndal (1976), Haron and Humble (1974), Steinmann and Oppenrieder (1985), Enderle (1985, 1988), Luijk (1986; 1988), Steinmann and Lohr (1989), Harvey (1989), Webley (1988), and Schlegelmilch and Houston (1989). To date, however, a large-scale empirical cross-country comparison of the use and content of corporate codes of ethics is still outstanding.

The differences between the United States (US) and Europe are also reflected in teaching and research. Most US business schools offer courses in business ethics and several specialized academic research centres have been established (De George 1987). The Harvard Business School, receiving a $30 million pledge from John Shad, ex-chairman of the Securities and Exchange Commission, provides one of the most spectacular recent examples of the US interest in the subject. According to *Fortune* magazine (1987) the money will be used to incorporate business ethics in the curriculum in an attempt to convince Harvard Business School students that 'ethics pays'. In Europe, few business schools offer courses on business ethics. In the UK, for example, the first course of this kind was offered to MBA students at the London Business School in 1987. And, although there are individuals at a variety of European universities who have an interest in business ethics, there are currently only three research centres specifically focusing on business ethics: the Institute of Business Ethics and the King's College Business Ethics Research Centre, both in London, as well as the Forschungsstelle für Wirtschaftsethik at the University of St Gallen.

The distinctions between the United States and Europe, however, may not be confined to the academic sector. While the widespread adoption of written codes of ethics by US companies is well documented (Cressey and Moore 1980; Foundation of SWGSB 1980; Ethics Resource Center 1980), European companies do appear to be far less enthused about the use of such codes. Indeed, it is known that various UK companies regard corporate codes of ethics as the latest import from Wall Street and therefore of little relevance to British industry. Others voice concern that codes of ethics are too broad to be of any use (Schlegelmilch and Houston 1989). Overall, there is little empirical evidence that permits a direct comparison between the usage of corporate codes of ethics in the United States and Europe. The European data that does exist is confined to a description of practices of British companies (Schlegelmilch and Houston 1989) and thus may not adequately reflect company practices in continental Europe.

This study attempts to redress this information gap by extending the Schlegelmilch and Houston (1989) survey of the top 200 British firms to the largest 200 French and 200 West German companies. In addition to contrasting the proportion of European and US companies with corporate codes of ethics, a detailed content analysis provides insight into the distinctive approach to certain questions of business ethics in Europe. A number of propositions are developed that explain differences in the adoption of codes and shed light on some of the national characteristics found in corporate codes of ethics.

The chapter is organized in two parts. The first part describes the methodology and compares the number of European firms with codes of ethics to the corresponding US figures. It also provides information on code titles, timing of adoption, and US affiliations of the responding European firms. The second part of the article includes the detailed content analysis which identifies those parts of the codes of ethics that transcend culture and those that are culture-specific.

19.2   A SURVEY OF 600 EUROPEAN FIRMS

19.2.1 Data

During 1988, 600 mail questionnaires were dispatched to the chairmen of the 200 largest French, British, and West German companies, respectively. For France and West Germany, the addresses were obtained from the ELC *International Business Directory* (1988), and for Britain from the *Times* Top 1000 (1986/7) listing. A sample of large companies was chosen, since an earlier study (Melrose-Woodman and Kverndal 1976) found a positive relationship between company size and the existence of corporate codes of ethics. The three countries were selected because they are the three largest of the twelve countries in the European Community, representing nearly two-thirds of the volume Gross National Product. The fact that the authors are native speakers of French and German, and would thus be able to read and interpret the corporate codes of ethics easily, also guided the choice of countries.

The survey resulted in 207 (35 per cent) responses. Of these, 189 (91 per cent) could be used for the analysis, while 18 (9 per cent) were letters providing reasons for non-participation (see Table 19.1). The usable response rate of 32 per cent is in line with a 28 per cent response to a survey on business ethics of the Fortune 500 companies conducted in the US (Center for Business Ethics 1986).

Table 19.1 Breakdown of survey response

	Usable Responses	%
Britain	80	42
France	50	27
West Germany	59	31
Total	189	100

The most common reasons for not participating in the survey were references to 'company policy', 'lack of time', and 'insufficient resources'. None of the known characteristics of the non-responding companies (such as size or line of business) suggested any systematic differences between them and the responding firms.

19.2.2 Variables

It could not be assumed that the CEOs of the sampled British, French, and German companies would share a common understanding of the characteristics of corporate codes of ethics. A definition was therefore provided to create a common frame of reference. Based on Melrose-Woodman and Kverndal (1976), the following text was used for the British sample and accordingly translated into French and German: 'A statement setting down corporate principles, ethics, rules of conduct, codes of practice or company philosophy concerning responsibility to employees, shareholders, consumers, the environment or any other aspects of society external to the company.'

Following this definition, the CEOs were asked whether their companies had corporate codes of ethics. If yes, we requested a copy. Correctly anticipating that not all companies would be willing to disclose their codes to outsiders, the questionnaire also obtained information on the name of the document, the date of introduction, and the issues addressed in the codes.

Companies without codes were asked to indicate the likelihood of introducing one prior to 1990. The question was cast into a five-point scale ranging from 'very likely' to 'very unlikely.' To check whether the CEOs completed the questionnaires themselves, the respondents were asked to state their position in the company. The questionnaire finished with an open-ended comment section.

19.2.3 Survey results

(a) Codes of ethics: frequency of adoption in Europe

Seventy-eight (41 per cent) of the 189 companies responding to the questionnaire had introduced codes of ethics, while 111 (59 per cent) had not. The proportion of 41 per cent of companies with codes should be interpreted as an upper bound on the characteristics of the total population of interest. Indeed, since only about one-third of the companies replied to the mail survey, it is possible that non-coverage bias resulted in an overestimation of the true proportion of companies with codes. The lowest proportion of codes was found in the French sample, where only 30 per cent of the responding companies had written codes of ethics. In Germany and Britain the corresponding figures are 51 per cent and 41 per cent, respectively. The European results are in sharp contrast to US findings, where 75 per cent of the respondents to a survey of *Fortune* 500 companies (Center for Business Ethics 1986) stated that they had written codes of ethics. The difference between the US and Europe is statistically significant ($p < 0.01$).

It should be noted that we have treated US affiliates and affiliates of other European multinationals as part of the local sample; i.e., Procter and Gamble, France, for example, is treated as a French company. Were the sample purged of all foreign affiliates, so that only local companies remain in the local samples, the number of companies with codes of ethics would drop to 51. Thus 35 per cent of companies with codes have non-local parents. Removing such affiliates from the analysis and focusing only on companies that have their headquarters in the respective European countries changes our results as follows: 33 per cent of the companies in the reduced sample of 154 adopted codes of ethics, while 67 per cent did not. The lowest proportion of codes is still to be found in France, where 18 per cent of companies adopt them. The proportion of companies adopting codes in Germany and Britain drops to 47 per cent and 31 per cent, respectively, when affiliates of foreign parents are excluded.

Thus, foreign affiliates in the three countries reviewed are essentially to be found among the firms adopting codes. Moreover, most of these affiliates have US parents. In section 19.2.4 below, we provide a detailed analysis of the influence of US affiliations on the introduction of codes of ethics in Europe. Table 19.2 includes a comparison of the complete sample with a reduced one which excludes all foreign affiliates. In what follows, all results refer to the complete sample. Reference to the reduced sample is always made explicit.

The names of the companies with and without codes are included in the Appendix, with the exception of three companies who asked not to have their identities released. For the latter, only the country identification is provided. Also provided in Appendix 19.A at the end of the chapter is the national origin of all parent companies.

(b) Code titles, introduction dates and distribution of codes

In line with US findings, European companies with formal codes of ethics use a plethora of titles for these documents. However, with few

Table 19.2 Adoption of codes of ethics

	UK		France		W. Germany		Total	
	Number of Firms	%	Number of Firms	%	Number of Firms	%	Number of Firms	%
Complete Sample								
With Codes	33	41	15	30	30	51	78	41
Without Codes	47	59	35	70	29	49	111	59
Total	80	100	50	100	59	100	189	100
Reduced Sample (Excluding Foreign Affiliates)								
With Codes	20	31	7	18	24	47	51	33
Without Codes	45	69	31	82	27	53	103	67
Total	65	100	38	100	51	100	154	100

exceptions (for example, Esso (UK), Albright and Wilson (UK)), the word 'ethics' usually does not appear. Instead it is 'conduct', 'principle', or 'objectives' that are referred to. Typical are BASF's (WG) 'Unternehmensleitlinien', British Gas' 'code of conduct', or Lafarge Coppee's (F) 'Principes d'action'. Sometimes the documents are personalized. It is the 'Whitbread Way', 'Wir von Spar', or Francis Bouygues' 'Ce que je crois' that become ethical codes for the company.

With the remarkable exceptions of Zeiss, who introduced a corporate code of ethics as early as 1896, and Mobil France, whose code is dated 1945, the large majority of codes were introduced after 1984. Indeed, the median introduction date for our European sample is 1986. As can be seen in Table 19.3, the proportion of European companies with codes has risen from 14 per cent in 1984 to 41 per cent in 1988. Assuming that the companies who stated their 'likely' or 'very likely' intent to introduce codes prior to 1990 will indeed write up such documents, over 56 per cent of our sample of European firms will have adopted written codes by 1990. Excluding foreign affiliates does not change the timing of adoptions. The median introduction date remains 1986 with a large majority of introductions occurring after 1984.

While there is no sign that the surge of code introductions in Europe is about to subside, the difference in the proportion of codes adopted in Europe and the United States is likely to remain wide for years to come (Schlegelmilch 1989). Indeed, it would take another eight years, at present introduction rates, for 75 per cent of our sample to adopt codes of ethics. Thus, the spread of formal codes of ethics in Europe is unlikely to reach current US levels before 1996.

One of the key purposes of corporate codes of ethics lies in the fact that the company publicly commits itself to a set of core values

Table 19.3 The timing of code adoption in Europe

Date	Complete Sample		Excluding Foreign Affiliates	
	Number of Firms	% of Responding Sample	Number of Firms	% of Responding Sample
1984	27	14	11	7
1986	44	23	25	16
1988	78	41	51	33
1990	99	56	70	45

against which its actions can be measured. Although primarily directed towards employees, the majority of companies, therefore, also circulate their codes to external interest groups such as customers and suppliers. However, as many as 26 per cent (11 UK, 3 German, 6 French) of companies with codes restrict the circulation to management, boards of directors, or specific groups of employees only (e.g. Mobil Holidays (UK), Gesellschaft für Zahlungssysteme (WG), and Casino (F)).

19.2.4 US affiliations of responding firms

It is interesting to note that 19 (24 per cent) of the 78 European companies that have adopted corporate codes of ethics have US parents. In contrast, only 2 (1.8 per cent) of the companies without codes are subsidiaries of US parents. Based on this significant difference ($p < .01$), it is tempting to suggest that the writing of codes is an essentially American practice which has made its way to Europe via the subsidiaries of US firms. Table 19.4, constructed from information found in Dun and Bradstreet's (1988) *Who Owns Whom*, also shows that European firms adopting codes are found to have tighter affiliations with the United States than those who have not, when *having* a US subsidiary is considered together with *being* a US subsidiary. Thus, we finally determined that 22 per cent of European companies without codes have no US connection while only six per cent of those with codes are in this situation, a difference significant at $p < .01$.

There are, however, differences between the three European countries surveyed. In West Germany the proportion of firms with US parents among those with codes is only 18 per cent compared to 33 per cent in France. All European firms adopting written codes are more likely to have US connections, but the overall proportion of firms without US ties is significantly higher in France than it is in the other two countries. In France 26 per cent (13/50) of the companies in our sample do not have US connections. By contrast, only 14 per cent (8/59) of the West German sample and 10 per cent (8/80) of the

Table 19.4 Proportion of European companies with US parents or US subsidiaries

| | Companies Without Codes | | | | | | | | Companies With Code | | | | | | | |
| | Total Europe | | UK | | France | | WG | | Total Europe | | UK | | France | | WG | |
	No.	%	No.	%	No.	%	No.	%	No.	%	No.	%	No.	%	No.	%
All Companies	111	100	47	100	35	100	29	100	78	100	33	100	15	100	30	100
With US Parent	2	2	0	0	1	3	1	3	19	24	9	27	5	33	5	18
With US Subsidiaries	85	76	40	85	23	66	22	76	54	70	23	70	8	53	23	76
No US Connection	24	22	7	15	11	31	6	21	5	6	1	3	2	13	2	7

British are in this situation. Thus, the countries with the highest rate of code adoption, West Germany and Great Britain, are also those whose largest companies have the strongest US connections.

19.3   WHAT THE CODES CODIFY: DO CODES HAVE A NATIONAL IDENTITY?

19.3.1 An overview

Looking at the codes that were received, the great variety in appearance is striking. There are short creeds set out on both sides of a small plastic-coated card (e.g. Ford (WG)), lengthy typed documents (e.g. Brinkmann, (WG), Bouygues (F)), over-20-page-long pocket guides (e.g. Hoechst (WG)) and glossy booklets with company logos embossed on the cover sheet (e.g. Boots (UK), Carnaud (F)). Despite this diversity, three basic formats can be distinguished. First, there are regulatory documents giving staff specific advice on behaviour and conduct. These codes often include sanctions (termination of employment and/or reimbursement of damages) if there is a breach of the code. Among the companies with this kind of code are Mobil Holdings (UK), Albright and Wilson (UK), Petrofina (UK), British Gas (UK), Mobil Française (F) and Casino (F). Second, there are short and more widely phrased creeds including statements of aims, objectives, philosophy, or values. These codes are, for example, employed by Sainsbury's (UK), Henkel (WG), Ford (WG), Zahnradfabrik Friedrichshafen (WG), British Telecom (UK), DRG (UK), ICL (UK), Carnaud (F), Aeroports de Paris (F), and VAG (F). Often, these codes are not self-standing but appear in other policy documents or annual reports. Specific guidance on employee behaviour or sanctions is not stated in these kinds of documents. Third, there are elaborate corporate codes of ethics covering social responsibility to a set of stakeholders and a wide range of other topics. Companies using such codes include Boots (UK), Shell (UK), Reckitt and Coleman (UK), Ciba Geigy (UK), Esso (UK), BASF (WG), Wella (WG), Hoechst (WG), Lafarge Coppee (F), and Bouygues (F).

To analyse the content of the codes in more detail, we attempted a classification into seven subject categories: Employee Conduct, Community and Environment, Relationship to Customers, Relationship to Shareholders, Suppliers and Contractors, Political Interests, and Innovation in Technology. Comparative information on the content of US corporate codes of ethics was found in the Foundation of the Southwestern Graduate School of Banking's 1980 'Study of Corporate Ethical Policy Statements'. This study analyses policy statements of 174 US corporations, of which 134 are industrial corporations. Both small and large companies are surveyed. For comparability, we only compiled statistics for those industrial corporations whose sales exceeded $1 billion, thus picking out those companies that would appear on a list of the top 200 industrial corporations in the United States. As it turns out, most of the firms with codes were large: 118 of the total 134 industrial corporations with written codes of ethics had sales in excess of $1 billion in 1978. The study classifies codes content using categories that are comparable to ours. Five of the subject headings correspond exactly (Employee Conduct, Community and Environment, Customers, Suppliers and Contractors, and Political Interests). Only one category did not appear in the US survey: Relationship to Shareholders. Shareholders are mentioned in US codes but are not the object of a separate classification. For the last topic, Innovation and Technology, we matched our classification to the US category (Technical Research) which corresponded most closely to our heading.

The comparison of US data to the overall figures for our three European countries reveals striking differences between code contents in these two parts of the western world (see Table 19.5). All European codes address the question of employee conduct. Only 55 per cent of US companies do. By contrast, over 80 per cent of US codes refer to the customer, while only 67 per cent of European countries do. This is in keeping with the findings of Channon (1973) and Jamieson (1980) who refer to the 'American stress upon marketing' (Jamieson 1980: 107). Striking differences exist in relation to suppliers and contractors, as well as in political interests. Almost all US firms refer to relations with the US government in their codes, and 86 per cent of them mention relations to suppliers. By contrast, less than 20 per cent of European codes broach either of these topics. Thus, corporate codes of ethics of European firms are significantly different in content from those written by US firms. And this conclusion holds despite the fact that firms with US parents are included in our sample of European firms.

Codes within the three European countries also exhibit some differences in emphasis. Relations to customers is one of these, with France's high level of concern exceeding the US figure. In this and with regard to shareholders, the United Kingdom is an outlier with relatively little emphasis placed on the relations to shareholders or customers. A surprising result is the emphasis in West German codes on innovation and technology. Sixty per cent of codes mention it compared to only 20 per cent and six per cent in France and the UK, respectively.

19.3.2 Culture-free and culture-bound contents

Many ethical issues transcend national barriers. Fairness and honesty in a company's relations to the public are concepts found in corporate codes of ethics on both sides of the Atlantic. There are, however, two areas whose treatments are country-specific. Political issues are, not

Table 19.5 Subjects addressed in corporate codes of ethics

Subject	UK n = 33		France n =15		WG n = 30		Total European Countries		United States* n=118		Chi-square Significance
	No.	%	No.	%	No.	%	No.	%	No.	%	Europe vs. US
Employee Conduct	33	100	15	100	30	100	78	100	47	55	p < .01
Community and Environment	21	64	11	73	19	63	51	65	50	42	NS**
Customers	18	39	14	93	20	67	52	67	96	81	p < .05
Shareholders	13	39	11	73	18	60	42	54	NA	NA	NA***
Suppliers and Contractors	7	21	2	13	6	20	15	19	101	86	p < .01
Political Interests	4	12	3	20	5	17	12	15	113	96	p < .01
Innovation and Technology	2	6	3	20	18	60	26	33	18	15	p < .01

*US comparison is based on a survey of the Foundation of the Southwestern Graduate School of Banking (1980).

**NS = not significant.

***NA = no comparable data available.

surprisingly, one of these issues. More interestingly, employee relations are the second subject matter to reveal transnational differences.

(a) Ethical principles that transcend cultures

The outlook on many of the topics addressed in corporate codes of ethics is common to Europe and to the United States. Thus, companies in Europe and in the US ban the acceptance of gifts or bribes, promote the use of accurate records, and warn against conflicts of interest.

Despite noticeable differences in the attention given to *customer relations* in Europe and in the United States, the issues brought up are very similar. Customers, regarded as partners, should be provided with quality service and products at a fair price. Carnaud (F) states its 'obsession with the customer as a partner'. Hoechst (WG) stresses the 'spirit of mutual interest between customer and seller'. 3M (US) vows to produce 'quality goods and services that are useful and needed by the public'. 'Quality and reliability of products are essential parts of the John Deere (US) tradition'. Sainsbury (UK) aims to 'provide unrivaled value to our customers in the quality of goods we sell', while Flachglas (WG) wants to 'cement its name as a quality symbol for glass in the mind of customers'.

Shareholder interests are usually mentioned in relation to company profitability. Dow Chemical (US) uses 'profit . . . as the means to an end. . . . To ensure the prosperity of our employees and stockholders'. For BICC (UK) it is the obligation of the company to provide shareholders with 'a return on their investment which rewards their own financial risk'. Some companies are more specific, however. BASF (WG), for example, promises to maintain a capital-debt ratio that 'enables financial security and allows to take advantage of future growth opportunities'. Carnaud (F) explicitly vows to keep debt under control and to promote shareholder confidence.

Suppliers and contractors feature less frequently in European codes than they do in US codes. But the themes are the same: companies typically state their intention to be good partners. For Procter and Gamble (US), suppliers 'must be treated as the company expects to be treated . . . with fairness, without discrimination and as equals'. FAG (WG) aims at a 'lasting co-operation with suppliers'. Carnaud (F) refers to success resulting from 'real partnerships with our customers, our shareholders, our suppliers. . . .'

Community and environment includes topics such as protection and safety of the environment, donation to charities, dialogue with special interest groups, cultural activities, and pledges recognizing and accepting social responsibility. The following examples are typical. Hoechst (WG) states: 'All our products must be environmentally acceptable. . . . Never are economic considerations allowed to override safety.' Boots (UK) describes the Boots Charitable Trust established to 'exercise an independent judgment in supporting a large number of charities in a wide range of activities.' Exxon (US) 'has built a broad program of support to music, theatre, dance, film and visual art activities' while Lafarge (F) states its responsibility towards 'certain particularly underprivileged groups: the physically or mentally handicapped, minorities.'

Statements relating to *innovation and the use of technology* are also to be found in a code of ethics. These can be very specific. For example, Bouygues (F), whose code is summarized in a twelve-commandment sheet, states as its eleventh commandment the group's commitment to the use of advanced computerized information systems. More frequently, however, the statements are of a more general nature and establish the company's emphasis on Research and Development activities. 'The research effort of some 6,500 scientists and technicians around the world is the spark which generates an ongoing supply of new products and technology from Kodak' (Eastman Kodak (US)). Somewhat surprisingly, the subject is given much prominence in a large proportion of West German codes of ethics. Flachglas lists five objectives in its code, among which are the commitment to 'intensive research and development efforts that should support our technological position and foster innovations' and the aim to 'continue the development and implementation of new technologies' for which Flachglas is 'willing to take calculated risks'. Hoechst seeks to 'achieve peak performance . . . in research and development' while BASF includes a whole page of research guidelines in its code of ethics. The latter promises, among other things, to support 'research projects that are aimed at cost reductions.' Henkel, finally, also supports innovation and states: 'The Company develops the creativity of all its employees in order to improve its competitiveness. Research and development, including process development, must supply, in time, innovative products for the new needs of customers.'

But transnational differences relating to all the above subject areas are merely a matter of emphasis. There are no substantive differences in content.

(b) The culture-specific issues

Political interests, because of the differences in the sociopolitical environment across nations, will quite naturally receive different treatment from country to country. More intriguing are the differences in attitude towards the ethics of employee relations.

Political Interests. The relationship to federal and local governments figures prominently in US codes of ethics. Indeed, almost all of them mention the topic, some of them at some length. Aside from statements of a general nature pledging, for example, obedience 'both (to) the letter and the spirit of the law' (US Gypsum Co.), many organizations specify their policy toward compliance with securities laws and antitrust laws. The objective is typically to inform employees of the content of these laws and regulations and the sanctions resulting from a breach thereof. Thus, Kerr/McGee prepared a lengthy document which 'has been prepared in order to bring to your attention the principal rules of Anti-trust law which affect business operations'. Of course, with respect to such documents, the United States differs from Europe. The difference, however, just reflects a difference in the legal environment of business and not a distinctive *attitude* towards political issues.

US statements with regard to political interests do, however, reveal a distinctly American outlook towards the relation to government. While companies state their commitment to law-abiding behaviour, company declarations reveal an underlying mistrust of government intervention in the private sector. Thus, Dow Chemical states: 'We pay our taxes *gladly*, yes, but we do not pay them *blindly*. . . . We have the right to question the wisdom of regulatory zeal that has the effect of destroying the various freedoms it alleges to protect.' For Allied Chemical Corp., 'It is vital that the corporation speaks with one voice on matters involving relations with the Federal Government and Federal Government agencies.' Is Allied Chemical Corp. suggesting that the government would take advantage of conflicting signals? No statements with comparable overtones are to be found in Europe. Indeed, European codes do not mention government in any precise manner. They are content, when they include political issues at all, to make statements of a general nature. Bertelsmann (WG), for example, explicitly 'supports a free, democratic and socially responsible society,' as does Lafarge (F), while Wella (WG) 'welcomes political, social and cultural activities of employees.'

Employee Relations are mentioned in the corporate codes of all the European firms in our survey. Indeed, some of the codes are entirely devoted to employee conduct (for example, Audi (WG), Gesellschaft für Zahlungssysteme (WG), Mobil Holdings (UK), Petrofina (UK)). In the United States, by contrast, less than half of the corporate codes address the issue of employee relations. More importantly, however, the content and tone of these statements vary from country to country, both within Europe and between Europe and the United States.

Two kinds of statements are to be found in the employee conduct section of European codes: those that are designed as a guide to employee *behaviour* and those that seek to inform the employee as to the proper *attitude* to adopt within the company. Guides to behaviour include statements with regard to insider dealings, confidentiality or acceptance of gifts, and are found throughout Europe and in the United States. It is with regard to employee attitude that interesting differences between European countries emerge. German companies frequently address the employees' *right* of co-determination (Mitbestimmung) and the resulting shared *responsibility*. Stadtwerke Bremen comments that 'co-determination and shared responsibility support the social progress in our company.' Hoechst points out that 'cooperation is marked by a sense of joint responsibility'. Going further, German codes formulate the specific expectations the company has of its employees. Haniel expects, among other things, that 'employees set themselves demanding objectives, develop initiatives for their own training and development, the courage to openly state their personal opinions and to offer constructive solutions in case of conflicts.' Messer Griesheim similarly lists expectations in its code, including issues like the provision of information to other employees, reliability and loyalty, the acceptance of constructive criticism, and the requirement to further develop his own expertise as well as those of other employees. Bertelsmann expects that 'within a framework of critical loyalty, employees should identify with the tasks, objectives and behaviour of the firm.'

French and British firms, by contrast, tend to emphasize the importance of their employees to the organization as a whole. Rather than promoting a sense of responsibility, these firms promote a sense of *belonging*. Whitbread (UK) states that 'people are the company's most important assets'. Carnaud (F) seeks to promote professional growth of every individual. For Lafarge (F) and Bouygues (F), what distinguishes a company is its employees. The company's goals are collective ones. At Bouygues we are 'passionately entrepreneurial. This attitude is essential in the face of the growing dullness of company atmospheres'.

In the United States it is neither responsibility nor belonging that characterizes relations. US codes of ethics, when they mention employees, stress *fairness* and *equity*. Aside from the traditional equal opportunity and affirmative action statements, some US firms emphasize fairness in wages and treatment. Deere and Co., for example, states that 'good personal relationships cannot exist without equitable salary administration'. Union Carbide Corp. states as its established policy to 'provide compensation levels and individual salaries fully comparable to those provided by our competition for equivalent performance, required knowledge, skill, and accountability.' Commitment to employee education is also mentioned in American codes, and is treated as an issue of equal opportunity.

The overall tendency in Europe is thus to stress *employee responsiveness to company activities*, while in the United States it is the quality of *company policy towards employees* that is at the forefront of topics included in corporate codes of ethics. This difference is traceable to a more extensive legal protection of labour in Europe, as well as to the long-standing ethnic diversity of the US labour force. It is more difficult to trace intra-European differences in emphasis to fundamental national characteristics. Indeed, closeness is not exactly the characteristic that comes to mind when comparing French and British cultures. But, over the past fifteen years, both these countries have experienced economic decline, while West Germany, thanks to a strong export sector, avoided until recently the dramatic unemployment levels of its European trading partners. Responsibility is, however, somewhat of a German national characteristic. Indeed, West Germany has kept its inflation rate in check throughout the 1970s through disciplined avoidance of excessive wage increases. Again, economic success is achieved through the individual worker's sense of responsibility. Economic stagnation and a tendency to disassociate work from the individual's sense of identity in France and the UK can account for the 'dullness of company atmospheres' alluded to by Bouygues. In such circumstances British and French firms seem to want to instill a sense of hope and optimism among their employees. Promoting belonging here seems to be less a question of national character than a response to the tensions in the social fabric that are the result of poor economic conditions.

19.4 CONCLUSION

With few exceptions, European companies started only very recently to adopt corporate codes of ethics. However, while a large proportion of companies currently still without codes intend to introduce one prior to 1990, the 'ethics gap' (Schlegelmilch 1989) between Europe and the United States is likely to remain for years to come. At present introduction rates, it will take eight years for the proportion of European companies with codes (41 per cent) to reach the level of 75 per cent that was already reported for the US in the mid-1980s.

An analysis of the subjects addressed in corporate codes of ethics revealed significant differences between Europe and the United States, in particular with regard to employee conduct, supplier and contractor relations, as well as political interests. But differences in the contents of codes also exist between the three European countries. France, for example, stands out through the high proportion of codes that address customer relations (93 per cent), while German codes address innovation and technology more frequently (60 per cent) than the codes in any other country.

Despite the above differences, most ethical issues were found to transcend national barriers. The exceptions are the treatment of political issues and employee relations, both revealing transnational distinctions. While the differences in the treatment of political issues primarily reflect the different legal environments for European and US companies, the differences in the attitudes towards the ethics of employee relations were found to be less obvious. German companies tend to stress the shared responsibility of management and employees, codes in France and Britain aim to promote a sense of belonging, while US firms stress fairness and equity. Overall, therefore, European companies emphasize *employee responsiveness* to company activities, while firms in the United States stress *company responsiveness* to employee requirements of fairness and equity. From a managerial point of view, our findings indicate a growing pressure to introduce corporate codes of ethics to avoid manoeuvering the company into an 'ethical outsider' position. For multinational companies that are considering the introduction or extension of codes into different countries, the findings also raise the question of standardization of codes of ethics versus adaptation to different national environments. This concern is captured in a comment received from Bertelsmann (WG): 'A difficult task is the international transfer of such codes of ethic in growing multinational companies, if one does not want them to be entirely uncommitting/superficial.' Thus, considering the extension of codes into different countries, management needs to consider whether national identity is part of the company culture. If so, it will be more difficult to achieve a satisfactory standardization of codes across national boundaries.

With regard to future research, our study points towards three avenues. First, it would be desirable to enlarge the analysis by including data on the use and contents of corporate codes of ethics in the third large trading power of the non-communist world, Japan. This would provide additional evidence on the extent to which codes are employed outside the United States and Europe and would inform us as to whether such codes reflect specific Japanese characteristics. Second, an analysis should be made to determine the role of corporate codes in the overall attempt of companies to promote ethical standards. Are codes treated as alternatives to other measures (such as ethics committees or seminars) to foster higher ethical standards, or are they complements or even catalysts of such endeavours? Finally, and perhaps most importantly, work needs to be done to determine the effectiveness of different types of corporate codes of ethics in different organizational and national settings. Evidence along these lines could be directly transformed into normative managerial guidelines and would consequently be of great relevance.

19.5 REFERENCES

Bommer, M., Gratto, C., Gravender, J. and Tuttle, M. (1987) A behavioural model of ethical and unethical decision making. *Journal of Business Ethics*, 6, pp. 265–80.

Bond, K. (1984) *Bibliography of Business Ethics and Business Moral Values*, Omaha: College of Business Administration, Greighton University.

Bowie, N.E. (1979) Business codes of ethics: window dressing or legitimate alternative to government regulation?, in T.L. Beauchamp and N.E. Bowie (eds), *Ethical Theory and Business*, Englewood Cliffs, NJ: Prentice-Hall.

Center for Business Ethics (1982) *A Selected Bibliography of Business ethics Articles*, Waltham, MA: Bentley College.

Center for Business Ethics (1986) Are corporations institutionalizing ethics? *Journal of Business Ethics*, 5(2), pp. 85–91.

Channon, D. (1973) *The Strategy and Structure of British Enterprise*, Graduate School of Business Administration, Harvard University.

Cressey, D.R. and Moore, C.A. (1980) *Corporation Codes of Ethical Conduct*. Report to the Peat, Marwick and Mitchell Foundation, February.

De George, R.T. (1987) The status of business ethics: past and future. *Journal of Business Ethics*, 6(3), pp. 201–11.

Donald, G.J. (1986) *A Bibliography of Business Ethics, 1981–1985*, New York: Mellen Press.

Dun and Bradstreet International (1988) *Who Owns Whom: North America, Continental Europe and the United Kingdom*, London.

Dunfee, T.W. and Robertson, D.C. (1988) Integrating ethics into the business school curriculum. *Journal of Business Ethics*, 7, pp. 61–73.

ELC International (1988) *Europe's 15000 largest companies*, London.

Enderle, G. (ed.) (1985) *Ethik und Wirtschaftswissenschaft*, Berlin: Vahlen.

Enderle, G. (1988) *Wirtschaftsethik im Werden*, Stuttgart.

Ethics Resource Center (1980) *Implementation and Enforcement. Codes of Ethics in Corporations and Associations*, Washington, DC.

Ferrell, O.C. and Gresham, L.G. (1985) A contingency framework for understanding ethical decision making in marketing. *Journal of Marketing*, 49 (summer), pp. 87–96.

Fortune (1987) Shad the lawgiver, May 11, p. 54.

Foundation of the Southwestern Graduate School of Banking (1980) *A Study of Corporate Ethical Policy Statements*, Dallas, TX.

Friedman, M. (1970) The social responsibility of business is to increase its profits. *New York Times Magazine*, September 13.

Goodpaster, K.E. and Matthews, J.B. (1982) Can a corporation have a conscience? *Harvard Business Review*, January–February, pp. 132–41.

Harron, F. and Humble, J. (1974) *Social Responsibility and British Companies*, Management Centre Europe, Brussels.

Harvey, B. (1989) Business ethics in Great Britain, in H. Steinmann and A. Lohr (eds), *Unternehmensethik*, Stuttgart: Poeschel Verlag.

James, G.G. (1984) In defence of whistle blowing, in W.M. Hoffmann and J.M. Morre (eds), *Business Ethics. Readings and Cases in Corporate Morality*, New York: McGraw-Hill.

Jamieson, I. (1980) *Capital and Culture: A Comparative Analysis of British and American Manufacturing Organizations*, England: Gower Publishing Co.

Melrose-Woodman, J. and Kverndal, I. (1976) *Towards Social Responsibility: Company Codes of Ethics and Practice*, British Institute of Management Survey Reports, No. 28.

Nozick, R. (1974) *Anarchy, State and Utopia*, New York: Basic Books.

Rawls, J. (1971) *A Theory of Justice*, Cambridge, MA: Belknap Press.

Schlegelmilch, B.B. (1989) The ethics gap between Britain and the United States: a comparison of the state of business ethics in both countries. *European Management Journal*, 7(1), pp. 57–64.

Schlegelmilch, B.B. and Houston, J.E. (1989) Corporate codes of ethics in large UK companies: an empirical investigation of use, content and attitudes. *European Journal of Marketing*, 23(6), pp. 7–24.

Steinmann, H. and Lohr, A. (eds) (1989) *Unternehmensethik*, Stuttgart: Poeschel Verlag.

Steinmann, H. and Oppenrieder, B. (1985) Brauchen wir eine Unternehmensethik. *Die Betriebswirtschaft*, 2(45), pp. 170–83.

Stone, C.D. (1975) *Where the Law Ends*, New York: Harper & Row.

The Times (1986/1987) *Times Top 1000 Companies*, London: Times Books Ltd.

van Lujik, H.J.L. (1986) *When the Market Fails: The Morality of Economic Man*, Forschungsstelle für Wirtschaftsethik an der Hochschule St. Gallen für Wirtschafts-und Sozialwissenschaften, Beiträge und Berichte, No. 13.

van Lujik, H.J.L. (1988) Ethics in international business: a plea for business ethics networks. Paper presented at the round table on 'Ethics, Economics and International Business' at the XVIII World Congress of Philosophy, Brighton, United Kingdom.

Webley, S. (1988) *Company Philosophies and Codes of Business Ethics*, London: Institute of Business Ethics.

APPENDIX 19.A COMPANIES WITH AND WITHOUT CODES OF ETHICS

Nationality of Parent Company	Company Name	Date of Introduction
With Codes of Ethics (n = 78)		
Britain (n = 33)		
USA	Albright & Wilson	N.A.*
USA	Bass	1978
UK	BICC	1986
UK	Boots	1978
Canada	British Alcan Group	1978
UK	British Gas	1986
UK	British Rail	1983
UK	British Steel	N.A.*
UK	British Telecom	1987
USA	Cargill UK	1978
Swiss	Ciba-Geigy	1973
UK	Coats Viyella	1984
USA	Conoco[1]	1984
USA	Conoco UK[1]	1980
UK	DRG	1970
USA	Esso	1977
USA	Gulf Oil	1986
UK	ICL	1987
UK	Lex Service	1981
USA	Mobil	1978
Belgium	Petrofina	1985
UK	Reckitt & Coleman	1987
UK	Rowntree	1986/87
UK	Sainsbury	1985
Netherlands	Shell	1984
UK	South of Scotland Electricity Board	1979
UK	Taylor Woodrow	N.A.*
UK	Trafalgar House	1987
UK	United Biscuits	1988
UK	W.H. Smith & Son	1988
UK	Whitbread	1985
UK	Wimpey	N.A.*
USA	Woolworth	1984
France (n = 15)		
France	Aeroports de Paris	1985
France	Bouygues	1985
France	Carnaud	1983
France	Casino	1989
France	Coopagri Bretagne	1987
USA	Esso	1979
USA	IBM	1977
UK	ICI	1987
France	Lafarge Coppee	1977

Nationality of Parent Company	Company Name	Date of Introduction
France (continued)		
USA	Mobil Oil	1945
USA	Procter & Gamble	1987
France	Publicis	1986
Netherlands	Shell	1984
Germany	V.A.G.	1988
USA	Yoplait	1989
West Germany ($n = 30$)		
Germany	ANT Nachrichtentechnik	1988
Germany	AUDI	1984
Germany	BASF	1988
Germany	Beiersdorf	1978
Germany	Bertelsmann	1960
Germany	BMW	1985
Germany	Brinkmann	1987
USA	Dow	N.A.*
Netherlands	Enka	1987
Germany	FAG	1988
Germany	Flachglas	1986
USA	Ford	N.A.*
Germany	Gesellschaft für Zahlungssysteme	1985
Germany	Haniel	1987
Germany	Henkel	1987
USA	Hewlett Packard	1970
Germany	Hoechst	1988
Germany	Messer Grieshelm	1987
Netherlands	Philips	1986
Germany	Porsche	1981
USA	Procter & Gamble	N.A.*
Germany	Raab Karcher	1988
Germany	SPAR	1987
Germany	Stadtwerke Bremen	1986
Germany	VIAG	1988
Germany	Wella	1980
Germany	Zahnradfabrik Friedrichshafen	1986
Germany	Zeiss	1896
Germany	Firm X	1979
Germany	Firm Y	1980

[1] Conoco, although a subsidiary of Conoco UK, does not have its figures consolidated into its parent company's. Two separate questionnaires were sent and received.

*N.A. = Not Available

Nationality of Parent Company	_Company Name_

Without Codes of Ethics (_n_ = 111)

Britain (_n_ = 47)

UK	AMEC
UK	Blue Circle Industries
UK	Booker
UK	Bowater Industries
UK	British Caledonian
UK	British Coal
UK	British Shipbuilders
UK	Britoil
UK	BSC
UK	Bunge & Co.
UK	C & J Clark
UK	Cable & Wireless
UK	Costain Group
UK	Dalgety
UK	Davy Corporation
UK	Debenhams
UK	Glaxo
UK	Guiness
UK	Harrisons & Crossfield
UK	John Laing
UK	Johnson Mathey
UK	Ladbroke Group
UK	LRT
UK	Metal Box
UK	Nat. Freight Cons.
Swiss	Nestlé Holdings
UK	Nurdin & Peacock
UK	Ocean Tran. & Trading
UK	Palmer & Harvey
UK	Pearson
USA	Pergamon Press
UK	Pilkington Brothers
UK	Plessey
UK	Post Office
UK	Powell Duffryn
UK	Reed International
UK	Rio Tinto Zinc
UK	RMC Groups
UK	Rothmans International
UK	Rover Group
UK	S&W Berisford
UK	Scottish & Newcastle
UK	Sedgewick Group
UK	Simon Engineering
UK	Tesco
UK	Vickers
UK	Wellcome

Nationality of Parent Company	Company Name
France (n = 35)	
USA	Beghin-Say
France	Calberson
France	Club Mediterranee
France	Cogema
France	Compagnie General d'electricite
France	Conforama
France	CSEE Alsthrom
France	Dollfus Mieg
France	Enterprise Miniere et Chimique
France	Exor
Italy	Fiat
France	Grands Moulins de Paris
France	Guyomarch
France	L'Oreal
France	Labruyere Eberle
France	Lesieur
France	Lyonnaise des Eaux
France	Merlin Geurin
France	Michelin
France	Pechiney
France	Pernod-Ricard
France	Peugeot
France	Poliet
France	RATP
France	Roquette
France	Safic-Alcan
France	Sanders
France	Sanofi
France	Seita
France	Socopa
France	Spie Batignoles
Netherlands	Telecommunications Radioelectriques et Telephoniques
France	Union Laitiere Normande
France	Usinor Sacilor
France	Louis Vultton
West Germany (n = 29)	
Germany	AEG Kabel
Germany	Badenwerk
Germany	Deutsche Babcock
Germany	Dyckerhoff & Wildmann
Germany	Freudenberg & Co.
Germany	Haindl Papier
Germany	Heinrich Bauer Verlag
Germany	ISAR Amperwerke
Germany	Kssbohrer
Germany	Klöckner-Humboldt Deutz
Germany	Leybold
Germany	Melitta Gruppe
Germany	Neckarwerke

Nationality of Parent Company	Company Name
Germany	Otto Versand
Germany	Otto Wolff
USA	Philip Morris
UK	Rothmans
Germany	Ruhrgas
Germany	Ruhrkohle
Germany	Saarberg
Germany	Saarstahl Völklingen
Germany	Thyssen Stahl
Germany	Vereinigte Aluminium Werke
Germany	VEBA
Germany	VEBA Kraftwerke Ruhr
Germany	VEBA Oel
Germany	Vereinigte Elektrizitätswerrke Westfalen
Germany	Wegmann & Co.
Germany	Firm Z

20 *The need for moral champions in global marketing**

Lyn S. Amine

20.1 INTRODUCTION

Over the years, a number of scandals have come to light concerning production or marketing of potentially harmful products in less-developed countries (LDCs). Well-known examples from the 1970s and 1980s include high-dosage contraceptives sold over the counter; baby food promoted using high-pressure sales methods; continued sales of pesticides and high-tar cigarettes after forced withdrawal from western markets; inadequate health and safety precautions during production of asbestos; and the explosion of a chemical plant due to lax safety standards. One might reasonably wonder why well-educated, professionally-trained managers, who work for companies with international reputations, might take decisions that risk provoking censure by the world business community. Is it just the result of the 'profit motive' run rampant? Is it merely the 'ugly face of capitalism?' Or are there other reasons that might explain the apparent willingness of western managers to run the risk of jeopardizing the health and well-being of consumers in the developing world?

This chapter discusses these questions by framing the issues in the context of ethics and social responsibility in global marketing. Of particular interest here is the 'opportunity' for managers to become involved in dubious ethical decisions and practices when marketing potentially harmful products to consumers in LDCs.

Marketing in LDCs is often characterized by an imbalance of power because the foreign corporation controls access to information about the product, its use, likely effects of misuse, and the availability of safer alternatives. Consumers in LDCs may be vulnerable to exploitation in so far as they lack, to a greater or lesser degree, the basic skills and knowledge that typify consumers in western markets.

* Reproduced from the *European Journal of Marketing*, Special Issue on Marketing and Social Responsibility, 1996, 30 (5) by permission MCB University Press Ltd.

Also, the consumer environment in many LDCs lacks agencies and organizations to monitor company action, such as the EPA, FDA, Better Business Bureaus, and Consumers Union in the US.

Examples of the sort of problems and dangers that unsuspecting consumers might be exposed to were seen in Malaysia during the early 1980s (Newman 1980). Problems included adulterated products, use of known carcinogens, deceptive and misleading labelling, inadequate product information and warnings, phony discounts, short weights, unlicensed practitioners, and so on. Producers and marketers of such products included both domestic and foreign companies. When the latter were queried about their practices in Malaysia, some managers responded that they were doing their best in a largely under-regulated market place; others said that it was not their responsibility to act for the government which they claimed was conniving in the exploitation of its citizens. While this dismal picture has doubtless improved considerably in Malaysia and other LDCs since the early 1980s, the problem remains of how to define the role of global company managers in markets where consumers are vulnerable. In this chapter, it is argued that the role of managers in such a situation should be one of 'moral champions', committed to pursuing the best in ethical and moral decision making and behaviour.

The term 'vulnerable' is used here to describe consumers who, for various reasons, find themselves at a disadvantage relative to a global corporation in not being fully able to express, claim, or defend their rights as consumers. Since the Consumer Bill of Rights was issued in the US in the early 1960s, at least four basic rights have been identified: the right to safety; the right to be informed; the right to choose; and the right to be heard (i.e., to have one's interests fully and fairly considered in the formulation and administration of government policy).

Peter and Olson (1993) comment that even though this list appears to offer considerable protection, it assumes that consumers are willing to be involved in purchase and consumption of a product, and that they are able to defend their rights. This assumption may not hold true in the case of children, the elderly, or the uneducated poor because they may not have the necessary cognitive ability with which to defend their rights to information, choice, and due consideration. With regard to safety rights, the burden of responsibility would appear to fall on the sellers of goods and the local government or its agencies. Consumer vulnerability is particularly prevalent in LDCs, being associated with the poverty and illiteracy typical of lower levels of economic development. Even when willing to stand up for themselves, consumers in LDCs may not have the necessary education and confidence with which to express and claim their rights.

Company attitudes towards consumer vulnerability are of special interest at the present time as we see cigarette producers targeting the newly emerging democracies (NEDs) of Eastern Europe and the fast-growing populations of newly industrializing countries (NICs) in Asia. Faced with increasingly negative attitudes towards smoking in the USA and increasing regulation, cigarette producers are seeking new growth markets abroad. Here we can draw parallels with the cases of exploitation from the 1970s and 1980s cited above. For example, will vulnerable consumers in NEDs, where market infrastructure is still only embryonic and consumer protection not yet fully addressed, be exposed to similar risks of exploitation and deception? Will young people in Asian NICs who want to embrace a modern lifestyle and western values be misled by evocative advertising into equating known carcinogens with social emancipation? These are some of the questions that drive the thesis of this chapter that there is now, perhaps more than ever, a need for managers of global companies to become moral champions. If not, we may see repetitions of consumer exploitation that many champions believe should be relics of the past.

In order to portray the ethical implications of marketing potentially harmful products to vulnerable consumers abroad, a new descriptive model is presented that identifies relationships between the manager, the global company, its home market environment, a host market environment, the global business environment, and a target consumer. The goal is to show how different influences act on a manager to shape the character of the decisions he or she may take.

These influences may either promote or hinder high levels of ethical decision making. While the model is positive (describing how things are) and not normative (laying out how they ought to be), the author subscribes to the belief by Hunt and Vitell (1993: 782) that 'understanding how ethical decisions are made ('is') can contribute to making those decisions better ('ought').'

Each part of the model is discussed with reference to the literature on ethics and social responsibility in marketing. Previous contributions have been both conceptual and empirical. Conceptual work has been done on: developing rules of thumb and frameworks that lay out guidelines for ethical decision making (Laczniak 1983; Wotruba 1990); describing and modelling the ethical decision-making process and the influences on it (Bommer et al. 1987; Ferrell and Gresham 1985; Ferrell et al. 1989; Hunt and Vitell 1986, 1993); and developing scales for measuring personal ethical values and norms (Mayo and Marks 1990; Singhapakdi and Vitell 1991; Vitell et al. 1993). Empirical studies of managers have been carried out to describe and measure their ethical perceptions, attitudes and intentions (Hunt and Vasquez-Parraga 1993; Mayo et al. 1991). Also, cross-national comparisons have been reported on companies' use of ethical codes of conduct as well as the content of these codes (Langlois and Schlegelmilch 1990; Schlegelmilch and Houston 1989; Vogel 1992).

The chapter is organized in two parts. First, conceptual issues are addressed. The term 'moral champion' is defined and the descriptive model is presented. Relationships between the component parts of the model are discussed in the context of past research. In part two, the argument in favour of moral champions is developed. Possible counter-arguments are reviewed and refuted, and managerial implications of becoming a moral champion are addressed. In conclusion, a research agenda is presented listing some issues that require further attention.

20.2 CONCEPTUAL ISSUES

20.2.1 Definition of a 'moral champion'

Use of the term 'moral champion' in this article implies a high moral and ethical posture. According to Smith and Quelch (1991), ethicists identify three levels of duty to which people – and hence managers in organizations – are obligated:

1   avoid causing harm;
2   prevent harm;
3   do good.

They comment that negative duties are stronger than positive duties. This seems particularly appropriate in the context of any discussion of marketing potentially harmful products in LDCs, NEDs, and NICs. Smith and Quelch also point out that while it seems reasonable to expect businesses not to cause harm and to make efforts to prevent harm (in so far as it is within their control), there is less agreement on the need for companies to do good. McCoy's (1983) 'parable of the Sadhu' illustrates the type of moral conflict that an individual can face when trying to determine what is an appropriate ethical response in the face of human suffering. While taking part in an extended hike in the mountains of Nepal, McCoy's group of companions came upon an unconscious, almost naked Sadhu, an Indian holy man. Each climber gave the Sadhu help but none made sure that he would be safe. McCoy asks himself whether someone should have stopped to help the Sadhu to safety. Would it have done any good? Was the group responsible? McCoy's ability to help the Sadhu was tempered by his own physical problems at the time, the environmental constraints (due to being halfway up a mountain), and a general lack of consensus on what to do. McCoy draws parallels between this incident and the type of ethical decisions that managers face at work.

The parable of the Sadhu draws attention to key aspects of the model presented in Figure 20.1, namely the role of environmental influences and constraints; the impact of group membership on choices made by an individual; the type of decision-making process

Figure 20.1 An environmental model of factors affecting ethical decision making in global companies

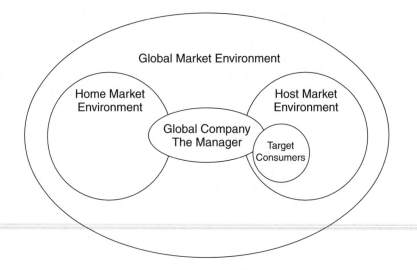

and rules that might be invoked; and finally, the impact of contingent factors such as a high-stress situation.

20.2.2 A model of ethical decision making in global companies

The model presented in Figure 20.1 represents an attempt to combine a micro-level analysis of individual ethical values and decision making with a macro-level analysis of the role of the company in its various external environments. An effort is made to examine the combined impact of macro- and micro-level factors on vulnerable consumers. Buller *et al.* (1991) previously developed a simple model featuring four levels of analysis (individual, corporate, societal, and global), based on earlier work by Owens (1983). However, their model did not incorporate any consideration of either the consumer or the different levels of national economic development in which global companies operate. The following discussion of the components of the model is firmly grounded in a review of the relevant literature.

20.2.3 Home market environment

The classical French comedy playwright, Molière, created an unforgettable character called Tartuffe, a wealthy but corrupt priest whose most famous statement was, '*Ce n'est pas pecher que de pecher en silence.*' In other words, sinning is not sinning if no one hears about it. Escaping notice in the US market is unlikely because, as Vogel (1992) points out, America is distinctive with regard to the unusual visibility of ethical issues. In the USA the promise of public scrutiny of corporate behaviour, the risk of public censure, and the inevitable enforcement of rules and laws are all strong motivators to keep company managers on the 'straight and narrow' path. Moreover, US consumers are sufficiently emancipated to take a continuing interest in the way companies conduct their business. Means of redress are institutionalized and frequently used. Yet, despite this stringent infrastructure, abuses of individual and company power have occurred and continue to occur (see Laczniak and Naor 1985 and Vogel 1992 for examples). Thus we see that it is not just in overseas markets that unethical behaviour occurs but also in highly policed home markets. Even though standards for ethical decision making and behaviour are clearly spelled out, some managers still opt to make unethical choices for private or corporate gain.

20.2.4 Host market environment

US commercial law is well known for its character of extra-territoriality (see Cateora 1993: 205–7 for details), whereby US managers operating abroad are held accountable at home for their actions. In the context of global marketing, one might assume that managers in US companies, where a high level of public scrutiny prevails, would choose to avoid any risk of censure by pursuing a consistent level of ethical behaviour abroad. If this is not the case, then we may suppose that they subscribe to Tartuffe's philosophy. In other words, they believe that 'out of sight' is also 'out of mind'. This belief may be all the stronger if a host market environment has a poorly developed or poorly policed legal infrastructure. In this instance, it may well be tempting to try to 'sin in silence'.

20.2.5 Global market environment

Ciulla (1991) has drawn attention to the variability that exists in legal and ethical values, attitudes, and standards even among the developed nations of the world, leaving aside the developing world. She cites comparisons of 'familial amoralism' in Italy, 'national amoralism' in Japan, and 'ethical imperialism' in the USA. This reminds us that there is no commonly accepted global code of ethics that applies to business (Buller *et al.* 1991). Clearly, managers operating abroad must make some accommodation to the nature of the foreign environment in which they are operating. However, as Shue (1981: 600) stated, 'No institution, including the corporation, has a general license to inflict harm,' even in places where local laws do not specifically outlaw such behaviour.

Competition is a key feature of the global market environment. Wotruba (1990) comments that 'competitors' actions seem intuitively to be a possible moderator of ethical decision making since questionable behaviours may be considered more necessary under intense competition.' Unfortunately, as Wotruba points out, research on this topic is lacking. In the global arena, competitors bring different national ethical standards into play. Thus a manager may feel compelled to compromise ethical standards learned at home in order to 'follow the crowd' and not lose ground in a foreign market.

20.2.6 Global company

It has been suggested that organizational structure and control systems combined in the past to hinder the adoption of social responsibility as a corporate value and as a 'modus operandi'. Ackerman (1975: 52) found that social issues pose three major dilemmas for corporations organized along divisional lines:

1   social demands subvert corporate-division relationships;
2   financial control systems are ineffective in explaining and evaluating social responsiveness;
3   the process for evaluating and rewarding managers is not designed to recognize performance in areas of social concern.

In other words, if headquarters management intervenes in divisional autonomy to recommend action by managers on a social issue, this may disturb the separation of power that has been instituted to promote economic performance. Moreover, social responsiveness by individual managers may well be inhibited because the 'payoff' is difficult to assess, according to traditional financial reporting mechanisms.

In the 1990s, solutions have been found to some of these problems through the personal inspiration and leadership of top management. The role of superiors and the availability of positive role models are important influences in the context of a corporation (Williams and Murphy 1990). Their influence can vary considerably from one company to another (Chonko and Hunt 1985) and can be either positive or negative, depending on the signals sent by the top executives (Kelly 1987). O'Toole (1991) gives examples of chief executive officers who have been able not only to promote a more socially responsible corporate culture, but also to ensure high levels of economic performance. The old dictum is proven true that 'where there's a will, there's a way'.

With regard to the global company as an institution made up of peer groups, research has been conducted to assess managers' perceptions of their peers' ethical behaviour. In the 1970s managers were reported to perceive their peers as being less ethical than themselves (Newstrom and Ruch 1975; Weaver and Ferrell 1977); in the 1980s few managers believed that their peers actually engaged in unethical behaviour (Chonko and Hunt 1985). Zey-Ferrell *et al.* (1979) reported that marketing managers' perceptions of what their peers did had a greater influence on their behaviour than their own personal ethical beliefs. More recent research by Vitell *et al.* reached the opposite conclusion:

> The ethical climate seemed to have little effect on one's acceptance of various norms. Apparently, this is an area where individual factors dominate and whether or not one's firm espouses the importance of ethical behavior is irrelevant. On the other hand, a sense of idealism and income level were both closely linked to acceptance of all the norms tested. Since income may be a surrogate measure of success, the results may indicate that those who were more successful tended to have stronger marketing-related norms.
>
> (Vitell *et al.* 1993: 336)

This last speculation does not seem to be borne out in real life if one recalls the ethical lapses of highly successful individuals like Ivan Boesky, Michael Milken, Frank Lorenzo and, most recently, Dan Rostenkowski. Moreover, contrary to Vitell *et al.*'s (1993) conclusion, Nichols and Day (1982) reported that individuals interacting in a group produce group decisions at a higher level of moral reasoning than the average of the individual members acting alone. Thus, at the present time it is difficult to determine on the evidence available whether managers in global companies are more or less likely to reach ethical decisions. In assessing the role of the company in influencing individual beliefs and behaviour, we should remember that individual ethics are also shaped by other organizations and are partly a result of the person's individual history and personality. Moreover, organizations do not reflect exactly the prevailing societal ethic. Finally, ethics are not static but change markedly over time (Buller *et al.* 1991).

20.2.7 The individual manager

Further comment is relevant concerning an individual's membership of different peer groups. McLean's (1978) theory of reference groups stresses that ethicists have failed to account for the pressure that multiple roles exert on members of modern society when they undertake ethical analyses. One of the roles often not taken into account is that of family member. Other sources of variability between individuals exist. For example, as Buller *et al.* state:

> It is possible for individuals from different backgrounds to have the same moral values, but to behave differently when faced with a common situation because of the reasoning process through which they apply the code.
>
> (Buller *et al.* 1991: 768)

Thus, we must differentiate between what a person thinks (which relates to personality) and how a person thinks (i.e. the cognitive style). Also, managers in companies from different nations may share similar values but differ in their actions, partly as a result of their information processing and decision making, and partly formative influences in both their home environment and overseas markets. These linkages are reflected in the model in Figure 20.1 by the overlaps between each component. The difference between the 'what' and the 'how' of individual ethical decision making has been greatly illuminated by the modelling done by Hunt and Vitell (1986; 1993). Their updated model specifically allows for differences in decision making that might occur between managers in the international setting. Hunt and Vitell draw attention to the impact of personal characteristics including one's religion, value system, belief system, strength of moral character, cognitive moral development, and ethical sensitivity.

Regarding values, 'organizational commitment' may be very important to company managers. Hunt and Vitell (1993) raise the question whether it is possible that 'individuals exhibiting high organizational commitment will then place such great importance on the welfare of the organization that they engage in questionable behavior' (if this were thought to be beneficial to the company). This situation poses a moral dilemma because of a conflict of duties. Ross (1930) identified six categories of *prima facie* duties (fidelity, gratitude, justice, beneficence, self-improvement, and non-maleficence (non-injury)) to various stakeholders. A manager's duty to do no harm to vulnerable consumers may be perceived to conflict with a duty of fidelity to the company (for example, by reducing discretionary costs such as informative advertising, or package warning labels in order to improve corporate economic performance). Shue (1981) warned that such a conflict can be avoided by always focusing on three important values: preserving a consumer's dignity, autonomy (freedom to determine one's own fate), and freedom of choice (to accept or reject a marketing offer). As Goodpaster and Matthews (1982: 141) stated 'Showing respect for persons as ends and not mere means to is central to organizational purposes is central to the concept of corporate moral responsibility.'

20.2.8 The overseas consumer

Consumer vulnerability is associated with low levels of economic development and lack of supervision of the market place. Consumers' emancipation is inhibited by the cumulative effects of the lack of education, lack of opportunities to acquire consumer skills through store and price comparison, lack of information about products and potential hazards, lack of availability of alternative choices, and so on. As a result, many consumers in LDCs, NEDs, and NICs may be completely unprepared or insufficiently armed to evaluate marketing offers made by any company, whether global or local. A current example of vulnerability is seen among urban consumers in Russia. Although generally well educated, they have little time or energy with which to monitor the actions of companies, being daily distracted by the continuing struggle to find basic necessities.

Based on the body of evidence available, we see that it is the interaction of three key variables that combines to produce decisions which might harm vulnerable consumers in distant markets. These are the company, its managers, and its market environments. With regard to the company, of particular importance are the corporate culture, the degree of enforcement of any corporate code of conduct, and the supervision and training of managers. In certain cases, a 'conspiracy of circumstances' may occur which fosters the risk of consumer exploitation. This is not to excuse or condone such behaviour; rather it is an attempt to explain how such abuses may arise.

Having described the parts of the model and how they interact, we have now established a conceptual basis on which to build an argument in favour of the need for moral champions in global marketing.

20.3 THE NEED FOR MORAL CHAMPIONS IN GLOBAL MARKETING

20.3.1 Aspects of ethical decision making

The fact that vulnerable consumers abroad have been and continue to be victimized is explained by Shue (1981: 599) in these words:

> [It] has a great deal to do with the discounting of the welfare of people across national boundaries, especially when the boundaries also mark cultural, ethnic, or racial differences. Harm to foreigners is simply not taken as seriously.

One may argue that discounting others' welfare results from an unequal interplay of deontological (process) and teleological (outcome) evaluations during decision making (see Hunt and Vitell 1986 for a full discussion). However, it seems more likely that it results either from a failure to identify the existence of an ethical dilemma or choice, or from a misplaced sense of loyalty in following the lead of superiors or trying to protect company interests.

Failure to identify a moral choice may result from a low level of cognitive moral development (see Kohlberg 1969 for details), or a lack of ethical sensitivity (Hunt and Vitell 1993), or a lack of strength of moral character (Williams and Murphy 1990). Candee (1975) showed that persons in moral development stages 3 and 4 were more likely to follow their superior in morally questionable action than were persons in stage 5 or 6. Ward and Wilson (1980) investigated how individual motivation (safety vs. esteem needs) interacting with the presence or absence of peer pressure affects the type of decisions taken by the individual. Esteem-motivated individuals do not submit to group pressure but display a consistent moral posture across situations. In contrast, safety-oriented individuals tend to acquiesce to group pressure and exhibit inconsistent moral action. However, when acting as individuals, both personality types make similar moral choices.

Donaldson (1985) developed an 'ethical algorithm' for use by managers in global companies. It is intended to help them distinguish between the justified and the unjustified application of moral standards to a foreign target market in cases where these standards differ from one's home country. The algorithm is based on specific recognition of the level of economic development in the target market. It answers the question: Is company practice (P) permissible for company (C) when (P) is acceptable in host country (B) but not in home country (A)? Application of the algorithm requires company managers to deliberate on the interactions between two of the three environments shown in Figure 20.1, to the benefit of the overseas consumer. The power of the algorithm 'lies in its ability to tease out implications of the moral presuppositions of a manager's acceptance of 'home' morality' (Donaldson 1985: 363). In this way, the temptation to rely on the simplistic argument of cultural relativity is excluded.

20.3.2 Arguments against the need for 'moral champions'

Numerous arguments can be raised against the thesis of this chapter. Five of the most common are listed below. The reader will recognize that the preceding discussion has already established a strong basis on which to refute these arguments.

1 *Moral projection.* Organizations do not and cannot have the same moral attributes as individuals.
2 *Levels of economic development.* Strikingly different levels of economic development are a reality of international business. The national government is at fault if it does not adequately protect its people. It is not the company's role or responsibility to stand in *loco parentis*. If a foreign company were to embrace higher legal, moral or ethical standards than the foreign government, this would smack of cultural imperialism or paternalism.
3 Why us? Playing the role of 'white knight' leads to lost profits and benefits only the competition. In simple terms, 'Why should we change when everyone else is doing it?'
4 *Conflict of duties.* A company's resources belong to its shareholders. It is they, not the managers, who should properly decide

on any act of social responsibility that may increase the company's cost of doing business.

5 *Competence and legitimacy.* Many managers are unsure about how to 'do good' and question what is legitimately within their purview as managers of a company operating in a foreign market.

Smith (1990: 56–60) identified four positions delineating the range of attitudes towards corporate social responsibility. The first two summarize the attitudes expressed in the five arguments listed above:

1 Profit maximization and social irresponsibility. Firms may do good through profit maximization (Adam Smith's 'invisible hand') but may also cause harm, would not act to prevent it, and are only doing good as a result of serving their self-interest.

2 Profit maximization tempered by the 'moral minimum' operating through self-regulation. This means avoiding causing harm. According to Smith and Quelch (1991), most firms and managers are at this stage.

3 Profit as a necessary but not sufficient goal, with affirmative action extending beyond self-regulation. This is where actively doing good begins to play a role and where being a 'moral champion' starts to be recognized.

4 Profit as a necessary but not sufficient goal, with social responsibility extending beyond self-regulation and affirmative action to include the championing of political and moral causes unrelated to the corporation's activities.

With reference to point four above, it is not the purpose of this chapter to recommend that companies become directly involved in political or moral causes in a foreign environment; this may be inappropriate or even illegal. Rather, it is the thesis of this chapter that there is a need to embrace a high level of moral care and concern for strangers in distant markets. This need cannot be reasoned away using simplistic arguments such as the five listed above.

Much of the current discussion about ethics and social responsibility in global business revolves around company policies about disclosure of information. What is needed is relevant and sufficient information for all stakeholders that will allow them to make informed choices and avoid being cast in the role of victims.

As Shue (1981: 599) asks: 'Why is informed consent not more appealing when it does in fact relieve a firm of the responsibility of having inflicted harm upon unsuspecting people?' Any decision by the company to withhold information from consumers overseas implies that the decision makers have other goals to accomplish which they consider of greater importance than the welfare of distant stakeholders. This article argues that such a position is indefensible.

20.4   CONCLUSION

On the basis of the literature review presented in this chapter, it is clear that there are significant gaps in our understanding of the issues raised. The new environmental model of factors affecting ethical decision making in global companies identifies specific domains in which further research can be conducted. As a conclusion to this discussion, an agenda for further research is presented.

■ Empirical research is needed to identify which global corporations have already adopted the stance of 'moral champions' and what results have been achieved, measured in both social and economic terms. The case study method would be an ideal medium to depict both the players, the type of market, and the type of decision-making procedures used to ensure full consideration and protection of all stakeholders, both at home and abroad.

■ We need to understand better how managers handle the 'what' and the 'how' of making decisions in the international marketplace. How do managers resolve conflicts of duties? How often do such conflicts occur in global marketing? What is the role of peer groups, both formal and informal, in shaping the individual decisions of managers? Also relevant is an examination of the role played by the chief executive officer in establishing an 'ethical climate' for decision making within the company.

■ Research attention should be directed towards measuring the impact of competition on a company's actions in foreign markets. Does greater intensity of competition exert greater pressure on managers of global companies to 'follow the crowd'? How do managers reconcile their market performance goals and priorities with due consideration for stakeholders, particularly those who are vulnerable to harm? How are profit motives evaluated relative to social responsibility goals?

■ With regard to markets in the developing world, is there any correlation between the existence and operation of governmental 'watchdog' agencies and a lower incident of consumer exploitation? If so, what types of 'policing' are most effective? Is there any evidence of a correlation between higher levels of consumer education and emancipation and a foreign company's commitment to involvement in socially responsible activities unrelated to its main line of business? At what level of national economic development does it become important for a global company to start thinking about its corporate image in the market as a socially responsible company?

Using the model, researchers can focus on a particular domain for further research effort and hypothesis testing, as suggested above. Research methods among companies might include case studies, surveys, or longitudinal tracking studies. The results of such research will add notably to our understanding of what it takes for companies to become moral champions in global marketing. Research of this type will also provide evidence of the likely payoffs from becoming moral champions, in terms of enhanced reputation, performance, consumer preference, and sales growth.

20.5   REFERENCES

Ackerman, R.W. (1975) *The Social Challenge to Business*, Cambridge, MA: Harvard University Press.

Bommer, M., Gratto, C., Gravander, J. and Tuttle, M. (1987) A behavioural model of ethical and unethical decision-making. *Journal of Business Ethics*, Vol. 6, pp. 265–80.

Buller, P.F., Kohls, J.J. and Anderson, K.S. (1991) The challenge of global ethics, *Journal of Business Ethics*, Vol. 10, pp. 767–75.

Candee, D. (1975) The moral psychology of Watergate. *Journal of Social Issues*, Vol. 31, Spring, pp. 183–92.

Cateora, P.R. (1993) *International Marketing* (8th edn), Homewood, IL: Irwin.

Chonko, L.B. and Hunt, S.D. (1985) Ethics and marketing management: an empirical examination. *Journal of Business Research*, Vol. 13, August, pp. 339–59.

Ciulla, J.B. (1991) Why is business talking about ethics? Reflections on foreign conversations. *California Management Review*, Vol. 34, No. 1, pp. 67–86.

Donaldson, T. (1985) Multinational decision-making: reconciling international norms. *Journal of Business Ethics*, Vol. 4, pp. 357–66.

Ferrell, O.C. and Gresham, L. (1985) A contingency framework for understanding ethical decision-making in marketing. *Journal of Marketing*, Vol. 49, Summer, pp. 87–96.

Ferrell, O.C., Gresham, L. and Fraedrich, J. (1989) A synthesis of ethical decision models for marketing. *Journal of Macromarketing*, Vol. 11, No. 3, pp. 55–64.

Goodpaster, K.E. and Matthews, J.B., Jr. (1982) Can a corporation have a conscience? *Harvard Business Review*, January–February, pp. 132–41.

Hunt, S.D. and Vasquez-Parraga, A.Z. (1993) Organizational consequences, marketing ethics and salesforce supervision. *Journal of Marketing Research*, Vol. 30, February, pp. 78–90.

Hunt, S.D. and Vitell, S.J. (1986) A general theory of marketing ethics. *Journal of Macromarketing*, Vol. 6, No.1, pp. 5–16.

Hunt, S.D. and Vitell, S.J. (1993) The general theory of marketing ethics: a retrospective and revision, in N.C. Smith and J.A. Quelch (eds), *Ethics in Marketing*, Homewood, IL: Irwin, pp. 775–801.

Kelly, C.M. (1987) The interrelationship of ethics and power in today's organizations. *Organizational Dynamics*, Vol. 16, Summer, pp. 5–18.

Kohlberg, L. (1969) Stage and sequence: the cognitive developmental approach to socialization, in D.A. Goslin (ed.), *Handbook of Socialization Theory and Research*, Chicago IL: Rand-McNally, pp. 347–480.

Laczniak, G.R. (1983) Framework for analyzing marketing ethics. *Journal of Macromarketing*, Vol. 3, No. 1, pp. 7–18.

Laczniak, G.R. and Naor, J. (1985) Global ethics: wrestling with the corporate conscience. *Business*, July–September, pp. 3–10.

Langlois, C.C. and Schlegelmilch, B.B. (1990) Do corporate codes of ethics reflect national character? Evidence from Europe and the United States. *Journal of International Business Studies*, Vol. 21, No. 4, pp. 519–39.

Mayo, M.A. and Marks, L.J. (1990) An empirical investigation of a general theory of marketing ethics. *Journal of the Academy of Marketing Science*, Vol. 18, No. 1, pp. 163–71.

Mayo, M.A., Marks, L.J. and Ryans, J.K. (1991) Perceptions of ethical problems in international marketing. *International Marketing Review*, Vol. 8, No. 3, pp. 61–75.

McCoy, B.H. (1983) The parable of the Sadhu. *Harvard Business Review*, September–October, pp. 103–8.

McLean, S.D. (1978) Ethics, reference group theory, and root metaphor analysis. *Andover Newton Quarterly*, Vol. 18, No. 4, pp. 211–21.

Newman, B. (1980) Consumer protection is underdeveloped in the Third World. *Wall Street Journal*, 8 April, pp. 1, 23.

Newstrom, J.W. and Ruch, W.A. (1975) The ethics of management and the management of ethics. *MSU Business Topics*, Vol. 23, Winter, pp. 29–37.

Nichols, M.L. and Day, V.E. (1982) A comparison of moral reasoning of groups and individuals on the defining issues test. *Academy of Management Journal*, Vol. 25, March, pp. 201–8.

O'Toole, J. (1991) Do good, do well: the business enterprise trust awards. *California Management Review*, Vol. 33, No. 3, pp. 9–24.

Owens, J. (1983) Business ethics in the college classroom. *Journal of Business Education*, April, pp. 593–9.

Peter, J. and Olson, J.C. (1993) *Consumer Behavior and Marketing Strategy* (3rd edn), Homewood, IL: Irwin.

Ross, W.D. (1930) *The Right and the Good*, Oxford, Clarendon Press.

Schlegelmilch, B.B. and Houston, J.E. (1989) Corporate codes of ethics in large UK companies: an empirical investigation of use, content, and attitudes. *European Journal of Marketing*, Vol. 23, No. 6, pp. 7–24.

Shue, H. (1981) Exporting hazards. *Ethics*, Vol. 91, July, pp. 579–606.

Singhapakdi, A. and Vitell, S.J. (1991) Research note: selected background factors influencing marketers, deontological norms. *Journal of the Academy of Marketing Science*, Vol. 19, Winter, pp. 37–42.

Smith, N.C. (1990) *Morality and the Market: Consumer Pressure for Corporate Accountability*, New York, NY: Routledge.

Smith, N.C. and Quelch, J.A. (1991) Pharmaceutical marketing practices in the Third World. *Journal of Business Research*, Vol. 23, No. 1, pp. 113–26.

Vitell, S.J., Rallapalli, K.C. and Singhapakdi, A. (1993) Marketing norms: the influence of personal moral philosophies and organizational ethical culture. *Journal of the Academy of Marketing Science*, Vol. 21, Fall, pp. 331–7.

Vogel, D. (1992) The globalization of business ethics: why America remains distinctive? *California Management Review*, Vol. 35, No. 1, pp. 30–49.

Ward, L. and Wilson, J.P. (1980) Motivation and moral development as determinants of behavioural acquiescence and moral action. *Journal of Social Psychology*, Vol. 112, pp. 271–86.

Weaver, K.M. and Ferrell, O.C. (1977) The impact of corporate policy on reported ethical beliefs and behaviour of marketing practitioners, in B.A. Greenberg and D.N. Bellenger (eds), *Contemporary Marketing Thought*, Chicago, IL: American Marketing Association, pp. 477–81.

Williams, O.F. and Murphy, P.E. (1990) The ethics of virtue: a moral theory for marketing. *Journal of Macromarketing*, Vol. 10, Spring, pp. 19–29.

Wotruba, T.R. (1990) A comprehensive framework for the analysis of ethical behavior, with a focus on sales organizations. *Journal of Personal Selling and Sales Management*, Vol. 10, Spring, pp. 29–42.

Zey-Ferrell, M., Weaver, K.M. and Ferrell, O.C. (1979) Predicting unethical behaviour among marketing practitioners. *Human Relations*, Vol. 32, No. 7, pp. 557–69.

PART IV
Business ethics resources

Appendix A
Addresses of centres and
institutes of business ethics

AUSTRALIA

Applied Ethics and Human Change
Queensland University of
 Technology
P.O. Box 284
Zillmere 4034
Tel. 07 864 2111

Colin Ash
Western Australian College
P.O. Box 217, Doubleview
Perth, WA 6019

Australian Institute of Ethics and the
 Professions
University of Queensland
St. Lucia, Queensland 4067
Tel. 011 61 7 871 8300

Barbara Bell
The Institute of Chartered Accountants in
 Australia
GPO Box 3921
Sydney, NSW 2001

Centre for Philosophy and Public Issues
University of Melbourne
Dept. of Philosophy
Parkville, Victoria, 3052
Tel. 61 3 344 5125

Colin R. Honey, Director
Kingswood Centre for Applied Ethics
The Hampden Road, Crawley
Western Australia 6009
Tel. 09 389 0389
Fax. 09 389 0388

Dr. Simon Lonstaff, Executive Director
The St. James Ethics Centre
GPO Box 3599
Sydney, NSW 2001
Tel. 02 232 6982

Hugon Waldemar Niemotko
4/84 Wellington Street
Bondi, NSW 2026

Dr. Michael W. Small
School of Management
Curtin University of Technology
GPO Box U 1987
Perth 6001

BELGIUM

K. Boey, Director
Centrum voor Ethiek
UFSIA
Prirsstraat 13
B-2000 Antwerpen

Chaire Hoover d'Ethique Economique et
 Sociale
Universite Catholique de Louvain
3 Place Montesquieu
1328 Louvain-La-Neuve
Tel. 32 10 473951
Fax. 32 10 473952

Vincent Commenne, Chairman
Service de recherche et information
 d'ethique et placement
Moensberg 101
B-1180 Brussels

P. Van Parijs
Senimaire Ethique des Affaires
U.C.L., 1, Chemin d'Aristote
B-138 Louvain-La-Nueve

BRAZIL

Maria Arruda
Departamento de Mercadologia
Fundacao Getulio Vargas
Escola de Administracao de Empresas
   de Sao Paulo
Av. Nove de Julho, 2029
CEP 01313 Sao Paulo, SP

Fundacao Instituto de Desenvolvimento
   Empresarial e Social (FIDES)
Rua Luiz Coelho 308 Cj. 11
CEP 01309 Sao Paulo, SP
Tel. (257) 3599 256 1212

Antonio Savio Passos Palazzo
Rua Rainha Guilhermina 90/204
Leblon
CEP 22441–120 Rio de Janeiro, RJ

Eduardo Vasconcellos, Dean
Universidade de Sao Paulo
Falculdade de Economia Administracao
   e Contabilidade
Caixa Postal 11.498
CEP 05499 Sao Paulo, SP

CANADA

Bruce S. Alton
Trinity College
6 Haskin Avenue
Toronto, ON M55 1M8

Jean Paulo Bellemare
P.O. Box 548
Trois-Rivieras
Quebec, PQ G9A 5J1

Conrad G. Brunk
Department of Philosophy
Conrad Grebel College
Waterloo, ON N2L 3G6

Canadian Centre for Ethics and Corporate
   Policy
George Brown House, 2nd floor

50 Baldwin Street
Beverly, Toronto, Ontario 551LA
Tel. (416) 348 8691

Centre for Applied Ethics
Michael McDonald, Director
University of British Columbia
Vancouver, BC V6T 1Z1

Centre for Accounting Ethics
University of Waterloo
School of Accountancy
Waterloo, ON N2L 3G1
Tel. (519) 885 1211 ext. 2770

Centre for Corporate Social Performance
Max Clarkson, Director
Faculty of Management
University of Toronto
246 Bloor Street West
Toronto, ON M5S 1V4

Centre for Professional and Applied
   Ethics
Arthur Schafer, Director
University of Manitoba
Winnipeg Manitoba R3T 2N2

S. Chojnacki, Librarian
University of Sudbury
Sudbury, ON PBE 2C6

Donald J. DeGrandis
Corporate Secretary
Northern Telecom Limited
3 Robert Speck Parkway
Mississauga, ON L4Z 3C8

K.C. Dhawan
Sir George Williams Campus
Concordia University
1455 De Maisonneuve Blvd.
Montreal, PQ H3G 1M8

Vincent DiNorcia
University of Sudbury
Sudbury, ON P3E 2C6

Guy Fleury
Management Catagory Programs
300 Laurier Ave. West
21st Floor, L'Estlanade
Ottawa, ON K1A 0M7

Jeffrey Gandz
University of West Ontorio
School of Business Administration
London, ON N6A 3K7

Grou de Recherche Ethos
Universite de Quebec a Rimouski
200 dea Ursulines
Rimouski, PQ B5L 3A1
Tel. (204) 474 9107

Ishtiyague Haji
Department of Philosophy
Simon Fraser University
Burnaby, BC V5A 156

Shannon Jung
Religion Department
Concordia College
Montreal, PQ H48 1R6

Cornelius Kampe
3 Riga Drive
Wolville, NS

B.E. Kent
Department of Philosophy
Simon Fraser University
Burnaby, BC V5A 156

Kevin Lockett
HRD Consulting Co.
14 Long Branch Avenue
Toronto, ON M8W 3H

Dr. Abbyann Lynch, Director
Westminster Institute for Ethics and
    Human Values
Westminster College
361 Windermere Rd.
London, ON N6G 2K3

Shirley Mancino
Government of Ontorio
Chairman's Office, 3rd Floor
Frost Bldg. South
Queens Park, ON M7A 1Z5

Alex C. Michalos
Institute of Public Affairs
Dalhousie University
Halifax, NS B3H 3J5

Peter Miller
Department of Philosophy

University of Winnipeg
Winnipeg, MB R3B 2E9

Chris Morris
Department of Philosophy
University of Ottawa
Ottawa, ON K1N 6N5

George J. Nathan
Department of Philosophy
Brock University
St. Catherines, ON

Occupational Ethics Group
Jack Stevenson, Co-Chair
Department of Philosophy
University of Toronto
Toronto, ON M5S 1A1

Jean Pasquero
Universite du Quebec a Montreal
1495 Rue Saint Denis, J-4205
C.P. 8888, Succ. 'A'
Montreal, PQ H3C 3P8

Deborah C. Poff
Department of Philosophy
University of Alberta
Edmonton, AB T6G 2E5

Timothy Reid
Ryerson Polytech Institute
21 Gerrard Street
Toronto, ON

David J. Roy
Centre of Bioethics
110 Avenue des Pins Quest
Montreal, PQ H2W 1R7

Hal Schroeder
School of Management
4401 University Drive
Lethbridge, AB T1K 3M4

Robert W. Sexty
Department of Management
Memorial University of Newfoundland
St. John's, NF A1C 5S7

Robin Sleep
Ryerson Polytechnical Institute
Philosophy – 50 Gould Street
Toronto, ON M5B 1E8

Taskforce on the Churches and Corporate
   Responsibility
129 St. Clair Avenue West
Toronto, ON M4V 1N5
Tel. (416) 923 1758

Bernard Wand
Carelton University
Department of Philosophy
Ottawa, ON K1S 5B6

Elizabeth Weber-Wheatony
Mont St. Vincent University
Halifax, NS

Westminster Institute for Ethics and
   Human Values
361 Windermere Road
London, ON N6G 2K3
Tel. (519) 673 0046

Barry Wheaton
Department of Religious Study
Mount Saint Vincent University
Halifax, NS

Richard Wolak, O.M.I
Newman Theological College
20 Gareth Place
St. Albert, AB T8N 3K5

Jacke Wolf
St. John's College
400 Dysart Road
Winnipeg, MB R3T 2M

CHILE

Sonia Godoy
Banco de Chile
Departmento de Recursos Humanos
Ahumada 251
Santiago

CHINA

Tong Wan Sheng
Director of Trade Research Institute of
   Beijing Business Academy
No. 11 Fucheng Road
Beijing
Tel. (01) 8417711 2631

Li Dianfu
Dean, Faculty of Accounting
Beijing Institute of Business
33 Fucheng Rd.
Beijing
Tel. (01) 8417711 ext. 2321/2323
Fax. (01) 8417834

CZECH REPUBLIC

Dr. Marie Bohata, Professor
Central Research Institute of National
   Economy
nam Hrdinu 4/1635
140 00 Prague 4

DENMARK

Peter Kemp
University of Copenhagen
Kobmagergad 50
DK-1150 Copenhagen

Peter Pruzan
Institute of Computer and Systems
   Sciences
DASY
Julius Thomsens Plads 10
DK-1925 Frederiksberg C

ENGLAND

Siobhan Alderson, Research Officer
Cranford School of Management
Cranford, Bedford MK430 AL

The European Business Ethics Network
Cheltenham & Gloucester College
Faculty of Business and Social Studies
Broadlands
P.O. Box 220, The Park
Cheltenham
Glos GL50 2QF
Tel. 01242 543233

Michael Blair
General Counsel
Securities and Investment Board
Gavrelle House
2–14 Bunhill Row
London EC1Y 8RA

Board for Social Responsibility
Chris Beales
Church House
Great Smith Street
London SW1P 3NZ
Tel. 0171 222 9011

Centre for Business and Public Sector
   Ethics
Rosemund Thomas
6 Croftgate
Fulbrook Road
Cambridge CB3 9EG

Peter Curwen
Reader in Public Policy
Sheffield Business School
Pond Street
Sheffield S1 1WB

Jim Fisher-Adams
25 Denning Road
Hampstead
London NW3 1ST

The Hinsky Centre
Mr Owen Nankivell
Westminster College
Oxford OX2 9AT

Ted Honderich
Department of Philosophy
University College of London
Gover Street
London NC13 6BT

Institute of Business Ethics
Stanley Kiaer, Director
12 Palace Street
London, SW1E 5JA
Tel. 0171 931 0495

Jennifer Jackson, Director
Centre for Business and Professional
   Ethics
The University of Leeds
Leeds LS2 9JT

Clare Lorenz
Lorenz Associates
5 Makepeace Avenue
London N6 6EL

Jack Mahoney
London Business School

Sussex Place
Regent's Park
London, NW1 4SA
Tel. 0171 262 5050
Fax. 0171 724 7875

Society for Applied Philosophy
Brenda Almond, Honorary Secretary
Social Values Research Centre
University of Hull
Hull HU6 7RX

Elaine Sternberg
18 Tamar House
12 Tavistock Place
London WC1H 9RA

C. Michael Wilkinson
Teesside Polytechnic
Middlesborough
Cleveland TS1 3BA

Marlene Winfield, Project Director
Conscientious Dissent at Work: Issues in
   Private Sector Employment
24 Patshull Road
London NW5 2JY

FRANCE

ACADI
Yves Cousin
47, rue de L'Universite
75007 Paris

Centre d'Ethique de L'Entreprise
J.L. Flinois
45, rue de L'Universite
75007 Paris

Economie et Humanisme
J.C. Lavigne
14, rue Antoine Dumont
F-69372 Paris

Ethique des Affaires
J. Mousse
E.D.H.E.C.
15, rue Monsieur
F-75007 Paris

European Baha'l Business Forum
George Starcher
Secretary General

35, Avenue Jean Jaures
73000 Chambery

Group Essec
Jean G. Padioleau
Avenue de la Grande Ecole
B.P. 105
95021 Cergy-Pontoise Cedex
Tel. 1 30 38 38 00

Antoine Verhuel
Group 'Project'
14, rue d'Assas
F-75006 Paris

GERMANY

Association for Ethics, Education and
  Management
Joachim Kreutzham, Executive Director
Hindenburgplatz 3
D-3200 Hildesheim

Betriebwirtschaftliches Institut
H. Steinmann
Friedrich Alex Universsitaet
Postfach 3931
Lange Gasse 20
D 8500 Nurenberg

Dietar Brinkmeirer
Bernadottestr 96
6000 Frankfurt 50

CIVITAS
P. Koslowski, Director
Forshungsinstitut für Philosophie
Lange Laube 14
3000 Hannover 1

Martin Gruschka
Lucrum & Co., Ltda.
Dethstr 5
1000 Berlin 30

Frank Simon
Wesfalische
Wilhelms Universität Münster
Lehrstuhl fur Allgemeine BWL
Am Stadtgraben 13
4400 Münster

Peter Eigen, Chairman
Transparency International

Hardenbergplatz 2
D-10623 Berlin

Wissenschaftszentrum Berlin für
  Sozialforschung
Meinolf Dierkes
Tegelorter Ufer 39
1000 Berlin

GHANA

Kwame Gyeke
Department of Philosophy
University of Ghana
Logon

HOLLAND

Patrick A. Wharton
D. Reidel Publishing Co.
P.O. Box 17
3300 AA Dordrecht

HONG KONG

Advisory Services Group
Ambrose W.T. Ng, Head
Corruption Prevention Department
25/F Fairmont House
8 Cotton Drive
Tel. 826 3228

Gael M. MacDonald, Associate
  Professor
Asia Pacific International
1301 Shun Tac Centre
200 Comaught Road, Central

Hong Kong Ethics Development Centre
1 F, Tung Wah Mansion
199–203 Hennessy Road
Wanchai
Tel. 2587 9812
Fax. 2824 9766

Prof. Gerhold K. Becker
Centre for Applied Ethics
Hong Kong Baptist College
224, Waterloo Road
Kowloon
Tel. (852) 339 7291
Fax. (852) 339 7379

Kam Hon-Lee
The Chinese University of Hong Kong
Shatin, NT

HUNGARY

Dr. Laszio Zsolnai
Department of Business Economics
University of Economics
Budapest 5, P.O. Box 489
H-1828

INDIA

P.S. Cholhan, President
Nopex
Great Western Building
130–32 Bombay Samachar
Bombay 400 032

B. H. Reporter
Jost's Engineering Co.
60 Sir Phirozeshah Mehta
Bombay 400 001

Xavier Intitute of Management
R. D'Souza, Director
Bhubaneswar 751 013
Tel. (0674) 52446

IRELAND

Dr. Elizabeth P. Tierney
Annacrivey Mews
Enniskerry, County Wicklow

ISRAEL

A. Barzel
Department of General Studies
Israel Insitute of Technology
Technicon City
Haifa
Dove Izaeli
Professor of Marketing & Business Ethics
Faculty of Management
Tel Aviv University
Tel Aviv, 69978

Daniel Jacobson
Department of Labor Studies

Tel Aviv University
Tell Aviv, 69978

A. Michael Maidan
Philosophy Department
University of Haifa
Haifa, 31999

Management Ethics Forum of the Israeli
    Management Centre
Simha Werner
4 Henreita Sold Street
Tel-Aviv

ITALY

Stafano Frega
Etica degli Affari
Prospecta Publisher
Via Tizino, n.11
Milan, 20145

POLITEIA
Lorenzo Sacconni, Director
Via Brera, 18
Milano, 20121

Mario Unnia
Prospecta
Via Tiziano 77
Milano, 20145

JAPAN

Mototoka Hiroike, President
The Institute of Moralogy
2–1–1, Hikarigaoka, Hashiwa-shi
Kashiwa City, Chiba-ken, 277

Institute of the Study of Social Justice
Anselmo Mataix, Director
Sophia University
7–1, Kioicho, Chiyoda-ku
Tokyo 102

Dr. Yukimasa Nagayasu
The Institute of Moralogy
Research Department, Economic
    Secton
2–1–1 Hikarigaoka, Hashiwa-shi
Kashiwa City, Chiba-ken 277

Ariyoshi Okumura, President
IBJ Capital Management Co., Ltd.
4–2 Marunouchi I-Choma
Chiyodo-Ku, Tokyo 100

Tohoku Gakuin University
Hiraku Hoshimiya
Tsuchitioi 1–3–1
Sendai 980

LUXEMBOURG

International Affairs
Law and Ethics Division
LUX Conference
SC, 74 rue Ermesinde
L-1469
Tel. (352) 47 471928

Uri R. Rau
5, rue Belaire
L-6111
Junglinster

MALAYSIA

Dr. J.L. Gupta
Department of Management
School of Social Sciences
University Sains Malaysia
11800 Pulau Pinang

Dr. Syed Azizi Wafa
Department of Management
School of Social Sciences
University Sains Malaysia
11800 Pulau Pinang

MALTA

Saviour Gauci
University of Malta
Department of Management
Msida

MEXICO

Juan Gerardo Garza
Instituto Tecnologico y de Estudios
Superiores de Monterrey
Sucursal de Correos 'J'
C.P. 64849 Monterrey, N.L.

Luisa Riveira
Apartado Postal 61–024
Colonia Juarez 06600

NETHERLANDS

Dr. Arie F. Brand, Dean
University of Twente
School of Management Studies
P.O. Box 217
7500 AE Enschede

Centre for Bioethics and Health Law
University of Utrecht
P.O. Box 80.105
3508 TC Utrecht

Marinus C. Doeser
Vrije Universitieit
Postbus 7161, 1007 MC
Amsterdam
Ethiek van Econimie en Bedrijf
E.J.J.M. Kimman
Rijksuniversiteit Limburg
P.O.B. 616
6200 MD Maastricht

European Business Ethics Network
Nijenrode University
Straatweg 25
NL 3462 BG Breukelen

European Institute for Business Ethics
Henk J.L. van Luijk, Director
Vac. Res. Ass.
Nijenrode University
Straatweg 25
3621 BG Breukelen
Tel. 31 3462 91290
Fax. 31 3462 91296

Dr. Wim L. Hanssen
Department of Management Studies
Agricultural University
Hollandse Weg 1
6707 KN Wageningen

Christelijke Hogeschool Wendescheim
W. Meykamp
Sector Hoge Economisch
Onderwijs
Postbus 10090
8000 GB Zwolle

NEW ZEALAND

Howard Russell
Marketing Insight
P.O. Box 2637
Auckland

I.C. Stewart
University of Auckland
Private Bag
Auckland

NIGERIA

Dr. John H. Boer
P.O. Box 261
Jos, Plateau

NORWAY

Heidi von Weltzien Hoivik, Provost
Norwegian School of Management
Ellen Kjos-Kendall
Personalkonsulent
Elias Smiths vei 15
Postboks 580 N-1301 Sandvika

Norwegian National Committee for
    Research Ethics in the Social Sciences
    and the Humanities
Gaustadalleen 21
N-0371 Oslo
Tel. 47 22 95 87 82

Arild Lillebo
Corporate Values 1990
P.O. Box 44
1345 Osteras

PERU

Jaime Pedreros Fitzgerald
Inclan 135 Of. 202
Lima, 18

PHILIPPINES

Patricia Lazaro
U.P. College Baguia
Baguio City 0201

SAUDI ARABIA

Fayez Ibrahim Habib
College of Administrative Sciences
King Saud University
P.O. Box 2459
Riyadh 11452

SCOTLAND

Action for Corporate Responsibility
Sheena Carmichael
4 Beau Gate
Glasgow G12 9EE

Jim Sieyes
Management Development
P.O. Box 30
Spanago Valley PA16 OAH

SINGAPORE

Dr. Dennis M. Ray
Nanyang Technological University
ENDEC SAB-NTU
Nanyang Avenue

SOUTH AFRICA

Dr. Albert Zandvoort
P.O. Box 7294
Pretoria 0001

Johann Liebenberg, Senior General
    Manager
Chamber of Mines of South Africa
P.O. Box 809
Johannesburg 2000

S.M. Motsuenyane, President
National African Federated Chamber of
    Commerce Industries
Privage Bag X81
Soshanguve 0152

SPAIN

Antonio Argandona, Professor
Instituto de Studios Superiores de la
    Empresa
University of Navarra
Av. Pearson 21
08034 Barcelona

E.S.A.D.E.
Jose M. Lozano
Avenida Pedrelbes 60–62
08034 Barcelona

Javier Gorosquieta
Professor of Business Ethics
Comillas University of Madrid
Centro Loyola de Estudios y
    Comunicacion Social
Pablo Aranda, 3
Madrid

Empresa y Humanismo
Kepa Miena Ormazabal
Universidad de Navarra
Edificio Central
E-31080 Pamplona

Dr. Domenec Mele, Professor
Instituto de Studios Superiores de la
    Empresa
Universidad de Navarra
Avenida Pearson 21
08034 Barcelona

Juan Trave
Esade Avenida
Pedralbes 60
Barcelona 08034

Marta Dalfo
Documentation Service
Instituto de Ciencias Para la Familia
Universidad de Navarra
Edificio Los Nogales
31080 Pamplona

SWEDEN

Dr. Thomas Brytting
FA-Counsel
Sturgatan 58
Stockholm A-10241

Olof Henell
University of Lund
P.O. Box 5136
Lund S-220 05

The Swedish Council for Management
    and Work Life Issues
Hans De Geer
P.O. Box 5042
Stockholm

SWITZERLAND

Institute for Business Ethics
University of St. Gallen
Guisanstrasse 11
CH-9010 St. Gallen
Tel. 41 71 302644
Fax. 41 71 302881

Institute for Social Ethics
Hans-Balz Peter, Director
Sulgenauweg 26
Ch-3007 Berne

Dr. Peter F. Mueller, President
Ethics & Business
Zurichbergstr. 46a
8044 Zurich

UNITED STATES

9 to 5, National Association of Working
    Women
614 Superior Ave. N.W.
Cleveland, OH 44113
Tel. (414) 274 0925
    (800) 522 0925

Accion International
120 Beacon St.
Sommerville, MA 02143
Tel. (617) 492 4930

American Council on Consumer Interest
240 Stanley Hall
University of Missouri
Columbia, MO 65911
Tel. (314) 882 3817

American Enterprise Institute for Public
    Policy Research
1150 17th Street, N.W.
Washington, DC 20036
Tel. (202) 862 5800

Arthur Andersen Centre for Professional
    Education
Herb Desch
1405 North Fifth Avenue
St. Charles, IL 60174
Tel. (708) 377 3100

Association for Practical & Professional
  Ethics
Brian Schrag, Executive Secretary
Indiana University
410 N. Park Avenue
Bloomington, IN 47405
Tel. (812) 855 6450

Association of Professional
  Responsibility Lawyers
c/o American Bar Association Centre for
  Professional Responsibility
541 North Fairbanks Court
Chicago, IL 60611
Tel. (213) 626 7300

Business Enterprise Trust, The
Kathleen Meyer
Executive Director
204 Junipero Sierra Blvd.
Stanford, CA 94305
Tel. (415) 321 5100

Business Ethics Section of the Academy
  of Legal Studies in Business
120 Upham Hall
Miami University
Miami, OH 45056
Tel. (800) 831 2903

Business Ethics Strategies, Inc./BEST
P.O. Box 1698
New York, NY 10011
Tel. (212) 691 1224

Business for Social Responsibility
1030 15th St. NW, Suite 1010
Washington, DC 20005
Tel. (202) 842 5400

Business, Government, and Society
  Research Institute
University of Pittsburgh
Katz Graduate School of Business
c/o B. Mitnick
261 Mervis Hall
Pittsburgh, PA 15260
Tel. (412) 648 1555

Carnegie Council on Ethics and
  International Ethics
Dr. Joel Rosenthal, President
Merrill House
170 East 64th Street
New York, NY 10021–7478

Tel. (212) 838 4120

Center for Academic Ethics
Arthur Brown, Director
Wayne State University
311 Education Building
Detroit, MI 48202
Tel. (313) 577 8290

Center for Advance Study in the
  Behavioral Sciences
202 Junipero Serra Blvd.
Stanford, CA 94305
Tel. (415) 321 2052

Center for the Advanced Study of Ethics
Dr. Edmund D. Pellegrino
Georgetown University
Healy Hall, Room 201A
Washington, DC 20057
Tel. (202) 687 8999

Center for the Advancement of Applied
  Ethics
Peter Madsen, Director
Carnegie Mellon University
Baker Hall
Pittsburgh, PA 15213
Tel. (412) 268 5703

Center for the Advancement of Ethics and
  Character
Kevin Ryan, Director
605 Commonwealth Avenue
Boston, MA 02215
Tel. (617) 353 3262

Center for Applied Christian Ethics
Dr. Allen Johnson, Director
Bible Department
Wheaton College
Wheaton, IL 60187
Tel. (708) 752 5886

Center for Applied Ethics
Pace University
Dyson College of Arts and Sciences
L. Hundersmarck
Department of Philosophy and
  Religious Studies
78 North Broadway
White Plains, NY 10603
Tel. (914) 422 4182

Center for Applied Ethics
Father Thomas Shanks, Director
Santa Clara University
Santa Clara, CA 95053
Tel. (408) 554 5319

Center for Applied Ethics
Duke University
Durham, NC 27706
Tel. (919) 660 5204

Center for Applied Philosophy and Ethics
Robert J. Baum, Director
332 Griffin-Floyd Hall
University of Florida
Gainesville, FL 32611
Tel. (904) 392 2084

Center for Applied & Professional Ethics
Dr. Roy Cebick, Director
Department of Philosophy
801 McClung Tower
University of Tennessee
Knoxville, TN 37996–0480
Tel. (615) 974 3255

Center for Applied & Professional Ethics
John F. O'Grady, Director
Department of Theology &
    Philosophy
Barry University
11300 Northeast Second Avenue
Miami Shores, FL 33161–6695
Tel. (305) 899 3779

Center for Biotechnology Policy and
    Ethics
Texas A & M University
College Station, TX 77843–4355
Tel. (409) 845 5434

Center for Business and Democracy
Richard Schram, Director
Goddard College
Painfield, VT 05667
Tel. (802) 454 8311

Center for Business Ethics
W. Michael Hoffman
Executive Director
Bentley College
Waltham, MA 02154–4705
Tel. (617) 891 3434

Center for Business/Religion/
    Professions
William Martin, Director
Pittsburgh Theological Seminary
616 N. Highland Avenue
Pittsburgh, PA 15206
Tel. (412) 362 5610

Center for Business, Society, and Ethics
Pete Matheson
Carnegie Mellon University
154 Baker Hall
5000 Forbes Avenue
Pittsburgh, PA 15213
Tel. (412) 268 5703

Center for Corporate Community
    Relations, The
Boston College
36 College Rd.
Chestnut Hill, MA 02167–3835
Tel. (617) 552 4545

Center for Corporate Public Involvement
1001 Pennsylvania Avenue, N.W.
Washington, DC 20004–2599
Tel. (202) 624 2425

Center for Creative Leadership
One Leadership Place
P.O. Box P-1
Greensboro, NC 27410
Tel. (910) 288 7210

Center for Ethics
Utah Valley Community College
Department of Humanities and
    Philosophy
800 West 1200 South
Orem, UT 84058
Tel. (801) 222 8000

Center for Ethics
The University of Tampa
Debbie Thorne, Ph.D.
401 W. Kennedy Blvd., Box 61–F
Tampa, FL 33606–1490
Tel. (813) 258 7415

Center for Ethics Across the University
David Ozar, Director ext. 8352
Loyola University of Chicago
6525 N. Sheridan Road
Chicago, IL 60626
Tel. (312) 508 8349

The Center for Ethics and Corporate
Policy
637 S. Dearborn St.
Chicago, IL 60605
Tel. (312) 508 8349

Center for Ethics in Public Policy and the
Professions
Dr. James W. Fowler
Emory University
Candler Library, Room 428A
Atlanta, GA 30322
Tel. (404) 727 4954

Center for Ethics and Religious Values in
Business
Oliver Williams, Co-Chairman
University of Notre Dame
College of Business Administration
Notre Dame, IN 46556
Tel. (219) 631 6685

Center for Ethics & Social Policy
Dr. Barry Stenger
Graduate Theological Union
2400 Ridge Road
Berkeley, CA 94709
Tel. (510) 649 2560

Center for Ethics Studies
Robert Ashmore, Director
Academic Support Facility, Rm. 336
Marquette University
Milwaukee, WI 53233
Tel. (414) 288 5824

The Center for Economic Conversion
222 View St., Suite C
Mountain View, CA 94041–1344
Tel. (415) 968 8798

Center for Law and Social Policy
Alan Houseman
1616 P Street, N.W., Suite 450
Washington, DC 20036
Tel. (202) 328 5140

Center for Media and Values
Elizabeth Thoman
1962 South Shenandoah Street
Los Angeles, CA 90034
Tel. (310) 559 2944

Center on Philanthropy
Dr. Warren F. Ilchman, Executive Director

Indiana University
550 W. North St.
Suite 301
Indianapolis, IN 46202–3162
Tel. (317) 274 4200

Center for Policy Research
Amitai Etzioni
The George Washington University
714 Gelman Library
Washington, DC 20052
Tel. (202) 994 8142

Center for Professional Ethics
John R. Wilcox, Director
Manhattan College
Bronx, NY 10471
Tel. (718) 920 0449

Center for Professional Ethics, The
Robert Lawry, Director
Case Western Reserve University
233 Yost Hall
10900 Euclid Ave.
Cleveland, OH 44106–7057
Tel. (216) 368 5349

Center for Professional Ethics
Rev. John A. Leies, Director
St. Mary's University
One Camino Santa Maria
San Antonio, TX 78228

Center for Public Policy and
Contemporary Issues
University of Denver
2301 South Gaylord Street
Denver, CO 80208
Tel. (303) 871 3400

Center for Religion, Ethics and Social
Policy (CRESP)
Philip B. Snyder, Coordinator
Cornell University
123 Anabel Taylor Hall
Ithaca, NY 14853
Tel. (607) 255 5027

Center for Research in Business and
Social Policy
The University of Texas at Dallas
Dallas, TX 75061
Tel. (214) 883 2013

Center for Study of Business and
  Government
Bernard M. Baruch College
City University of New York
17 Lexington Avenue
Box 348–A
New York, NY 10010
Tel. (212) 447 3420

Center for the Study of Ethics
Albion College
Albion, MI 49224
Tel. (517) 629 0529

Center for the Study of Ethical
  Development
206 Burton Hall
178 Pillsbury Drive
University of Minnesota
Minneapolis, MN 55455
Tel. (612) 624 0876

Center for the Study of Ethical Issues in
  Business
David Messick, Director
Kellogg Graduate School of Management
Northwestern University
2001 Sheradon Road
Evanston, IL 60208
Tel. (708) 491 8074

Center for the Study of Ethics
Elaine Englehardt, Ph.D
Utah Valley State College
800 West 1200 South
Orem, UT 84058–5999
Tel. (801) 222 8000 ext. 8129

Center for the Study of Ethics and the
  Professions
Dr. Vivian Weil, Director
Illinois Institute of Technology
Life Sciences, Room 166
3101 South Dearborne Street
Chicago, IL 60616–3793
Tel. (312) 567 3017

Center for Study of Ethics in Society
Michael S. Pritchard, Director
Western Michigan University
Dept. of Philosophy
Moore Hall Room 311
Kalamazoo, MI 49008–5022
Tel. (616) 387 4380

Center for the Study of Values
Dr. Frank Dilley
University of Delaware
Newark, DE 19716
Tel. (302) 831 2546

Center for Value Based Leadership
Charles Joyner, Director
55 Forest Drive
P.O. Box 819
Forest Knolls, CA 94933
Tel. (415) 488 0659

Center for Values and Social Policy
Dale Jamieson, Director
University of Colorado at Boulder
Dept. of Philosophy
Campus Box 232
Boulder, CO 80309–0232
Tel. (303) 492 6364

Center for the Teaching and Study of
  Applied Ethics
College of Law
University of Nebraska-Lincoln
P.O. Box 830902
Lincoln, NE 68583–0902
Tel. (402) 472 1248

Clearinghouse for Information About
  Values & Ethics
Organization & Human Systems
  Development
Directorate for Science and Policy
  Programs
American Association for the
  Advancement of Science
1333 H Street, NW,
Washington, DC 20005
Tel. (202) 326 6600
Fax. (202) 289 4950

Computer Ethics Institute
11 Dupont Circle, N.W., Suite 900
Washington, DC 20036–1271
Tel. (202) 939 3707

Committee on Ethics in the Public Service
National Academy of Public
  Administration
1120 G Street, N.W., Suite 850
Washington, DC 20005
Tel. (202) 347 3190

Committee on Professional Ethics, Rights
 and Freedom
Cathy Rudder, Executive Director
American Political Science
 Association
1527 New Hampshire Avenue, N.W.
Washington, DC 20036
Tel. (202) 483 2512

Common Cause
Ann McBride
2030 M Street, N.W., Suite 300
Washington, DC 20036
Tel. (202) 833 1200

Computer Professionals for Social
 Responsibility
P.O. Box 717
Palo Alto. CA 94302
Tel. (415) 322 3778

Conference Board, The
Jack Wirts, President
845 Third Avenue
New York, NY 10022
Tel. (212) 759 0900

Corporate Social Responsibility
Commission for Church in Society
Edgar G. Crane. Director
8765 W. Higgins Road, Ninth Floor
Chicago, IL 60631–4190

Council on Economic Priorities
Alice Tetter-Marlin, Director
30 Irving Place
New York, NY 10003
Tel. (212) 420 1133

Council for Ethics in Economics
Paul M. Minus, Director
Trinity Church, 3rd Floor
125 East Broad Street
Columbus, OH 43215–3605
Tel. (614) 221 8661

Council of Ethical Organizations
Mark Pastin
Chair and President
1216 King Street, Suite 300
Alexandria, VA 22314
Tel. (703) 683 7916

Defense Industry Initiative on Business
 Ethics and Conduct

c/o A.R. Yuspeh, Coordinator
Howrey & Simon
1299 Pennsylvania Avenue, N.W.
Washington, DC 20004–2402
Tel. (202) 783 0800

The Elmwood Institute
P.O. Box 5805
Berkeley, CA 94705
Tel. (510) 848 1127

Emerson Electric Centre for Business
 Ethics
John P. Keithley, Director
School of Business Administration
Saint Louis University
3674 Lindell Blvd.
St. Louis, MO 63108
Tel. (314) 977 3891

Environmental Investor Network
410 N. Bronson Ave.
Los Angeles, CA 90004–1504
Tel. (213) 466 3297

Environmental Program for Business
 Managers
New York University
48 Cooper Square
New York, NY 10003
Tel. (212) 998 7215

Environmental Report
707 State Rd., Suite 102
Princeton, NJ 08540
Tel. (609) 683 0187

Ethics in Public Service Network
c/o K. Denhardt
University of Central Florida
Department of Public Administration
Phillips Hall, Room 102
Orlando, FL 32816–1395
Tel. (407) 823 2604

Ethics, Inc.
6609 Midhill Place
Falls Church, VA 22043
Tel. (703) 536 1711

Ethics & Development Network
Colorado State University
Fort Collins, CO 90523
Tel. (709) 491 1101

Ethics Institute, The
Capital University Law and Graduate
    Centre
665 South High Street
Columbia, OH 43215–5683
Tel. (614) 445 8836 ext. 221

Ethics Institute/The Right Thing, Inc.
    (TRT)
1025 Connecticut Avenue, N.W., Suite 217
Washington, DC 20036
Tel. (701) 807 1162

Ethics Officer Association
c/o Centre for Business Ethics
Bentley College
175 Forest Street
Waltham, MA 02154–4705
Tel. (617) 891 2575

Ethics Resource Centre Inc.
Michael Daigneault, Director
1120 G Street, N.W., Suite 200
Washington, DC 20005
Tel. (202) 737 2258

Forum for Corporate Responsibility
William Stemper, Director
593 Park Avenue
New York, NY 10021
Tel. (212) 758 2245

Forum for Policy Research
Dr. Ted Goertzel
Rutgers, the State University of New
    Jersey
Department of Public
    Administration
401 Cooper Street
Camden. NJ 08102
Tel. (609) 225 6311

Foundation for Public Affairs
19th St. N.W., Suite 200
Washinton, D.C. 20036
Tel. (202) 872 1750

Freedonia Group
3570 Warrensville Ctr Rd., #201
Cleveland. OH 44122–5226
Tel. (216) 921 6800

Global Environmental Management
    Initiative
2000 L St. N.W., Suite 710

Washington, DC 20036
Tel. (202) 296 7449

Goldberg Centre for Managing Values
    and Society
Dr. Jay Halfond, Director
101 Hayden Hall
Northeastern University
Boston, MA 02115
Tel. (617) 373 3239

Great Lakes Centre, Inc.
410 Alexander St.
Rochester, NY 14607
Tel. (716) 461 5490

Hall Centre for Humanities
Bill Andrews, Director
University of Kansas
211 Wadkins Home
Lawrence, KS 66045
Tel. (913) 864 4798

Hastings Centre, The
Daniel Callahan, Director
255 Elm Road
Briarcliff Manor, NY 10510
Tel. (914) 762 8500

Henry Salvatori Centre
Charles R. Kesler, Director
Claremont McKenna College
Pitzer Hall
850 Columbia
Claremont, CA 91711
Tel. (909) 621 8201

Warren W. Hobbie Centre for Values and
    Ethics
Dr. Lawrence Brasher
Catawba College
2300 West Innes Street
Salisbury, NC 28144–2488
Tel. (704) 637 4429

Hoffberger Centre for Professional Ethics
Dr. Alfred Guy, Director
University of Baltimore
1420 N. Charles Street
Baltimore, MD 21201–5779
Tel. (410) 837 5324

HUC-UC Centre for the Study of Ethics
    and Contemporary Moral Problems
Dr. Barry Kogan

Hebrew Union College and The
  University of Cincinnati
3101 Clifton Avenue
Cincinnati, OH 45220
Tel. (513) 221 1875

The Hudson Institute of Santa Barbara
3463 State Street. Suite 520
Santa Barbara, CA 93105
Tel. (800) 582 4401
Fax (805) 569 0025

Human Economy Centre
Mankato State University
Department of Economics
MSU 14
P.O. Box 8400
Mankato, MN 56002-8400
Tel. (507) 389 2969

Human Economy Network, The
Professor Don Cole
Economics Dept.
Drew University
Madison, NJ 07940
Tel. (201) 408 3429 ext. 3429

Humanities and Philosophy Dept.
Utah Valley Community College
800 West 1200 South
Orem, UT 84058
Tel. (801) 222 8000

Humanities and the Professions
  Program
Martha Martini, Associate Director
Brandeis University
Waltham, MA 02254-9110
Tel. (617) 736 3424

Indiana University Centre on
  Philanthropy
550 West North St., Suite 301
Indianapolis, IN 46202-3162
Tel. (317) 274 4200

Institute for Absolute Ethics
Mr. McNair, Director
A Division of Executive Leadership
  Foundation
2193 Northlake Parkway
Bldg. 12, Suite 107
Tucker, GA 30084
Tel. (404) 270 1818

Institute of Applied Ethics
David N. James, Director
Department of Philosophy
Old Dominion University
Norfolk, VA 23529-0083
Tel. (804) 683 3861

Institute for Business Ethics
Laura B. Pincus, Director
DePaul University
One East Jackson Blvd., Suite 7003
Chicago, IL 60604-2287
Tel. (312) 362 8895

Institute of Business Ethics
Glen Howard, Chairman
301 East 47th Street
Suite 20-M
New York, NY 10017
Tel. (212) 832 8348

Institute for Business, Ethics, and Public
  Issues
Dr. Betty Stead, Director
College of Business Administration
University of Houston
4800 Calhoun Road
Houston, TX 77204-6283
Tel. (713) 740 4560

Institute for Business and Management
  Ethics
Dr. Samuel M. Natale, Director
Iona College
715 North Avenue
New Rochelle, NY 10801
Tel. (914) 633 2269

Institute for Christian Ethics
Stetson University
P.O. Box 8367
DeLand, FL 32720-3757
Tel. (904) 822 7364

Institute of Consumer Responsibility
6506 28th Avenue, N.W.
Seattle, WA 98115
Tel. (206) 523 0421

Institute for Ethics and Policy Studies
Craig Walton, Director
University of Nevada, Las Vegas
4505 Maryland Parkway
Las Vegas, NV 89154-5049
Tel. (702) 895 3463

Institute for Global Ethics, The
Rushworth M. Kidder, President
P.O. Box 563
11–13 Main St.
Camden, ME 04843
Tel. (207) 236 6658

Institute for Leadership and Continuing
Education
Katherine Oakley, Director
College of St. Catherine
P.O. F8
2004 Randolph Avenue
St. Paul, MN 55105
Tel. (612) 690 6219

Institute for Philosophy and Public Policy
Mark Sagoff
University of Maryland
3111 Van Munching Hall
College Park, MD 20770
Tel. (301) 405 4753

Institute for the Study of Applied and
Professional Ethics
Ronald M. Greene, Director
Dartmouth College
6031 Parker House
Hanover, NH 03755
Tel. (603) 646 1263

Institute for Sustainable Forestry, The
P.O. Box 1580
Redway, CA 95560
Tel. (707) 923 4719

Interfaith Centre on Corporate
Responsibility
Mr. Tim Smith, Director
475 Riverside Drive, Room 566
New York, NY 10115–0500
Tel. (212) 870 2295

International Association for Business
and Society
c/o Sage Publications, Inc.
2455 Teller Road
Newbury Park, CA 91320
Tel. (805) 499 0721

International Association for Business on
Society
Steven N. Brenner
Management Department

Portland State University
Portland, OR 92707–0751
Tel. (503) 725 4768

International Centre for Ethics in
Business
Richard De George, Director
School of Business
University of Kansas
Lawrence, KS 66045
Tel. (913) 864 3976

International Reform Federation
205 Tuckerton Road
Suite 200, Braddock Building
Medford, NJ 08055
Tel. (609) 985 7724

International Society of Business,
Economics, and Ethics
University of Kansas
c/o R.T. DeGeorge
Department of Philosophy
Lawrence, KS 66045–4148
Tel. (913) 864 3976

International Society for Ecological
Economics
University of Maryland
P.O. Box 1589
Solomons, MD 20688
Tel. (410) 326 0794

Investor Responsibility Research Centre
Margaret Carroll, Executive Director
1350 Connecticut Avenue, N.W.
Suite 600
Washington, DC 20036–2102
Tel. (202) 234 7500

Josephson Institute for Advancement of
Ethics
Rosa Maulini, CEO/CFO
4640 Admiralty Way, Suite 1001
Marina Del Rey, CA 90292–5179
Tel. (310) 306 1868

Kegley Institute of Ethics
Christopher Meyers, Director
California State University at Bakersfield
9001 Stockdale Highway
Bakersfield, CA 93311–1099
Tel. (805) 664 3149

Kennedy Institute of Ethics
Robert Veatch, M.D., Director
Georgetown University
1437 37th Street, N.W.
Washington, DC 20057
Tel. (202) 687 6774

Labor Research Association
145 W. 28th St., 6th Floor
New York, NY 10001–6191
Tel. (212) 714 1677

Law, Medicine, and Ethics Program
George Annas, Director
Boston University School of Public
  Health
80 East Concord Street, A-509
Boston, MA 02118
Tel. (617) 638 4626

Lincoln Centre for Ethics
College of Business
Arizona State University
Tempe, AZ 85287–4806
Tel. (602) 965 2710

Marion W. Isbell Endowment for
  Hospitality Ethics
William E. Miller, Director
School of Hotel and Restaurant
  Management
Northern Arizona University
Box 5638
Flagstaff, AZ 86011
Tel. (520) 523 2845

Media Ethics
c/o Mass Communication
Prof. Emmanuel Paraschos
Emerson College
100 Beacon Street
Boston, MA 02116–1596
Tel. (617) 351 7808

Minnesota Association for Applied
  Corporate Ethics
Andrew R. Apel, Director
College of St. Catherine
2004 Randolph Avenue
St. Paul, MN 55105
Tel. (612) 690 6819

Minnesota Centre for Corporate
  Responsibility
Robert McGregor

1000 LaSalle Ave.
Minneapolis, MN 55403–2005
Tel. (612) 962 4000

Minnesota Ethical Practices Board
S. Centennial Building, First Floor
658 Cedar Street
St. Paul, MN 55155
Tel. (612) 296 1720

Minnesota Network for Institutional
Ethics Committees
2221 University Avenue S.E. Suite 425
Minneapolis, MN 55414
Tel. (612) 331 5571 ext. 473

Kathleen Dean Moore, Chair
Department of Philosophy
Oregon State University
Hovland Hall 208
Corvallis, OR 97331–3902
Tel. (503) 737 2955

National Association of Environmental
  Prof.
5165 MacArthur Blvd. NW
Washington, DC 20016
Tel. (202) 296 1500

National Humanities Centre
Robert Connor
7 Alexander Drive
Research Triangle Park, NC 27709
Tel. (919) 549 0661

National Institute for Engineering Ethics
National Society of Professional
  Engineers
Jimmy Smith
1420 King Street
Alexandria, VA 22314–2715
Tel. (703) 684 2840

Northwest Ethics Institute
Raymond T. Cole, Executive Director
P.O. Box 15901
2729 Northeast 87th Street
Seattle, WA 98115–3455
Tel. (206) 623 1572

Olsson Centre for Applied Ethics
R. Edward Freeman
Colgate Darden Graduate School of
  Business Administration
University of Virginia

P.O. Box 6550
Charlottesville, VA 22906–6550
Tel. (804) 924 7247

Organizational Ethics Associates
3505 Arborcrest Court
Cincinnati, OH 45236
Tel. (513) 984 2820

Poynter Centre for the Study of Ethics in
    American Institutions
David H. Smith, Director
Indiana University
410 N. Park Avenue
Bloomington, IN 47405
Tel. (812) 855 0261

Principled Economics Institute
Mose Durst, President
2840 College Ave. Suite E
Berkeley, CA 94705
Tel. (510) 548 0532

Program in Applied Ethics
Lisa Newton, Director
Fairfield University
Fairfield, CT 06430
Tel. (203) 254 4000 ext. 2282

Program in Applied Ethics
John Carroll University
University Heights
Cleveland, OH 44118
Tel. (216) 397 4466

Program in Applied and Professional
    Ethics
301 Gordy Hall
Dept. of Philosophy
Ohio University
Athens, OH 45701–2979
Tel. (614) 593 4596

Programs in Business Ethics
William W. May, Director
School of Religion
University of Southern California
Los Angeles, CA 90089–0355
Tel. (213) 740 0276

Program on Ethics and Public Life
Henry Shue, Director
Cornell University
117 Stimson Hall
Ithaca, NY 14853–7101
Tel. (607) 255 8515

Program in Ethics and the Professions
Professor Dennis Thompson, Director
Harvard University
79 Kennedy Street
Cambridge, MA 02138
Tel. (617) 495 1336

Program for Ethics, Science and the
    Environment
Dept. of Philosophy
Oregon State University
Corvallis, OR 97331–3902
Tel. (503) 737 5648

Program in Ethics in Society
c/o Dept. of Philosophy
Stanford University
Stanford, CA 94305–2155
Tel. (415) 723 0997

Project on Corporate Responsibility
1609 Connecticut Avenue, N.W.
Washington, DC 20009

Public Citizen
Joan Claybrook
2000 P Street, N.W. Suite 600
Washington, DC 20036
Tel. (202) 833 3000

Public Policy Centre
Barbara Brown Zikmund, President
Hartford Seminary
77 Sherman Street
Hartford, CT 06105
Tel. (203) 232 4451

Public Policy Research Centre
University of Missouri at St. Louis
8001 Natural Bridge Road
Room 362SSB
St. Louis, MO 63121
Tel. (314) 553 5273

Research Centre on Computing and Society
Southern Connecticut State University
501 Crescent Street
New Haven, CT 06515
Tel. (203) 397 4423

Resources for Ethics and Management
Michael Rion, Principal and Founder
80 Sherman Street
Hartford, CT 06105
Tel. (203) 521 9233

Robert K. Greenleaf Centre, The
Larry Spears, Executive Director
921 E. 86th Street Suite 200
Indianapolis, IN 46240
Tel. (317) 259 1241

Henry Salvatori Centre
Prof. Charles Kelser
Claremont McKenna College
Pitzer Hall
Claremont, CA 91711
Tel. (909) 621 8201

Silha Centre for the Study of Media
    Ethics and Law
Donald Gillmor
University of Minnesota
School of Journalism
206 Church Street, S.E.
111 Murphy Hall
Minneapolis, MN 55455–0418
Tel. (612) 625 3421

Social Investment Forum
P.O. Box 57216
Washington, DC 20037
Tel. (202) 833 5522

Social Philosophy and Policy Centre
Fred Miller
Bowling Green State University
Bowling Green, OH 43403

Society for the Advancement of
    Socio-Economics
Richard Coughlin, Executive Director
2808 Central S.E.
Albuquerque, NM 87106
Tel. (419) 372 2536

Society for Business Ethics
Ronald Duska
Philosophy Department
Rosemont College
1400 Montgomery Ave.
Rosemont, PA 19010
Tel. (610) 527 0200 ext. 2346

Social Investment Forum
430 First Avenue North
Suite 290
Minneapolis, MN 55401
Tel. (612) 333 8338

Social Issues in Management (SIM)
Section of the Academy of Management

Pace University
Ken Cooper, Secretary/Treasurer
P.O. Box 39
Ada, OH 45810
Tel. (914) 923 2607

Society & the Profession: Studies in
    Applied Ethics
Lewis Hodges, Director
Washington and Lee University
Lexington, VA 24450
Tel. (703) 463 8786

Society of Whistleblowers
c/o G.W. Brown
5111 Hillrose Drive
Baxter, TN 38544
Tel. (615) 432 6046

Stein Institute of Law and Ethics
Fordham University School of Law
140 West 62nd Street
New York, NY 10023–7485
Tel. (212) 636 6838

A. Alfred Taubman Centre for Public
    Policy
Policy and American Institutions
Thomas Anton
Brown University
Box 1977
Providence, RI 02912
Tel. (401) 863 2201

TOES (The Other Economic Summit)
Winnifred Armstrong
400 Central Park W. #5P
New York, NY 10025
Tel. (212) 865 3078

University Centre for Human Values
Amy Gutman, Director
Louis Marx Hall
Princeton University
Princeton, NJ 08544–1006
Tel. (609) 258 4798

Vesper Society, The
Claude Whitmyer
151 Portero Avenue
San Francisco, CA 94103
Tel. (415) 648 2667

Warren W. Hobbie Centre for Values and
    Ethics
Dr. J. Lawrence Brasher, Director

Catawba College
2300 W. Innes Street
Salisbury, NC 28144–2488
Tel. (704) 637 4429

William B. and Evelyn Burkenroad
   Institute for the Study of Ethics &
   Leadership in Management
Arthur P. Brief, Director
A. B. Freeman School of Business
Tulane University
New Orleans, LA 70118–5669
Tel. (504) 865 5662

VENEZUELA

Dr. Rogelio Perez-Perdomo
Professor of Business Ethics

Instituto de Estudios Superiores de
   Administracion
Apartado Postal 1640
Caracas 1010–A

Vladmir Yackovlev, Executive
   Development Manager
Education & Training Centre of
   Petroleios
Apartado Postal 52042
Caracas 1050

WEST AFRICA

A.E. Ogaba-Otokpa
Buiness Research Management
P.O. Box 2384
Kano, Nigeria

Appendix B
Business ethics related sites on the World Wide Web

URLS (Web site addresses) are constantly changing. All of these were correct at time of going to press.

Academy of Management
Pace University
P.O. Box 3020, Briar Cliff Manor
New York, NY 10471

Director Nancy Urbanowixz
E-Mail nancy@academy.pace.edu
Phone 914-923-2607 **Fax** 914-923-2615
Web http://www.aom.pace.edu/

Association for Practical and Professional Ethics
410 North Park Avenue
Bloomington, IN 47405

Director Brian Schrag
E-Mail appe@indiana.edu
Web http://ezinfo.ucs.indiana.edu/
~appe/home.html

Committed to encouraging high quality interdisciplinary scholarship and teaching in practical and professional ethics.

The Beard Center for Leadership in Ethics
A.J. Palumbo School of Business
Administration
Duquestne University
Pittsburg, PA

Director Jim Weber
E-Mail weberj@duq2.cc.duq.edu
Phone 412-396-5475
Web http://www.depaul.edu/ethics/
beard.html

Hosts semi-annual distinguished speakers series, ethics workshops for executives from small and medium sized organizations.

Better Business Bureau
CBBB National Headquarters
4200 Wilson Boulevard, Suite 800
Arlington, VA 22203-1804

Web http://www.bbb.org

Helping consumers and businesses to maintain an ethical marketplace

British Petroleum's 'What we care about'
BP American Building
200 Public Square
Cleveland, OH 44114-2375

Phone 216-586-4141 **Fax** 216-586-4050
Web http://www.bp.com/care.html

The Business Enterprise Trust
204 Junipero Serra Blvd.
Stanford, CA 94305

E-Mail bet@betrust.org
Phone 415-321-5100 **Fax** 415-321-5774
Web http://www.betrust.org

Nonprofit organization that seeks to shine a spotlight on acts of courage, integrity, and social vision in business.

| **Business Ethics Teaching Society** | **Web** | http://www.usi.edu/bets |

University of Southern Indiana –
School of Business

| **The Caux Principles** | **Web** | http://www.arg.co.uk/ethical business/main.archive.htm. |

Goal: to set a world standard against which business behaviour can be measured.

The Centre for Applied Ethics	**Director**	Michael McDonald
	E-Mail	mcdonald@ethics.ubc.ca
Columbia	**Phone**	604-822-5139 **Fax** 604-822-8627
Computer Science Building,	**Web**	http://www.ethics.ubc.ca/

The University of British
Columbia
Computer Science Building,
227-6356 Agricultural Road,
Vancouver, BC
CANADA V6T 1Z2

A lot of information on ethics and related topics – highly recommended.

Center for Business Ethics	**Director**	W. Michael Hoffman
Adamain Graduate Center,	**E-Mail**	cbeinfo@bentley.edu
Room 108	**Phone**	617-891-2981 **Fax** 617-891-2988
Bentley College	**Web**	http://www.bentley.edu/resource/ cbe/
Waltham, MA 02154-4705		

Conduct conferences, publishing of proceedings, consulting for business and education organizations in setting up guidelines, programmes on business ethics.

Centre for Applied	**Director**	Jennifer Jackson
Christian Ethics	**E-Mail**	j.c.jackson@leeds.ac.uk
University of Leeds	**Phone**	011-44-113-233-3280
Department of Philosophy		**Fax** 011-44-113-233-3265
Leeds LS2 9JT	**Web**	http://www.wheaton.edu/CACE
UNITED KINGDOM		

Center for Professional Ethics	**Director**	John Wilcox
Manhattan College	**E-Mail**	jwilcox@manhattan.edu
Manhattan College Parkway,	**Phone**	718-862-7442 **Fax** 718-862-8016
Riverdale	**Web**	http://www.manhattan.edu/special/ prethics/corporat.html
New York, NY 10471		

Ethics training for organizations

Center for the Study of Ethics	**Director**	Vivian Weil
in the Professions	**E-Mail**	csep@charlie.cns.iit.edu
Illinois Institute of Technology	**Phone**	312-567-3017 **Fax** 312-567-3016
3101 S. Dearborn Street,	**Web**	http://www.iit.edu/~csep/
Room 166		

Life Sciences Bldg
Chicago, IL 60618-3793

Intercollegiate Ethics Bowl, Online Ethics Code project and publications. Links to other sites.

Ciba's Vision **Web** http://www.cibasc/com/index.html

Corporate Conduct Quarterly **Director** Jay A. Sigler
Rutgers University **E-Mail** ccq@clam.rutgers.edu
401 Cooper Street **Phone** 602-225-6353 **Fax** 602-225-6559
Camden, NJ 08102 **Web** http://camden-www.rutgers.edu/ccq/
A practical guide for corporate ethics and compliance

EthicScan Canada Limited **Web** http://www.interactive.yorku.ca/
P.O. Box 54034 ethicscan/start.html
Toronto, Ontario **Phone** 416-783-6776 **Fax** 416-783-7386
CANADA M6A 3BU
Business ethics, research, and consulting clearing-house that monitors the social and environmental performance of 1500 companies in Canada.

European Business Ethics **Director** Alison McGregor
Newtork – UK **Web** http://www.nijenrode.nl/research/
Cheltenham & Gloucester College eibe/eben/index.html
Faculty of Business Studies, **Phone** 011-1242-543-233
Broadlands **Fax** 011-1242-543–205
P.O. Box 200, The Park
Cheltenham, Glos GL50 2QF
United Kingdom

Gaia's Hive: The Ethics **Phone** 800-306-2426/514-687-2500
Resource Center **Web** http://www.per2per.com/
2325 Riverview Street (site currently under construction)
Eugene, OR 97405
Involved in developing profitable ways to apply the powerful tools of ethics.

The Heartland Institute **E-Mail** think@heartland.org
800 East Northwest Highway, **Phone** 847-202-3060 **Fax** 547-202-9799
#1080 **Web** http://www.heartland.org
Palatine, IL 60067
Nonprofit, nonpartisan organization – applies cutting edge research to state and local public issues.

Institute for Business and **Director** Laura B. Pincus, J.D.
Professional Ethics **E-Mail** lpincus@wppost.depaul.edu
DePaul University **Phone** 312-362-8895 **Fax** 312-362-6973
DePaul Center, 7002or 7033 LC **Web** http://www.depaul.edu/ethics/
Chicago, IL 60614

Institute for Global Ethics **Phone** 800-729-2615/207-236-6658
USA Headquarters **E-Mail** wethics@globalethics.org
P.O. Box 563 **Web** http://www.globalethics.org/
Camden, Maine 04843
Independent, nonsectarian and nonpolitical organization dedicated to elevating public awareness and promoting the discussion of ethics in a global text.

The Institute for the Study of Applied and Professional Ethics
Dartmouth College
6031 Parker House
Dartmouth Collge
Hanover, NH 03755

Director	Ronald M. Green
E-Mail	ethics.institute@dartmouth.edu
Phone	603-646-1263 **Fax** 603-646-2652
Web	http://www.dartmouth.edu/artsci/ ethics-inst/

Big site with a lot of information – future projects include developing undergraduate course in ethics.

International Business Ethics Institute
1129 20th Street, NW
Suite 400
Washington, D.C.

Pres	Lori A. Tansey
E-Mail	info@business-ethics.org
Phone	202-296-6938 **Fax** 202-296-5897
Web	http://www.business-ethics.org/

Nonprofit, nonpartisan education organization – founded in response to the growing need for transnationalism in the field of business ethics.

Katallattein
C/O DIBIT
Instituto Scientifico H. San Raffael
Via Olgettina, 58–20132
Milano, Italy

Director	Lorenzo Sacconi
E-Mail	sacconl@dibit.hsr.it
Phone	011-39-2643-4841
	Fax 011-39-2-2643-2765
Web	http://www.nijenrode.nl/research/ eibe/eben/homepages/inst-italy.html

Management Training: Courses on Ethics and Economics in Management

KPMG Business Ethics Practice

Director	Dr. Larry A. Ponemon
E-Mail	lponemon@kpmg.com
Phone	201-307-7947
Web	http://www.us.kpmg.com/ethics/

Mission is to be a facilitator of the best and brightest thinking taking place on business ethics, a place where business leaders can turn for guidance.

Lockheed Martin's 'Setting the Standard'
Lockheed Martin Corporation
P.O. Box 34143
Bethesda, MD 20827–0143

Director	Carol R. Marshall
E-Mail	Vice President – Ethics & Business
Web	http://www.lockheed.com/ethics/

Provides a guide to company's Code of Ethics and Business Conduct.

Markkula Center for Applied Ethics
Santa Clara University
Santa Clara, CA 95053

Director	Tom Shanks, S.J.
E-Mail	tshanks@scuacc.scu.edu
Phone	408-554-5319
Web	http://www.scu.edu/ethics/

Center designed as a source of information and to encourage dialogue on contemporary ethical issues – special feature: ethics and the election ballot '96.

Murray G. Bacon Center for Ethics in Business
Iowa State University
318 Carver Hall
Ames, IA 50011-2063

Director	Dr. Charles B. Shrader or Dr. Arthur A. Smith
E-Mail	cshrader@iastate.edu
Phone	515-294-3050
Web	http://www.public.iastate.edu/ ~BACON_CENTER/

Navran Associates	**Director**	Frank J. Navran
3037 Wembley Ridge	**E-Mail**	fj@navran.com
Atlanta, GA 30340-4716	**Phone**	800-635-9540/770-493-8886
		Fax 770-439-4162
	Web	http://www.navran.com/

Full service management training and consulting company specializing in three areas: applied (business) ethics, employee empowerment, and total service quality management.

Olsson Center for Applied	**Director**	R. Edward Freeman
Ethics	**E-Mail**	freemane@darden.qbus.
Darden Graduate School of		virginia.edu
Business	**Phone**	804-924-7133 **Fax** 804-924-3889
P.O. Box 708	**Web**	http://www.darden.virginia.edu/
Newcomb Hall Station		research/olsson/olsson.htm
Charlottesville, VA 22904		
List of books on ethics.		

The On-Line Journal of Ethics	**Web**	http://www.depaul.edu/ethics/
		ethg1.html

Students for Responsible	**E-Mail**	Mail@SRBnet.org
Business	**Phone**	415-561-6510 **Fax** 415-561-6461
Presidio Mail Post	**Web**	http://www.SRBnet.org/
P.O. Box 29221		
San Francisco, CA 94129-0221		

Student organization – believe that they can and should be in the forefront of the changing role on business in the society.

Transparency International	**Director**	Mr. Fritz Heimann
1615 L. Street, N.W.	**E-Mail**	TIUSA@aol.com
Suite 700	**Phone**	202-682-7048 **Fax** 202-857-0939
Washington, D.C. 20036	**Web**	http://www.transparency.de/

Coalition against corruption in international business transactions – headquarters in Berlin.

Wharton Ethics Program	**Director**	Thomas Donaldson
2203 Steinberg Hall	**E-Mail**	tomascol@wharton.upenn.edu
Dietrich Hall	**Phone**	215-898-1166 **Fax** 215-573-2006
Philadelphia, PA 19104-6369	**Web**	http://www.wharton.upenn.edu/

To produce outstanding research on ethical issues confronting business managers.

Woodstock Theological Center	**Director**	James L. Connor, S.J.
Georgetown University	**E-Mail**	
P.O. Box 571137	**Phone**	202-687-3532 **Fax** 202-687-5835
Washington, D.C. 20057-1138	**Web**	http://guweb.georgetown.edu/
		woodstock

Involved in various business ethics seminars and publications

The WWW Ethics Center for	**Web**	http://www.cwru.edu/affil/
Engineering & Science		wwwethics/

Appendix C
Examples of credos and corporate codes of ethics

A.G. EDWARDS AND SONS, INC. ETHICS STATEMENT

The highest standard of ethical conduct is expected of all A.G. Edwards personnel. When faced with possible conflicts of interests, we should give preference to the client and the firm over our personal interests. We should not, without management approval, use the firm of our positions in it for personal gain other than our direct compensation.

AIRBORNE EXPRESS – STATEMENT OF VALUES

Airborne's Values are the foundation for the corporate drive to excel.

- Customer satisfaction is the top priority of every employee and the purpose of every job. Cost effective ongoing achievement of customer satisfaction is the foundation of our business.
- Strategies, goals and objectives, established to ensure consistent customer satisfaction, corporate financial health, and employee development support, are clearly defined, communicated, and understood.
- Management believes in, promotes and pursues excellence throughout the organization. Excellence is expected in the quality and quantity of work done by every employee in every function, both for our customers and our fellow employees. 'Doing it right the first time' is the dominant pattern in every activity.
- Initiative and ingenuity applied to the conduct of business and the resolution of problems are encouraged and supported throughout the organization.
- The roles and responsibilities of every employee are clearly defined. Aggressive co-operative fulfillment on behalf of our customers and in support of Airborne strategies and goals is valued and commendable.
- Reward structures recognize contribution to and achievement of results that enhance customer satisfaction, improve cost effectiveness and strengthen profitability.

ALLIED SIGNAL, INC. VALUES

- Customers: Our first priority is to satisfy customers.
- Integrity: We are committed to the highest level of ethical conduct wherever we operate. We obey all laws, produce safe products, protect the environment, practice equal employment, and are socially responsible.
- People: We help our fellow employees improve their skills, encourage them to

take risks, treat them fairly, and recognize their accomplishments, stimulating them to approach their jobs with passion and commitment.

- Teamwork: We build trust and world-wide teamwork with open, candid communications up and down and across our organization. We share technologies and best practices, and team with our suppliers and customers.
- Speed: We focus on speed for competitive advantage. We simplify processes and compress cycle times.
- Innovation: We accept change as the rule, not the exception, and drive it by encouraging creativity and striving for technical leadership.
- Performance: We encourage high expectations, set ambitious goals, and meet our financial and other commitments. We strive to be the best in the world.

AMERICAN PROTECTIVE SERVICES, INC. PHILOSOPHY ON STANDARDS OF ETHICS

To conduct ourselves with unfailing commitment to the highest ethical and professional standards. To always treat others as we would like to be treated.

ARMSTRONG WORLD INDUSTRIES, INC.

Our Operating Principles:

To respect the dignity and inherent rights of the individual human being in all dealings with people.

To maintain high moral and ethical standards and to reflect honesty, integrity, reliability and forthrightness in all relationships.

To reflect the tenets of good taste and common courtesy in all attitudes, works, and deeds.

To serve fairly and in proper balance the interests of all groups associated with the business – customers, stockholders, employees, suppliers, community neighbors, government and the general public.

BAXTER HEALTHCARE CORPORATION VALUES

Respect: We will treat all individuals with dignity and respect and be honest, open and ethical in all our dealings with customers, with shareholders and with each other.

Responsiveness: We will strive continually to understand and meet the changing requirements of our customers through teamwork, empowerment and innovation.

Results: We will consistently keep our commitment to provide value to our customers, to shareholders and innovation.

CBI INDUSTRIES, INC. GUIDING PRINCIPLES

- To prudently manage our assets to provide a fair return to our shareholders.
- To be continually responsive to the changing needs of our customers.
- To emphasize the importance of our employees by: Providing an environment where people realize their full potential, where they feel good about their work, are challenged and well trained, and are able to grow both professionally and personally, thereby maximizing their contributions. Promoting employee ownership to enhance a mutuality of interest with other shareholders. Developing and

maintaining appropriate compensation, benefit and retirement programs to promote long-term employment.

- To encourage innovation which improves our business processes, practices, and products and services, in order to achieve a clear competitive advantage.
- To foster a work environment which emphasizes integrity, quality, safety, training and productivity as important and ongoing practices throughout CBI.
- To develop close relationships with our suppliers, treating them with fairness and respect, enabling them to support our commitments to our customers.
- To carry out work consistent with responsible behavior toward the environment.
- To encourage and support the activities of our employees in civic, social and professional organizations where they live and work.

CHRYSLER CORPORATION CORE BELIEFS AND VALUES

Customer Focus: Delighting our customers stands above all other values and requires:

- Exceptional products
- Exceeding expectations in quality, service, value, and things gone right
- Pleasing purchase experience
- Quick, satisfactory redress of grievances
- Effective, responsive communication
- Building trust through integrity

Inspired People: Our success will be achieved only through inspired people, operating in an environment based on:

- Mutual trust and respect
- Openness and candor
- Empowerment and teamwork
- Innovation and risk taking
- Encouraging and valuing diversity
- Integrity

Continuous Improvement: Our culture must be based on the continuous improvement of core processes in all aspects of the business by:

- Embracing change
- Eliminating waste and bureaucracy

THE CLOROX COMPANY PRINCIPLES

- We will maintain within the organization the flexibility to take full advantage of our opportunities and make the best use of our strengths and resources.
- To most effectively develop, manufacture and market our products, we have established profit centers and the centralized staff functions to support them. When justified by promising business opportunities, we will establish new profit centers and sales organizations, and new central staff services groups.
- We will delegate responsibility with accountability to the lowest practical level with the proper balance of management control to assure optimum coordination and use of our resources world-wide.
- We will encourage an innovative spirit throughout the organization.
- We will encourage our people to take the initiative in their work, understanding

that some risk is involved, but also that the potential benefits to the business often outweigh such risks.

- We continually will focus on productivity improvement, cost reduction, and quality in our operations.
- We will strive for and encourage throughout the entire Company a working alliance among all levels of the organization to achieve our common goals. We will use the 'team approach' in all our work.
- Every job in our organization should permit us to earn respect and recognition, to maintain individuality and dignity, and to experience the deep satisfaction of working with others for a common purpose.

COACHMEN INDUSTRIES, INC. PRINCIPLES

How we accomplish our mission is as important as the mission itself. Fundamental to success for the Company are those basic values which have guided our progress since our founding.

- Our Corporate motto is 'Dedicated to the Enrichment of Your Life'. This means we will do our best to provide quality products and services which will improve the lifestyle of our interests.
- Our word is our bond. Our dealers and suppliers are our partners. We endeavor to practice the Golden Rule in all of our relations with others.
- Quality is our first priority. We must achieve customer satisfaction by building quality products. This will allow us to compete effectively in the marketplace. We will always remember: No sale is a good sale for Coachmen unless it fulfills our customers' expectations.
- Customers are the focus of everything we do. As a Company, we must never lose sight of the commitment we make to those who buy our products. Our deep-seated philosophy is that 'Business is good where it is invited and stays where it is well cared for'.
- Integrity is our commitment. The conduct of our Company's affairs must be pursued in a manner that commands respect for its honesty and integrity.
- Profits are required for the company to grow and flourish. Profits are our report card of how well we provide customers with the best products for their needs.

COMPUTER SCIENCES CORPORATION MANAGEMENT PRINCIPLES EXCERPT

We will maintain the highest standards of ethics and business conduct, and operate at all times within the laws of the United States and all other countries in which we do business.

THE FINOVA GROUP CODE OF CONDUCT EXCERPT

In general, the Company strives to provide a safe, healthful and productive work environment. Each employee has a personal responsibility to other employees and to the Company to help eliminate actions or circumstances that undermine the work environment.

Ethical business conduct requires that even the appearance of inappropriate behavior be avoided as well as the behavior itself. The appearance of impropriety can often be avoided by complete and early disclosure of events to appropriate individuals within FINOVA. Disclosure and approval received before the fact will frequently avoid questions with regard to subsequent conduct. In conducting your affairs and the affairs of the Company, you should remember that over-disclosure is preferable to under-disclosure.

- **Conflicts of Interest:** FINOVA policy regarding a possible conflict of interest is based on the principle that an employee's business decisions must be made in the interests of FINOVA. In reaching these decisions, an employee cannot be influenced by personal or family considerations that consciously or unconsciously affect his or her judgment as to what is in the best interest of the Company.

    A potential conflict if interest exists of a FINOVA employee has any direct or indirect business, financial, family or other relationship with customers, competitors, suppliers or consultants/contractors that might impair the independence of any judgment the employee renders on behalf of the company.

- **Entertainment or Gifts:** Business decisions by Company employees are expected to be made only on the basis of quality, reputation, service, price and similar competitive factors. Therefore, good judgment and moderation must be exercised in the acceptance of entertainment and gifts to avoid even the appearance that a business decision has been influenced.

- **Securities Laws and Insider Information:** FINOVA policy requires full compliance with laws. Insider trading and unauthorized disclosure of information are strictly prohibited.

- **Company Records:** FINOVA's books and records must accurately reflect all measurable transactions affecting the Company, including the disposition of Company assets.

- **Confidential Information:** Employees shall at all times during the period of their employment and thereafter keep in confidence all non-public information of FINOVA. Non-public information refers to information of a confidential, proprietary, or secret nature related to FINOVA's business.

- **Information Security:** FINOVA employees have a fiduciary duty to preserve, increase the effectiveness and reliability of, and account for FINOVA information and information systems. This means that FINOVA employees must take appropriate steps to ensure that information and information systems are properly protected from a variety of threats such as error, fraud, embezzlement, sabotage, terrorism, extortion, industrial espionage, privacy violation, and natural disaster.

- **Suppliers:** FINOVA's relationships with suppliers and vendors are to be based on fundamental concepts of honesty, fairness, mutual respect and nondiscrimination. We encourage continued supplier support of all kinds that will enhance our, and their, prosperity and build sound, long-term relationships. At the same time, we respect and value healthy competition for our business. Therefore, purchasing decisions by employees must be made solely on the basis of quality, reputation, service, cost and similar competitive factors. Anyone who buys goods or services, or who in any way influences such buying, must maintain the highest standards of ethical conduct, objectivity and independence when choosing suppliers or negotiating contract terms in order to achieve the best price, value and contract terms for FINOVA.

Other topics covered in the code are:

- Antitrust
- Bribes, Kickbacks and Rebates
- Company Property
- Compliance with Laws
- Employment Practices
- Environmental Compliance
- Employee Retirement Income Security Act
- Health and Safety

- Political Contributions
- Sales and Marketing
- Taxation
- Off Duty Conduct
  (Source: FINOVA Code of Conduct Booklet)

GEORGIA GULF GUIDING PRINCIPLES

All applicable laws and regulations will be adhered to with special emphasis on meeting or exceeding environmental and safety standards.

Relationships with customers, stockholders, employees, suppliers and the communities in which we operate will be conducted in a fair, open and ethical manner. Never ending process improvement will be practiced in order to provide quality products and services which meet the needs of our customers.

Equal opportunity for advancement will be provided to all employees in an atmosphere of open communication, trust, respect, and support.

Competitive compensation and benefits, including incentive and equity pro-grammes based upon company profitability and long-term growth, recognizing both team work and individual achievement will be offered to all employees.

THE GILLETTE COMPANY VALUES

We will live by the following values:

- People: We will attract, motivate and retain high-performing people in all areas of our business. We are committed to competitive, performance-based compensation, benefits, training and personal growth based on equal career opportunity and merit. We expect integrity, civility, openness, support for others and commitment to the highest standards of achievement. We value innovation, employee involvement, change, organizational flexibility and personal mobility. We recognize and value the benefits in the diversity of people, ideas, and cultures.
- Customer Focus: We will invest in and master the key technologies vital to category success. We will offer consumers products of the highest levels of performance for value. We will provide quality service to our customers, both internal and external, by treating them as partners, by listening, understanding their needs, responding fairly and living up to our commitments. We will be a valued customer to our suppliers, treating them fairly and with respect. We will provide these quality values consistent with improving our productivity.
- Good Citizenship: We will comply with applicable laws and regulations at all government levels wherever we do business. We will contribute to the communities in which we operate and address social issues responsibly. Our products will be safe to make and to use. We will conserve natural resources and we will continue to invest in a better environment.

HORMEL FOODS CORPORATION COMPANY VALUES

Our mission will be accomplished by focusing on values relating to our consumers, customers, employees, shareholders, suppliers and the communities we serve.

Consumers – We strive to:

- anticipate, listen and respond to consumer desires for innovative new products
- develop loyal consumers through continuous improvement of product quality and consistency

- be a trustworthy provider of wholesome, nutritious and good tasting food products of excellent value

Trade Customers – We strive to:

- provide service that is innovative, responsive, reliable, courteous and professional
- develop partnerships with our customers to assure mutual success
- provide quality products supported by innovative and effective marketing programmes

Employees – We seek to provide an environment in which:

- all employees trust and respect one another
- teamwork and positive attitudes are commonplace
- all ideas are valued, respected and recognized
- continuous improvement, innovation and prevention are a way of life
- everyone strives to satisfy customers at all times

Shareholders – We are committed to:

- long-term profitability and growth
- providing optimum economic value for our shareholders
- a satisfactory return on assets employed
- making sound economic decisions based on thorough risk and return assessments

Suppliers – We develop mutually beneficial supplier relationships built on:

- trust and respect
- optimization of total value through innovation, technology and process involvement
- quality, price and service

Communities – We serve our communities by:

- operating modern, clean, safe and efficient facilities which add value to the community
- our active participation and leadership in community affairs
- leading and supporting community and national efforts to improve the environment

JOHNSON CONTROLS, INC. VISION

Our creed: We believe in the free enterprise system. We shall consistently treat our customers, employees, shareholders, suppliers and the community with honesty, dignity, fairness and respect. We will conduct our business with the highest ethical standards.

KELLOGG COMPANY PHILOSOPHY

Integrity and Ethics: Integrity is the cornerstone of our business practice. We will conduct our affairs in a manner consistent with the highest ethical standards.

LEVI STRAUSS & COMPANY ETHICAL MANAGEMENT PRINCIPLES

We need leadership that epitomizes the stated standards of ethical behavior. We must provide clarity about our expectations and must enforce these standards throughout the corporation.

MARTIN MARIETTA CORPORATION CREDO

Our foundation is INTEGRITY. We conduct our business in an open and forthright manner in strict compliance with applicable laws, rules, and regulations so that we are correctly perceived to be an ethical organization of dedicated and competent individuals of high integrity and credibility producing quality products and services that contribute significantly to our communities and to our nation.

MARTIN MARIETTA CORPORATION CODE OF ETHICS AND STANDARDS OF CONDUCT

Martin Marietta Corporation believes in the highest ethical standards. We demonstrate these beliefs through our commitments – commitments we are dedicated to fulfill.

- To our employees we are committed to just management and equality for all, providing a safe and healthy workplace, and respecting the dignity and privacy due all human beings.
- To our customers we are committed to produce reliable products and services at a fair price that are delivered on time and within budget.
- To the communities in which we live we are committed to be responsible neighbors, reflecting all aspects of good citizenship.
- To our shareholders we are committed to pursuing sound growth and earnings objectives and to exercising prudence in the use of our assets and resources.
- To our suppliers we are committed to fair competition and the sense of responsibility required of a good customer.

MOBIL CORPORATION VALUES EXCERPT

We value ethics to conduct our business to the highest ethical standards and in compliance with all applicable laws and regulations.

OKLAHOMA NATURAL GAS COMPANY CORE VALUES

Ethics: Our actions are founded on trust, honesty, and integrity through open communications and adherence to the highest standards of business ethics.

PET INCORPORATED VALUES

- Ethics and compliance with all applicable laws
- Consumer and customer driven in the development and delivery of all products and services
- Good citizenship in all the communities where we have operations

- Company-wide continuous improvement activities using a team approach
- The development and training of our employees
- An environment which supports the creativity and initiative of all our employees
- Equal opportunities for all employees
- Fulfillment of our commitment – what we say we do, and we do do

PRINCIPAL FINANCIAL GROUP CORE VALUES EXCERPT

Ethics: We operate in an ethical and legal manner. We are dedicated to being honest and straightforward in our dealings with customers, the public and each other

Social Responsibility: The Principal is a responsible member of the communities in which it operates. We do our best to support society, the global community, the economy, the insurance and financial services industries, and the nations, states and local communities where our employees and customers work and live.

ROCKWELL INTERNATIONAL CORPORATION CREDO

We believe maximizing the satisfaction of our customers is our most important concern as a means of warranting their continued loyalty.

We believe in providing superior value to customers through high-quality, technologically-advanced, fairly-priced products and customer service, designed to meet customer needs better than the alternatives.

We believe Rockwell people are our most important assets, making the critical difference in how well Rockwell performs, and, through their work and effort, separating Rockwell from all competitors.

We believe we have an obligation for the well-being of the communities in which we live and work.

We believe excellence is the standard for all we do, achieved by encouraging and nourishing:

- Respect for the individual
- Honest, open communication
- Individual development and satisfaction
- A sense of ownership and responsibility for Rockwell's success
- Participation, co-operation and teamwork
- Creativity, innovation and initiative
- Prudent risk-taking
- Recognition and rewards for achievement

We believe success is realized by:

- Achieving leadership in the markets we serve
- Focusing our resources and energy on global markets where our technology, knowledge, capabilities and understanding of customers combine to provide the opportunity for leadership
- Maintaining the highest standards of ethics and integrity in every action we take, in everything we do

We believe the ultimate measure of our success is the ability to provide a superior value to our shareowners, balancing near-term and long-term objectives to achieve both competitive returns on investment, and consistent increased market value.

WARNER-LAMBERT COMPANY CREED

- To our customers: We commit ourselves to anticipating customer needs and responding first with superior products and services. We are committed to continued investment in the discovery of safe and valuable products to enhance people's lives.
- To our colleagues: We commit ourselves to attracting and retaining excellent people, and providing them with an open and participative work environment, marked by equal opportunity for personal growth. Performance will be evaluated candidly, on the basis of fair and objective standards. Creativity, speed of action, and openness to change will be prized and rewarded. Colleagues will be treated with dignity and respect. They will have the shared responsibility for continuously improving the performance of the company and the quality of work life.
- To our shareholders: We commit ourselves to providing fair and attractive economic returns to our shareholders. We are prepared to take prudent risks to achieve sustainable long-term corporate growth.
- To our business partners: We commit ourselves to dealing with our suppliers and other business partners fairly and equitably, recognizing our mutual interests.
- To society: We commit ourselves to being responsible corporate citizens, actively initiating and supporting efforts concerning the health of society and stewardship of the environment. We will work to improve the vitality of the world-wide communities in which we operate.

Above all, our dealings with these constituencies will be conducted with the utmost integrity, adhering to the highest standards of ethical and just conduct.

Appendix D
Example of an ethics audit
report: The Body Shop*

D.1 MEASURING UP

The Body Shop publishes its first Values Report this January. This Report comprises three statements covering the Company's track record on the environmental, animal protection and the human relationships within our business.

D.1.1 The road ahead

The Body Shop is a large, multi-local business. It is not a one-woman show, but a global operation with franchisees running their own businesses and thousands of people working towards common goals. It is a curious, committed and passionate work in progress.

We want it to be obvious for anyone to see why we do what we do – and how we do It. This applies to every level of our business, from the manufacture and marketing of skin and hair care products to our activities as a socially responsible company. But we've had to make our own roadmap – there are few signposts along the way. Our Values Report is an ambitious document which defines our future challenges. There is much in the Report that delights us but more than a little that we are very disappointed by.

There is clearly a lot to take in at once. So, we've summarized it to give a sample of the highlights and low points. The title says it all. This is our – and your – yardstick to assess The Body Shop performance. It is only the first of many.

D.1.2 Why?

In January 1996 The Body Shop releases more details on its ethical activities than ever before.

It has done this because:

■ The Company believes that business has a moral responsibility to tell the truth about itself and face up to things that need to change;
■ The Body Shop is a high profile advocate of social and environmental causes. Sometimes this kind of advocacy upsets people, so if a company wants the licence to campaign on public issues it must demonstrate its own commitment to reflection and self-improvement on issues like environmental protection, animal protection and human rights;

* Reproduced from *The Values Report 1995*, with the permission of The Body Shop International PLC.

■ For The Body Shop to continue to mix business with politics, cosmetics with campaigns, it has to take its supporters and stakeholders (including customers, employees and suppliers) along with it.

> I would love it if every shareholder of every company wrote a letter every time they received a company's annual report and accounts. I would like them to say something like: Okay, that's fine, very good. But where are the details of your environmental audit? Where are the details of your accounting to the community? Where is your social audit?
>
> (Anita Roddick, BODY AND SOUL 1991)

D.1.3 What?

The instrument used to release details of our ethical performance is called the *Values Report 1995*. Each component of the Report has an element of independent verification in line with established best practice where this exists. There are three components:

(a) Social audit

A social audit requires measurement of performance against policies, internal management systems, programmes and targets, stakeholder expectations and external benchmarks. During 1994/5 The Body Shop worked with the New Economics Foundation (NEF) on a consultation process with our stakeholders. The results, verified by NEF, are published in the Social Statement.

(b) Environmental audit

The Environmental Statement section of our Report covers issues at our principal operating sites in Watersmead (Littlehampton, UK), Wick (Littlehampton, UK) and Wake Forest (North Carolina, USA).

In all three cases our environmental management systems and data have been subject to external verification (audit) in line with the provisions of the EU Eco-Management and Audit Scheme (EMAS). The Environmental Statement also includes information from international markets around the world.

(c) Animal protection audit

The Animal Protection Statement section of our Report includes an independently verified assessment of our Against Animal Testing procedures and purchasing criteria according to International Standards Organisation standard ISO 9002. This standard is aimed particularly at assessing conformance to specified requirements by a company's suppliers.

D.1.4 How?

If the word 'audit' conjures up for you the drier areas of high finance, you should know that in recent years many new types of audit – environmental, medical, and ethical – have emerged which have little to do with money, and everything to do with responsible management. The Body Shop approach to ethical business operates on three levels:

(a) Compliance

The first step is to take into account the responsibilities of business not to abuse people, the environment or animals wherever the Company operates. This means opening up to defined standards of human rights, social welfare and worker safety, environmental protection and, where relevant, wider ethical issues like animal protection.

(b) Disclosure

The second step is for companies to go beyond compliance with standards and be open about their records on social, environmental and animal protection. This transparency develops relationships of trust and sets an example.

Only through public disclosure can a real process of dialogue and discussion with stakeholders be achieved and the right direction charted for the future. The *Values Report 1995* also includes a report on our approach to Ethical Auditing.

(c) Campaigning

The really committed socially responsible business takes the third step after compliance and disclosure. This is to play an active part in agitating and campaigning for positive change in the way the business world works, with the ultimate aim of making a positive impact on the world at large.

It requires a political outlook to campaign. This does not mean party politics but it does require the conviction of stakeholders to come together on a common platform to fight for a fairer world (listed on the back page are some areas we have campaigned on).

D.2 OUR SOCIAL STATEMENT

D.2.1 How do you measure the way people think?

How do you measure the way people think? That is the overriding challenge of social auditing, which tries to apply tangible measures such as numbers and statistics to intangible human thoughts and emotions. The Body Shop began looking for a way to measure its social performance in 1993.

We could quantify our social impact in obvious ways: numbers of people employed, statistics on equal opportunities, pay and benefits, amounts of money given to charity. But we needed more than that. What opinions do people have about the quality of The Body Shop's environmental and social mission or the quality of the Company's contribution to the community? And what people should we be asking? Which stakeholder views are most important?

Because there was no international precedent and very few people with real experience in this field, we spent a year working out how to audit our impact on people. The experiences of three other organizations proved invaluable: Ben & Jerry's, the US Ice cream manufacturer, Traidcraft, the UK fair trade organiza-tion and Sbn, the Danish regional bank. All three had a good track record in public disclosure and though they all used different methods appropriate to their organizations, they had each been successful.

Keeping these successes in mind, we worked with the New Economics Foundation, a UK-based think tank, to tailor a social audit methodology that would be appropriate to an organisation as large and complex as The Body Shop. Our audit involved a mix of focus groups, market research-style questionnaires, face-to-face interviews and data collection. The information was collected group by group from each of our stakeholders – staff, customers, franchisees, suppliers and so on – so that is the way it appears in the final Social Statement. In all, more than 5,000 people were consulted.

What follows are some of the highlights and low points, together with an indication of what the Company is doing to address problems. The results will continue to be discussed in focus groups during 1996 so that future action plans can be fine-tuned and prioritised with the on-going aim of making The Body Shop more efficient, more accountable and still more effective.

D.2.2 Employees

(a) Good news

83 per cent of employees agreed with the founders' statement that 'Our success depends on the commitment, skill, creativity and good humour of our employees'

93 per cent of employees either agreed or strongly agreed that The Body Shop lives up to its mission on the issues of environmental responsibility and animal testing.

79 per cent of employees either agreed or strongly agreed that working for The Body Shop has raised their awareness of pressing global issues.

75 per cent of employees say they are proud to tell others they are part of The Body Shop.

71 per cent of employees enjoy their job.

(b) Bad news

45 per cent of employees were quite or very dissatisfied with the way The Body Shop encourages them to obtain qualifications.

26 per cent of employees could not recall ever having had a job appraisal.

23 per cent of employees felt the best way for them to develop their career was to change companies.

53 per cent of employees either disagreed or strongly disagreed that the behaviour and decision-making of managers was consistent throughout the Company.

(c) The future

- A new strategy for learning and development (including the issue of in service qualifications)
- Reinforcement of career development
- Reinforcement of new appraisal procedures
- Improved internal communications, particularly via managers
- Now initiatives on equal opportunities

D.2.3 International franchisees

(a) Good News

100 per cent of international head franchisees agreed or strongly agreed that The Body Shop does not test or commission tests on animals and that the Company takes active steps to make its business more environmentally responsible.

96 per cent of international franchisees said The Body Shop mission of dedicating its business to the pursuit of social and environmental change is important to them.

78 per cent of international franchisees agreed or strongly agreed that The Body Shop reasoning for campaigns is usually well communicated and thoughtful.

91 per cent of international franchisees were either satisfied or very satisfied with communications on environmental management and auditing.

(b) Bad news

43 per cent of international franchisees either disagreed or strongly disagreed that head office departments or divisions responded to inquiries and information needs quickly.

43 per cent of international franchisees were dissatisfied with the efficiency of communications on things that affect their market.

39 per cent of international franchisees either disagreed or strongly disagreed that they received frequent feedback on their performance from The Body Shop.

35 per cent of international franchisees had no opinion or disagreed that The Body Shop portrays its business practices accurately to the public.

(c) The future

- Improved performance feedback
- Reinforcement of understanding of information audit procedures for ensuring accuracy of public statements
- Closer involvement of international franchisees in marketing and customization of retail practice

D.2.4 Local (sub-)franchisees

(a) Good news

94 per cent of UK and 73 per cent of US local franchisees either agreed or strongly agreed that The Body Shop campaigns effectively on human rights, environmental protection and animal protection.

90 per cent of UK and 80 per cent of US local franchisees felt that the Company provides reliable and honest information to them on social, environmental and animal protection issues.

81 per cent of UK local franchisees are quite or very satisfied with the service levels of product deliveries.

97 per cent of US local franchisees agree or strongly agree that The Body Shop mission is important to them.

(b) Bad news

41 per cent of UK and 61 per cent of US local franchisees were dissatisfied with the frequency of feedback on performance.

More than one-fifth of local UK and US franchisees expressed no opinion on the majority of issues related to doing business with The Body Shop.*

43 per cent of UK and 64 per cent of US local franchisees disagreed that The Body Shop sales divisions communicated their long-term strategy clearly to the franchisees.

(c) The future

- Development of better indicators of performance for both franchisees and sales divisions

- More involvement of franchisees in decision-making
- New initiatives on communications

D.2.5 Customers

(a) Good news

The Body Shop scored an average of 9 out of 10 for its against animal testing stance among British customers.

The Body Shop scored an average of 7.8 out of 10 for its commitment to environmental responsibility.

The Body Shop scored an average of 7.5 out of 10 for campaigning effectively on human rights, environmental protection and animal protection.

(b) Bad news

Many customers in the US and UK are still confused by what is natural.

UK customer complaints rose from 18.3 per 100,000 transactions in 1992/93 to 20.9 per 100,000 transactions in 1994/95.

(c) The future

- Better indicators for monitoring customer satisfaction
- A special initiative on customer education on natural ingredients
- Improved audit of this area in future years

D.2.6 Suppliers

(a) Good news

95 per cent of suppliers agree or strongly agree that The Body Shop takes active steps to make its business more environmentally responsible.

93 per cent of suppliers believe the Company campaigns effectively on human rights, environmental protection and animal protection.

75 per cent of suppliers either agreed or strongly agreed that The Body Shop business practices reflect a high standard of ethics.

Prompt payment, clarity of delivery and purchase order requirements and fairness of quality assurance arrangements were all recognised by 80 per cent or more of suppliers.

(b) Bad news

One-fifth of suppliers disagreed or strongly disagreed that The Body Shop purchasing and logistics functions are well structured and efficient.

28 per cent either disagreed or strongly disagreed that it is easy to identify the right decision-makers within The Body Shop.

8 per cent of suppliers claimed to have experienced ethically corrupt behaviour in their dealings with individual members of The Body Shop staff.

(c) The future

- A code of conduct for purchasing staff to ensure probity at all times
- Improvements in business forecasting
- Improvements in communication with and support for suppliers

D.2.7 Communities in Trade Not Aid partnerships

(a) Good news

There was consensus from Trade Not Aid partners consulted by an independent organisation that there had been 'a range of social gains from The Body Shop relationship.'

Spending on both Trade Not Aid raw materials and Trade Not Aid accessory items increased by approximately one-third between 1993/94 and 1994/95. In 1994/95 more than £2 million worth of accessory items was purchased from Trade Not Aid suppliers.

In February 1995 there were 12 Trade Not Aid suppliers.

(b) Bad news

Forecasting of future ordering volumes from Trade Not Aid suppliers has been problematic for The Body Shop. This has caused difficulties for some suppliers.

Some of the Trade Not Aid links are not commercially viable in the conventional sense and have a high level of dependency on orders from The Body Shop.

(c) The future

- Improvements in business planning and forecasting to increase our purchasing
- Establishment of formal trading agreements with Trade Not Aid suppliers
- Improvements in methods for assessing the social benefits of trade links

D.2.8 Shareholders

(a) Good news

90 per cent of shareholders agreed or strongly agreed that The Body Shop takes active steps to make its business more environmentally responsible.

76 per cent of shareholders agreed or strongly agreed that the Company's business practices reflect a high standard of ethics.

78 per cent of shareholders were satisfied with the information they receive on The Body Shop financial performance.

75 per cent of shareholders either agreed or strongly agreed that the Company's annual report and accounts provide a comprehensive picture of The Body Shop overall performance.

(b) Bad news

29 per cent of shareholders either disagreed or strongly disagreed that the Company enjoys the trust of the financial community.

33 per cent of shareholders either had no opinion or disagreed that The Body Shop has a clear long-term business strategy. The Body Shop share price fell from a high of £2.63 on 11 May 1994 to a low of £1.68 on 8 February 1995, ending the financial year 1994/95 at £1.82.

(c) The future

While The Body Shop remains a public company it will:
- aim to maximise shareholder interests while also balancing the needs of other stakeholders

- develop and build relationships with shareholders and prospective shareholders
- operate a progressive dividend policy

D.2.9 Community involvement

(a) Good news

In 1994/95 The Body Shop directly employed staff gave an estimated 19,500 hours to projects in the community.

87 per cent of recipients of funding from The Body Shop Foundation ('The Foundation') either agreed or strongly agreed that The Body Shop takes active steps to make its business more environmentally responsible.

More than 90 per cent of The Foundation grantees were satisfied with: (i) the dedication to issues, (ii) integrity and transparency and (iii) clarity and competence of individuals who they dealt with in The Body Shop Foundation.

In 1994, The Body Shop donated 2.3 per cent of pre-tax profits to charity. This compares favourably with other UK companies, eg: 2.16 per cent for the Co-operative Bank and 0.44 per cent for Boots.

(b) Bad news

75 per cent of The Body Shop employees do not participate actively in the community volunteering programme.

Nearly half of grantees either disagreed or strongly disagreed that it was easy to identify the right decision-makers in The Body Shop Foundation.

Nearly one-third of grantees felt that The Foundation decision-making was unnecessarily slow.

26 per cent of grantees disagreed that The Body Shop Foundation communicates its grant making policy clearly in selected areas.

(c) The future

- Launch of a new six-point plan for the encouragement of community volunteering
- Formalization of arrangements for community liaison around The Body Shop's principal operating sites
- Implementation of a ten-point plan by The Body Shop Foundation to improve effectiveness and communications
- Introduction of better performance indicators and service standards for the Foundation

D.2.10 Campaigns (and relations with non-governmental organizations)

The Body Shop has taken public stances on moral issues for many years. The issues have embraced the environment, animal protection and human rights. Sometimes the campaigns have sparked international controversy, for example our two year campaign for ecological and economic justice for the Ogoni in Nigeria. Sometimes they have helped raise public consciousness, like our persistent campaigning against animal testing in the cosmetics industry. Sometimes they sink without a trace. Here are some of the recent highlights and low points of our public campaigning.

(a) Campaign highlights

We collected more than 3 million petition signatures from 927 shops in 30 countries around the world calling for stricter enforcement of the Convention on International Trade in Endangered Species. The petitions were delivered personally to US Secretary of State Bruce Babbitt.

With Greenpeace, Amnesty International, Friends of the Earth and others, we lobbied in 10 countries for justice for the Ogoni and the release of Ogoni leader Ken Saro-Wiwa. Parliamentary support and international awards for Ken Saro-Wiwa followed.

In an opinion survey 83 per cent of non-governmental campaign groups in the UK agreed or strongly agreed that The Body Shop takes active steps to make its business environmentally responsible.

80 per cent of non-governmental organisations identified The Body Shop mission to dedicate its business to the pursuit of social and environmental change as important to them.

74 per cent of organisations were satisfied with the dedication to issues of individuals they dealt with at The Body Shop.

(b) Campaign low points

The barbaric execution of Ken Saro-Wiwa and eight other innocent Ogoni leaders by the Nigerian military authorities and the inaction of Shell to intervene on their behalf.

36 per cent of non-governmental organisations were quite or very dissatisfied with The Body Shop delivery on what we said we would do in a 'timely and effective manner'.

Only 37 per cent of non-governmental organisations agreed that it was easy to find the right decision-makers in The Body Shop.

(c) The future

- Better indicators of performance in campaigns
- Better communications with campaign partners and the wider community of campaign groups

Footnote All of our commitments for the future are just a sample of what we intend to do. They are listed here simply for illustrative purposes. The full lists of commitments for each stakeholder group may be found in the Social Statement available on The Body Shop Internet site www.think-act-change.com

D.3 OUR ENVIRONMENTAL STATEMENT

D.3.1 Can a company ever be environmentally friendly?

Can a company ever be environmentally friendly? No, is the simple answer. But a company can go a long way towards it by minimizing the impact it makes. One crucial thing it needs to do is measure the impact. The Body Shop has been doing this for four years.

The Company's fourth Environmental Statement follows in the tradition of previous publications. Like the first three Green Books, it was prepared in line with the European Union Eco-Management and Audit Scheme (EMAS) – the toughest international environmental standard available. The Statement was independently verified and contains many targets for the future.

The Environmental Statement describes progress and challenges in each of the ten main areas of our environmental policy.

D.3.2 Thinking globally

(a) Our policy

The Body Shop International's business is the manufacture and retailing of skin and hair care products. We have developed this policy as a constant reminder of our responsibilities to act in order to protect the environment both globally and locally. We want to do things better than they have been done before and we want to include our staff franchisees, subsidiaries and suppliers in making that happen.

(b) Progress and challenges

In April 1992 The Body Shop International franchisees committed themselves to implement a programme of environmental management based in their own operations around the world. Every franchisee committed to undertaking an environmental review by 28 February 1994. This was achieved. Based on calculations for 1994/95, our international markets (excluding the UK and the US) were responsible for energy use contributing an estimated 37,775 tonnes of CO_2 towards global warming. 15,196 tonnes of CO_2 were due to air freighting alone.

(c) The future

■ We have committed that by the year 2000 the proportion of export freight going by air will be reduced to no more than 2.5 per cent of total export freight.

D.3.3 Achieving excellence

(a) Our policy

Sound environmental management is both good house-keeping and good sense. Through regular reviews and assessments of our operations around the world, we will set ourselves clear targets and time-scales within which to meet those targets.

(b) Progress and challenges

In 1994/95 our three main manufacturing and headquarters sites in the UK and the US were all audited and externally verified to European Union Eco-Management and Audit regulation standards. This was the fourth time around for our principal site at Watersmead, Littlehampton but the first time for our Wick, Littlehampton and Wake Forest, North Carolina sites. The details of environmental performance on these sites are all contained in the 1995 Environmental Statement.

(c) The future

■ Our vision is that one day The Body Shop will be totally environmentally accountable – not just in UK and US Company facilities, but in every franchised shop, every office, every warehouse and every manufacturing facility around the world. To this end we have committed that by 1997 all principal UK and US operating sites will be audited and verified to EMAS standards – this will include verification of our Glasgow soap-making facility Soapworks. By 1998, all of our manufacturing markets will produce independent environmental statements, and by the year 2000 all international markets will do the same.

D.3.4 Searching for sustainability

(a) Our policy

Sustainable development is about achieving a fairer and safer world for future generations. At all levels of operation – in our head office, in our manufacturing facilities; in our subsidiaries and franchises, and in our retail outlets around the world – we will try to use renewable resources wherever feasible and we will conserve natural resources where renewable options are not available. This will apply in particular to our purchasing which will be supported by a system of product stewardship including ecological assessments of our products and packaging.

(b) Progress and challenges

At 28 February 1995, 86 per cent of our spending with raw materials and stock suppliers (excluding accessory items) for manufacturing on our Watersmead site was covered by our environmental rating scheme. For the first time, in 1994/95, 19 suppliers reached a three star rating in the scheme. More than 50 per cent of raw materials spending for Watersmead was covered by our Ecological Life Cycle Assessment programme which requires very detailed research on the environmental sustainability of ingredients used in The Body Shop Products.

(c) The future

■ We have committed to completing on-site ethical audits of all our third party contract manufacturers by 1998. We have said that by the year 2000, all of our T-shirts will be made from cotton certified as organic, or other environmentally acceptable fibres. Also by the year 2000, we will double the number of raw materials suppliers with a three star rating in the environmental rating scheme and all wood used for products and shop fitting will be certified as sustainable.

D.3.5 Managing growth

(a) Our policy

The quest for economic growth is the cause of much environmental and human exploitation. Our future planning will be balanced between the environmental implications of our business and economics. We will devote increasing efforts to establishing non-exploitative trading arrangements with communities in less developed countries as a means to protecting their cultures and their environments.

(b) Progress and challenges

The New Economics Foundation has calculated that for every £1,000 value added to the British economy 0.22 tonnes of the global warming gas CO_2 is emitted to the atmosphere. The Body Shop operations in the UK contribute 0.18

tonnes CO_2 per £1,000 value added or 0.14 tonnes if the Company's investment in renewable energy is taken into account.

(c) The future

■ The Body Shop has committed that by 1997 it will agree a timetable for compensating for all electricity needs of factories, warehouses and head offices in the UK through investments in renewable energy.

D.3.6 Managing energy

(a) Our policy

Global warming, acid rain, nuclear waste – problems caused by the misuse and abuse of energy resources provide urgent reasons to achieve the highest possible energy efficiency in our operations. We will work towards replacing what we must use with renewable resources.

(b) Progress and challenges

In 1994/95 The Body Shop Watersmead site consumed 535 kWh (units) of electricity for every 1,000 packs of product distributed from its UK warehouse. This compares with 850 kWh in 1991/92 – a 37 per cent reduction over four years. But electricity and gas use on the three main sites was still responsible for CO_2 emissions of 9,243 tonnes during the year. The Body Shop investment in wind energy was responsible for replacing 3.15 million kWh into the UK national grid – or approximately 32 per cent of the electricity consumption of the Watersmead and Wick sites combined. Shops in the UK used an average of 39,237 kWh during 1994/95 – 18.6 per cent less than in 1991/92. The UK distribution fleet of 12 trucks consumed 438,598 litres of fuel and were responsible for emissions of 1,165 tonnes of CO_2.

(c) The future

■ We have committed that by the year 2000, all UK shops will reduce their average annual energy use to 35,000 kWh. By the year 2010, the UK distribution fleet will eliminate or compensate for all of its CO_2 emissions through tree planting and other initiatives.

D.3.7 Managing waste

(a) Our policy

We believe that wealthy societies have an urgent and overwhelming moral obligation to avoid waste. As a responsible business we adopt a four-tier approach: first reduce; next reuse; then recycle; and finally, as a last resort we will dispose of waste using the safest and most responsible means available.

(b) Progress and challenges

In 1994/95 The Body Shop consumed nearly 50 million litres of water on its three main sites. In 1994/95 543 tonnes of cardboard was recycled on the three main sites along with 42.5 tonnes of office paper and 137.5 tonnes of polyethylene and polypropylene packaging. In 1994/95 985,410 refills were given to UK customers and 2.39 million containers were collected for recycling. In 1995, we commenced trials of a new in-store refill bar in eight countries.

(c) The future

■ The Body Shop has committed that by 1998, the annual disposal of surplus stock will be no more than two per cent of the cost of sales from the BSI warehouse to franchisees and Company shops. The number of refills in UK stores will increase to five per cent of customer transactions and the recovery of recyclable plastic will increase to 10 per cent of plastic issued. By 1999 the number of UK customers given a plastic carrier bag will reduce to 40 per cent.

D.3.8 Controlling pollution

(a) Our policy

Pollution is a special form of environmental abuse – it is more than exploitation; it involves degradation and despoliation. Environmental damage is an inevitability of most industry practice, but we are committed to protecting the quality of the land, air and water on which we depend.

(b) Progress and challenges

At the end of 1995, construction of an ecological waste water treatment plant was being completed on the Watersmead site to complement the existing ultrafiltration treatment plant. In 1994/95 the average amount of organic material being discharged to the public sewer from the Watersmead site was 398 kg Chemical Oxygen Demand per week, compared with 399 kg per week in 1991/92. This represented 31.5 per cent of the legally permitted maximum.

(c) The future

■ By the year 2000, ecological waste water treatment systems will also be installed on the Wick and Wake Forest sites, and all solid waste arising from waste water treatment on the Watersmead site will be used on-site through ecological treatment processes.

D.3.9 Operating safely

(a) Our policy

The reputation of any business rests an safety – for staff, for customers and for the community in which the business operates. We will minimize risk in every one of our operations – from ensuring the safety and quality of our products to good neighbour policies in the communities where we work. We will maintain emergency plans to safeguard the environment within our workplace in the event of fires, floods or other natural disasters.

(b) Progress and challenges

During 1994/95 all emergency plans for our main operating sites were updated.

(c) The future

- Emergency plans will continue to be updated on a regular basis.

D.3.10 Obeying the law

(a) Our policy

The minimum requirement for any responsible business is to observe legal requirements and regulations wherever the Company operates. We will ensure that environmental laws are complied with at all times and in the event of difficulties these will be reported to the appropriate regulatory authorities.

(b) Progress and challenges

During 1994/95 we experienced difficulties complying with part of our waste water permit for the Wick site and on one occasion failed to comply with our waste water discharge permit on the Watersmead site. The regulator, Southern Water, was directly involved in both cases.

(c) The future

- With the upgrading of waste water treatment facilities on both Wick and Watersmead sites in 1995/96, we expect compliance with permit conditions not to pose difficulties in the future.

D.3.11 Raising awareness

(a) Our policy

Our mission is to forge a new and more sustainable ethic for business. We want our efforts to set a precedent far others. We are committed to continuous education for our staff on environmental issues. We are committed to freedom of information and full public disclosure of the results of our environmental assessments.

(b) Progress and challenges

Staff numbers trained on environmental topics continued to rise in 1994/95. There are now six basic training packs in circulation covering energy, waste, green consumerism, transport, water and sustainability. International environmental campaigns were run in many markets in 1994/95 – most notably on the Convention on Trade in Endangered Species which raised three million petition signatures world-wide. Markets joined environmental groups around the world to campaign on issues as diverse as waste and energy efficiency, recycling, and endangered species. In 1994 we published our third environmental statement.

(c) The future

- The Body Shop has committed to run three major international environmental campaigns by the year 2000.

We believe that public disclosure of environmental performance is a vital prerequisite for more sustainable operations in industry.

(Anita Roddick)

D.4 OUR ANIMAL PROTECTION STATEMENT

D.4.1 Can a skin and hair care company really protect animals?

Can a skin and hair care company really protect animals? Yes. The Body Shop believes it has a moral responsibility for animal protection. The term 'animal protection' encompasses a wide range of issues and philosophies embracing animal rights and animal welfare. The Body Shop approach to animal protection focuses on our Against Animal Testing policy and our support for organizations trying to prevent the extinction of species in the wild. We are also concerned about the use of animal derived ingredients in our products.

Since 1986, The Body Shop has maintained systems to ensure that suppliers of raw materials comply with the Company's strict policy of opposition to animal testing in the cosmetics and toiletries industry. For many years monitoring of suppliers has been based on six-monthly declarations of compliance with The Body Shop purchasing rule which each manufacturer must complete for each ingredient which they supply for inclusion in the Company's cosmetic and toiletry products.

In 1994, The Body Shop also devised a supplier rating system similar to its environmental rating system. This scheme looks at a wide range of criteria, for example support for non-animal testing research and level of involvement in the pharmaceutical industry (which may require animal testing for regulatory reasons).

In early 1995 The Body Shop subjected all of its supplier monitoring procedures to independent assessment against an International Standards Organisation quality management standard ISO 9002. To achieve this standard an organization must be able to satisfy the assessor that written procedures and systems are followed and if problems arise they are dealt with immediately. The Body Shop believes that independent assessment is the key to consumer confidence in the non-animal testing claims of the cosmetics and toiletries industry. Lots of companies make claims about not testing on animals, but it is undeniable that most materials have been tested by someone, somewhere at some time. The only real way to judge a company is on the basis that: (i) it does not test or commission animal tests on finished products; (ii) it does not test or commission animal tests on raw materials; and (iii) it has auditable systems for exerting pressure on suppliers to cease testing and that these systems can be independently assessed.

The Body Shop Against Animal Testing Policy is updated in line with what we believe is best practice and in discussion with animal welfare groups around the world.

At December 1995, the policy was as set out opposite. In each policy area we describe the progress the Company is making together with challenges we see for the future.

D.4.2 Against animal testing

(a) Our policy

The Body Shop is opposed to the use of animals in testing raw materials or products for the cosmetics and toiletries industry. We aim to eliminate the use of such tests world-wide and campaign to that end

We neither test our products or ingredients on animals, nor do we commission others to do so. We never have and we never will

We campaign to end animal testing in the cosmetics industry:

by increasing staff and public awareness of the issue. We actively promote our opposition to animal testing by making educational information and full product details available to our customers:

by linking with animal protection organisations ground the world, to lobby to end animal testing in the cosmetic industry.

(b) Progress and challenges

In 1995, a new in-store leaflet was produced on animal testing and endangered species. The leaflet explained The Body Shop Against Animal Testing Policy and how they are implemented. In 1994/95, The Body Shop continued to support the British Union for the Abolition of Vivisection in their campaign to make the European Union 'ecolabel' include animal welfare criteria. Sadly, this campaign has still not succeeded. The Company successfully lobbied European Commission officials and the UK government on product labelling under the European Union Cosmetics Directive. Mainstream industry had been arguing for labelling measures which would have effectively prevented The Body Shop and other companies from using campaign messages on products.

(c) The future

■ In 1996 the Company will promote an international campaign aimed at securing a global ban on animal testing of cosmetics. Pressure needs to be especially strong in Europe and North America, where many of the world's most powerful lobbies for continued testing exist. This campaign will be done in full consultation and concert with colleagues in the animal welfare movement.

D4.3 Alternative tests

(a) Our policy

We promote and use existing alternative tests and financially support their further development:

The ratification of alternatives will be a great step forward in ending animal testing. We will continue to support those initiatives which will most effectively achieve this end.

We ensure product safety by using existing ingredients and conducting non animal testing. We also use human volunteers to evaluate products prior to launch and monitor customer response in use.

(b) Progress and challenges

The Body Shop Foundation has supported research into alternatives to animal testing since 1991. From 1995, £20,000 per annum for three years is going to the Dr Hadwen Trust for research on skin sensitivity.

The Body Shop employs non-animal laboratory test methods to establish the safety of its own products alongside human volunteer tests and examination of the scientific literature. Between April and April 1995, 417 tests were carried out on members of staff who volunteered for preliminary 'safety-in-use' tests on 85 products. 1539 safety-in-use tests were carried out on staff volunteers for 123 products. 645 external volunteer patch tests were carried out by independent laboratories (103 products) alongside 70 internal volunteer patch tests (27 products).

(c) The future

■ As only a small part of the cosmetics and toiletries industry, The Body Shop does not have the scientific and technical leverage of the big companies. Scientific breakthroughs on alternatives to animal testing will depend largely on regulatory agencies and the large cosmetics companies accepting the technical flaws and limitations of animal testing. Our main contribution will continue to be one of example – producing popular innovative products which work, which do not compromise consumer safety and which do not depend on animal tests.

D4.4 Pressure on supplies

(a) Our policy

We pressure our suppliers to stop animal testing:

We require suppliers of raw materials for use in our cosmetics and toiletries to provide written confirmation every six months that any raw material they supply complies with our purchasing rule. We reject any raw material which fails to achieve this standard.

We conduct research among suppliers as to their overall stance on the issue of animal testing in the cosmetics and toiletries industry.

(b) Progress and challenges

Between October 1990 and April 1995, the number of Against Animal Testing declarations required from suppliers increased 241 per cent – from 535 to 1292. This reflects an ever-expanding product range and ingredient listing.

In our detailed research into practices of our suppliers for our rating scheme we found that 87 per cent of raw ingredient suppliers said they did not conduct tests but only 57 per cent said they did not commission animal tests. Of course those still involved in animal testing do not do it for The Body Shop, and indeed must not have done animal tests on materials supplied to the Company in a specified time frame. Nevertheless, there is still work to do. 38 per cent of The Body Shop's raw material suppliers wanted more information on non-animal testing alternatives.

(c) The future

- The Body Shop has said that by 1997 the Company will establish a formal network for suppliers to use and fund alternatives to animal testing procedures.

In early 1996, The Body Shop will announce an updated Against Animal Testing policy which reflects recent discussions with animal welfare groups. The new policy will include developments of our purchasing rule for suppliers.

D.5 ANIMAL PROTECTION

D.5.1 Wider issues

(a) Animal by-products

The Body Shop is conscious that animal protection in the cosmetics and toiletries industry goes beyond the animal testing issue. For example, some raw materials may be derived from bees, i.e. honey and wax, from sheep wool, i.e. lanolin or as by-products of the dairy and meat industry, i.e. milk, gelatin or hair. Whilst The Body Shop has never taken an active vegetarian stance, there have been important occasions where the company has sought to avoid a material which may have animal protection implications. Avoidance of natural musk (from deer) and spermaceti (from whales) were obvious choices for The Body Shop. Less simple have been choices around animal by-products where the primary use of the animal has not been for the cosmetics industry and where there has been no evidence of inhumane farming practices.

(b) The future

■ As part-of the Company's commitment to ethical sourcing of raw materials The Body Shop has conducted significant amounts of research into the sources of ingredients which may have an animal protection dimension. As a result the company has committed to full ethical sourcing of lanolin by 1998 and full ethical sourcing of all other by-products by the year 2000.

The question is not, can they reason? Nor, can they talk? But, can they suffer?

Jeremy Bentham

D.6 20 YEARS OF DEFINING MOMENTS

D.6.1 Highlighting our steps towards accountability

1976 First branch of The Body Shop opens in Brighton, England.

1977 First franchise issued.

1978 First international franchise opens in Brussels – in a kiosk!

1984 The Body Shop listed on the London Stock Exchange. Anita wins Veuve Cliquot Businesswoman of the Year Award.

1985 First campaign is run – 'Save the Whale', with Greenpeace UK.

1986 Campaign with Friends of the Earth raising awareness of global environmental issues. Environmental and Community Project Department set up at HQ. The Body Shop starts monitoring its raw materials suppliers to ensure they meet the Company's 'against animal testing' purchasing rule.

1987 Acid Rain Campaign is launched.

1988 Ozone or No Zone Campaign is launched. Amnesty International and The Body Shop join forces. First shops open in the USA. Soapworks opens in Easterhouse, Glasgow.

1989 Homeless Campaign in association with Shelter is launched. Stop The Burn Campaign to halt burning of Brazilian rain forests is launched. One of the First Trade Not Aid programmes begins with General Paper Industries in Nepal. The Body Shop starts to formally review its environmental performance.

1990 First shop opens in Japan. Purpose-built workplace nursery opens at UK Head Office. The Body Shop Charter is launched. Against Animal Testing Campaign is launched (2.6 million signatures collected in the UK). Once is Not Enough refill and recycle Campaign is launched. Romanian Relief Drive begins. The Body Shop launches the LEAP project with the Industrial Society and Shelter to break 'no home/no job' cycle in Britain's inner cities. The Body Shop Foundation is launched.

1991 The Yellow Ribbon Campaign for John McCarthy is run. Letter-writing Campaign with Amnesty International is launched. Brazil Nut Conditioner is launched – our first product containing an ingredient sourced from the Brazilian Amazon. The Body Shop help launch The Big Issue. The Body Shop receives Whitbread Award for Employee Volunteering. UK shops fund-raise for RSPCA to help wildlife affected by Gulf Oil slicks. Reviews become more formalised – progress checks are made against the Company's policies and goals on protecting the environment.

1992 The Key Issue campaign highlights homelessness as an election issue.

Department Environmental Advisers are launched at UK Head Office. The Body Shop becomes the first UK company to issue an environmental statement in line with EMAS. Refill, Recycle Campaign runs in UK shops. Against Animal Testing Campaign continues. The Body Shop formalises its audit process for health & safety at work. Voter Registration Drive in USA signs up more than 40,000 voters. Community store opens in Harlem. The first independently validated statement on its environmental performance, 'The Green Book', is published.

1993 'The Green Book 2', our second environmental audit statement, is launched. Our values on trial. The Body Shop wins Dispatches High Court Libel Case. Our AIDS/HIV awareness programmes are launched in the US and UK. 1,000th branch of The Body Shop opens in Spain. The Body Shop campaigns for strictest criteria for EC's eco-labelling scheme. Campaign to support Ken Saro-Wiwa and the Ogoni people of Nigeria starts. Plans start for a social audit, an ambitious check on the quality of human, relationships and social policies relevant to people associated with the Company.

1994 The Body Shop enshrines its values in its Memorandum and Articles of Association. 'Thwart Thorp' Campaign against Government decision to open nuclear reprocessing plant is run. First Violence Against Women Campaign is launched in Canada. Investment is made in a wind farm in Wales. The Body Shop aims to become energy self-sufficient in the UK. No Time To Waste home environmental audit Campaign is launched. First social audit commences involving a range of stakeholders. CITES world-wide endangered species Campaign is run in 30 markets – 3 million petition signatures are collected. Information audit function established to check accuracy of printed material and public statements produced by the Company. Values and Vision 1994 is published. The five audit areas (animal protection, environment, health & safety, social audit and information audit) are united in a combined 'ethical Audit' department answering to the Chief Executive. The department is responsible for distilling all relevant information into regular performance reports for distribution to the Company's stakeholders. The Body Shop joins UK retailers in marking world Aids Day. Fair Trade department launched at UK Head Office.

1995 Women's Rights campaigns run in several markets. Domestic Violence Campaign launched in UK, US and Singapore. 'Would You Do It In Paris?' Campaign against French nuclear testing in the Pacific is launched in Australia and New Zealand and supported by 12 markets. The Body Shop co-ordinated international protest at the sentencing and execution of Ken Saro-Wiwa and eight other Ogoni leaders. Ethical audits conducted across The Body Shop International operations in preparation for publication of the Values Report. The Report and the processes leading to it are subjected to external independent validation (or 'verification') where appropriate using the toughest available international standards.

1996 The Body Shop launches its first fully integrated *Values Report*, consisting of independently verified statements on the Company's performance on social, environmental and animal protection issues. The Body Shop Approach to Ethical Auditing is also published.

> The Body Shop sets itself very tough standards and has an exceptionally ambitious mission – to dedicate its business to the pursuit of social and environmental change. So measuring how well the Company matches up to its ideals has been a huge challenge. Doubtless our Values Report can be improved and we look forward to feedback. But in the long run I hope ethical audits and reports will be seen not just as exercises in openness but vital components of running efficient, effective and sustainable companies in the 21st century.
>
> (Dr David Wheeler, General Manager, Ethical Audit)

D.7 FOR MORE INFORMATION

The *Values Report 1995 (including: Animal Protection Statement ' 95, Environmental Statement '95, Social Statement '95 and The Body Shop Approach to Ethical Auditing '95) is available on The Body Shop Internet site: www.think-act-change.com*

Questions should be addressed to: Ethical Audit, The Body Shop International, Watersmead, Littlehampton, West Sussex BN17 6LS.

Unless otherwise stated, 'The Body Shop' refers to The Body Shop International PLC in the UK. These audits primarily focus on The Body Shop operations in the UK. All of our retail markets around the world are committed to the same core values and long term goals. While international markets are in various stages of development and achievement, The Body Shop family is committed to extending audit processes globally in coming years.

D.8 ACKNOWLEDGEMENTS

Reproduced from *The Values Report 1995* with the permission of the Body Shop International PLC.

Appendix E
Companies offering ethics consulting

The Adderly Page Group. Ltd.
1232 South Batavia Av., Suite 200
Batavia, IL 60510 3012
Phone: (630) 513 7311
Fax: (630) 513 7383

Canyon Consulting Corp.
5740 Feather Bush Dr.
Gold Canyon, AZ 85219
Phone: (602) 983 5000

Dale Biron Consulting
38 Miller Av., Suite 189
Mill Valley, CA 94941
Phone: (415) 381 2858
Fax: (415) 389 8566

The Center for Executive Re-Invention
Phone: (800) 491 1106

The Ethics Resource Center
1120 G St. N.W., Suite 200
Washington, DC 20005
Phone: (800) 777 1285
Fax: (202) 737 2227

FTP Consulting Services, Inc.
402 Fourth St., Suite 2
Dell Rapids, SD 57022
Phone: (605) 428 4270
Fax: (605) 428 5506

Great Lakes Center, Inc
410 Alexander St.
Rochester, NY 14607
Phone: (716) 461 5490

The Hudson Institute of Santa Barbara
3463 State St., Suite 520
Santa Barbara, CA 93105
Phone: (800) 582 4401
Fax: (805) 569 0025

The Larimer Center for Ethical Leader-
ship, Inc.
524 S. Cascade, Suite 1
Colorado Springs, CO 80903
Phone: (719) 636 8983
Fax: (719) 636 5175

The Negotiation Skills Company
P.O. Box 172
Pride's Crossing, MA 01965
Phone: (508) 927 6775
Fax: (508) 921 4447

Performance Parners
15 Montgomery Av.
Takoma Park, MD 20912
Phone: (800) 364 9380

Index